From Allies to Enemies

From Allies to Enemies

~ VISIONS OF MODERNITY, IDENTITY, AND
U.S.-CHINA DIPLOMACY, 1945–1960

SIMEI QING

HARVARD UNIVERSITY PRESS
Cambridge, Massachusetts, and London, England   2007

Library of Congress Cataloging-in-Publication Data

Qing, Simei.
    From allies to enemies: visions of modernity, identity, and U.S.-China
diplomacy, 1945–1960 / Simei Qing.
        p.   cm.
    Includes bibliographical references and index.
    ISBN-13: 978-0-674-02344-4 (alk. paper)
    ISBN-10: 0-674-02344-7 (alk. paper)
    1. United States—Foreign relations—China.   2. China—Foreign
relations—United States.   3. United States—Foreign relations—1945–1989.
4. Cold War.   I. Title.
E183.8.C5Q26   2006
327.7305109'045—dc22   2006043662

Dedicated to the memory of my parents

Contents

Acknowledgments   *ix*

Introduction: Cultural Visions and Foreign Policy   *1*

1   Perceptions and Realities: Chinese and American Visions of
Modernity and Identity   *10*

2   Straining the Relationship: Truman and the
Reconstruction of China after World War II   *33*

3   Disillusionment and Polarization: The Failure of the
Marshall Mission and Deepening Divisions in Nationalist
China   *57*

4   New American Strategies: Debates over the
Chinese Communist Party and Taiwan
in the Truman Administration   *95*

5   Two Sides of One Coin: The CCP's Policies toward the
Soviet Union and the United States   *113*

6   From Adversaries to Enemies:
Military Confrontation in Korea   *143*

7   Inducement versus Containment:
U.S. China Policy under Eisenhower   *169*

8   The Foundation of New China: Conflicting CCP Visions
    of Industrialization in the 1950s   *205*

9   Mao's Magic Weapon: From a Gradualist Political Program
    to the Hundred Flowers Policy   *228*

10 Becoming First-Class Citizens of the World:
    China's Diplomacy of Peaceful Coexistence   *253*

    Conclusion: Ways of War and Peace   *297*

    Notes   *309*

    Primary Sources   *381*

    Index   *387*

Acknowledgments

Now that this work is finally completed, after many years of research and many revisions, I want to thank all my teachers, friends, colleagues, and students, as well as the institutions that have encouraged and supported me through all these years. The research conclusions are, of course, my responsibility.

As the thought of this work began to evolve, the U.S. Institute of Peace provided a Peace Scholar Award, which made it possible for me to work in the National Archives in Washington, D.C., and in the Chinese National Archives for an entire year. A predoctoral fellowship from the Social Science Research Council/John D. MacArthur Foundation on International Peace and Security enabled me to undertake a two-year interdisciplinary training program on cultural and comparative sociology at Princeton University. The Center for International Security and Cooperation at Stanford University supplied an office and all necessary support, as well as a highly stimulating intellectual environment.

While I cannot list all of the archivists and librarians who helped to facilitate my research in the United States and China, I do want to express my great appreciation to those archivists and librarians in the United States at the National Archives, the Eisenhower Library, and the Truman Library, as well as their counterparts at the second National Archives of China, whose professional help was essential to the completion of this study.

A special thanks to many of my students at James Madison College,

Michigan State University, who have challenged my arguments, compelled me to rethink some of my theoretical interpretations, and enthusiastically cheered me on over the years.

I am grateful for the assistance of two able and scrupulous copy editors, Kate O'Neill and David Rumohr, who worked on this manuscript before I submitted it to the Press. They not only helped me improve the quality of this work, but went beyond the call of duty to offer their insights and critiques throughout the tedious process of making revisions and meeting deadlines.

I received outstanding guidance from members of the Department of History at Michigan State University. Bill H. Hixson taught me about modern and contemporary American history with profound insight. Donald Lammers guided me through the complex history of European foreign relations and first introduced me to the fascinating field of cognitive psychology in the study of world politics. Lewis H. Siegelbaum taught me the social historian approach to Soviet studies and the study of European history. He also offered important support, as both a teacher and a friend.

During the course of writing and revising this work, I benefited immensely from the advice and suggestions of the following scholars, who took the time to read the manuscript or parts of it at its various stages of evolution: Gordon H. Chang, Su-Ya Chang, Kathleen Conzen, John W. Coogan, Bruce Cumings, Anna Graham, Norman A. Graham, Michael Guyer, David Holloway, Akira Iriye, Otto Koester, Steve I. Levine, Sean McEnroe, Michel Oksenberg, Gilbert Rozman, Michael Schaller, Michael Schechter, Philip West, Allen S. Whiting, and Robert Wuthnow. In numerous conversations on American–East Asian relations, international history, and my methodology during my research, I also benefited greatly from the advice and suggestions of these scholars: Guy Alitto, Steve Averill, Gene Burns, Thomas Christensen, Paul A. Cohen, He Di, Roger Dingman, Prasenjit Duara, Rosemary Foot, Michael Gasster, Alexander George, Peter Hays Gries, Gu Ning, Harry Harding, Charles W. Hayford, Richard Hellie, Michael H. Hunt, Jia Qingguo, Madeline Levine, John Wilson Lewis, Li Jingjie, Li Shenzhi, David G. LoRomer, Michael Lund, Doug Merwin, Niu Jun, Robert Ross, Sheng Zhihua, Gordon T. Stewart, Tao Wenzhao, Nancy Tucker, Frederick Wakeman, Wang Jisi, Kathryn Weathersby, Xiong Zhiyong, Xue Litai, Zhang Baijia, Shu-Guang Zhang, Zhu Ruizhen, and Zi Zhongyun.

I am especially indebted to Akira Iriye for his persistent emphasis on the study of the cultural dimension of international relations. From the very beginning of this work he has given me valuable advice and genuine encouragement. I am grateful to Michel Oksenberg, my mentor during my SSRC/MacArthur fellowship years, for first encouraging me to adopt an interdisciplinary approach, particularly the approach of cultural and comparative sociology, to the study of U.S.-China diplomacy. Gilbert Rozman, my mentor during the SSRC/MarArthur interdisciplinary training program at Princeton University, read several early drafts of the manuscript. He taught me about the comparative sociology of international relations and offered detailed suggestions and honest critiques. Robert Wuthnow warmly invited me to join his workshop on comparative religion and cultural studies at Princeton University and taught me about cultural sociology. David Holloway, who taught me international relations theory at Stanford University, helped me to pin down the theoretical questions of this study and offered valuable help whenever I needed it. Gordon H. Chang not only shared with me his unusual insights on U.S.-China relations, but also offered his advice and tough criticism of this work over the years. Michael Schaller read various versions of this manuscript and offered his thoughtful criticism throughout the revision process. John W. Coogan shared with me his unique expertise on the history of international relations and provided thoughtful advice on my research. I am especially grateful to Zhu Ruizhen, Russian interpreter for Mao Zedong and Zhou Enlai from 1954 to 1966 and editor of the private papers of Shi Zhe, Russian interpreter for Mao and Zhou from 1948 to 1953, who guided me through the primary sources on the Korean War and Sino-Soviet relations. My special thanks also to Shen Zhihua, who shared with me his research findings on the Korean War in the Russian archives and oral history on Sino-Soviet relations in China. My deep appreciation to Norman A. Graham, who has been a wise mentor at James Madison College and the toughest of critics of my manuscript; he has never intervened in my research findings, even if he sometimes disagreed with my arguments. Thanks also to Steve I. Levine for reading all the different versions of this manuscript, for sharing with me his incredible insights and knowledge of the history of U.S.-China relations, for persistently encouraging me to pursue historical truth, and for his friendship in all weather—bad as well as good—over the years.

My heartfelt thanks to Elizabeth Gilbert at Harvard University Press and John Donohue at Westchester Book Services, who have brought this work to its completion. John and his colleagues helped me to clarify my methodological approach, sharpen my arguments, remove repetitive sections, and refine the presentation of every chapter in this work. Without their outstanding professional work, this book would not stand as it is today.

I could not have completed this work without the advice of Warren I. Cohen. Through all my ups and downs he has always trusted and supported me, even when I disagreed with him in my studies and research conclusions. He always pushed me to pursue historical truth with intellectual honesty and integrity. I owe a great intellectual debt to him for his guidance in my studies of American diplomatic history and U.S.-China relations.

Kathleen McDermott, my editor at Harvard University Press, helped me through the most difficult stage of this work: meeting the challenge of rising above my years of research in the archives and developing this work for a much broader readership. From articulating the main thesis to reorganizing the supporting primary sources, her advice was crucial at every step of its completion. I feel fortunate to have had the opportunity to work with her on this project.

When I showed Warren Cohen my final manuscript, he told me that my parents must have been very proud of me at that moment. I could not hold back my tears. My parents taught me that historical inquiry should never be done for the sake of pursuing personal fame and wealth, but to pursue historical truth, regardless of its popularity at the time. This book is dedicated to their memory with their daughter's love.

From Allies to Enemies

Introduction

Cultural Visions and Foreign Policy

Could American misunderstanding of international affairs profoundly influence the destiny of modern democracy in the United States? Yes, it could, argued Walter Lippmann in his classic study *Public Opinion* (1922). He pointed out that while citizens in earlier democratic societies lived in small communities and made decisions on domestic policies, citizens in modern democracies are asked to make judgments on critical issues of war and peace. Yet when the public interprets international affairs, the major problem is, "We do not first see, and then define, we define first and then see." In observing world events, citizens often create for themselves a pseudo reality that is more consistent with their preexisting beliefs, misconceptions, or prejudices than with the *actual* reality of the world. Lippmann, one of the leading journalists in America in his time, asked whether a free press would help address the problem of "hidden subjectivity" in the public's interpretations of foreign affairs. It might not, he argued. In media coverage of international affairs, "news and truth may no longer be the same thing." It was not that editors or reporters "deliberately tried to suppress the truth." Rather, "the chief censor and the chief propagandist are hope and fear in their own minds."[1]

Misunderstanding and misperception in international relations is a critical and complex phenomenon. It is also, in many cases, not unilateral.[2] This book constitutes the first comprehensive endeavor to compare American perceptions of China's economic and political reconstruction efforts and foreign-policy intentions with the reality in China in the important period between 1945 and 1960. During that time, U.S.-China relations deteriorated rapidly: the strategic allies became adversaries, and then irreconcilable enemies.

This book asks one question: Did this drastic deterioration result from an inevitable conflict between the two countries' vital national interests and moral principles that was therefore doomed to take place? Or instead, was the transition from allies to enemies created by the fallout from counterproductive foreign policies on both sides, the bitter fruit of repeated misjudgments of each other's intentions, or the fatal consequences of an illusion—the perceived incompatibility of national interests and principles?

To address the question, this book studies the United States' China policies from both the inside out and the outside in. The former requires one to understand American visions and aspirations (i.e., U.S. policymakers' China policies and strategies) entirely on their own terms. To study the United States' China policies from the outside in is to investigate any significant gaps between U.S. interpretations of Chinese foreign-policy objectives and actual Chinese intentions.

The purpose of this study is not, therefore, just to ask why a specific policy was made, but to go further: to ask how it could become so counterproductive as to generate exactly the opposite of its desired and expected outcome. The answer to the question of why a specific policy was made usually involves issues of power, ideology, domestic politics, or policymakers' personalities. But to explore how a policy could be counterproductive, one needs to delve more deeply, revealing those rarely examined assumptions that might be so ingrained in mainstream policy debates that the general public, and even most policymakers, are not conscious of them. In the broadest terms, this is a study of the critical role of deeply anchored visions in the origins of human military conflicts.

Increasingly, scholars in this field have called for a comprehensive comparison between U.S. interpretations of Chinese intentions and China's actual foreign-policy goals.[3] As Michael Hunt and Steven Levine point out, without such a comparison, "one cannot fully understand American actions, provide cogent evaluations of American views, or properly judge American policy." They emphasize that American scholars should be especially on guard against seeing China and Asia through the lenses of the American value system and instead try their best to view China and Asia through Chinese and Asian eyes.[4] This is what Paul A. Cohen persistently argues in his thesis of a China-centered approach. The term *China-centered*, he emphasizes, is employed not to place China at the center of the universe but "to understand what is happening in that history in terms that are as free as possible of imported criteria of significance." Otherwise, he says, we may present a so-called Chinese reality, defined "too much by the historian's own innermost reality, and too little by the reality of the people he or she is writing about."[5]

Moreover, scholars in this field continue to stress the importance of examining the different philosophical or cultural assumptions underlying policy debates on both sides. As Michael Schaller emphasized, we must examine those deep-seated policy assumptions underlying U.S.-China interactions that had led to war and confrontations in the past.[6] Nations, like individuals, do have "visions, dreams, and prejudices about themselves and the world that influence their relationships," emphasizes Akira Iriye. He urges scholars of international relations to be "aware of the 'imagined' nature of a given 'reality.'" "All realities in a way are imagined realities, products of forces and movements that are mediated through human consciousness." In his view, study of those "most highly valued beliefs" or "latent, if not always clearly articulated" cultural visions that "underl[ie] such interactions" is "long overdue."[7] Or, in Gordon H. Chang's view, the new research agenda should focus on the elusive but important "cultural context of diplomacy" in U.S.-China relations. Policy analyses are conducted through "cultural filters." "Can one deny that there is a realm of social ideas, images, beliefs, and sentiments, which are distinct from, but still influence, the formal expressions of power and policy?"[8]

In studying the making of America's China policies from both the inside out and the outside in, or studying why there were persistent counterproductive policies on both sides, the major methodological challenge is twofold. First, how can one present core American policy assumptions on their own terms, without their being filtered through Chinese beliefs or interpretations? Likewise, how can one present core Chinese policy assumptions on their own terms, without filtering them through American categories and paradigms? Second, how can one go beyond the conscious frameworks of past participants, view them from a distance, and analyze what the participants might not have been consciously aware of when they assessed each other's intentions?

This challenge is analogous to investigating a dispute or debate between two individuals. The investigator must first explore and come to understand the mindset and positions of each party involved. Because the participants may become so immersed in the specific content of the debate that they are hardly aware of their own predispositions, the investigator, "taking a distanced perspective," may be in a better position to "analyze what the participants are taking for granted."[9]

This book adopts an interdisciplinary approach to this methodological challenge. It redefines how core assumptions and cultural predispositions are apprehended or examined, thereby building a connection between cultural studies and international security studies.[10]

Official versus Informal Ideology

The concept of core policy assumptions is not identified with official ideology. *Ideology* here refers to officially declared value systems, such as democratic capitalism and Marxist socialism. For instance, if one argues that in the 1950s, the policy assumptions of the leaders of the Chinese Communist Party (CCP) were grounded in Marxist socialism or communism, then we need to understand how they defined or interpreted this ideology.

During the 1950s, most Americans loathed socialism/communism, identifying it with a grim police state that ruthlessly repressed individual liberties. By contrast, when the great American educator John Dewey first visited China in 1920, he exclaimed: "The best and the brightest here all embrace, in one way or another, socialist ideas!" Chinese interpretations of socialism in the early twentieth century, long before the birth of the CCP, overwhelmingly focused on the ideals of nonaggression among nations and economic justice in society. Sun Yat-sen, the leader of the 1911 republican revolution and the father of Chinese democracy, wrote in 1907 that, with the rise of the socialist movement in Europe, humanity would no longer tolerate "the law of the jungle": "Humanity would hold out its hands to help the poor and the underprivileged, to safeguard the basic human dignity for everyone in the world, regardless of his race, sex, class, and nationality."[11]

The point here is: to discover underlying core policy assumptions, one should not take ideological rhetoric or labels, such as liberal capitalism and Marxist socialism, at face value. That is, one should not simply assume that the countries being studied hold to identical definitions of these ideological concepts or that there are homogenous interpretations within each nation or unvarying understandings even in an individual's mind. To imagine such a fixed set of definitions of socialism and capitalism, and to impose them uniformly on the minds of

Chinese and American policymakers, will not help to reveal the core assumptions made in U.S.-China diplomacy. Steven Levine emphasizes that in gaining an understanding of the foreign-policy objectives of the People's Republic of China (PRC), its informal ideology is more important than its official one. "An informal ideology," according to Levine, is "the complex of cultural values, preferences, prejudices, predispositions, habits, and unstated but widely shared propositions about reality that conditions the way in which political actors behave." An informal ideology, then, is "implicit, unconscious, or only partly conscious," and "a more powerful factor" in understanding the PRC's foreign policy objectives.[12] To identify core policy assumptions in U.S.-China diplomacy in the Cold War, clearly one needs to go beyond the ideological rhetoric to uncover the cultural predispositions that shaped or conditioned the distinctive indigenous interpretations of official ideologies.[13]

Cultural Predisposition and Political Behavior

The concept of cultural predisposition is not equated with the internalized worldviews of individuals. The reason is that doing so would make it impossible to study cultural assumptions at empirical levels, since an individual may not be conscious of the assumptions he or she makes, and even "sustained questioning of the individual" is unlikely to reveal them.[14] In the words of Alastair Iain Johnston, despite the "centrality" of the relationship between cultural ideas and political behavior, "it is an exceedingly difficult causal connection to show empirically."[15]

In order to study cultural predispositions at empirical levels, *culture* is redefined in this book. According to the disciplines of cognitive psychology[16] and contemporary cultural analysis,[17] culture can be viewed as a "moral classification system" in defining norms and deviances in society, or invisible moral and political parameters in the mainstream public debates. To discover this moral classification system, one must trace intellectual discourses in a nation over a rather long historical period. By determining the moral parameters of mainstream discourse since the beginning of the modern era (the period from the mid-eighteenth through the mid-twentieth century) and comparing them with those of mainstream debates in the contemporary age, one may then indirectly discover an individual's internalized cultural assumptions.

Such a definition of culture has its limitations, however. Its data are more about patterns of thought than about individuals' private ruminations. If culture has shaped us as a single species, so, too, has it shaped us as separate individuals. That is, in the study of culture, as Clifford Geertz emphasizes, "we must descend into detail, . . . to grasp firmly the essential character of not only the various cultures but the various sorts of individuals within each culture, if we wish to encounter humanity face to face."[18]

The concept of cultural predisposition in this study thus encompasses both the moral parameters of the mainstream discourse or the broad patterns of thought in the mainstream society, and individual worldviews or individuals' differing interpretations of their cultural heritage.

The Role of Cultural Visions of Modernity and Identity in Policymaking

The role of cultural values and beliefs in policymaking is twofold: they sometimes *follow* policy decision, functioning as policy justification or rationalization. At other times, however, deep-rooted cultural values may *precede* the decision, functioning as policy predispositions or policy rationality.[19]

For instance, after U.S. president Richard Nixon's historic trip to China, "the powerfully negative images of China and the Chinese that had dominated the center of the stage in American thinking about China for some twenty years" were, suddenly, replaced by "the highly positive views that had been quite out of view all this time." Here, the positive image of the PRC in the media and the public *followed* Nixon's policy decision. According to Harold Isaacs, a pioneer in image studies, when the national interest is at stake, policymakers may "first set their policy toward another state and then develop the image" of that state, which would support, justify, or rationalize such a major foreign policy shift in front of the media and the public.[20]

This study intends to inquire whether deeply embedded cultural assumptions may function as policy rationality, or filter systems whereby one selects and interprets the information about other nations' domestic developments and foreign-policy intentions. In this regard, conceptions of modernity and identity may play a particularly important role in the interactions between Western and non-Western countries. The search for modernity and new identities began in most non-Western, developing societies in the mid-nineteenth century, when reformers tried to transform their countries from agricultural to industrialized nations. Heated debates have emerged in modern times about what kinds of new economic and political systems a non-Western country should attempt to establish and how, in effecting such profound and far-reaching transformations of the country's economy, polity, and foreign policy, a non-Western society should redefine its new identity.[21] In these wide-ranging debates of unprecedented intensity, cultural conceptions of modernity and identity have often evoked deep political passions, religious fervors, and different intellectual convictions in non-Western societies.

To further confound a better understanding of this extraordinarily complex process of historical quest for modernity and new identity, there was a continual belief in the mainstream American discourse throughout the nineteenth and the first half of the twentieth century; that is, modernization meant Westernization. As Isaacs wrote in his pioneering study on American images of China and India in the 1950s, "The images of Asia and of Asian-Western relationships persisting in the minds of men educated and conditioned primarily to an Atlantic-Western-white view of the world certainly have a major place in the slowness and pain with which major American policy makers have reacted to the new realities in Asia since 1945." Based on extensive interviews at that time, he also concluded that "Different as they are in qualities of mind and character, this seems to apply both to Dean Acheson and to John Foster Dulles, i.e., it appears at all extremes of competence in the leadership of our public life."[22]

It is obvious that in the turbulent encounters between Western and non-Western societies during the nineteenth and twentieth centuries, as Judith Goldstein and Robert Keohane write, "policy outcomes can be explained only when interests and power are combined with a rich understanding of human beliefs" at much deeper levels.[23] Thus "efforts by social scientists to dispense with the study of national heritage have met with failure," according to Gilbert Rozman. "Some assumed that national differences are of little or no consequence only to discover that class struggle and modernization assume unexpected forms in non-Western countries." As he further states, "Neither socialism nor capitalism is as all-embracing a category for interpreting a country's development as many once thought. The historical slate is not wiped clean, and particularly in East Asia, its effects are becoming widely visible."[24]

In short, with its approach to core policy assumptions and cultural predispositions, this methodology aims to explore the long-term, implicit, and underlying issues in U.S.-China diplomacy, which may well transcend the Cold War framework and may continue to exist in the background of U.S.-China interactions in the post–Cold War world.

In the post–Cold War era, it is especially important to go beyond the ideological framework of the Cold War to reexamine the origins of U.S.-China antagonism. As Robert Jervis put it, "psychologists have shown that 'where one and only one hypothesis is operative with no competing alternatives, it tends to be more readily confirmable.' " Thus "to expose implicit assumptions and give themselves more freedom of choice, decision-makers should encourage the formulation and application of alternative images."[25] To learn from U.S.-China confrontations in the Cold War, our first step should be to study U.S.-China diplomacy from alternative conceptual frameworks. As Albert Einstein reflected, "The significant problems we face cannot be solved at the same level of thinking we were at when we created them."[26]

Although the United States has engaged in three major wars in Asia since the beginning of the 1940s, two of them with the Chinese, Americans and Chinese still "do not have any understanding of one another comparable to the understanding . . . between Americans and Europeans," laments Ernest May.[27] The title of David Lampton's most recent book on U.S.-China diplomacy expresses this current relationship: *Same Bed, Different Dreams* (2000).[28] In his preface to the fourth edition of *America's Response to China* (2000), Warren I. Cohen writes that he could only pray that the next edition of his book would not tell "a sad tale of how two nations," which have "no vital interests in conflict," "stumbled into war."[29]

Does the current difficult relationship between China and America have anything to do with the past? Yes, it does. An important legacy of U.S.-China relations during "the critical decade" following 1945 was, according to Harry Harding, "to help create and reinforce a set of mutual perceptions that still have a significant, although often unrecognized, impact to this day."[30] Or, as Robert S. Ross put it, "Many of the factors that prolonged and exacerbated conflict between the United States and China in the 1950s and the 1960s may also bedevil U.S.-China relations in the post–Cold War era."[31]

Historians of U.S.-China relations bear a special duty and responsibility at the dawn of the twenty-first century to study the roles of deep-seated assumptions or cultural visions of modernity and identity in the origins and developments of U.S.-China confrontations, because historical studies on this important subject may have a profound impact on the future evolution of U.S.-China relations. These historical inquiries may either help confirm flawed policy assumptions of the past, thus perpetuating policymakers' mistakes, or help uncover flawed assumptions that led to past conflicts and wars, thus laying down a more solid foundation for U.S.-China relations in the years to come.

CHAPTER ONE

Perceptions and Realities

Chinese and American Visions of
Modernity and Identity

Controversy between cultural universalism and particularism in American discourse has existed since the beginning of the modern era. Cultural universalists believe in the "enlightenment mode of history"; that is, that "time overcomes space—a condition in which the other in geographical space, will *in time,* come to look like an earlier version of us." Cultural particularists, in contrast, argue that quests for modernity have taken place in and varied according to different social and cultural environments, "in response to unique circumstances." It is thus impossible to engage in global "intercultural communications" concerning different quests for modernity and identity.[1]

A deeper examination of this controversy reveals two opposing underlying assumptions about people's desires in non-Western, developing societies. According to the universalists, the peoples in these societies, like those in the United States, are "yearning" for individual civil and political liberties. However, the particularists claim that the majority of people in developing societies are "indifferent" to, or at least "unenthusiastic" about, the ideal of individual freedom. Clearly, this debate reveals conflicting assumptions about the desires of people in the non-Western, modernizing world.[2]

Which of these assumptions is more consistent with reality? To address this question, this chapter compares Chinese and American visions of individual freedom, the market economy, and democracy in the modern era, when Chinese reformers—from Taiping rebels, to constitutionalists, to republican revolutionaries—began their earnest, comprehensive search for modernity and a new identity in China.

Before we address this underlying issue in the controversy, important questions must first be answered: How shall we distinguish between people's desires and government's? When analyzing people's desires, how shall we distinguish between the ephemeral and the constant, the digressive and the meaningful? A historical analysis of the long-term pattern of habits of mind may help solve the problem. For the purpose of this inquiry, however, a historical approach alone is not sufficient. The major focus here is *not* a detailed yet separate intellectual history of Chinese and American cultural values, which could not provide any basis for comparison. Instead, it is designed as a structured comparison of *mainstream* Chinese and American discourses on modernity and new identity. To provide a basis for analysis, it focuses particularly on how both sides drew the boundaries between the private and the public realms. For example, in Chinese and American discourses, how were basic concepts such as the individual, the state, and the common good defined? How did the symbolic borders between the public and the private sectors negotiated? How did these symbolic boundaries change over time? And how did these different constructions of private-public relationships shape different economic and political blueprints in modern times?

In short, this chapter aims to answer these questions: first, whether the two peoples had identical definitions of freedom, democracy, socialism, and capitalism, or whether there were interpretations outside the tradition of the mainstream discourse across the Pacific; and second, whether there were shared basic human concerns and moral values.

Discourses on Individual Freedom, National Freedom, and Internationalism in the Modern Era

By the turn of the century, most modern Chinese reformers agreed that individual freedom was the key to the West's rapid growth in the modern age. They also agreed that the core of this ideal was freedom of conscience. Zhang Taiyan, the intellectual spokesman of the 1911 republican revolution, wrote that individual freedom meant, above all, freedom of conscience; that is, all "supreme" ideological authorities must be abandoned. He thus argued that "a blind embrace of the generally acknowledged truth" from the West, like a blind embrace of

Confucianism in the past, might severely jeopardize the individual's free thought and that every individual must have the sacred freedom to pursue whatever he or she values most, without imposed constraints from any "supreme" ideological authorities.[3]

If there was wide consensus among modern Chinese reformers on the vital importance of individual liberty to China's place in the modern world, there was no agreement on how to construct the relationship between individual rights and group rights. Many believed this relationship should be one of mutual dependence and complementarity. For instance, in his first Chinese translation of John Stuart Mill's work in 1898, Yan Fu purposely changed the original title, *On Liberty,* to a new title: *On the Relationship between Group Rights and Individual Rights.* As Yan wrote in his introduction, the relationship is similar to that between a unit and the whole, or between a cell and the human body. Neither one can exist without the other. According to Liang Qichao, one of the leaders in the constitutionalist movement, both one's desire for independence and one's desire for harmony with the group are inherent in human nature. Thus this relationship should not be considered to be antagonistic or contradictory.[4] As he wrote, "to build a strong and free China, every Chinese must be strong and free first."[5] On the other hand, "Human evolution is first of all the evolution of social groups, not isolated individuals."[6] Or as Kang Yuwei, the founder of the constitutionalist movement, emphasized, if individual liberty is the precondition for national liberty, national freedom gives meaning and purpose to individual freedom. In his words, "the essence of pursuing individual freedom lies in the harmony and unity between the individual, the nation, and the common good of humanity."[7]

For others, however, this relationship was mutually antagonistic. Hong Xiuquan, the leader of the Taiping peasant rebellion (1850–1865), believed that all individual self-interests must be suppressed to serve the grand cause and urgent needs of the Taiping revolution. Some leading liberal scholars, too, constructed this relationship in terms of mutual antagonism, but their focus was on the individual's rights. In his 1918 work "On Ibsenism," Hu Shi, one of the leading writers in the May 4th movement, first proposed that cultivation of "a form of self-serving principle" was much more important than serving the interests of the society. He quoted Ibsen as saying: "You should feel that your own self-interest is the most important thing in the world." In his view, one should be aware of the immense danger inherent in the public realm, which "favors dictatorship or absolute conformity, often uses arbitrary power to ruin individuality." As he argued, whenever there was a conflict between the individual and the group, the individual's rights must be protected first.[8] If Hu was more concerned about the societal pressures for individual conformity, he nonetheless did not openly embrace the supremacy of the individual's self-interests, as Ibsen did. Like other modern Chinese reformers, Hu also defined society as "Big Me" and individuals as "Small Me": "The Small Me has a great responsibility for the immortal Big Me's timeless past and timeless future," he wrote. He thus implied that individual freedom might not be an end in itself. In this sense, he vaguely agreed with, or ambiguously conformed to, the moral parameter within which the debates on freedom took place.[9]

Regardless of these different interpretations of the private-public relationship, modern Chinese reformers shared common ground: they treasured above all China's national freedom. According to Sun Yatsen, the quest for modernity in the West originated from its great intellectual rebellion against papal rule in medieval times; thus the Western concept of modernity put its primary emphasis on individual freedom. By contrast, Sun argued, China had not had a rigid religious system similar to that of papal rule, and China's quest for modernity originated in its great struggle for national freedom.

Modern Chinese history since the Opium War taught Chinese people that they could never enjoy individual freedom without first achieving their national freedom, Sun emphasized. Due to the loss of national freedom after the Manchu invasion and occupation, and particularly after the Opium War, "our ancient morality and civilization have not been able to manifest themselves and are now declining." Since a foundation was "essential to expansion," "we must talk nationalism first if we want to talk internationalism or cosmopolitanism."

He persistently reminded his fellow countrymen of a common phrase in ancient China, "Rescue the weak, lift up the fallen": "If we want China to rise to power, we must not only restore our national standing, but we must also assume a great responsibility towards the world. If China cannot assume that responsibility, she will be a great disadvantage not an advantage to the world, no matter how strong she may become." Clearly, individual freedom, national freedom, and a new internationalism were intertwined with one another in many modern Chinese reformers' conceptions of modernity and new identity. And the cornerstones were national freedom and equality in the world.[10]

* * *

Across the Pacific, in drafting Virginia's "Act for Establishing Religious Freedom," Thomas Jefferson wrote one of the most brilliant pleas for freedom of conscience. At the center of Jefferson's definition was a concept of human dignity based on "each person's possession of a soul in the likeness of God."[11]

Moreover, individual freedom is also defined as the liberty to pursue individual wealth. As Alexander Hamilton argued, "freedom to hold and dispose property is paramount." In his view, this concept of freedom represented a Common Man's rebellion against the hereditary aristocracy of England, which had assumed for centuries that the right to wealth flowed in the bloodstream.[12]

Furthermore, the ideal of individual liberty is also interpreted in American discourse as the full expression of unique individuality. As Ralph Waldo Emerson wrote, "the word *masses* is most dreadful," since the poorest and the humblest equally possesses a unique individuality.[13]

Clearly, in the American vision, the ideal of individual freedom is not equated with selfishness or a free individual doing whatever he or she wants without thought of the larger community. In fact, defining the boundary between individual rights and group rights is a critical issue in the American conversation on individual liberty. And that conversation is marked by two divergent constructions: one may be called atomism, the other organicism.[14]

Atomism defines the whole as the sum total of its parts. To use a metaphor, group rights can be considered as analogous to a heap of billiard balls. A billiard ball retains its essential characteristics when separated from the heap, the whole of which is no more than the sum total of all the billiard balls. The common good is thus each individual's maximal pursuit of self-interest and freedom. Organicism, on the other hand, views the relationship between an individual and a group as that of a cell and a multicellular organism. The organism is *not* equivalent to the sum total of the component cells. "If one may describe the behavior of a group of billiard balls from one's knowledge of any one of them, no amount of knowledge about an individual cell would enable one to say anything about the organ of which it is a part." In this view, while an individual's rights and freedom should be vigorously protected, group rights and freedom should be protected as well.[15]

In spite of these different interpretations of this private-public relationship, both sides believe that the pursuit of an individual's rights and happiness should be an end in itself. Put another way, in mainstream discourse in America, the ultimate moral judgment is individual freedom. As Louis Hartz argues, America as a nonfeudal society lacks a socialist tradition, which Europe has. It was "born equal," as Alexis de Tocqueville said. The American society "begins with Locke, transforms him, and stays with Locke." Or, as Seymour Martin Lipset writes, "the emphasis in the American value system has been on the individual. . . . America began and continues as the most anti-statist nation."[16]

While many scholars affirm the central place of individual liberty in the American Creed, a question still remains: does it do justice to the complexity of the mainstream discourse in modern America? In *Contested Truths,* Daniel Rodgers raises this question. He argues that the major issue in understanding American political culture is not just to identify keywords, such as *individual rights* and *private property,* but to trace how the same keywords have been used for essentially different ends. "The crucial contest" is thus over the meaning of the same word. It is this recurrent struggle over "a relatively small number of words" that have shaped political talk in America, and "disguised its powerful conflicts under a misleading veneer of sameness." In particular, Rodgers focuses on the key phrase "individual freedom" in postwar American political debates. In the mind of the New Deal left, freedom should include a new "economic bill of rights," while in the view of political centrists, freedom should be "everything that fascism and communism were not" in the Cold War. According to the civil rights activists, rights and freedom were swept up into "a common cry of protest." Nonetheless, Rodgers concluded that most of the time in the mainstream discourse, "freedom" was employed to defend individuals' political and civil liberties.[17] In this regard, as J. David Greenstone emphasizes, while there are profoundly different forms of liberalism in the overarching Lockean consensus, individual liberty defined as individualism or individual civil and political rights is at the core of the American value system.

The American value system, with its primary emphasis on individual civil and political rights, is not only embedded in the tradition of Lockean liberalism, but also ingrained in the ideal of "liberal peace" proposed by Immanuel Kant (1724–1804) and developed by President Wilson. According to Kant, the key to lasting peace on earth is "liberal peace" or the construction of a pacific federation among liberal republics organized on the principle of respecting and protecting individual rights.

In America's response to World War I and Russian revolution, Wilson further developed the Kantian ideal of "liberal peace." The Wilsonian goal became "the attainment of a peaceful liberal capitalist world order under international law, safe both from traditional imperialism and revolutionary socialism, within whose stable liberal confines a missionary America could find moral and economic preeminence." To build enduring peace in the world, he urged America to be the champion of "making the world safe for democracy."[18]

Thus what were the similarities and differences in Chinese and American discourses on individual freedom and national freedom and internationalism in the modern era? Both modern Chinese and American reformers believed that individual liberty meant freedom of conscience. This shared interpretation across the Pacific demonstrated a common human desire against ideological and religious monism. And both sides believed that humanity must end wars of conquest and achieve enduring peace on earth. However, there were important differences. In the American vision, the sanctity of individual freedom or individual civil and political rights centered squarely at the core of modernity, identity, and Wilsonian liberal internationalism.

In contrast, Chinese cultural heritage, from the concept of Yin-Yang balance in I-Ching to the Confucian Golden Mean doctrine, tends to construct the relationship between an individual and the group as "mutually complementary."[19] Moreover, as Sun Yat-sen emphasized, China's quest for modernity originated from its struggle for national freedom. Thus in China's concept of modernity, the ideal of individual freedom became an integral part of national freedom, and the Great Commonwealth on earth.

The Chinese and American visions of freedom and internationalism clearly had their different strengths and weaknesses. Chinese mainstream discourse in the modern era failed to emphasize the gravely counterproductive consequences of an absolutist construction of the public-private relationship. The major weakness is not that the "common good" rather than individual liberty became the ultimate moral judgment in China's quest for modernity; it is that many modern Chinese reformers were not fully aware of the far-reaching impact of their philosophical assumptions on their economic and political blueprints. Thus, when the call for national salvation and an end to widespread social sufferings became urgent, many of them subconsciously as well as consciously perceived the relationship between individual rights and the common good as mutually contradictory. A severe limitation on individual rights could be legitimized in the name of the nation and the people, without serious challenge from the intellectual community. As Li Zehou, a prominent Chinese philosopher, reflected on this major weakness in Chinese discourse in the modern era: "From the Northern expedition, civil wars, to the War of Resistance, several generations of Chinese intellectuals therefore started with patriotism and liberalism, and ended up with patriotism and social revolution."[20]

On the other hand, a major shortcoming in the mainstream American discourse in modern times is its failure to emphasize the profound impact of moral absolutism on America's perceptions of the world, particularly non-Western, developing societies. According to public polls taken in major Western democracies, 50 percent of Americans believed in moral absolutism, as compared with 36 percent of Britons, 24 percent of the French, 26 percent of Germans, 42 percent of Italians, 19 percent of Swedes, and 30.5 percent of Canadians. This fervent faith in absolute morality can be attributed to America's religious exceptionalism, one that was referred to by Edmund Burke as "sectarian Protestantism." As Seymour Martin Lipset points out, "Americans are utopian moralists who press hard to institutionalize virtue, to destroy evil people, and eliminate wicked institutions and practices." In particular, "they tend to view social and political dramas . . . as battles between God and the Devil." Or, as Everett Ladd put it, "To understand the American ideology, we need to see individualism not as a dimension of individual character but rather as a *moral* standard by which social institutions and practices are judged" in the world.[21]

These different ways of drawing the boundary between the private and the public realms, different parameters within which the mainstream discourse took place, and different strengths and weaknesses in conceptions of freedom, modernity, and internationalism profoundly shaped Chinese and American blueprints of the modern economy and polity.

Discourses on the Modern Economy

Three competing visions emerged in the Chinese discourse on the modern economy: an economy of absolute egalitarianism/radical populism, a competitive private economy with public guidance, and a mixed economy with private, cooperative, and public enterprises coexisting in China's modernity.

While an economy of absolute egalitarianism was the rallying cry of all poor peasant rebellions, it was most vigorously articulated by Hong Xiuquan in the midst of social suffering unprecedented since the Opium War. Hong imported a foreign religion—Christianity—as the official ideology of the Taiping rebellion to justify or legitimize this economic system. He proposed the concept of the village commune, wherein no individual should own private property, wherein the principle of "from each according to his ability, to each according to his needs" should prevail, and wherein there should be no more appalling poverty.[22]

Clearly, Hong's economic blueprint emphasized the government's role in enforcing an egalitarian society. The root of all social upheavals—economic ills and political corruption—lay in the great gap between the rich and the poor, he said. In his view, if the government could take charge of all private property and distribute it equally among the people, the problem would be solved. There would be no private commerce, no private trade, or, in Hong's words, "no merchants to exploit the common people." The national and the local authorities would take care of everyone and everything in society.

This radical populist approach to China's economy was historically appealing to poor peasants during profound social crises, as witnessed by many Taiping rebels' reactions to an alternative moderate economic blueprint. Hong Rengan (Hung Jen-gan), the new prime minister in the late stage of the Taiping rebellion, proposed that to boost the declining urban economy in Taiping-controlled areas, industry and commerce should be encouraged to develop through the initiatives of private enterprises. The economic power of private capital would be checked by public institutions, including the government. However, to the peasant rebels this moderate blueprint represented surrender to the rich and powerful in the towns and cities. Consequently, his new economic blueprint could not be implemented.[23]

On the other hand, according to Liang, Kang, and other constitutionalists, a modern Chinese economy must be a private economy with public guidance. That is, China's incipient industrialization must be left to "the genius of private enterprise." They argued that public enterprises had too often been ineffective and unproductive, as proved by the corrupt state enterprises of the 1860s and 1870s, and by the Qing dynasty's failed efforts to nationalize the railroad in the early twentieth century. "What was the result of all these efforts? We actually killed the sheep (private industry) to feed the tiger (the Qing dynasty)." These constitutionalists emphasized that in a competitive private economy, the emergence of one big corporation at least could not stop competition from others. If the government became the "sole monopoly," then, "no one would ever have the power to compete with a government-owned enterprise."[24]

Liang and Kang, however, endorsed not a capitalist free-enterprise system but a private economy with public guidance. It was crucial, they said, to utilize public guidance to address the problem of unequal distribution in China's development. In their view, the state must take the lead and cooperate with private enterprise to implement social-welfare programs: "The state should provide occupation for the unemployed, to teach a new profession to the unemployable. These social welfare programs not only can help the economy, but can also contribute to social order and gratify humanitarian feelings."[25]

Thus according to Liang and Kang both market competition and state intervention were necessary in the modern economy. Whether there should be more state intervention or market competition would depend on the specific situations in China. When state intervention brought about too many controls in the market, market competition would have to be strongly encouraged. When the market competition produced a gap between rich and poor, there would have to be more emphasis on public guidance.[26]

Chinese heritage put great emphasis on fair distribution of wealth, they stated. It was thus a serious mistake to think primarily of making China a powerful nation at the expense of people's welfare. "When the people are destitute, the nation can never be truly prosperous and powerful. . . . The interest of the state and that of the people are inseparable," asserted Kang. And the best way to promote both was "to give priority to the latter."[27]

The revolutionary nationalists put even greater emphasis on the issue of social justice in China's modern economy. As Sun Yat-sen proclaimed in 1913, "The railroads, public utilities, canals, and forests should be nationalized and all income from the land and mines should be in the hands of the state. With all this money in hand, the state can therefore finance the social welfare programs."[28]

After World War I, Sun Yat-sen proposed a coexistence between private, cooperative, and public enterprises in the modern economy. He emphasized the mixed economy, or the principle of people's livelihood, was neither a capitalist free-enterprise economy nor a socialist planned economy. In his view, while the free-enterprise system was effective for increasing wealth, it lacked the concept of fair distribution; and if the socialist planned economy emphasized fair distribution of wealth, it was not effective for rapid industrial growth. A combination of both, he argued, would be the best economic system for China. He particularly emphasized that the concept of fair distribution, unlike that of redistribution of wealth, opposed class warfare and embraced class reconciliation. But the only way to achieve class reconciliation in China's industrialization was to establish farsighted economic policies or to implement the Principle of People's Livelihood. That is, at an early stage in China's industrialization, Chinese economic policy should promote social/economic justice or use "peaceful means" to prevent the "intensifying of class warfare."[29]

These competing Chinese economic blueprints clearly shared one goal: to regard individual economic rights as part of human dignity, as well as the foundation of national freedom. Moreover, they also shared the view that the government must assume its responsibility to achieve the goal of both rapid growth and social justice in the modern economy.

In the United States, by contrast, the vision of a free-enterprise system dominated the mainstream discourse on the modern economy. Western Europe in the eighteenth century witnessed intense debates on the meaning of modernity, particularly the impact of a commercial revolution on modern society. At one end of the spectrum, Jean-Jacques Rousseau denounced luxury, corruption, and modern commercial society. He warned that modern man's obsession with the pursuit of individual wealth would lead to empty individualism, economic inequality, and the disintegration of human community. At the other end of the spectrum, Bernard de Mandeville openly embraced luxury and corruption, believing in the notion of "private vice, public good." In the middle were the French philosopher Voltaire and English author David Hume. They held a positive view of the modern commercial economy, arguing that the structural consequences of commercial development had come about with the decline of the rigid feudal order of rural society. But they also saw the modern economy as "circumscribed," always "bringing with it evils as well as blessings." In particular, they feared that the new "savages" spawned by the debased conditions of the laboring masses were bad candidates for citizens in a republican polity.[30]

The debates in Europe had an important impact on America's founding fathers. Jeffersonians were particularly alarmed by the possible dark side of a modern economy. As Thomas Jefferson argued, a society with large numbers of the landless poor could undermine the foundation of the young republic. How to avoid the emergence of a "landless poor" in America? State intervention was out of the question. To Jefferson, an ardent believer in a "minimal state," the solution was "expansion across space," or westward movement and free trade. Its objective was to create a society of independent, prosperous yeoman farmers, so that the new republic could remain at "the middle stage of modernity, between the first rude, barbarous and the last refined, corrupt stage of advanced modern economy."[31]

The Federalists were, however, more impressed by David Hume's emphasis on the progressive nature of the modern economy. Alexander Hamilton never doubted that the real disposition of human nature was toward luxury. He agreed with Locke that the marketplace was a fair playground, in which the more talented can excel and receive their rewards accordingly. Thus the modern market economy, through its mechanism of material incentives, would be the best engine for rapid industrialization. The crux of Hamilton's arguments was that political liberty and economic equality could not coexist in the modern economy. Equal political freedom could give all citizens an equal opportunity to become unequal in the marketplace and make "each man zealous to achieve for himself."[32]

In the early twentieth century, the rise of the progressive movement focused on the widening gap between rich and poor in the modern economy. "The industrial system based on an unchecked free market took men from the bench and field and chained them to the machine," claimed the progressive reformers. Perhaps this was the price society had to pay for rapid industrialization. But the time had come to make a change, they emphasized. Theodore Roosevelt's New Nationalism programs aimed to use mild government intervention to establish legislation on "graduated income and inheritance taxes, workmen's compensation, regulation of the labor of women and children, and a stronger Bureau of Corporations." But Woodrow Wilson called New Nationalism programs "new slavery," saying they would only regulate, rather than dismantle, the monopoly of big corporations, thus making Americans more dependent on the government.

In the Great Depression, Franklin D. Roosevelt's New Deal further introduced the concepts of the "positive state" into the mainstream discourse. The New Dealers/modern liberals and modern conservatives sharply differed on whether the state should put more income taxes into the public realm. For the modern conservatives, the purpose of the American national economy was "to maximize personal consumption." For the New Dealers/modern liberals, on the other hand, maximizing personal consumption "precisely is the root of our trouble." A major function of the state in the economic field was, in their view, to use governmental resources (mainly from income taxes) to reconstruct the public realm.[33]

The New Dealers/modern liberals emphasized, however, that their ideas were fundamentally different from those of the Left with respect to the role of the state in the marketplace. In their view, the Left ignored the possibility of unlimited political power concentrated in the hands of the government. The concept of the positive state, they believed, was thus "the best means to check both unlimited economic power in the hands of private monopolies and unlimited political power in the hands of the government."[34]

Therefore, modern liberals stated that they shared a common ground with modern conservatives; that is, their faith in the major role of private ownership and marketplace in the modern economy and their confidence in the great merit of a free enterprise system in America.

What were the similarities and differences between Chinese and American discourses on a modern economy? Both modern Chinese and American reformers were primarily concerned with how to construct the relationships between political liberty and economic equality, and between rapid growth and social/economic justice. However, in these mainstream discourses, each side advocated very different solutions.

The Taiping rebels' radical populist economic blueprint of employing a centralized state to eradicate private economy and enforce an absolute egalitarian society was surely alien to mainstream America. On the other hand, the Hamiltonian concept of irreconcilability between political liberty and economic equality was clearly alien to the mainstream Chinese discourse. The Chinese constitutionalists' blueprint of a private economy with public guidance, or its emphasis on the balanced role between state intervention and market competition in the modern economy, was more similar to the concept of the social market in continental Europe rather than that of the liberal market in the United States.

Most important, Sun's principle of people's livelihood—the republican revolutionaries' blueprint of a mixed economy—was even further removed from the American belief in the fundamental virtue of private ownership in the modern economy.

These major differences can be attributed to their vastly different assumptions with regard to the relationship between political liberty and economic equality. In the mainstream American discourse, the importance of political liberty or individual civil and political rights holds the highest place. In the mainstream Chinese discourse, individual civil and political rights, individual economic rights, and national rights to develop could not be separated from one another, but were dependent upon one another in the modern economy. Thus if Sun's principle of people's livelihood represented a middle ground between the radical populists and the constitutionalists in the Chinese milieu, he appeared to be a "social radical" in the American setting, as Woodrow Wilson dubbed him.

Discourses on the Modern Polity

From the mid-nineteenth century through the early twentieth century, before the rise of the CCP, two major competing visions emerged in the Chinese discourse on the modern polity: the radical populist polity and democracy. After the rise of the CCP (1921) and before the war of resistance (1937), three major political blueprints competed in China: a united front between Sun Yat-sen's Kuomintang (KMT) and the CCP, a parliamentary system excluding the CCP, and Chinese soviets in rural China excluding the KMT.

In Hong Xiuquan's blueprint for the Taiping peasant rebels, an economic system of absolute egalitarianism clearly required a concentrated political power to enforce its implementation. Thus, according to Hong, elected officials in the village commune should be in charge of everything from the military to agricultural production and from politics to education to make sure the most hated phenomenon in rural China—the gap between rich and poor—would never occur in the Heavenly Kingdom on earth.

In the late nineteenth century, the constitutionalists envisioned a constitutional monarchy in China, after the model of Meiji Japan. However, Chinese intellectuals increasingly rejected this concept and turned instead to the ideal of democracy and republicanism. As Sun declared, Chinese republican revolutionaries must never entertain the notion of becoming "new emperors" after the revolution, like the peasant rebels had over the past 2,000 years. Otherwise, "we would cause China's subjugation and genocide in today's world." Sun rejected the argument that a democratic polity could never take root in China because the Chinese tradition was "contradictory with the democratic ideals." He emphasized that the ideal of people's sovereignty was a central theme in the Confucian/Taoist heritage. It contributed to the creation of the first national civil-service-exam system in world history, a system based on meritocracy rather than on aristocracy, as well as on the concept of universal rights to education. The ideal of people's sovereignty in Chinese heritage also engendered a new interpretation of "the mandate of heaven," which offered moral sanctions to poor peasants' rights to armed rebellion to overthrow a decadent dynasty, he argued. China's polity must therefore be "modernized" by combining the best from the Chinese and the Western heritages, particularly the incorporation of the Western concepts of institutional checks and balances and rule of law, into the modern Chinese political system.[35]

If the 1911 democratic revolution led by Sun brought down the last Manchu dynasty, it did not produce a new China. Instead, in Sun's words, it brought about a "sham parliamentary system" led by Yuan Shikai, which was followed by warlordism and national disintegration. It was in the aftermath of the failed 1911 revolution that Sun articulated a theory of democratic transition in China. He proposed three stages of evolution. In the first stage, military rule, the major task was to eliminate the warlords and achieve national unity through military force. In the second stage, tutelage rule, there should be a "strong political leadership," made up of dedicated intellectual reformers, that was "willing to assume the hardship and risks of modernization" and to lead "an extraordinarily tough transition." In this stage, the major task was to employ this "political leadership" to carry out village and county elections, to help the villagers understand the rule of law, due process, and other major concepts of democracy and constitutionalism. Tutelage rule was crucial for China's democratic transition, he said, since "a democratic façade" after the republican revolution of 1911 was brought about by "our neglect of such a 'revolutionary process' and a reckless advance to parliamentary government." The third stage, constitutional rule, should bring full democracy in China. After every village and every county had fair, effective elections, there should be direct provincial elections; and after every province had successful direct elections, a multiparty system and the national election would naturally follow. He emphasized that the voting rights in the West were for a very long period of time limited to property owners, males, and white people. In contrast, he said, with this gradualist, bottom-up approach, voting rights would be immediately extended to the poor peasants, women, and minorities in China. "How can human rights ever be developed in China? The only way is to organize the common people, village-by-village, and county-by-county." In the short run, this democratization process might appear to be slow, he said. But in the long run, he argued, this approach would be the best way to build a genuine democratic polity in China.[36]

By the late 1910s, many urban intellectuals, particularly college students, became disillusioned with the failure of the 1911 republican revolution and impatient with Sun's gradual approach to full democracy in China. They began to turn to anarchism as a faster way to reform the Chinese polity. Voluntary student organizations mushroomed. Their basic idea was to build democracy immediately by "destroying the boundary between manual and mental labors, making every manual laborer study, and making every intellectual do manual work." The most famous anarchist organization at the time was the Beijing Labor-Study Mutual Aid League. Within the league, all things produced belonged to the community. In a few months, however, the league was dissolved.[37]

The collapse of the league and other, similar anarchist organizations in urban centers shook the Chinese intellectual community. If the constitutionalist reform, the democratic revolution, and anarchist experiments all failed to produce a democratic polity in China, how could the old Chinese political structure ever be replaced? As Shi Cuntong—a former anarchist of the Beijing Labor-Study Mutual Aid League—recalled, the answer seemed clear to many: "We must first of all employ radical means to make a total, thorough change of the entire nation."[38]

Many anarchists were quickly attracted to the Russian Revolution of 1917. As Sun himself observed, young students in Beijing and other cities "rushed" to Russia to "learn everything about socialism and communism." Cai Hesen, a former anarchist who later became one of the CCP founders, wrote at the time: "We realize that we cannot implement anarchism immediately, because there are two antagonistic classes in the current world." So "we must use the means of socialism or communism" to reach "the ends of anarchism in the future."[39]

According to others in the socialist movement, such as Mao Zedong and Zhou Enlai, the major issue was not only class division but, more important, the existence of a most powerful landed elite in the countryside. The total revenue of the Manchu government was merely 2.4 percent of the gross national income, and the rest was mostly in the hands of the landed elite. As long as they controlled the agricultural revenue, "the Chinese state would never be able to transfer the agricultural accumulation to industrial investment," as the Meiji government had done in Japan.[40]

From this perspective, Chinese political reform must start with a land revolution. "China was neither able to abolish the landed aristocracy through a French-style revolution, nor able to begin her industrialization through a Japanese-style constitutional monarchy," Zhou Enlai wrote after he had studied in Japan and Europe. Why? "Because China's landed elite was too powerful. The landed elite accounted for 10 percent of the rural population." A land revolution was not only the best way to achieve China's political reform and industrialization, he argued, but also the "only way" to achieve China's national freedom. "For the past one hundred years all modern Chinese reformers were trying to find a way to end the age of national humiliation. But they all failed," he maintained. Among all political parties in China, the CCP was the only one that saw "the intimate connection between national liberation and social revolution" and was therefore "determined to carry out a social revolution to achieve national freedom."[41]

Meanwhile, during the early 1920s, Sun and his followers continued to champion a democratic polity and a gradualist, bottom-up approach to full democracy. With the establishment of the CCP in 1921, Sun urged building a united front between the KMT and the CCP. He emphasized that these two parties—one with urban China as its base, the other with the poor peasants as its major constituency—should become "equal partners" in China's new polity. He thought this unity was particularly important in organizing village elections and building local assemblies in rural China. "Foreigners have always laughed at us, claiming that the Chinese are like 'a sheet of loose sand,' thus 'hopeless.' " He repeatedly told the members of both parties that the unity of these two parties should be the "best answer" to the skeptical foreigners, and the "best guarantee" for building a genuine, rather than a sham, democratic polity in China.[42]

With the death of Sun Yat-sen in 1925 and the collapse of the united front between the KMT and the CCP in 1927, new types of grassroots organizations emerged that were entirely different from what Sun had envisioned. The landed elite now dominated the elections of county assemblies organized by the KMT government. As a British scholar observed, since the KMT had no political organizations among poor peasants, with the communists out of the way, "the little finger of the local landlord is now thicker than the loins of the KMT government in Nanjing." The election was thus distorted. The entire apparatus fell into "the hands of the old ruling groups," often "through the use of the votes of their clan dependents or the votes of terrorized tenants."[43]

On the other hand, in communist-controlled areas, the incorporation of poor peasants into political struggle, without institutional checks, "ruralized" the political process. Many poor peasant associations in the CCP area in this period enjoyed quasi-judicial powers, as traditional rural secret societies, guilds, and clans had done. These poor peasant organizations greatly encouraged "the arbitrariness of justice," as "exemplified in the summary execution of bandits and the drumhead justice against the 'bad gentry.' " Thus the CCP movement, based on the direct participation of poor peasants, had "a built-in anti-legalist mechanism and strong anti-intellectual sentiments," which demonstrated surprising similarity to many of the political characteristics of the Taiping peasant rebellion.[44]

Most Chinese reformers, however, understood the importance of the spiritual transformation of Chinese people as the foundation of the modern polity. According to Hong Xiuquan, the Christian ideal, as he interpreted it, should be the basis of the new political system. In Liang Qichao's view, rule of law must be "balanced" by rule of man. Without a "new citizenry," he wrote, all reform programs could merely alleviate the symptoms of China's political illness, but could not effect a "permanent cure." Liang's view was shared by Sun. The eventual triumph of a democratic polity in China, as Sun argued, "lies in the morality of its citizens."[45]

China not only needed a bottom-up approach to full democracy, but also needed new generations of intellectuals who would be selflessly dedicated to serving the people, the nation, and world peace and harmony. Only with the creation of a "moral citizenry," combined with the rule of law and divisions of power, could China's democratic polity have a more solid foundation.[46]

In America, the central concern underlying visions of a modern polity was which system could best protect individual rights to private property and free expression. For the founders, the answer is a political system of checks and balances and the Bill of Rights as enshrined in the Constitution.

The basic principle of checks and balances in the modern polity is that "sovereignty must be limited, no matter where sovereignty resides, in a monarch, a class, or a people." If the Federalists feared, above all, "power lodged in the majority," Jeffersonians feared "power lodged anywhere else." As Jefferson argued, "honest republican governments" should be "so mild in their punishment" of people's rebellions, "as not to discourage them too much." "A little rebellion now and then is a good thing, and as necessary in the political world as storms in the physical." It is much better that people be restless than that they be lethargic—for "lethargy in the people means death for republics." This does not mean that Jefferson endorsed the French concept of direct democracy. On the contrary, he, like the Federalists, championed the basic principle of checks and balances in the polity.[47]

Moreover, Jefferson believed in the plasticity of the human mind. He was convinced that freedom of religion and freedom of conscience, rather than self-cultivation and moral education, were the best way to create a republican citizenry. Thus, the Constitution set up a legal framework for democratic compromise and tolerance among the citizens. Its ultimate objective was to protect its citizens' essential civil and political rights. It is important to note that, at that time, these rights were not applied to African Americans, Native Americans, or women.

As Alexis de Tocqueville keenly observed in 1835, the rise of voluntary organizations at the grassroots level further contributed to the consolidation of America's democratic polity. In these voluntary associations, he saw the "spiritual affinity" between sectarian Protestantism and individual liberty. Indeed, he believed that religion is "more needed in a democratic republic than in any other. How is it possible that society should escape destruction if the moral tie is not strengthened in proportion as the political tie is relaxed? And what can be done with a people who are their own masters if they are not submissive to the Deity?"[48]

What, then, were the similarities and differences between Chinese and American mainstream discourses of democracy in the modern era? While both modern Chinese and American reformers agreed that kings or emperors should not—must not—rule and that sovereignty must reside in the people, there were essential differences in their discourse on the modern polity. First, they differed in their constructions of human nature. In the U.S. Constitution, "the soul-craft behind the state-craft has been Presbyterian," reflecting a belief in the "original sin" of human beings. The authors of the Constitution had anticipated "every evil of human nature, every by-path to power that history traced."[49] In the Chinese cultural heritage, there is optimism about human nature and a persistent emphasis on the possibility of eradicating human selfishness through self-cultivation and moral education.[50] Thus modern Chinese reformers often underestimated the danger of the reemergence of a new ideological monism inherent in the creation of a "moral citizenry."[51] Put another way, the "spiritual transformation" of the Chinese people must be combined and preconditioned by a Chinese bill of rights. With such a constitutional guarantee, China's emphasis on Yin-Yang balance or "harmony between the opposites" in its philosophical thinking could be complemented by a system of institutional checks and balances found in a modern polity. A more important difference in Chinese and American visions of a modern polity was Sun's theory of gradual democratic transition and his call for a united front between the KMT and the CCP to carry out land revolution and village mobilization. This vision of China's democratic transition was obviously foreign to middle-class America in the modern era.

In 1924, when Sun Yat-sen contemplated a new economic system in China, he called it a system of people's livelihood. It would be neither a capitalist system nor a socialist system, he said, but a mixture of both. China needed capitalism to generate wealth, and China also needed socialism to achieve fair distribution of wealth. In his view, only when the majority of the Chinese people could get rich together would China be able to achieve its industrialization. Only after China completed its industrialization, he said, could the country achieve "national freedom," and make its contribution to a new world order of peace, justice, and harmony.[52]

In 1984, when Deng Xiaoping, the leader of the CCP, reflected on China's economic reform, he talked about "building socialism with Chinese characteristics." China was to open up in order to learn from the West and encourage a portion of the Chinese people to get rich first. However, in China's modernization drive, he emphasized, the majority of the Chinese people must get rich together. When China's gross national product (GNP) reached $1 trillion, Deng saw two ways to distribute the wealth. In a capitalist system, only 10 percent of the Chinese people would be extremely wealthy, while the majority would remain "mired in poverty and backwardness." In a socialist system, "all the Chinese people would lead a relatively comfortable life." Deng declared: "This is why we want to uphold socialism." Deng defined socialism as a means of mobilizing all Chinese people to achieve China's modernization, rather than waging class warfare between workers/poor peasants and the intelligentsia, or between villages and colleges. Deng's ultimate goal for China's modernization was the achievement of national freedom and equality. "Nothing short of a world war" could tear China away from that goal, he stated, "and even if a world war broke out, we would engage in reconstruction after the war."[53]

While Sun and Deng employed different rhetoric and addressed different audiences, their economic blueprints revealed essential similarities. Both attempted to build a modern economic system in China in which there would be no polarization between rich and poor. Both regarded the ultimate goal of China's modernization to be its national freedom and equality in the world and the Great Commonwealth on earth. That is, their "core assumptions" or visions were remarkably similar, highlighting some enduring themes in China's historical quest for modernity and a new identity, ones deeply conditioned by China's cultural heritage, societal conditions, and position in the international system, and profoundly different from American visions of modernity and identity.

First, at the heart of the American cultural heritage is the sanctity of individual civil and political rights, or the concept that every individual is created in the image of God. Thus at the core of modernity is a philosophical or moral "dichotomy between individualism and collectivism."[54] Even the New Deal, which incorporated a belief in the positive state and economic justice into its programs, did not intend to transcend the moral/political parameters of individualism or individual civil and political liberties.

In contrast, the Chinese cultural heritage conceptualizes the universe as a system of Yin-Yang balance and harmony, of mutual benefit and dependence. Accordingly, Chinese mainstream discourse since the modern era has placed a strong emphasis on the mutual complementarity of the private and public sectors, or mutual benefit and dependence among individual civil and political rights, individual economic rights, and national rights to develop.[55]

In the mainstream American discourse on modernity, there is a broad consensus that no middle ground can or should be struck between these two oppositional categories of individualism and collectivism. On the other hand, in the mainstream Chinese discourse on modernity, there is a persistent belief that a middle ground can and should be found between the private and public realms. Such a profound difference between Chinese and American core concepts of modernity, obviously, would have a substantial impact on both sides' definitions of socialism and capitalism, and on their blueprints for reconstructing China's economy and polity.

Second, America is one of the few nations that has never had a feudal heritage; therefore it is one of the few nations that has never had a mainstream socialist movement. From the beginning of the republic, the northern states in the United States emerged as a vibrant middle-class society. A major political challenge in the United States has been how to appeal to the mainstream middle-class society in the cultural tradition of Lockean liberalism, as well as the religious tradition of sectarian Protestantism.

In contrast, a major political challenge in China since the modern era has been how to bring peasants and intellectuals/entrepreneurs, or rural and urban China together; in essence, how to strike a balance between the public and the private sectors to achieve China's freedom and modernization. Those divergent blueprints for China's economic and political reconstruction either favored the poor peasantry, as in the Taiping rebellion, or the urban and rural elites, as in the KMT's programs after Sun's death, or coalitions between rural peasantry and urban intelligentsia, as in Sun's Three Principles of the People. In this regard, Chinese cultural heritage created a unique intellectual space, wherein the efforts to build a genuine partnership between rural and urban China's vastly different economic priorities and political demands, and between a distinctive form of Chinese nationalism and world peace and harmony, as Sun championed, could enjoy the overwhelming support of the greatest majority of the Chinese people in the long run.

Third, in American worldviews, the ideal of individual freedom, or the sanctity of an individual's civil and political rights, is regarded not only as the highest fulfillment of human aspiration but as the vital foundation for long-standing peace in the world. In particular, since the end of World War II, many Americans who witnessed the horror of the Holocaust have asked why more was not done to prevent this human tragedy. This vivid historical memory has strengthened Kant's ideal of liberal peace and Wilsonian liberal internationalism in U.S. foreign policy debates since 1945. The most powerful moral conviction in America, bridging a range of ideologies, was that the American people must stand up to new Nazi Germanys, to new totalitarian ideologies, to avoid another human tragedy and a new world war.

In Chinese worldviews, the Great Commonwealth or universal peace, justice, and harmony is the ultimate human paradise on earth. Both the basic concept of Yin-Yang balance and the Golden Mean doctrine point to a more polytheistic world outlook.[56] In particular, in the wake of World War II, after more than 100 years of resistance against foreign invasions, there were no ideals in China that could generate more intense passions and appeal to more Chinese people than the ideals of national freedom, China's modernization, and world peace and harmony. The most powerful moral conviction in China following the war, spanning the spectrum of ideologies, was that the Chinese people must stand up to imperialism and concentrate on China's modernization drive.

In summary, neither the concept of cultural universalism nor that of cultural particularism, neither the ideal of individualism nor that of collectivism, is rich or complex enough to interpret the aspirations of Chinese reformers to freedom, social justice, and democracy in the modern era. Restated, Chinese and American visions of modernity and identity were neither identical with each other nor antagonistic to each other. Rather, they overlapped. Both modern Chinese and American reformers shared similar human concerns on how to build a modern economy, polity, and a new world order, but they formulated very different blueprints to reach their goals. Their principal differences cannot be simply explained by official ideologies, such as Christianity (Taiping peasant rebels' official ideology), democracy (the official ideology of Sun Yat-sen's KMT), socialism (the CCP's official ideology), and capitalism (the official ideology of Chiang Kai-shek's KMT). Instead, each country's deep ocean of historical currents played a much more vital role in shaping the contours in which the mainstream Chinese and American discourses on modernity and identity took place.

When World War II was over, China's quests for modernity and new identity marched on with extraordinary vigor and passion. To what extent were these profoundly different Chinese and American visions of modernity and identity to shape U.S.-China interactions, subconsciously as well as consciously, in the post–World War II and the Cold War era?

CHAPTER TWO

Straining the Relationship

Truman and the Reconstruction of
China after World War II

After World War II, mainstream American visions of a new world order were founded on a belief in political and economic freedom in the international arena. Most Americans genuinely believed that a free-trade system based on free enterprise, accompanied by universal political liberty, would guarantee enduring peace and prosperity in the post–World War II era.

Given this world outlook, how did U.S. president Harry S. Truman's administration attempt to reconstruct Nationalist China's polity and economy and integrate blueprints for China's incipient industrialization and democratization into the broad American visions of global peace and order in the post–World War II era? More important, when mainstream American visions interacted with mainstream Chinese visions, why did America's China policies produce the opposite result from what the Truman administration anticipated and intended?

The Bretton Woods Monetary Agreement was one of the pillars of the American plan for a new international system, and its first application was the negotiation, from April 1945 to November 1946, of the Commerce, Navigation and Friendship Treaty with the KMT government.

In the treaty for the United States' relinquishment of extraterritorial rights in China, signed January 11, 1943, the two countries agreed to enter into negotiations for concluding a modern commercial treaty as soon as the war was over. On April 2, 1945, the U.S. State Department presented to the KMT government a draft treaty, and in September negotiations began. Both Nationalist China and the United States attached great importance to these negotiations. On the American side, it was the first attempt to apply the basic principles of the Bretton Woods agreement to a developing nation with the aim of using it as a model for subsequent negotiations.[1] On the Chinese side, it was considered a symbol of China's independence and sovereignty after the unequal treaties and extraterritoriality had been abolished by the Allies; moreover, there was a strong desire to use these negotiations as China's first step toward entrance into the world family on an equal basis.

One year later, however, Chinese intellectuals and entrepreneurs, who had been the principal supporters of China's integration into the world economy, turned their back on the KMT government and the Truman administration. How did commercial treaty negotiations generate the first split between the KMT government and the urban Chinese middle class and trigger the first anti-American outcry in urban China in the postwar years? It is important to note that the American negotiators were FDR New Dealers, who aimed to create a new international order under which, they believed, the American economy would prosper most but the world poor would also benefit. So what went wrong in the negotiations between the Truman administration and the KMT government?

This chapter will begin with an examination of both Nationalist Chinese and American visions of China's incipient industrialization in the postwar era, with a focus on the Truman administration's efforts to reconstruct Nationalist China's economy and bring it into the free-trade, free-enterprise style of the New Deal. It will then discuss why there was a conflict of visions between Nationalist China, particularly its emerging middle class, and the Truman administration regarding China's postwar economic reconstruction. It will be followed by a discussion of the impact of this conflict on the major policy differences in the treaty negotiations. Finally, it will examine the implications of this treaty for the split between the KMT government and the urban Chinese middle class, as well as for the eruption of anti-American sentiments in urban China in the post–World War II years.

American Visions of China's Industrialization

Before World War II was over, the American business community demonstrated an unusual interest in participating in China's postwar economic reconstruction. On October 9, 1944, at the 31st National Foreign Trade Convention in New York City, the chair of the Far East Session made the following remarks:

> I have been listening for some years at these National Foreign Trade Conventions to the story of the good brotherhood between North America and South America, to the story of Europe, of Africa, and I always wondered if sometime in our lifetime we would begin to talk of the greatest area of future possibilities in the world, the Far East, with a population of over a billion people or twice the population of Europe; probably four times the area in square miles. . . . I cannot help thinking that in the future the great traffic of America, as regards its foreign trade, will be with Asia.[2]

This sentiment was not unique among American businessmen. In 1943, the Sino-American Industrial and Commercial Association was established. By October 1945, the members of the association numbered more than 370 units, nearly all of them big industrial and commercial companies in the United States.[3]

Intimately tied to the desire to participate in China's postwar economic reconstruction were the American business community's perceptions of China's industrialization. On December 22, 1944, the National Foreign Trade Council and the China-American Council of Commerce and Industry, Inc. (formerly the Sino-American Industrial and Commercial Association), sent the State Department a joint memorandum, "American Approach to the Development of Chinese-American Trade and Industry." They stated, "The views in this memorandum are those of the widest organized groups of American businessmen interested in China and are believed to be basic and fairly representative of the enlightened American businessmen's point of view" as to China's industrialization. In this memo, they explained what type of industrialization they preferred to see in China and what kind of preconditions China should provide to guarantee American businessmen's maximum participation there.[4]

First of all, they claimed, China's tariff and other trade barriers should be reduced "as much as is practicable": "It is of prime importance that China join with other nations in promoting a restoration of world trade on a non-discriminatory basis." Such a reduction of the tariff was "essential" for their participation in China's industrialization and for integrating China into the free-trade system.

The second important condition for their participation, they maintained, was that the Chinese government not depend mainly on extensive U.S. government loans, but instead on American private capital as the major source of financing for China's industrialization. A great potential danger could be involved in such intergovernmental loans, they argued. "Once a loan is made, it becomes a direct obligation of the Chinese government to service it in dollars with a definite schedule of interest payments and installments of principal." Since the amount of funds required for postwar reconstruction in China was so huge, the intergovernmental loans would soon "present really serious fiscal problems" for the Chinese government. Private capital, in contrast, would relieve the Chinese government of such fiscal obligations. If private resources could be enlisted in the form of direct investments by American enterprises or investments in Chinese companies, they maintained, the obligation of the Chinese government would be limited to providing only "(a) reasonable security and healthy conditions for the earning (by Americans investors) of a moderate return by way of interest or dividends and (b) foreign exchange to cover that portion of earnings which needs to be remitted as dividends and interest, plus amortization of such capital as in the forms of loans." And they further pointed to the areas in China where they were willing to provide private capital: heavy industry, light industry, mineral exploration, transportation, communication, and public utilities, among others. In short, they were eager to invest in almost every sphere of China's economic reconstruction.

The third important condition for their participation in China's industrialization, they said, was full-scale privatization in China. "American business is committed to one fundamental conviction. This is, simply stated, that in the long run, greater and more efficient results can and will be obtained by the fullest enlistment of free private enterprise with government encouragement, than by primary reliance upon government." Of course, ideology was not the only reason for such insistence on China's privatization. There was also a very practical consideration: American businessmen were confident that, given nondiscriminatory treatment, they could successfully compete with Chinese private enterprises. But if there were a wide range of public, or state, enterprises in China, the prospect for them would be very different. "The prospect of government entering into direct competition would operate as a serious deterrent to any substantial investment for private account. Hence, the field of private enterprise in China should be unequivocally reserved" for foreign investment, since American private capital surely did not want to compete with state enterprises. Therefore, they claimed, "if there is general agreement on the desirability of attracting private venture capital to China, this should be formalized on the basis of definite assurances concerning the areas in which private enterprise may operate. The larger the area of commercial and industrial activity that can be defined as the accepted field of private enterprise, the greater will be the inducement to private enterprise" of the United States.[5] Among these three conditions, a free-enterprise system in China was regarded as the most important precondition for the realization of the first two.

What were the State Department's views of the reduction of tariffs, American private investment, and privatization in China's postwar economic reconstruction? Officials there did not entirely agree with the business community's many recommendations.

First of all, State Department officials maintained that, since China's tariff was "generally low," "the emphasis in the case of China should be against the creation of any discrimination in the application of Chinese tariffs and drastic increases in the present tariffs." These officials were advocating the same conditions that Secretary of State John Hay had asked for in his Open Door Notes in 1899 and 1900: low tariffs and equal treatment of all great powers in China.

Second, while State Department officials agreed that the majority of investment should come from American private capital, they posited that U.S. government loans were necessary, particularly for developing China's public utilities. "The most rapid development of the public utilities, particularly transportation, should be of the utmost importance to China, both for purposes of industrial growth and achievement of political solidarity," they argued, and the U.S. government "should be most willing to provide assistance on a long term basis."

Third, they agreed with the American business community that private, not state, enterprise should dominate industry and commerce in postwar China. They shared the business community's belief that a rapid privatization of Nationalist China's industry and commerce would not only yield "a larger total overall production of wealth," but also "be most conducive to the maintenance of democratic institutions within the country."[6]

However, there were significant differences between the State Department and the American business community with regard to privatization in China. Whereas the American business community demanded the least possible intervention from the KMT government, State Department officials preferred moderate intervention from the state to ensure fair distribution of wealth in China's economic reconstruction. Their argument was that an extreme form of privatization without any accompanying social policies could cause economic inequality, and thus political instability. They warned, "There is danger that in the process of turning back public enterprises to private hands, an enlarged concentration of economic power will result." It followed, then, that social policy must be incorporated into the general economic policies in Nationalist China's postwar reconstruction, "so that increased social output will redound to the advantage of the general population rather than toward further concentration of wealth and economic power in the hands of the few." They pointed out: "This type of growth tending to promote economic equality is most conducive to the proper functioning of a private competitive economy and to political and economic stability." Therefore, while Nationalist China should establish a free-enterprise system, "a certain amount of governmental planning is essential under the circumstances existent in China."[7]

In short, different blueprints for China's economic reconstruction had been drawn up in Washington. The American business community urged a laissez-faire market economy in China. The State Department instead asked for a free economy of a moderate nature in China, a free-enterprise system of the New Deal type. What emerged was "moderate plans within a framework of freedom." As New Dealers of the FDR era, the State Department negotiators were confident that if this blueprint for China's industrialization were fully implemented, China's economy would be strengthened, the gap between rich and poor narrowed, political stability restored, and Nationalist China integrated into the American-led liberal international economic system.

Chinese Nationalist Visions of China's Industrialization

Chiang Kai-shek published *The Theory of China's Economy* in 1943, presenting his own thoughts on China's industrialization. The basic theme of his book was that the reconstruction of China should follow neither the Western nor the Soviet economic models but rather Sun Yat-sen's Principle of People's Livelihood.

"The Western theory of free economy" was "founded on lust, particularly the lust of the 'small me,' " he said. "And economic development from such a foundation may lead to the destruction of reason and humanity." In contrast, he stressed, Sun Yat-sen's Principle of People's Livelihood, like Chinese traditional economic theories, was "founded on reason and the common good."

Moreover, the state's role in economic development, he said, was better defined in Sun's principle and Chinese traditional economic theory than it was in either Western or Soviet economics. Indeed, "European laissez-faire economics is against state intervention in people's economic activities; while Marxist economics wants to eliminate all individual economic freedom." He said both went to "extremes." From Confucius to Sun Yat-sen, Chiang said, Chinese economic theories took a middle ground concerning the state's role in the economy. That is, the state should actively promote people's desires to get rich, not trying to eliminate these desires, but also help to check people's "selfish lust" and achieve a fair distribution of wealth in society. "If the former can be called 'kindness,' the latter 'justice.' " In this connection, he remarked that "many Chinese economists only adored foreign economic doctrines, either Western or Soviet economic theories." Sun Yat-sen's Principle of People's Livelihood was popular with the Chinese people, Chiang argued, because it was consistent with the moral order of Chinese cultural tradition, which valued the common good, social engineering, reason, and humanity in economic development. And so he believed that in the post–World War II era, China must follow Sun Yat-sen's principle in the country's industrialization.[8]

In the closing months of 1944, one year after the publication of Chiang's book, the Supreme National Defense Council, the most important executive branch of the KMT government in wartime China, passed a resolution, "The General Principles Regarding China's Postwar Industrialization." The "General Principles" attempted to define the relationships between public and private enterprises and between foreign and Chinese capital.

With respect to the relationship between public and private enterprises, the resolution provided for a mixed economy, rather than a free-enterprise system. The Supreme National Defense Council explained, "This mixed economy is both different from Soviet socialism which regards private enterprises as exceptions, and free capitalism which considers public enterprises as exceptions."

Enterprises falling within the public sphere were as follows: (1) post and telegraphic administration, (2) munitions works, (3) mints, (4) main railway lines, and (5) large hydraulic power stations. The private sphere comprised the entire field of business aside from the five just listed. The "General Principles" proposed that foreign capital would be welcomed in all those spheres reserved for private enterprises in China. The public enterprise also welcomed foreign investment in the form of loans, but foreign management would not be allowed.[9]

But the KMT Sixth Congress refused to accept the "General Principles" as the guidelines for China's industrialization. On May 19, 1945, it passed a resolution, "Industrial Reconstruction Program in Postwar China" ("Reconstruction Program"), which was sharply critical of the "General Principles" and demanded greater restriction of private enterprise and foreign direct investment, or a "more comprehensive pursuit of Dr. Sun Yat-sen's Principle of People's Livelihood." In particular, a younger group within the KMT Sixth Congress complained that the "General Principles" did not provide sufficient protection for indigenous Chinese industry and commerce. They thus recommended that the government tighten regulations of foreign investment in China for ten to fifteen years, which was to be considered a transitional period.[10] Their views were shared by a number of high-ranking government officials, including Sun Fo, the president of the Legislative Yuan (the Chinese parliament).[11]

Chinese private entrepreneurs enthusiastically joined the debates about economic reconstruction. Through the Chinese Industrial Association, which comprised almost all the important wartime industrialist organizations in Nationalist China, they presented a different approach to China's industrialization.[12] Chinese entrepreneurs supported Sun Yat-sen's Principle of People's Livelihood, or the model of mixed economy. They believed that since "the territorial extent, population, and state of industrial under-development of China are so enormous," there would be "boundless possibilities for economic reconstruction in all fields." Thus, "a division of public and private enterprises on a rational basis would give both sectors fairly extensive spheres of operation without any particular obstacles to private initiative and capital."[13]

However, Chinese entrepreneurs did not totally agree with either the "General Principles" or the "Reconstruction Program" of the Nationalist Government. They wanted larger private spheres for Chinese private industry and commerce; in this regard, they were more in favor of the "General Principles" issued by the Supreme National Defense Council. Yet they also demanded more restrictions on foreign capital and more protection from the KMT government in their competition with foreign companies; in this respect, they were more in favor of the "Reconstruction Program" of the Sixth Congress of the KMT. They particularly advocated that "foreign companies of a highly competitive nature should not be welcomed by the Chinese government." Only those foreign enterprises "which require high technique and heavy equipment and which cannot be supplied from Chinese sources should be highly welcomed."[14]

On September 25, 1945, Chiang Kai-shek issued a confidential order to the general secretaries of the Supreme National Defense Council asking them to "compare the similarities and differences between these different proposals, to weigh the advantages and disadvantages of each of them, and to present a unified blueprint for China's industrialization." He particularly suggested that there should be a middle ground between the "General Principles" and the "Reconstruction Program." For instance, the spheres for public enterprises could be larger than those in the "General Principles" but smaller than those in the "Reconstruction Program."[15]

In their report of October 17, 1945, however, the general secretaries of the Supreme National Defense Council recommended adopting the "General Principles" as the guiding principles of China's postwar economic reconstruction. They argued that the "Reconstruction Program" of the KMT Sixth Congress tried to establish more governmental controls and regulations, "thus it implies restrictions within a planned economy." In contrast, the "General Principles" only enumerated certain important rules without too many regulations, "thus it implies encouragement for free development of private and foreign enterprises within the general framework of a planned economy," or "freedom within a plan."

Furthermore, they argued that although one of China's goals in its industrialization was to develop public capital, this goal could only be "achieved step by step." Thus the sphere for public enterprise in the "General Principles" should be regarded as the beginning stage of such a development, which could be "expanded in the later stages."

There was still another important reason for the adoption of the "General Principles," they stressed. It provided the best way "to get rid of the common shortcomings" of public enterprises, through the private corporation system. In all public enterprises, the government could only exercise its power of administrative supervision; beyond this, the government would not be allowed to exercise its power, any more than a shareholder had a voice regarding the company's management, finance, and personnel. That is to say, "all government officials are not allowed to participate in management of the enterprises of which they are in charge." If this plan could be implemented as required by the "General Principles," it would "greatly promote the spirit of free competition and speed up the development of public capital." According to the Supreme National Defense Council's report, "In order to develop public capital in the future, we must first prevent the development of bureaucratic capital; otherwise, government officials can take advantage of their positions to control public enterprises. They would be tempted to accumulate their own private capital, or bureaucratic capital, rather than real public capital." They repeatedly stressed to Chiang that such important regulations concerning "the banning of bureaucratic capital and the development of real public capital" were absent from the "Reconstruction Program" of the KMT Sixth Congress.

On top of all these arguments, the report reminded Chiang that when the "General Principles" were announced, "they won acclaim from American industrial and commercial circles," whereas when the "Reconstruction Program" had been announced, "it evoked doubts and suspicions on the American side." Since China's economic reconstruction needed foreign capital, "we cannot afford to ignore public opinion overseas." The report also assured Chiang that, "we might as well start from the 'General Principles.' After the basic industrial structure is built, we can further expand the sphere for public enterprise gradually, and reach the goal of the 'Reconstruction Program' regarding the development of public capital eventually."[16]

On January 5, 1946, Chiang Kai-shek approved the recommendations of this report, and the "General Principles" of the Supreme National Defense Council became the blueprint of Nationalist China's industrialization drive, not without disagreement, however. Chinese industrialists asked for an expansion of the private sector and for more governmental protection from foreign competition. The KMT Sixth Congress wanted more governmental protections for Chinese indigenous industry and commerce, in addition to stricter constraints on private capital so as to "avoid the worst form of capitalism." The moderate reformers in the Supreme National Defense Council took a centrist position, proposing a "fair division" between private and public enterprises and between foreign capital and Chinese capital. In spite of these important differences, the basic consensus among the Nationalists was that China should have a transitional stage of ten to fifteen years to enter the world free-trade system, and that Sun Yatsen's Principle of People's Livelihood, rather than the American economic model, should guide China's industrialization, to achieve a better balance between rapid growth and fair distribution of wealth as China's economy grew.

Conflicting Visions

In both Nationalist China and the United States, the more extreme proposals for China's industrialization did not become the official positions. In Washington, the New Dealers' blueprint at the State Department prevailed. In China, the Supreme National Defense Council's "General Principles" became the guiding document for China's economic reconstruction. However, there were still profound differences between these two visions.

These differences were manifested at the meetings between representatives of the KMT government and the State Department before the commercial treaty negotiations started. The meetings were held in Chungking, the wartime capital of Nationalist China. The Chinese delegation included governmental officials and representatives from the Chinese Industrial Association and from the intellectual community, which was headed by Wong Wenhao, the minister of economic affairs. The American delegation included State Department officials and representatives from the American business community, as well as prominent American economists. The delegation was headed by Charles Remer, an economic consultant at the State Department and a leading American scholar on foreign investment in China. The purpose of these meetings was an exchange of ideas between the two nations concerning the reduction of tariffs, foreign investment in China, the state's role in China's industrialization, and which model China should follow.

Most Chinese participants argued that China needed a transitional period of ten to fifteen years to reduce its tariffs. Within this transitional period, China should have the right to adopt "a reasonably high tariff" to protect its infant industry and commerce. They argued that in the nineteenth century, the United States was "an outstanding example of protectionism." In comparison, Nationalist China's demand was "a moderate protective tariff."[17] Sun Fo said that China would remove or lessen high protective tariffs as soon as its industry reached maturity, "at the conclusion of which China could become a member of the world free trade system."[18] As an American Embassy official observed, "The need of protection for Chinese infant industries was indeed emphasized by almost everyone of the Chinese delegation at the conference."[19]

The Chinese delegates clearly expressed their desire that intergovernmental loans, rather than foreign private capital, should be the major financial source of China's economic reconstruction. Wong Wenhao compared China's post–World War II situation with that of 1895 to make his point. When the Sino-Japanese war of 1895 was over, he said, the Chinese recognized their weakness and had a strong desire to bring foreign private capital into their country. Russia was favored as a source of such capital, because many Chinese felt that Russia was against Japan. China thus gave Russia the rights to build railways, to open mines, to start banks, and to do business in China. But by the end of the nineteenth century, the British, French, Germans, and Italians all demanded rights and concessions in China. Within a short time, China descended into the most miserable situation in its history. In this connection, Wong used the phrase "the danger of death from a sincere welcome to foreign private capital." There was no doubt that Chinese national sentiment underwent a significant change during the war of resistance, he stressed. Now the Chinese were, once again, eager to attract foreign capital into China, in order to build up a modern nation as soon as possible. However, he warned, "We must see that the public opinion here may be against foreign capital coming in freely once more." Therefore, "the general interest of the United States will probably be best served by making available to the Government of China a long-term loan at a low rate of interest."[20]

Of course, this did not mean that the Chinese participants were not interested in foreign direct investment in China. They were. They were eager to attract foreign private capital into China, to revitalize Chinese industries. However, in this regard, they also had important differences with their American counterparts, the chief of which centered on whether foreign direct investment should be allowed to compete with all Chinese private industries without any intervention from the Chinese government. The American participants insisted that because five industrial fields had already been singled out for the sphere of public enterprises, foreign private capital must be permitted to compete with Chinese entrepreneurs in the rest of the industrial fields. But the Chinese participants disagreed. In their opinion, "foreign investment in China was not free from political designs in the past." Thus "it will take time for the foreign investors to prove that they are now a different lot, different from their ancestors, and prepared to meet the Chinese on equal ground." Moreover, in their view, "the question of direct foreign investment in competitive industries cannot be considered wholly from an economic point of view." For example, if a foreign cotton mill successfully displaced a Chinese competitor by reason of its efficiency, the net effect on the welfare of the people would probably be beneficial, since it might provide cheaper and better textile goods to consumers, but "a case like this cannot be used to justify the free exploitation of the Chinese market without any guidance except the incentive to make a profit." In the words of Koh Tsung-fei at the Ministry of Communication, "Carried to the extreme, this kind of unlimited competition could work great havoc in China. One large foreign plantation, for instance, may displace thousands of small farm holdings, and half a million peasants may be thrown out of work." He emphasized that "from purely economic considerations, it cannot be denied that large and mechanized farming is more efficient." However, "the concomitant disturbance of the society is too serious and economic benefits should not be the only consideration."[21]

Most important of all, the sharpest difference occurred between Chinese and American participants with respect to the state's role in the economy, or the issue of privatization. For the Chinese delegates, Sun's Principle of People's Livelihood, or a mixed economic model, would offer the best chance for achieving harmony between rapid growth and economic justice. For the State Department, however, a free-enterprise system with moderate governmental intervention would be most conducive to that goal.

While the New Deal had surely contributed to social and economic justice in America, the Chinese delegates argued that it might not produce similar results in China. And the reason was simple: America was an industrialized nation and a middle-class society, while China was a developing country, with over 90 percent of the population living in impoverished villages.

According to Remer, the Chinese insistence on a mixed economy, rather than a free-enterprise system, was "most troubling." In his memo to the State Department, he sharply criticized the Supreme National Defense Council's "General Principles" for China's industrialization, or its division into public and private sectors. He also sharply criticized Chiang Kai-shek's *The Theory of China's Economy*. Chiang's theory, he said, was nothing more than "the Kuomintang's embrace of nationalistic socialism," which had been developed "in the midst of War and under conditions of increased governmental power."

At this point, Remer particularly targeted Sun's Principle of People's Livelihood. He emphasized that in the United States, economic planning was usually associated with the Soviets; but in Nationalist China, it was associated with Sun Yat-sen. The Chinese refused "to look beyond Sun's writings for any other sources," and "only when the 'General Principles' were read with Sun's writings in mind, could the underlying structure of ideas in the 'General Principles' become clear." Remer complained that Sun Yat-sen was "too powerfully" influenced by European socialist ideology. "He took it for granted that the socialism he had in mind could be created in the Chinese scene and he gave too little attention to the individualism which is a necessary support for the liberal aspects of his socialist state." Thus, in his view Sun's Principle of People's Livelihood was not at all a middle ground between individual rights and group rights, as Sun himself proclaimed, but a "disguised form of collectivism." In his words, "Dr. Sun's Principle of People's Livelihood, while it pays lip service to private enterprise, is really concerned with the establishment of public enterprise on a grand scale, and with the securing of foreign capital for that purpose."

Remer argued that some KMT governmental officials did not agree with the "General Principles" or Sun's Principle of People's Livelihood and preferred to install a free-enterprise system in China, but they were in the minority. Without America's help, they could not prevail in the KMT government.[22]

State Department officials agreed that even though "a certain amount of governmental planning is essential under the circumstances existent in China," it should only function within the framework of a free-enterprise system. They claimed, "It is believed that China's 'mixed economy' proposals are not in full accord with our objective in China's economic reconstruction."[23]

The key issue is not that China and the United States had different blueprints for China's economic reconstruction, but how their major differences were interpreted in both countries. Remer believed that the different Chinese and American visions had to be viewed in the context of the worldwide ideological competition between American individualism/liberalism and Soviet collectivism/communism in the post–World War II era. Thus he could not understand why Sun's Principle of People's Livelihood was neither American individualism nor Soviet collectivism. Perceiving the different visions in the light of "ideological rivalry" between the United States and the Soviet Union, the Truman administration concluded that it had no other alternative but to win over Nationalist China to the American model of economic development.[24]

Major Policy Differences in Commercial Treaty Negotiations (September 1945–November 1946)

In the course of commercial treaty negotiations, the conflict of visions was immediately transformed into major policy differences between these two nations. The first major difference was over China's mixed economic model. For the State Department negotiators, Nationalist China must establish a free-enterprise system in the New Deal style, which was essential not only for the world free-trade system but also for China's own economic development. They did not believe that a mixed economy could provide "compensating advantages to the Chinese economy."[25]

The second major difference was over the question of national treatment; that is, the American business community should enjoy the same rights and privileges as the Chinese when doing business in China. The American negotiators demanded "national treatment" for all Americans doing business with China in commerce, finance, and corporations. Chinese negotiators, however, believed that within the transitional period of ten to fifteen years, Americans should enjoy most-favored-nation treatment, rather than national treatment, in China.[26]

The American negotiators maintained that their demand was consistent with the general thinking of the UN Monetary and Financial Conference at Bretton Woods. If the provisions on corporations in this treaty with China were much wider in scope than those in any of the older treaties with any other nations, it was because these provisions were introduced with an eye toward "the overwhelming importance of corporations" or free enterprises in the postwar era "as a form of business enterprise" and were "intended as a forerunner for future treaties." Moreover, they argued that this national treatment was reciprocal: all Chinese doing business with the United States would receive "national treatment" in America.[27]

But the Chinese negotiators argued that the industrialization of China was just beginning. Although the draft treaty presented by the State Department did follow "the principle of equality and reciprocity as much as possible," in its actual application, not all of its provisions would be to "the equal advantage" of both parties, because of the differences in their stage of economic development.[28]

How could Chinese businessmen doing business in the United States, they asked, compete successfully with their American competitors, who were equipped with all the most advanced technologies? Furthermore, they argued, because of the provisions of U.S. immigration law, this regulation on reciprocity was "by no means actually reciprocal." Lee Kan, the principal Chinese negotiator, argued, "In spite of the liberal wordings, no Chinese (not already in the United States) can come to the United States and actually enjoy the rights enumerated in the treaty except: (a), quota immigrants (100 odd), and (b), 'treaty merchants.' For instance, a Chinese intending to engage in manufacturing activities in the United States solely for domestic (American) sales cannot actually be admitted into the United States except as a quota immigrant." The quota was 107 annually for Chinese, whereas China did not have a quota for Americans. Moreover, "in spite of the apparently reciprocal national treatment, Chinese corporations would actually be treated as 'foreign corporations' in the United States," because under the American federal system, each state in the United States had its own laws regulating corporate activities from outside the state. Thus the small number of Chinese who were allowed within the quota limit to enter the United States to do business there, would, in fact, never receive the same treatment as their American competitors in any state, argued the Chinese negotiators. Since differences "do exist between national treatment as conferred upon Americans in China and upon Chinese in America," they suggested that it might be "best to accord to corporations the same provisions as embodied in the United States–Norway Treaty and other modern United States treaties"; that is, to give the most-favored-nation treatment rather than national treatment to foreign businessmen.

The third major difference was over the issue of whether the most-favored-nation treatment should be conditional or unconditional. With unconditionality, all the rights and privileges accorded to one nation by China under most-favored-nation provisions "would be accorded immediately and unconditionally, or immediately and without request or compensation," to all the rest of the nations that had treaty relations with China. "The principle of equality of treatment in its unconditional and unlimited form," argued the American negotiators, would be the best defense against "spheres of interest," or "spheres of influence," thus eliminating one of the most important sources of conflict among the great powers. In other words, all the trading and investment advantages the United States or other powers might gain in China with the unconditionality of most-favored-nation provisions would be to the advantage of all powers doing business in China. Hence, a concert of power could be established in the Far East, realizing the objective of John Hay's Open Door policy at the end of the nineteenth century.

For the Chinese negotiators, however, an express statement of the most-favored-nation treatment in its unconditional form would be unacceptable for political and psychological reasons in postwar China. The national sentiment in China was "overwhelmingly" in favor of conditionality, they maintained. For many Chinese, it was important that these rights and advantages accorded to foreigners be "subject to conditions and requirements as prescribed by present and future Chinese laws." In reality, "without an express declaration, most-favored-nation provisions of a Sino-American treaty not expressly conditional would in practice be applied unconditionally, and, therefore, the practical result would be the same, whether or not the statement were included."[29]

By March of 1946, the negotiations came to an impasse over these major differences: a free-enterprise system versus a mixed economic system, national treatment versus most-favored-nation treatment, and the most-favored-nation treatment in its unconditional form versus its conditional form. How to break the impasse?[30]

The State Department officials conceded that some of the Chinese arguments were reasonable. For instance, the problem of U.S. immigration law regarding Chinese entrance into this country did jeopardize the nature of "equality and reciprocity" in the treaty. Thus, they tried to persuade the Senate Foreign Relations Committee to make certain revisions to the Chinese immigration law, to calm down the "fierce opposition" from the Chinese side. Following the Sino-American Treaty of 1880, which provided for a suspension if not absolute prohibition of the immigration of Chinese laborers and for the inadmissibility of Chinese other than laborers, the U.S. Congress passed, from 1882 to 1913, a series of exclusion laws that imposed particularly severe restrictions upon Chinese. The Chinese Exclusion Laws continued to exist even during World War II, when China and the United States were allies. The Nationality Act of 1940 reaffirmed the Chinese Exclusion Law of 1880, and, consequently, the ineligibility of Chinese and other East Asians for naturalization and their general inadmissibility to the United States under the Immigration Act of 1924. So the Chinese were subject not only to discriminatory measures applying to East Asians in general but to numerous special and exclusive types of discrimination.[31]

Bishop Paul Yu-pin, the Roman Catholic leader in China, told American journalists, "If your attitude of superiority continues, if the Far East becomes convinced that the United States has forfeited her moral right to leadership and is fixed in her determination to look down upon the colored races, I can foresee only a prospect which makes me tremble at its horrors." And he lamented, "Here the legislature of the greatest of the United Nations, the one to which China looked for true understanding, reaffirms a racist law of the most insulting and stringent kind. . . . We do not wish to have you open your country to a flood of Chinese immigrants. But we do object to being branded not only as being inferior to you, but as inferior to all the other nations and races in the world without exception. And this is precisely what your Chinese Exclusion Law does."[32]

Deeply concerned about the Chinese protests against the Chinese Exclusion Law, the State Department had presented to Congress a suggested revision of the Chinese Exclusion Law before the negotiations started. Congress accepted the suggested revision, and before World War II was over, a new Chinese Immigration Law, giving Chinese immigration a minimum quota rather than total exclusion, was established.[33]

However, the Chinese negotiators were by no means happy with this minimum quota when they compared it with the quota the United States accorded to other countries and with China's own immigration law regarding Americans (no quota, no restriction of any kind). The State Department then suggested to the Senate Foreign Relations Committee that the American side should at least include in the commercial treaty "some assurance" about immigration, such as a most-favored-nation clause, and a provision against discrimination on account of race, creed, or color. "We felt," as the State Department officials told the Senate Committee, that this provision "might assist the Chinese in selling the treaty to their own people without involving any important commitment on our part."

This suggestion was immediately rejected by the Senate. As Senator Tom Connally, Democratic chairman of the Foreign Relations Committee, told the State Department officials, "We have already done too much for the Chinese. We have given them food, money, equipment and training for their troops. . . . We have already changed our immigration laws to let some Chinese in, and that was already a great step to take."[34]

The American negotiators recommended using a U.S. government loan as a bargaining chip to bring the KMT government to terms.[35]

On November 8, 1946, the treaty was signed. Regarding the issue of national treatment, the KMT government agreed to give American businessmen substantial rights and privileges that would be less than national treatment but more than the most-favored-nation treatment (except in finances and mining, in which only most-favored-nation treatment would be accorded). The State Department agreed that the treaty would leave U.S. states free to make any laws they wanted about landholding but provided that if any state or territory of the United States should discriminate against the Chinese, China would not be obliged to grant citizens or corporations of that state or territory any better treatment with respect to landholding than the Chinese received in that state. With respect to the issue of conditionality of most-favored-nation provisions, the KMT government accepted the most-favored-nation treatment in its unconditional form. Most important, the State Department did not push the KMT government to abandon Sun Yat-sen's Principle of People's Livelihood publicly. However, the KMT government pledged to implement a privatization plan, on the American model of economic development, as rapidly as possible.[36]

Urban Chinese Middle-Class Protests against the Signing of the Treaty

As soon as the signing of the treaty was announced, a stunned American Embassy in Chungking reported that the treaty was received "at best approval with reservations, and at worst—in the Independent and Liberal left-wing press—with an attitude of hostility." And even in those newspapers controlled by the KMT government, "each favorable comment was almost invariably accompanied by an apology for the anticipated criticism."[37]

Shanghai's *Da Gong Bao,* which the American Embassy regarded as an "independent conservative" paper, published an editorial on November 11, 1946, arguing that the new treaty, though equal in form, was in reality "almost a new unequal treaty in which the old fashioned most-favored-nation clause has been revived." The disparity in strength of the two parties would give the United States "unequal advantages." It asked, if "not even England dares to maintain wholesale free trade with the United States, how can China?" But the editor wrote that the United States should not be blamed for the signing of the treaty. Instead, the Chinese should be surprised that "the Chinese Government has not striven to protect our industry, economy and livelihood against

American high speed industrial competition in our own homeland." In closing, the editorial warned that if "the unequal Sino-British treaty of 1840 managed our semi-colonial destiny for a century," then the new Sino-American commercial treaty "will dispose of our destiny for another 100 years."[38]

Even the Shanghai newspaper *Hsin Wen Pao,* which was controlled by the KMT C-C (Chen Lifu–Chen Guofu) group, admitted that, "Only when our country has become industrialized and foreign trade is properly developed shall we be able to take full advantage of opportunities conferred on us by this new treaty." Only then would the new treaty be "mutually beneficial and equal."[39] The centrist KMT *Chen Yen Pao* urged the United States "to refrain from adopting an attitude of selfishness as adopted by great powers in the past and from exploiting China economically."[40]

In Chungking, the capital, public opinion was "overwhelmingly" against the treaty, the American Embassy there noted.[41] Li Kwei-an, member of the Chungking City Council, for instance, stressed that "under present conditions of chaos and war and with our backward state of scientific and technical development, how can we reciprocate?" Shu Chung-lin, another member of the Chungking City Council, agreed: "With such disparity of power and strength between the two nations, any talk of reciprocity is futile. The conclusion of the treaty can only be interpreted in terms of equality between a sheep and a wolf—a sheep is inviting a wolf to come in and live with it on a basis of reciprocity and equality."[42]

The majority of industrialists and bankers in Chungking were angry about this treaty. Jo Shih-yen, manager of Min Sheng Shipping Company, commented, "A full grown man and a child agree that they should each carry a load of twenty catties in a race of perfect equality. Do you think this is real equality? In navigation, for example, have we ships to sail to American ports, even though we are permitted to do so?"[43] Wong Mo-hang, manager of Jeh Shing Chuang Bank, remarked, "This treaty provided equality in theory but not in practice. Its implementation means a fatal blow to the national industry and commerce of China."[44] Yen Kung-fu, director of the Chungking Banking Association, claimed, "The fragile Chinese banks, like boats, will have their bottoms torn out on the rocks when they begin to face the competition of the well-established and powerful American banking houses. This treaty provides for equal but predestined chances in a race for economic domination between the rich and the very poor. The outcome is obvious."[45] Shieh Ting-hsing, head of the Economic Investigation Office of the Szechuan Provincial Bank, also criticized it: "The treaty only quickens the process of colonization of China into a dependent country."[46]

The leading intellectuals in Chungking all expressed their "great indignation" at the treaty. Li Tze-shang, an economist and writer, argued, "The treaty is more far reaching in its scope than the previous 'unequal treaties,' even though extraterritoriality and inland navigation rights are not a part thereof. Because of the huge differences in national wealth and in the stage of advancement in industrialization, the starting points are entirely different. Therefore, no real equality can be provided by such a treaty."[47] Teng Chu-min, one of the most respected academics in urban China and a leading member of the Democratic League, asserted, "The treaty is the most unequal treaty China has ever signed with a foreign power since the Manchu Dynasty," and "the Chinese people should resist such a perfidious treason to the last in order to preserve national independence, both politically and economically."[48]

The independent centrist newspaper *Shang Wu Jih Pao* urged the Legislative Yuan to veto the treaty:

> We are of the opinion that the treaty has only the outward appearance of equality and reciprocity. . . . Should we follow the footsteps of the half-witted Manchu Dynasty by signing such a treaty bringing the nation to the status of a semi-colony? The cordial friendship between America and China should be cultivated and developed, to that every Chinese agrees. But handing over the national interest and future as a gift is a totally different thing. . . . In the name of the nation and the people, we implore the members of the Legislative Yuan, for the interests of the nation, to exercise their veto power on this particular occasion.[49]

The Chinese business community, the Chinese intellectual community, and metropolitan governmental officials all protested the signing of this treaty. In February 1947, when an American professor visited China, he was "surprised to find how many businessmen and financiers, along with intellectuals, in China believe that the Kuomintang government is beyond any hope."[50]

The signing of the treaty thus created a situation in Nationalist China that was the opposite of American China policy objectives throughout the treaty negotiations: it alienated the urban Chinese middle class and generated the first eruption of anti-American outcries in urban China in the postwar years.

Interests, Visions, and Counterproductive China Policy

The Truman administration was astonished and perplexed by the anti-KMT, anti-American outcries sweeping urban China. When the Truman administration used the leverage of a U.S. government loan to force the KMT government to come to terms, it believed that the American liberal vision for China's industrialization would win the popular support of urban Chinese and would make Nationalist China a "shining example" in the "ideological competition" between American individualism and Soviet collectivism in the post–World War II world. How can one explain such a counterproductive American policy toward China during the postwar years?

One could argue that this policy should be attributed to the Senate Foreign Affairs Committee's racist attitudes toward the Chinese, or to its refusal to make more concessions on the Chinese immigration quota, as suggested by the State Department. This argument underscores the problem of racism in America's China policy debates at that time. But the anti-American outcry in urban China did not focus entirely on the issue of Chinese immigration to the United States. It centered more on the fate of China's incipient industrialization and the possible destruction of the Chinese people's livelihood.

One may also argue that it could be attributed to American policymakers' obsession with foreign markets, particularly the China market. To avoid economic recession and ensure "full employment and prosperity in the United States" in the postwar years, the Truman administration was determined to open up more foreign markets. The Truman administration also wanted to improve the lot of the overseas poor as an integral part of that expansion of American free enterprise, or "the New Deal version of Woodrow Wilson's reforming expansionism."[51] Though this can explain what drove the Truman administration's China policy in the commercial treaty negotiations, it nonetheless cannot explain why the outcome was so contrary to the goal. That is, it cannot explain how the Truman administration could unintentionally dismantle the China market, triggering the split between the Nationalist government and the urban middle class, thus ruining its own chances of long-term economic opportunity in China without anticipating or even recognizing the possibility of such dire policy consequences.

What happened was that the Truman administration not only fundamentally misjudged urban China's economic conditions, but also urban Chinese aspirations, which were shaped in Chinese historical, socioeconomic, and cultural environments. Although both Nationalist China and America believed that China should be integrated into the world economy and that China should achieve a balance between rapid growth and economic justice in its industrialization drive, their blueprints for achieving that objective were very different. Moderate Nationalist Chinese reformers saw Sun Yat-sen's Principle of People's Livelihood, or a mixed economy, as the best way to achieve their goal. American reformers saw a New Deal–style free-market economy as the best means to that end. Also, because the major policy assumption underlying Washington's position was that economic reconstruction plans for Nationalist China must be viewed in light of the American/Soviet ideological rivalry, rather than in the context of China's historical quest for modernity and new identity, the United States rejected the idea of a ten- or fifteen-year delay in China joining the free-trade system and of a mixed economy based on Sun's principles. In the minds of American negotiators, there could be no middle ground between individualism and collectivism. And with the Chinese economy worsening rapidly in the aftermath of signing the treaty, the State Department, from 1947 to 1949, put even greater pressure on the KMT government to speed up privatization programs.

In the 1950s, both Washington and the KMT on Taiwan learned, at least partially, from this experience. When drafting the blueprint for Taiwan's industrialization in the mid-1950s, Yin Chung-jun, the architect of Taiwan's "economic miracle," emphasized that to achieve both rapid industrial growth and a fair distribution of wealth, it was crucial to follow Sun's Principle of People's Livelihood. The American free-economy model was appropriate for the American setting, he claimed, but it might not generate similar results in the extremely impoverished economic environment of Taiwan. "The economic system of People's Livelihood" was, Yin stressed, "a mixture of capitalism and socialism."[52] When State Department officers and congressmen frowned over the "socialist components" of Taiwan's economic blueprint, Karl Rankin, American ambassador to Taipei, urged Washington to endorse it. He stressed in his memo that while he himself was a believer in the American system of "free enterprise," he did not think it could work well in Taiwan at that time.[53] In 1962, W. W. Rostow, an economic adviser to President John Kennedy, indicated that Taiwan's economy was poised to "take-off." In 1991, the World Bank's report on East Asia emphasized that among the "four little dragons," Taiwan's economy had two distinctive characteristics: one was its sustained higher growth rate, the other was its "fair distribution of wealth."[54] In its public-relations campaign in Washington from the late 1950s through the early 1990s, however, Taiwan decided to "clothe" its "economic miracle" in the American model of "free enterprise," rather than emphasizing Sun's principles.[55]

In retrospect, the origin of U.S.-China antagonism in the post–World War II era could not be attributed simply to a clash of national interests. It was *against* America's best interests to prompt the split between the KMT government and the urban Chinese middle class. It was *against* America's best interests to have an eruption of anti-American sentiment sweep urban China. It was *against* America's best interests to contribute to the collapse of the Nationalist Chinese market. To a great extent, the origin of U.S.-China animosity was generated by a clash of deeply ingrained assumptions about what kind of economy modern China should have. When the nations' different visions were perceived through the colored lens of worldwide ideological rivalry between American individualism and Soviet collectivism, Washington was unable to perceive urban Chinese aspirations. The Chinese reality was misconstrued, and so were the American concepts of economic and security interests, and American China policy became counterproductive to its initial objectives.

CHAPTER THREE

Disillusionment and Polarization

*The Failure of the Marshall Mission
and Deepening Divisions in
Nationalist China*

From the end of 1945 to the end of 1946, while the Truman administration tried to integrate Nationalist China into the world free-trade system, it also attempted to bring it into the world democratic system. General George Marshall, an American national hero in World War II, was appointed by President Truman as his personal envoy—replacing General Patrick Hurley, who had resigned—to mediate between the Chinese Nationalists and the CCP. Marshall's mission was to help establish a representative government in postwar China.[1]

America's liberal solution failed to work in Nationalist China. According to General Albert C. Wedmeyer, who had been Hurley's aide in previous mediation, the Marshall mission was doomed to fail. He candidly told Marshall that Chiang Kai-shek was simply "a feudal lord," and the Chinese communists were "Marxist-Leninist ideologues." Because of this, there was "no chance" for Marshall to succeed in his mediation. The Chinese documents demonstrate, however, that neither the KMT nor the CCP was monolithic in the postwar years, and that from the start, neither Chiang nor Mao intended to have a civil war.

The failure of the Marshall mission was by no means predetermined. More importantly, one critical issue he never mentioned was the drastic change of attitudes toward the United States among the urban Chinese in the aftermath of the Marshall mission. How could urban Chinese, who were so overwhelmingly in favor of the Marshall mediation at the beginning, end up so profoundly disillusioned with American policy toward China? Their major complaint was not that America intervened in China's political reconstruction but that this intervention was based on "a subjective understanding of the Chinese situation." In other words, to explain the failure of the Marshall mission, one needs to explain why the KMT, the CCP, and, more surprisingly, the Third Force—a collection of several political parties that claimed to be the voice of the urban Chinese middle class, particularly the intelligentsia and entrepreneurs—all changed their attitudes in the course of the Marshall mediation.

The following discussion will focus on the dynamic interactions between American and Chinese visions of democracy in the postwar years, with the primary concern being why the Truman administration's ideal of liberal democracy, as applied to postwar China, could deepen the isolation of the KMT government in Chinese society. This chapter will first identify two divergent American views on how to analyze the Chinese political situation in the postwar years—one held by the War Department, and the other by the Far Eastern Bureau at the State Department. It will then discuss the Chinese Nationalists', the Chinese Communists', and the Third Force's conceptions of China's political reconstruction and examine the impact of the various American concepts of a liberal solution in China on the attitudes of the KMT, the CCP, and the Third Force during the Marshall mediation. It will further explore why the ruptures between the KMT state and the incipient civil society, and between the KMT state and the poor peasantry were further widened in the wake of the Marshall mission. Finally, it will look at how the Third Force changed its perceptions of the nature of America's China policy, and why the polarization between the KMT state and Chinese society gave rise to anti-KMT, anti-American sentiment in urban centers, a political development the Truman administration did not intend to generate and did not anticipate.

American Visions of Political Reconstruction in Postwar China

What kind of political system should the United States help build in postwar China? The U.S. War Department called for an "effective and unified" government, the State Department, for a "democratic China." A democratic China, as a State Department memo argued, was of "the utmost importance to the success of the United Nations and for world peace." A China "disorganized and divided either by foreign aggression or by violent internal strife" attributable to the absence of a democratic system would be "an undermining influence to world stability and peace, now and in the future." Truman shared the State Department's view of America's political objectives in China, and the goal of the Marshall mission was therefore to build a representative government in postwar China.[2]

There were profound differences within the Truman administration concerning how to deal with the CCP in Nationalist China in the post–World War II era. The War Department and the U.S. Navy considered the Chinese Communists the tools of the Soviet Union and advocated helping the KMT armies move into North China and Manchuria, even though such aid for the KMT "amounts to at least indirect support of Chiang Kai-shek's activities against the dissident forces in China." If the United States gave up its support for the Nationalists, the War Department warned, the Communists would enter North China and Manchuria, which, in turn, would pass to Soviet control. Then "Russia will have achieved in the Far East approximately the objectives Japan initially set out to accomplish." The impact of such a result on the United States would be "at least as grave militarily as any situation likely to arise due to continued U.S. support of the National Government."[3]

Marshall agreed with this assessment. For him, it was clear that the major obstacle in his mediation would be the Chinese Communists: "I will assume that the Communist group will block all progress in negotiations as far as they can, as the delay is to their advantage." The longer the delay, "the less probability" of the KMT government's being able "to establish a decent semblance of control over Manchuria."[4]

However, the Far Eastern Bureau at the State Department held that the Marshall mission must treat both the KMT and the CCP on equal terms, so that the CCP would not be driven into Russian arms. "It is necessary to bring the Chinese Communist elements, other dissident elements and the National Government of China into a unified government." If this were *not* done, "we could expect Russia to ultimately take control of Manchuria and maintain a dominant influence in North China." Thus they urged Marshall not to give exclusive support to the Nationalist government, but instead retain effective bargaining power with both sides, to "induce the Central Government and the Communist Government to get together." As Secretary of State James Byrnes told Truman, "If the Communist Government agrees to concessions which would appear to be acceptable, while the Central Government refuses to give ground, the Central Government would be informed that the assistance which we could otherwise give to China would not be given." Further, "We would be forced to deal directly with the Communists in so far as the evacuation of Japanese from

North China was concerned." If the CCP failed to grant concessions while the KMT conceded "what appeared to be necessary to meet the views of the U.S. Government," then "full support would be given the Nationalist Government and we would move its armies into North China as required."[5]

The essential question was, Should the United States take sides in China during the Marshall mediation? The War Department was a proponent of the United States supporting the KMT. The Far Eastern Bureau's position, however, was that choosing sides in China was "unwise" because it could cause America to lose its bargaining power with both sides and, even worse, help seal the relationship between the CCP and Moscow, which "we foresee and fear."

These different approaches to the CCP in the Marshall mediation were not based on different strategic objectives in China. On the contrary: the policy goal of each department was to reduce the Soviet influence in Manchuria. But their profoundly different analyses of the Chinese situation, particularly their very different underlying assumptions concerning the nature of the CCP movement in Nationalist China, affected their policy proposals. Was the CCP's popularity based on its land-reform program in rural China? Or was it the result of Moscow's instigations?

In the view of the War Department, the Navy, and Marshall before he went to China, the communist movement in China was "a cut-and-dried made-in-Moscow movement." The key to bringing the CCP to terms was therefore to make a deal between Washington and Moscow. They reasoned that if Stalin would agree to the American terms, so would the CCP.[6]

John Carter Vincent and the Far Eastern Bureau he headed believed, however, that the communist movement in China derived its strength not from Moscow's support but from the Chinese people's dissatisfaction with the "illiberal policy" of the KMT government and, in particular, with that government's "failure to alleviate agrarian distress." In Vincent's words, Americans should keep in mind that "fifteen years of intermittent efforts to eliminate the Chinese Communists by the Nationalist Government's force when they were receiving no support from Russia had certainly not proved successful."[7]

The Far Eastern Bureau suggested that "the only practical manner" in which to meet the challenge of the CCP movement should be twofold: (1) to "nourish and encourage the Communist movement to grow in our direction," since America could not "starve out the popular movement which the Communists represent," and (2) to reform the KMT government: "If the Nationalist Party showed as much zeal for bringing good government to China as it was showing for eliminating opposition," argued a memo from the Division for Chinese Affairs, "there would be no question but that it could 'out-compete' the Communists in gaining support of the Chinese people."[8] In particular, it warned that "the basic problem of agrarian reform" had rarely received "any active attention" from the KMT.[9] As a result, the peasants now supported the Chinese Communists in North China.[10] Given the popularity of the CCP movement in China, "a reduction of the influence of the Chinese Communists might be more readily achieved," if the KMT government "took them in" on a minority basis rather than try to "shoot them all." Such a representative government, which included the KMT, the CCP, and the Third Force, "moving ahead with American support in the job of rehabilitation and reconstruction," could have a much better chance "to cut the ground out from under the Communists, even though they were in the Government."[11] Therefore, the Far Eastern Bureau recommended that Marshall use the bargaining power of American economic or military aid to force the so-called extremists within both the KMT and the CCP to make concessions and compromises and to build a democratic coalition government, which should immediately begin reform measures, with "relieving the rural devastation" as the first step.

Truman was skeptical of the Far Eastern Bureau's analysis of the Chinese situation and the nature of the CCP movement in China. Throughout the war years, Truman had believed that "the Commies in China not only did not help us but on occasion helped the Japs."[12] Moreover, he did not believe that the CCP was largely an indigenous movement. As he argued, "I was never taken in by Stalin's declaration at Potsdam that 'the Chinese Communists were not really proper Communists.' " Truman was convinced that Stalin wanted a civil war in China and that the CCP would be his tool in this "dangerous endeavor."[13]

The president believed that neither the Soviets nor their puppet, the CCP, should ever be allowed to replace Japan in control of Manchuria and China. This was not just an issue of strategic importance, he emphasized, but a matter of fundamental principle for America. "The police state of Communism is no different from the police state of the Nazis," he told Margaret Truman. As a Jacksonian democrat, he was determined to fight for the rights of the "common people," particularly those of the middle class in America, in China, and all over the world. As he declared later in the Truman Doctrine, "it must be the policy of the United States to support free people who are resisting attempted subjugation by armed minorities or by outside pressures."[14]

Therefore, in his instructions to the Marshall mission to China, Truman set down a confidential policy "bottom line." Even if the KMT government refused to concede ground to the CCP, the Marshall mission should continue to support the KMT and help it to transport troops into North China and Manchuria.

Marshall tried to clarify and confirm this point in his memo to Truman before he left for China:

> I stated that my understanding of one phrase of my directive was not in writing but I thought I had a clear understanding of the President's desires in the matter, which was that in the event that I was unable to secure the necessary action by the Generalissimo [Chiang Kai-shek], which I thought reasonable and desirable, it would still be necessary for the U.S. Government, through me, to continue to back the National Government of the Republic of China. . . .
>
> The President stated that the foregoing was a correct summation of his direction regarding that possible development of the situation.[15]

Different Chinese Visions of Democratic Reform in Postwar China

The KMT's visions of democracy in postwar China were closely related to their concepts of a new polity in the second Republic between 1927 and 1937. During that period they revised or reinterpreted Sun Yat-sen's political theory of democracy, formulating a new approach to China's democratic reform that emphasized the role of the rule of law but deemphasized the role of land reform in Nationalist China's political reconstruction.

In 1927, the KMT established the second Republic of China. The first had been established in the wake of the 1911 republican revolution. The second was born after the collapse of the united front between the KMT and the CCP. The Nationalist vision of the political system, as the KMT claimed, was "a modern state with a powerful government backed by a sound citizenry and able to take its place among the advanced nation-states of the world." For the KMT, this one-party state would represent the stage of "tutelary rule," as proposed by Sun Yat-sen in his Theory of Democratic Transition. It was a transitional stage between the first period, military rule (for unification of the nation), and the third one, constitutional rule (full democracy).

The KMT writers of the late 1920s and the early 1930s almost unanimously rejected the notion of the parliamentary political system "either on the grounds of Chinese experience since 1912 or on the grounds that the parliamentary systems of the West were themselves a cover for the capitalist exploitation of the population." The KMT, however, in the words of Hu Hanmin, the party's leading theoretician between 1927 and 1931, had no desire to hold power forever. On the contrary, he declared, the party intended to "hand power back to the people." The KMT officially announced in 1929 that the period of political tutelage would last for a total of six years ending in 1935.[16]

For the KMT leadership, the major task of the second Republic was national unification and reconstruction, particularly the introduction of the rule of law. Before the establishment of the second Republic in 1927, the Special Courts had been established to deal with warlords and alleged counter-revolutionaries in the Nationalist revolution (1924–1926). These were provincial legal institutions controlled directly by KMT party members. The Special Courts run by the KMT were finally abolished and an independent judiciary was established in 1929. The judicial reforms in this period placed great emphasis on the sanctity of due process and protection of private property. For the party leadership, these reforms were important, both for preserving social stability and for ending foreign privilege. The KMT intended to show the world's great powers that the Chinese legal system was "up to date and effective," in order to abolish extraterritoriality in China. By the end of the 1920s, "a certain right of remonstrance was enjoyed by party organizations and by business and other public figures, and the press was largely uncontrolled," observed a British scholar. From 1927 to 1937, before the Japanese invasion, the KMT gradually won the support of the urban population, particularly entrepreneurs and intellectuals.[17]

The KMT's plan to reconstruct rural China was a failure. For Sun Yat-sen, the KMT's major task in the stage of the tutelage rule would be educational; specifically, the training of the people in the exercise of their political rights through social organization and mobilization. Since the Communists had played an important role in mass movements, the KMT now regarded all social organizations with deep suspicion. All mass movements were actually suspended after December

1927. A new, orthodox view of social organization emerged within the KMT. According to Dai Jitao, a leading conservative theorist of the KMT, the role of social organization in the period of destruction (military rule) was to create an instrument against the warlords. In this period of reconstruction (tutelage), it was no longer needed. Hu Hanmin agreed. "Is it wise," he asked, "for the Kuomintang going on to lay fires in its own rear in the period of reconstruction?"[18]

In rural China, where political and social authority was diffused among half a million villages, no amount of well-drafted legislation by the KMT was likely to change anything, unless the Nationalist government was prepared "to train and to protect local democratic organizations," observed a British scholar at that time. In fact, the very revenue necessary for reform depended on the ability of the KMT to reform the abuses of the land tax. Without effective democratic control at the village level, as Jack Gray commented, "the central government had no means whatever of penetrating the thousand-year-old jungle of local bargains, compromises, evasions, and misappropriations which made up the land-tax system." Even the moderate legislation designed to secure a reduction of rents by 25 percent became a dead letter. Furthermore, to eliminate the CCP movement in the countryside, the KMT government reimposed on the village the hated *pao-chia* system of mutual surveillance, and this, in the hands of the local landed elite, "made any sort of democratic growth, however moderate, virtually impossible." Increasingly, the KMT was concerned only with maintaining order and collecting such taxes as they could in rural villages; they planned to "ensure their own survival by compromising" with the landed elite. Some leading KMT members were deeply worried about the abandonment of Sun's major social-organization programs in rural China. For instance, Chen Gongbo, the head of the Central Organization Department, told the party that a survey of partial registration of the party membership showed that within the KMT, "military and political circles now seem to predominate," businessmen and students "come next," and peasant and worker elements were "the least numerous." For him, "this certainly departs too far from Sun Yat-sen's emphasis on the peasants and workers."

So in the second Republic, the KMT was, on the one hand, relatively successful in building legal frameworks, protecting private property rights, and recruiting industrialists and intellectuals in urban centers. On the other hand, it did little to help China's peasants rise from poverty. Sun Yat-sen's land-reform program was entirely neglected in the second Republic.[19]

Caught up in the national crisis presented by Japan's invasion of Manchuria in 1931, the KMT did not end its tutelage rule in 1935 as it had promised. During the War of Resistance, a second united front between the KMT and the CCP was established. Thus before the end of the war, when the KMT attempted to transform the tutelage rule into the constitutional rule, a question arose: what should the KMT do about the CCP in the post–World War II era? For the KMT leadership, the consensus was that the KMT should "build a representative government of the people, by the people, and for the people at the earliest possible date, in accordance with the teachings of Dr. Sun Yat-sen."[20] However, the KMT was sharply divided over the CCP–KMT relationship.

Chiang Kai-shek, in his book *China's Destiny* (1943), a blueprint for China's political reconstruction in the postwar era, proclaimed that both Nationalists and Communists should continue their cooperation to build China into a democratic country. In his words, "only then shall we not be ashamed of being the descendants of the Chinese nation."

> I believe that we are all patriots who love our country, and that no matter how much we may have fought each other in the past, there is no reason why we cannot give up our personal prejudices and animosities for the sake of the nation. This would allow our internal politics to be unified and our Government to proceed along the right road, so that foreigners would not look down upon us as a backward nation and inferior people.

However, he insisted that to join the national government, the Communist armed forces must first surrender to the *current* KMT government as soon as the war was over, because as long as the Communists did not do so, the political transition from tutelage rule to constitutional democracy could not be implemented. "Everyone condemned those territory-grabbing warlords as counter-revolutionary. Can we now call these disguised warlords and new feudalists genuine revolutionaries?" He claimed, "If there is no willingness to alter the habit of feudal warlordism, and abandon completely the partition of territory by force of arms, then no matter how lenient our attitude may be, it cannot produce any result and no reasonable solution can be found" in the postwar era.[21]

The most powerful groups within the KMT, the "C-C" and the military factions, opposed a representative government in postwar China that included the CCP, even if the CCP gave up its armed force to the KMT government. This group urged Chiang to eliminate the CCP on the battlefield *before* constitutional democracy could be established in China. For them, the origin of the CCP movement in China was pure and simple: "Communism originated from Soviet imperialism, which has encroached on our country."[22] As General Bai Chongxi, a military hero in the War of Resistance and later the defense minister of the KMT government, told Chiang Kai-shek, "We must take advantage of the victory in the war of resistance to win our war against the Communist bandits, once for all." In his view, the democratic election could generate such cutthroat factional rivalries within the KMT that before the election could be held, the CCP movement must first be "stamped out" through the KMT's "superior military forces."[23]

Sun Fo argued that the CCP should be invited to join the national government in postwar China but that it should give up its armed force to the new coalition government rather than to the current KMT government.[24] The Communist problem in China should be solved only through "political and peaceful means." He particularly emphasized that except for those "hotheads" in the KMT, "opposition to a military solution of the problem is well-nigh universal" in China. The KMT could not afford to ignore "the fervent hopes and aspirations of the entire Chinese nation" for peaceful cooperation between the KMT and the CCP following World War II. He declared that it was time for the KMT, the CCP, and the Third Force to establish a coalition government in order to realize Sun Yat-sen's lifelong dream to build a true democracy, a people's democracy, in China.[25]

The Political Science Group of the KMT, which included most of the intellectuals in the party, largely agreed with Sun Fo's view. They might not like the Communists; yet, they did not believe that the Communist problem could be solved through military force in China. Wu Dingchang, the head of the Group and the chief of the staff of the KMT government, argued in a confidential memo to Chiang Kai-shek that Chiang should invite Mao Zedong, chairman of the CCP Central Committee, to Chungking to discuss the issue of peaceful cooperation in postwar China. Negotiation with the CCP and a search for a political solution would be, he asserted, the "best way" and the "only way" to undermine the Communist influence, and to build a united, democratic China.[26]

Chiang Kai-shek partially agreed with this argument. As he told his generals, "from a purely military point of view, you are right, that is, before we can build a constitutional democratic polity, we must eliminate the Communist bandits." However, "from a political point of view, it is not a right thing to do, particularly through our military forces in the aftermath of the war of resistance." He emphasized that "the political pressures from urban populations for Nationalist-Communist cooperation are overwhelming. And there are also sharp divisions of opinions within our own party. We must act with the greatest caution on this issue. We cannot use military measures to solve the Communist problem in the postwar era."[27]

In short, within the KMT there were three different views regarding the KMT-CCP relationship in postwar China. One was to terminate the KMT-CCP cooperation and to eliminate the CCP movement as soon as the War of Resistance was over. The second was just the opposite: to continue this cooperation, and to let the CCP surrender its armed force to a new coalition government that would include the KMT, the CCP, and the Third Force, rather than to the current KMT government. The third view was to continue this united front, with the CCP first surrendering its armed force to the current KMT government, rather than to the new coalition government. Chiang Kai-shek supported the third view. In August 1945, Chiang sent three letters to Mao in Yanan, inviting Mao to come to Chungking to discuss "peaceful cooperation" between the KMT and the CCP. Chiang did intend to use "political means" to solve the CCP problem. But he also intended to persuade Mao to give up the CCP's armed force to the KMT government, *before* the CCP could join a new coalition government in postwar China.

The CCP's Seventh Party Congress was convened between April 23 and June 11 in Yanan, the headquarters of CCP-controlled areas during the War of Resistance. Its purpose was to put forward the CCP's vision of China's reconstruction. Since February 1945, the CCP Central Committee had met several times to prepare for this important gathering, particularly Mao's political report to the Seventh Congress, entitled *On Coalition Government*.

The CCP's theory about the nature of the Chinese political system changed during the War of Resistance, evolving from one of proletarian dictatorship to one of New Democracy, as proposed by Mao in 1939. And so in addition to the CCP's primary emphasis on land reform in rural China, it placed great emphasis on its united front not only with the KMT, but, more important, with the Third Force in urban China.

According to Mao, his report *On Coalition Government,* delivered to the Seventh Party Congress, was an expansion of the Theory of New Democracy. The major difference here was, he said, that he elevated the roles of private capitalism and the coalition government in China's economic and political reconstruction.

Mao's new emphasis on coalition government was, to an extent, intimately tied to his increased belief in the necessity of developing private capitalism in postwar China. While "as a historical trend, capitalism is going downward," he wrote, it was still of "vital importance to develop capitalism" in the underdeveloped world, particularly in China. Unfortunately, he told the Congress, there was "widespread fear" over the development of capitalism within the party, due to the "negative impact of populist ideology," or the ideology of peasantry, upon many party members. "To build a system of New Democracy is our party's general guiding principle for a long historical period," he emphasized. Thus "blind opposition" to capitalist development in postwar China could be "highly detrimental to the implementation of our program of New Democracy." He stressed that the CCP must "distinguish" between its guiding principle of New Democracy and the peasants' ideology of populism. "The CCP must elevate the peasants to a more advanced level, rather than reducing the CCP to the level of populism." He also theorized a direct link between the development of capitalism, China's industrialization, and the CCP's destiny in postwar China. The development of capitalism would contribute greatly to China's industrialization, he said. And China's industrialization would be directly connected with the CCP's future. "If our party could not accomplish China's industrialization, could not address the major concerns of big cities, our party would die," he warned. "In the past twenty-five years, we were unable to address these issues. In the following twenty-five years, should we still not try our hardest to address these issues, we would be doomed to perish."[28] And to develop capitalism and to achieve China's industrialization, Mao claimed, the CCP should "warmly welcome all foreign investments" in postwar China:

> To develop Chinese industry, we need a huge amount of capital. Where can we get so much capital? We can get it only from two sources: one is Chinese people's own accumulation; the other is foreign aid and foreign investment. . . . It is thus highly beneficial to both Chinese people and peoples of foreign nations to build up a China that can enjoy lasting domestic

and international peace, wherein China can concentrate on thorough political and land reforms. Only through such reforms can China develop
large-scale light and heavy industries and modern agriculture. On that
basis, foreign capital will have a huge Chinese market to invest in.[29]

Furthermore, Mao's new emphasis on coalition government was also
directly related to his optimistic assessment of the U.S.-USSR relationship. During the first stage of the Seventh Party Congress, or before
the end of May 1945, he was particularly convinced that British-U.S.-
Soviet cooperation would be the "predominant international trend" in
the post–World War II world. Given such a "favorable" international
environment, the "progressive forces" within the KMT could have an
"upper hand," and Chiang Kai-shek could be "forced to reach compromises with us."[30] He told the Seventh Party Congress that there
could be three different types of coalition government in postwar
China. One was the Greek type, which would exclude the CCP, or a
government mainly dominated by the KMT; another was the Polish
type, which would exclude the KMT, or a government largely dominated by the CCP; and the third type was a coalition government made
up of the KMT, the CCP, and the Third Force. He predicted that this
third type of coalition government might emerge in postwar China.
While such a coalition government would still be influenced by Chiang
Kai-shek, "we must join it." So long as there was such a coalition
government, the national government's major policies would be discussed by the KMT, the CCP, and the Third Force. Then, it would
be "harder for Chiang Kai-shek to carry out his own policies." And
it would be "easier to make our policies known to the Chinese
people."[31]

This does not mean, however, that Mao and other CCP leaders
shifted away from the core of the CCP's political blueprint in the
Theory of New Democracy. At the center of the CCP's vision of China's
political reconstruction was still the critical role of land reform. Clearly,
the CCP's and the KMT's political blueprints differed sharply on this
issue. In Chiang's view, the precondition for China's democracy was
national unification based on law and order. In the CCP's view, in
contrast, the precondition for China's democracy was land reform.
Without fundamental social change, particularly in rural China, Mao
asserted, there could never be true democracy, law and order, or national unity. The greatest majority of the Chinese people were peasants,
he said. "To forget Chinese peasants, there would be no Chinese democratic revolution, or any revolution." Indeed, "should we forget the

word of peasantry, we would be entirely useless in China, even if we read through all Marxist books!"[32] Mao asked, "Why did the democratic experiment of the 1911 revolution fail so quickly? Why was there national chaos instead of national unity in the wake of the Republican revolution? It was because there was no profound social change in rural China, and the majority of the rural population was indifferent to or uninterested in the political change in urban centers." Mao proclaimed that democracy and national unification could never be achieved in China without nationwide land reform.[33]

Mao's confidence about a continued united front between the KMT and the CCP in postwar China, however, suffered two major setbacks in June and July 1945. First, six members of the U.S. delegation to Yanan, who had praised the CCP's system of New Democracy in their reports to Washington, were all prosecuted after they returned to the United States. The other was the public statement of General Patrick Hurley, President Truman's new envoy to China, that his objective was to support Chiang Kai-shek "completely" and "make no contacts" with the CCP. Although the CCP's suspicion of the Truman administration began to grow, Yanan had not yet changed its overall expectations of continued compromises between Washington and Moscow, or the continuation of the Yalta international system. It still hoped that the Truman administration might change its current China policy. The CCP leadership still believed that the CCP's struggle against the KMT would continue to be primarily political, rather than military.[34]

With these two setbacks before the conclusion of the Seventh Party Congress and afterwards, the CCP leaders also began to fear that a Greek type of coalition government, which would exclude the CCP, could prevail. The memories of the White Terror, which took place after the collapse of the first united front between the CCP and the KMT in 1927, were now looming large in Yanan. Few in the CCP could forget the White Terror. In just one month in 1927 in Shanghai alone, "as many as four thousand of their comrades were killed."[35] Members of the CCP and their sympathizers were hunted down, arrested, and executed, sometimes with their bodies exposed on the streets or their heads hung on the city gates as ominous warnings to the rest of the population.[36] At one of the meetings, Mao talked about Hong Xiuquan, vowing that the CCP would rather die than surrender, as Hong and his fellow Taiping revolutionaries had heroically done. "When Chairman said these words, he was clearly emotional," observed one of the participants at that meeting.[37]

To avoid the worst in postwar China, Mao decided to place more big cities in the CCP's hands, or to negotiate with Chiang from a "position of strength." On August 10, 1945, with the prospect of the Soviet army's entry into the Chinese theater, the CCP Central Committee issued a confidential circular, asking the CCP's troops to "seize this opportunity to take over big cities and key transportation routes in Southeast China," such as Nanjing and Shanghai.

Just one week later, Mao's concept of coalition government and his military strategy were to undergo another primary change, prompted by the signing of the Friendship and Alliance Treaty between the Republic of China and the USSR on August 14, 1945. Four days after the Soviet Red Army entered Manchuria, this treaty was signed in Moscow. For the first time in Soviet history, Moscow officially recognized the Chiang Kai-shek government as the *only* legitimate national government in China. In return, the Chiang Kai-shek government agreed to create an "exclusive naval base" at Port Arthur on Liaoning Peninsula, which would be used "only by Chinese and Soviet military and commercial vessels." The Port Arthur base was to be "under the jurisdiction of a Sino-Soviet Military Commission." The commission would consist of two Chinese and three Soviet representatives. The chairman was to be appointed by the Soviets, and the vice chairman, by the Chinese. The Soviets were responsible for defense of the port, and the agreement on Port Arthur was to last for thirty years, with the Soviet Government returning Port Arthur naval base to China in 1975.[38]

This treaty decisively altered Mao's strategy of "entering the negotiations with big cities in our hands." According to this treaty, the Japanese army could only surrender its occupied Chinese territory, particularly the big cities, to the Chiang Kai-shek government. As Mao told his comrades, "We initially thought that we would enter peace negotiations with the KMT Government under two different conditions: either to enter it with big cities, or without. Now we will have to enter the negotiations without any big cities."[39] On August 22, 1945, a confidential circular of the CCP Central Committee and the Military Committee explained why military strategy would have to shift from the goal of occupying "big cities" to taking over "small cities and the countryside."

Seven days later, however, the CCP leadership again changed its military strategy. By the end of August, it further realized that according to the treaty, the Soviet army would also return to the Chiang Kai-shek government all the territory it had taken from Japan. Accordingly, in its confidential circular of August 29, 1945, the CCP leadership focused entirely on Manchuria. It stressed that the Soviet army would soon withdraw from Manchuria and return it to the Chiang Kai-shek government, and that the CCP troops must "rapidly" and "immediately" enter Manchuria and that they should "take dirt routes, and occupy the countryside and the small and medium sized cities." It ordered, "Do not ask the Soviet Army to help us." It would be fine "as long as the Soviet Army does not resolutely oppose our movements." However, if the Soviet army was "resolutely against some movements of ours," then, "we must take into account their oppositions, and make retreat, so that the Soviet Army would not be entangled in the matter of international law." It strategized that it would be better if the CCP troops in Shandong province could enter the Northeast from the sea routes. And "the sooner, the better."[40] The critical importance of Manchuria for the CCP's political position in postwar China seemed to be very clear to the CCP leadership. In Mao's words, as long as the CCP could have Manchuria, the largest industrial base in China at the time, "the Chinese revolution would have a solid base, no matter what might happen in the future."[41]

With the signing of this treaty, Stalin also increased political pressure on the CCP to enter immediately peace negotiations with the KMT government. On August 22, 1945, Stalin's letter arrived in Yanan, urging Mao to accept Chiang Kai-shek's three letters of invitation and go to Chungking without further delay. In Stalin's words, "China should take the path of peaceful development. Mao Zedong should go to Chungking to negotiate with Chiang Kai-shek. If a civil war breaks out in China, the Chinese nation and Chinese people will be completely ruined."[42] Stalin's instruction to the CCP in 1926 had influenced the party's decision to give up its military force to the KMT, which had resulted in the loss of 90 percent of the CCP's base areas in the White Terror that had followed. How should the CCP respond to Stalin's instructions this time? Meanwhile, support for Chiang's invitation among urban Chinese was overwhelming. An editor of the prestigious Shanghai Da Gong Bao wrote, "Everyone is watching closely the attitudes of Yanan. Our nation must be unified, otherwise our victory in the War of Resistance is not complete."[43]

At an enlarged Politburo meeting on August 23, 1945, Mao said that he must go to Chungking to negotiate with Chiang, stressing, "The urban Chinese are all watching us." He suggested some modifications of the Theory of New Democracy and his notion of coalition government. In view of new developments in the international situation, the CCP should not insist on its leadership in the coalition government. Instead, it could now recognize the leadership of the Chiang Kai-shek government.[44]

The CCP's concept of coalition government underwent significant changes in 1945: from hope for the best, to fear for the worst, and to both hope for the best and prepare for the worst. However, its paramount task remained the same throughout this period: to build a system of New Democracy, rather than one of proletarian dictatorship. The nature of the CCP-led revolution, or the system of New Democracy, in Mao's words, was anti-imperialism and antifeudalism, not anticapitalism. "The revolutionary classes" thus included not only poor peasants and the working class, but also private entrepreneurs, urban intellectuals, and all the "progressive forces" within the KMT. Therefore, the CCP's vision of economic and political reconstruction in postwar China was, as Mao proclaimed, "to pursue Sun Yat-sen's ideals, rather than carrying out socialist or communist revolution." When many party members complained that the Seventh Party Congress put too much emphasis on Sun Yat-sen, Mao replied,

> Did I talk too much about Sun Yat-sen in my report? No. Lenin also asked us to develop his ideas. Sun's will before his death in 1925 put the greatest emphasis on awakening masses and uniting with all other peoples and nations that treat us as equal. These two basic principles we entirely agree with. His talks on democracy are the best, which are shared by ordinary Chinese people. We should uphold Sun Yat-sen as our banner, as Americans today are upholding Washington and Lincoln as theirs. Within our party, there is widespread dissatisfaction toward Sun Yat-sen, which we must overcome.

When should this system of New Democracy be changed to that of socialism and communism? Mao said that it would depend on "one standard only." That "only standard" was not from "rigid quotes from Marxist books," he emphasized, but based on "Chinese reality"—specifically, whether this system could "promote the rapid development of production forces in China," or China's rapid economic development. As long as the system of New Democracy could do so, it should exist, and exist "for a long historical period."[45]

In sum, before the Marshall mission, the CCP's blueprints for political reconstruction of postwar China had three key components: first, the implementation of nationwide land reform; second, the continuation of the united front with both the KMT and the Third Force; and third, taking precautions to avoid the worst should that front collapse. And the precaution was twofold: having a base area in Manchuria and submitting the CCP armed force not to the current Chiang Kai-shek government but to a new coalition government.

"The social base" of the Third Force was, as Shi Fuliang, a Shanghai journalist, wrote, "the Chinese middle class, which include national entrepreneurs, artisans, white-collar office staff members in the industrial and commercial sectors, the intellectuals, small landowners, rich farmers and self-sufficient farmers. In one word, we are the force of the middle class."[46]

The political program of the Third Force was to build a democratic polity in China. For the Third Force members, "the crux of this democratic polity is not just a new constitution and new elections." The constitution could become "a piece of empty paper," and the election could be "manipulated and monopolized by the KMT." The core of a "genuine democratic polity" in China, they emphasized, was "a coalition government including the KMT, the CCP, and the Third Force." Zhang Dongsun, a prominent Third Force theorist and a liberal professor at Beijing University, wrote that only with such a coalition government could the best interests of the rich, the poor, and the middle class be "compromised, balanced and checked" in postwar China. As he wrote,

> In today's China the KMT represents the interests of the wealthy and the powerful, such as the big capitalists and the big landlords; the CCP represents the interests of the poor and the underprivileged, such as poor peasants and workers; and the Third Force represents the interests of the middle class, such as university professors, high school teachers, lawyers, doctors, journalists, entrepreneurs and middle merchants. If these parties can work together, then, all Chinese people's interests can be taken into account in the new government's policies. . . . Without checks and balances among these three major political forces, there will never be true democracy in China.[47]

For many in the Third Force, the CCP movement could not be eliminated through military power in China. They argued that "as long as there is poverty, there will be Communists in China."[48] Moreover, the CCP's theory of New Democracy was "basically consistent with our own blueprint in this stage of China's development." Since the CCP did not formulate "unrealistic policies" such as the rejection of private property and national capitalism in the postwar era, the CCP should be regarded as "our friend, good friend." Compared with the KMT, indeed, "those Communists are at least genuine about their ideals and about China's reform." The CCP movement could be a problem in the future, "when the Communists want to eliminate all the capitalists and carry out a socialist revolution." But who could know what China would be like decades from now? they asked. "Maybe by then every Chinese will have food to eat, clothes to wear, and the living standard will be greatly raised." When China "becomes a prosperous nation, will the Communists still want to have a socialist revolution? Will any one still want to follow them to stage such a revolution? Not a chance." And so for them, the best way to avoid a socialist revolution in China was to make the CCP "part of the new coalition government" and "to implement economic policies with a socialist spirit." If the CCP were isolated from the democratic process and the problems of people's livelihood were not solved, then, "we are planting the seeds of a socialist revolution in the future."[49]

If the Third Force's political blueprint was a democratic coalition government including the KMT, the CCP, and the Third Force, there was no agreement among them on how important land reform would be in postwar China. For many liberal economists in urban centers, the major issue in rural China was not a matter of land reform, but a lack of scientific methods for growing crops.[50] For others, however, "an immediate radical revolution in the countryside should head the national agenda."[51] There were still others who urged a fundamental change in land relationships in the rural areas yet believed that this goal could be achieved through peaceful, reformist means. As Ruji Qing, a prominent nonpartisan democrat and a president of the American and Canadian Students' and Scholars' Association in the 1930s, argued, the fundamental change in rural China could take the form of exchanging the landlords' land for shares of state-owned factories. In that way the landlords could be transformed peacefully into shareholders in the industrial and commercial sectors, while many of the state-owned industries could be privatized rather than falling into the hands of corrupt government officials. He believed that if the rights of the poor peasants were well protected in the land-reform efforts, and the property of the landed elite dismantled in a peaceful way, "China's unity and democracy will have a solid foundation in the postwar era." He warned that a lack of land reform would be suicidal for the KMT:

Eighty percent of China's population is peasants. . . . If they have little to eat, little to wear, little to support their spouses, and are totally helpless at times of illness and death, how can we talk about China's peace and democracy? When they are forced to the corner, they will rebel, as they did in the past thousand years of Chinese history. If the Government attempts to suppress such rebellions by armed forces, the armed forces sooner or later will rebel against the Government, since 90 percent of the solders are made up of the peasants themselves. . . . The Emperor Qin had the strongest army at his time, which had conquered six states and unified all China in 200 BC, but his dynasty collapsed just as a high-rise building on the sand, when a poor peasant army rose against his son's dynasty.[52]

Clearly, in the postwar years, the Third Force championed peaceful cooperation between the KMT and the CCP in a new democratic system. The majority of the Third Force believed that the post–Sun Yat-sen KMT represented the interests of the rich, the CCP represented the interests of the poor, and the Third Force represented the interests of the middle class in China.[53] Many Third Force members felt it was their sacred responsibility to bring the KMT and the CCP together, to build a "true democracy" in Nationalist China.[54]

In summary, while the KMT, the CCP, and the Third Force all pledged to build a democratic political system in postwar China, they divided over two crucial issues. First, should the CCP surrender its military force to the current KMT government or to a new coalition government consisting of the KMT, the CCP, and the Third Force? Second, should the CCP be allowed to take over some of the Japanese-occupied areas, particularly in Manchuria? In these two primary controversies between the KMT and the CCP, the majority of the Third Force sympathized with the CCP's position, attributable to the CCP's land-reform program and the legacy of Sun Yat-sen's Three Principles of the People. Therefore, the fate of the Marshall mission depended to a great extent on how successfully it could address such deep-rooted divisions in Nationalist China.

The Marshall Mediation in China

On August 26, 1945, Mao arrived in Chungking. Before Marshall's arrival, the KMT and the CCP had had two rounds of negotiations. The first, between Chiang and Mao, lasted from August 28 to October 10, 1945.[55] On October 10, 1945, the Double Ten Agreement was signed in Chungking, declaring that a Political Consultative Conference (PCC) was to convene to discuss the establishment of a coalition government in China. It also announced that unsolved issues, such as the disposition of the CCP's military forces, should be determined by the PCC.[56] The second round of the KMT-CCP negotiation, between

Chiang and Zhou Enlai, began on October 20 and ended on November 25, 1945. Chiang, upset at the KMT's defeat in the KMT-CCP military "showdown" in early October,[57] sent a confidential order to the KMT army commanders on October 13, two days after the signing of the Double Ten Agreement, instructing the KMT troops to "abolish all Communist-controlled separatist regimes" as quickly as they could, in order to "defeat the Communist conspiracy to destroy China's national unity."[58]

Chiang's confidential order fell into the CCP's hands on November 2, 1945, when the Liu Bocheng–Deng Xiaoping army captured a KMT army commander. The CCP leadership decided to seize this opportunity to launch a "propaganda campaign" to win the support of the urban population. The CCP Central Committee's telegram to Zhou emphasized, "Our goal is to win over the middle class between the CCP and the KMT in urban China. As long as our most fundamental interests are not jeopardized, we must be as flexible as possible."[59]

On December 15, 1945, Marshall arrived in China and began his mediation between the KMT and the CCP. When he arrived, the KMT-CCP negotiations had just reached an impasse. Urban Chinese, particularly the Third Force, were overjoyed by his arrival. As an editorial of Shanghai's *Da Gong Bao* wrote, "We are so grateful that this great American national hero is willing to help bring peace and democracy to our motherland. He left his family before Christmas to come here, to help the Chinese people. Should we feel ashamed? Yes, we should. Why do we Chinese still need an American mediator to solve our own problems?"[60]

On January 10, 1946, with Marshall's effective mediation, the PCC convened in Chungking. On January 31, the PCC passed a resolution declaring that a democratic coalition government including the KMT, the CCP, and the Third Force was to be established in China. Both the nationalization of the armed forces and the convention of the National Assembly should take place *after* the new coalition government was established in China.[61] On this critical and most controversial issue between the KMT and the CCP, George Marshall clearly endorsed the united position of the CCP and the Third Force.

The PCC Resolution thus triggered an angry uproar within the conservative factions of the KMT. For them, it was indeed "a coup against our party." Some KMT Central Standing Committee members even proposed prosecuting the PCC delegates of the KMT, particularly Sun Fo, for their "criminal behavior."

However, Chiang Kai-shek told his generals that he would support the PCC Resolution. "China needs peace," he said, "and the KMT needs to co-operate with the non-KMT members to guarantee peace in China."[62] The urban Chinese's sympathy for the CCP could be partially attributed to the "loss of the revolutionary spirit" within the KMT, claimed Chiang. The PCC Resolution should be treated as a "wake-up call" for the party. He told the party militants, "Many party members have entirely lost their revolutionary spirit of 1911. The condition of our armed forces is appalling. . . . American reports from the battle-fields are telling me more truth. This Political Consultative Conference gave the KMT a strong stimulus. It will do us good if we can reflect on it, not fight against it."[63]

On the other hand, the CCP and the Third Force applauded the PCC Resolution, which, indeed, met their major demands. Mao immediately sent a message to Marshall expressing his "deep appreciation" for Marshall's "fairness" in his mediation.[64] At this stage of the new democratic revolution, the CCP could consider following the American path, Mao told his comrades: "In theory we support socialism, but at present we do not intend to put it into practice. We should study American democracy and science so that China can carry out agricultural reform, achieve industrialization, protect freedom of enterprise and other individual rights, and realize eventually the goal of establishing an independent, free, strong and prosperous new China." Mao also asked Zhou to tell Marshall that he would like to visit the U.S., since "there are so many things I could learn from America."[65]

On February 1, 1946, a CCP Central Committee's confidential circular proclaimed that "the new stage of peaceful, democratic development in China has arrived." It emphasized that the PCC Resolution was to implement "the principles of the division between the party and the army, and between the party and the government," to establish "the parliamentary system and the cabinet system," to provide self-government in local areas, and to hold "popular elections of provincial governors." From now on, "our party and our army will be legalized." The CCP would join the national government, and its army would be integrated into the national military force. "In today's situation, this would be the only way to make the KMT agree to integrate its troops into a unified, national military force." As Zhou Enlai told his comrades, the CCP should take the path of the French Communist Party, which, by integrating its army into a national army, greatly consolidated its political power in France.[66]

On February 5, 1946, in its confidential circular, the CCP Central

Committee further stressed that the major thrust of China's revolution would shift from military struggle to "non-military, parliamentary struggle." It particularly emphasized that "the major danger" within the CCP was now "the narrow-minded outlook among many of our comrades."[67]

On February 6, a CCP Intelligence Department memo reported, "The Soviet Union, Great Britain, the United States, and Canada are all pleased with the PCC Resolution." Moreover, "according to Sun Fo and key members of the Political Science Group, Chiang would not change his position on the PCC Resolution despite the KMT militants' outrage against it." The CCP Central Committee urged that "we should now cooperate with Chiang Kai-shek, Sun Fo . . . and members of Political Science Group, and isolate the C-C and military cliques within the KMT." The CCP Central Committee thus decided to stop its propaganda war against the KMT, as proposed by Sun Fo and the "Political Science Group."[68]

After the conclusion of the PCC Resolution, the most critical issue was how to nationalize the Chinese army under a new coalition government. Marshall suggested a KMT-CCP army ratio of 5:1.[69] He also proposed that after six months the new coalition government should take a certain number of KMT and CCP troops and "carry out an experimental merger" to establish a new national army eventually.[70]

On February 12, 1946, at the CCP Central Committee meeting on Marshall's proposal of military unification, Mao expressed serious doubts. "We want unification without being wiped out. The separation of party from army is not the most dangerous thing. Merger and re-deployment of troops is the most dangerous. Now only by managing things well can we ward off danger." He acknowledged: "The nation-wide unification of forces is something that in principle we must support, but we must look very concretely at the steps to bring it about."[71] Zhou, on the other hand, believed that Marshall's proposal was "acceptable," since it was very close to the CCP's own proposal of a KMT-CCP army ratio of 9:2. He told his comrades, "General Marshall reminds me of General Stilwell," who had been military adviser to Chiang Kai-shek in World War II and sharply critical of Chiang. Marshall was "fair" to the CCP on the issue of the KMT-CCP troop ratio and nationalization of the armed forces. "Only after Zhou made repeated representations and explanations," Zhang Bijia emphasizes, "did the Central Committee finally decide to accept" Marshall's proposal. On February 21, Zhou informed Marshall of the CCP Central

Committee's decision to accept "in principle" his proposal regarding the merger. He also told Marshall, "Chairman Mao spoke highly of your efforts to modernize China's military force and to bring China onto the path of democracy."[72]

However, Chiang Kai-shek was dismayed by Marshall's proposal. He complained in his diary that this plan, which would preserve eighteen divisions of the CCP's troops in the new national army, even more than the CCP had requested, was "the biggest loss of our government." However, with the CCP's decision to accept it, Chiang had no choice but to offer his endorsement. On February 25, 1946, Marshall's plan to nationalize the Chinese armed forces was formally agreed on by the KMT government and the Central Committee. According to the PCC Resolution, each participating party of the PCC should convene a plenary meeting of its central committee, to ratify the PCC Resolution and the Agreement of Nationalization of Chinese Armed Forces.

Between March 1 and March 17, 1946, at the KMT Central Committee's meeting, the KMT conservative militants revolted against the ratification. For them, this new coalition government would "eventually destroy the KMT." The majority at the session thus opposed ratifying the PCC Resolution but expressed a willingness to "revise" it.

The key revision proposed that under the new constitution the power of the executive branch must not be responsible for the legislative branch. In this way, Chiang's power would not be "seriously weakened by the CCP and the Third Force." Chiang, troubled by Marshall's military nationalization program, favored the KMT conservatives' proposal for a drastic increase of presidential power in the new coalition government.[73]

With enormous pressure not only from KMT conservatives but from Chiang Kai-shek himself, Sun Fo, the KMT's chief negotiator at the PCC, appealed to Zhou and the Third Force for concessions. The negotiators from the Third Force, particularly the Democratic League, refused flatly. Zhou, however, agreed to compromise. As he told the Third Force negotiators, "Politics is a very realistic matter. We cannot only see the trees while losing sight of the whole forest. We must find a way to make the PCC Resolution work in China."

On March 15, 1946, Zhou informed the KMT delegation that the CCP delegation would agree to the revision of the PCC Resolution concerning the relationship between the executive and the legislative branches in the new constitution. In exchange, Zhou insisted, the KMT should make a public pledge to the nation that it would ratify the PCC Resolution immediately and make no further demands for revisions.[74]

Zhou's concession, however, was quickly overturned by Mao Zedong and the CCP Central Committee. On March 18, 1946, Mao expressed his "deep concerns" over Zhou's position. The KMT conservatives were now determined to oppose the PCC Resolution. "Under such circumstances, we should not join the new government in Nanjing."[75]

The CCP Central Committee's position was popular with many of its high-ranking military officers as well as with the rank and file. Some of them had been suspicious of the KMT's motivations from the moment the negotiation began. Immediately after the KMT declined to ratify the PCC Resolution, two prominent military leaders, Li Fuchun and Huang Kecheng, wrote to Mao, asking whether "making continued concessions" to the KMT was the best way to protect the CCP's interests. "Chiang Kai-shek and the KMT will not put down their swords because of our substantial concessions," they said. "The KMT's massacre can break out anytime now." Their recommendation was that the CCP should give up trying for a political solution and instead "settle the KMT-CCP conflict on the battlefield."[76]

Nonetheless, Mao did not yet want to go so far as to give up on finding a political solution. From mid-March through June 1946, he was still convinced that Moscow and Washington could achieve reconciliation in China and that Marshall would force Chiang and KMT conservatives to make concessions to the CCP sooner or later. Mao was also convinced that Chiang probably had two goals in mind concerning the CCP. The first was his long-term goal of eliminating the CCP; the second was his short-term goal of preserving the CCP on a temporary basis. The best way to force Chiang to stick to his short-term goal was, in Mao's mind, to demonstrate the CCP's power and strength, rather than to make continued concessions to the KMT. When the Soviet troops began to withdraw from northeast China in mid-March through June 1946, Mao decided, "We must speak from a position of strength, to force Chiang to come to terms at the negotiation table."[77]

In Chiang's view, the Soviet withdrawal from Manchuria represented the best opportunity for the KMT to eliminate the CCP's military forces there. If the KMT could eradicate the CCP's army in Manchuria now, as he told Marshall, it would be much easier to abolish the rest of the

CCP forces south of the Great Wall. Chiang was confident that Washington would support his military campaigns against the CCP in that area, which was strategically important to America. Moreover, since Chiang's political appointments in Manchuria had mostly gone to the Political Science Group, it now claimed that the Nationalist government "must assert its sovereignty in the Northeast" and that "no separatist regime should ever be allowed" in that industrial heartland of Nationalist China.[78] Beginning in mid-March 1946, Manchuria was thus chosen as the testing ground by both the CCP and the KMT.

From March 11 until April 18, 1946, Marshall was back in Washington, reporting to Truman on the Chinese situation. In mid-March, with the Soviet military withdrawal from Manchuria, the KMT immediately took over Shengyang, the most important industrial city in the Northeast. Its next target was Changchun, one of the largest cities in Manchuria. On April 18, when Marshall returned to China, the CCP army had just overtaken Changchun. Mao hoped that Marshall's return, combined with the CCP's show of military strength, would force Chiang to retreat at the negotiating table. Thus despite opposition from Zhou and Lin Biao, the commander-in-chief of the CCP army in Manchuria, Mao ordered the CCP troops to defend Changchun. In May 1946, however, KMT troops took back the city.[79]

The eruption of the civil war in Manchuria put Marshall in a political dilemma. The War Department's objective for the Marshall mission was to help the KMT become the dominant force in Manchuria without causing a civil war in China. This prompted Marshall to press the CCP to withdraw from the major cities there; meanwhile, he also pressed Chiang to stop attacking the CCP forces in Manchuria.

In his private reports to Truman, however, Marshall spoke more candidly about the causes of the CCP-KMT military conflict in Manchuria. He disagreed with Chiang's argument that the CCP's military campaign was the major cause of the civil war. As Marshall wrote, the Communist military campaign "grew out, in my opinion, from the following circumstances: the Communists became fearful of the good faith of the Government" in carrying out the PCC Resolution. This doubt was "stimulated by the anti-Communist demonstrations" which at times resulted in "physical attacks on Communist meetings, newspaper offices and individuals." Nonetheless, the CCP military campaign in Manchuria was at least partially responsible for the collapse of the PCC Resolution, because it "strengthened the position of irreconcilable elements within the Kuomintang," wrote Marshall. Right after the CCP's takeover of Changchun, Marshall found that "the irreconcilables" of the KMT were "firmly in the saddle," and Chiang took the position that "the Communists were in league with the Soviet Government and could not be relied upon to keep any agreements." The KMT conservatives "would have been opposed to the PCC resolution under any circumstances," he said, but the CCP's military campaign in Changchun offered them a perfect excuse.[80]

The major obstacle to his mediation in Manchuria was, Marshall told Truman, the "irreconcilables" within the KMT. If, before he came to China, he had thought that the CCP would be the major obstacle to a democratic coalition government, by now he had altered his view. Throughout his mediation, he told Truman, he had been "deeply disappointed at the belief, freely expressed, by some of the Government military officials and some politicians that the Communists can be quickly and easily crushed." Marshall called such a view "a gross underestimate" of possible consequences of a civil war for the KMT, since "a long and terrible conflict would be unavoidable."[81]

On June 10, 1946, Chiang publicly changed his position concerning a political solution for the KMT-CCP conflict in China. He pledged to solve the Communist issue through military means in one year: "Before today I advocated a political solution in China. But now I have decided to give up a political solution. . . . Now let me give you my word that I will end military campaigns against the Communists in one year, and restore industrial production in two years. Comrades, please trust my words, I can achieve all these goals in three years."[82]

On June 26, 1946, in Washington, the House Foreign Affairs Committee "reported favorably on the military assistance bill to the Chiang Kai-shek Government." One day later, the Truman administration announced that the United States was to provide the KMT government with $51.7 million in "pipeline" equipment.

Marshall was appalled at the news from Washington: "These moves, coming at the most critical stage in my negotiations, are causing difficulty and embarrassment." He warned that the KMT conservative militants were "utilizing recent American measures as a basis" for pressing Chiang to push forward with "a campaign of extermination" against the Communists all over China. On the other hand, the CCP was now convinced that "American economic and military support to the KMT Government will continue" no matter whether the KMT government offered the CCP "a fair and responsible basis for settlement of military and political differences." In early July of 1946, Marshall reported to Truman that it would be impossible for him to continue his mediation in China.[83]

On the Eve of Civil War: Mao's "Intermediate Zone Theory" and the Soviet Union

On February 9, 1946, Stalin told a voters' meeting in Moscow that as long as the capitalist system still existed, war could never be avoided. On March 5, former British prime minister Winston Churchill, in his speech at Fulton, Missouri, on the postwar international situation, called for building an alliance among English-speaking peoples to "resist communism" in the post–World War II world.

The Truman administration began to emphasize more vigorously the importance of an "open door" policy to China including, in particular, Manchuria. Moscow was angry about Washington's public rejection of Russia's "special interest" there which, in Stalin's mind, was promised by the Yalta Agreement. Moscow's attitude toward the CCP's role in Manchuria began to change. The Soviets urged the CCP to stop KMT troops from occupying Manchuria and also encouraged a CCP force to reoccupy Shenyang in northern China.[84]

KMT conservatives were thrilled by the increased tension between Moscow and Washington. To raise morale within the KMT, they began to predict confidently that a third world war would soon break out between Washington and Moscow over China and that the United States would send its troops to help the KMT defeat the CCP in the expected Chinese civil war.

For Yanan, Moscow's message was much more complicated than it appeared. The CCP leadership was pleased to see Moscow's change of heart toward the growth of the CCP's power in Manchuria. But it was also aware that the Soviet leadership did not want to see a Chinese civil war whereby the USSR might be dragged into a direct military conflict with the United States. As Stalin told his Chinese comrades, should a civil war break out in China, Washington could send troops to help the KMT safeguard the United States' critical interests, especially to the south of the Great Wall, as guaranteed by the Yalta Agreement. Thus, regardless of Stalin's rhetoric on capitalism and war, the CCP leadership understood that Moscow would do everything to avoid such a military showdown. That was why, as Hu Qiaomu recalled, Stalin sent urgent oral messages to Zhou Enlai, asking him to report to the CCP Central Committee that a civil war between the KMT and the CCP could mean a war between the United States and the USSR.[85] Throughout 1946, because of precisely the same concerns or fears, Moscow "explicitly" asked the Greek Communists to give up their armed force and emphasized "the inadvisability of the armed confrontation alternative." According to the Yalta Agreement, Greece was, like China south of the Great Wall, not assigned to be within the "sphere of influence" of the Soviet Union.[86]

Meanwhile, there were heightened and widespread anxieties among the Third Force members, as well as within the CCP. Was a third world war soon to break out? Could a Chinese civil war spark off a deadly confrontation between the United States and the USSR? Should the CCP concede more to the KMT to avoid a new world war?

Within the context of all those concerns and worries, domestically and internationally, Mao proposed his intermediate zone theory. The intermediate zone referred to the developing countries in Asia, Africa, and Latin America. Mao's major hypothesis was twofold. First, the United States would not fight a third world war with the Soviet Union, until it could control the intermediate zone and that the U.S.-USSR relationship would continue to be dominated by rivalries and compromises in the post–World War II era. Second, Moscow's compromises with the United States did not require the revolutionary forces in the intermediate zone to make similar concessions in their domestic struggles. On the contrary, the more resolute their revolutionary struggles became, the more unlikely it was that a third world war, sparked by the United States and the USSR, would ever take place.

According to Hu Qiaomu, Mao's secretary at that time, the two goals of Mao's intermediate zone theory were to reject the KMT conservatives' claim that a third world war would soon erupt and, more important, to avoid the fate the CCP had suffered in 1927, which many believed could be attributed to the CCP leadership's blind following of Stalin's instructions. As Hu wrote, "Stalin wanted us to make more concessions to avoid a war between the Soviet Union and the United States during that time. But the 'intermediate zone theory' told us that Moscow's compromises with Washington should not require the revolutionaries in the 'intermediate zone' to make similar concessions in their domestic struggles."[87]

Mao's "People's War Theory" and the United States

According to Soviet sources, after March 1946 the Red Army offered important military aid to the CCP's fourth field army in Manchuria, which included over 700,000 rifles, 12,000 machine-guns, 37,000 various cannons, 600 tanks, 800 airplanes, and 2,000 trucks. According to the military commanders of the fourth field army, however, their troops never received that much military equipment. Liu Yalou, chair of the joint chiefs of staff at the fourth field army, recalled, "While the general impression was that the Soviet Red Army left us lots of military equipment, it was an incorrect one. In fact, we were so poorly equipped at the time that we were compelled to write a letter to the CCP headquarters, suggesting that the Central Committee ask the Soviet Red Army to give us military aid before its withdrawal from Manchuria." However, the CCP headquarters declined this request. "Chairman Mao sent us a letter, which I read and which should still be in the chairman's papers, emphasizing that Chinese revolution should depend upon its own forces to win victory, and no one should be ever allowed to utilize the name of the CCP Central Committee to ask for anything from the Soviet Red Army." In the name of the fourth field army, Liu collected 1 million tons of crops in northern Manchuria to exchange for Soviet weapons. "During our most difficult time" in the civil war, he said, "it was the Korean comrades under Kim Il-Sung who provided us the most valuable military aid, from weapons to logistic support."[88]

Regardless of the controversy over Soviet military aid to the CCP in Manchuria during the civil war, Moscow probably did intend to offer military support to the CCP force in Manchuria after March 1946, without being dragged into a direct military confrontation with the United States. The question is, of course, how many of these weapons actually reached the hands of the fourth field army. Moreover, no matter how much Moscow tried to support the CCP force in Manchuria, its military aid could not be compared with Washington's aid to the Chiang Kai-shek government. The Truman administration also landed 90,000 of its marines in China, guarding the major communication lines for the KMT government in northern China.[89] Given the differences in military forces between the CCP and the KMT in mid-1946, "The Soviets initially did not believe that we could win the civil war," Hu Qiaomu wrote[90] (see Table 3.1).

By mid-1946, Mao knew a civil war could no longer be avoided. The CCP leadership reached a critical decision. Its strategy must be shifted from "seeking peace through fighting" after March 1946 to "preparing for full-scale civil war." Hu wrote, "For over twenty years when I worked at Chairman Mao's side, I saw only two decisions over which he so agonized he could not make up his mind. Many in the party knew the chairman did not sleep and eat for three days and nights

Table 3.1 Comparison of Strength between the CCP and the KMT, July 1946

Item		Number	Ratio or Percentage
Troops (soldiers)	CCP	1,200,000	
	KMT	4,300,000	3.58:1
Territories (sq. km.)	CCP	2,285,800	23.8
	KMT	7,311,720	76.2
Cities	CCP	464	23
	KMT	1,545	77
Population	CCP	136,067,000	28.5
	KMT	338,933,000	71.4

Source: Peng Ming, ed., *Zhongguo xiandaishi ziliao xuanji, 1945–1949* (A Selection of Contemporary Chinese Historical Documents, 1945–1949), vol. 6 (Beijing: Zhongguo renmindaxue chubanshe, 1989), p. 181.

before he made the decision to enter the Korean War. But few knew in mid-1946 how much he was agonizing over the decision to break up with the Chiang Kai-shek government." As he acknowledged, in Yanan, "many of us were nervous about the huge military aid the KMT had been receiving from the United States, wondering whether we could ever win a war with the KMT, which had so many advanced weapons." It was in this context that Mao proposed his "people's war theory" to raise the morale within the party and the Third Force, when the CCP's military power was clearly inferior to that of the Chiang Kai-shek government.[91]

At his talk in Yanan with American correspondent Anna Louise Strong in August 1946, after Mao emphasized that the war between the KMT and the CCP would not trigger a world war between the United States and the Soviet Union, Strong raised a question: "But suppose the United States uses the atom bomb? Suppose the United States bombs the Soviet Union from the bases in Iceland, Okinawa, and China?" Mao replied, "The atom bomb is a paper tiger which the U.S. reactionaries use to scare people. It looks terrible, but in fact it isn't. Of course, the atom bomb is a weapon of mass slaughter, but the outcome of a war is decided by the people, not by one or two new types of weapon." Mao then proclaimed: "Take the case of China. We have only millet plus rifles to rely on, but history will finally prove that our millet plus rifles is more powerful than Chiang Kai-shek's airplanes plus tanks."[92]

This disparity in military power between the KMT and the CCP would soon change. Such a rapid change could be attributed not just to Mao's military strategy but, more decisively, to deepening divisions between the Nationalist state and Chinese society.

Polarization of the Nationalist Government and Chinese Society

In late June 1946, more than 100,000 people in Shanghai poured into the streets to protest the outbreak of civil war in China. The demonstrators elected a prestigious group of twelve liberal intellectuals and entrepreneurs to deliver their petition to the KMT government in Nanjing. When the petitioners arrived in the Nanjing train station, they were beaten by KMT secret agents and had to be hospitalized. One month later, following the assassination of professors Li Gongpu and Wen Yiduo, two leading members of the Democratic League, millions of students and professors poured into the streets in all the major cities in China, and the roar against the KMT "resounded through the skies."[93]

In August 1946, Chiang asked Marshall's view on whether the United States would recognize a new government in China that did not include the CCP, as required by the PCC Resolution. For the Bureau of Far Eastern Affairs at the State Department, the answer was "no." In his memo to Undersecretary Dean Acheson, John Carter Vincent argued that "the real substance" of Chiang's question was "whether we would give material support to a coalition government of the type he has in mind." And "if I thought any good . . . would come from all-out support of Chiang" when he was engaged in large-scale civil war in China, "I would be for it, but I can see only trouble, trouble coming" from such support. He concluded, "I think we must . . . try to avoid seeing the Chinese situation as all black or white."[94]

Marshall was sympathetic with this view. However, given "the bottom of line" of the president's policy concerning his mediation in China, there was little he could do. In November 1946, the Constitutional Assembly convened to design a new constitution, without the participation of the CCP and the Democratic League. Marshall admitted that "reactionary KMT leaders' domination is evident" at the Assembly.[95]

Luo Longji, vice president of the Democratic League, lamented to the American Consulate in Shanghai that "the Constitutional Assembly is only a farce, since 130 million in Communist areas plus supporters of the Democratic League are not represented." In his view, "The Constitutional Assembly merely gives the United States an excuse to back the Kuomintang," and he was "greatly surprised that Ambassador John Leighton Stuart regards it as a step toward constitutional government" in China. For Luo, it was a "step backward," since "the Communists and the Democratic League cannot accept a constitution made by others." From now on, he said, compromise would be made "much more difficult by the unilateral Constitutional Assembly." Despite the KMT's belief that "the Democratic League is Red-run," in fact, "the League holds an independent position, from which it has tried to mediate" between the KMT and the CCP. He stressed that the CCP's forces "cannot be annihilated by military power, no matter what cities they lose right now."[96]

Robert Ward, the American Consul in Shanghai, reported to the State Department that he had known Luo for years and believed that Luo was speaking to him "truthfully." Ward believed, "In his opposition to the KMT Government, he faithfully reflects the still inarticulate feelings of a large majority of the class of Chinese intellectuals." While Luo was not a Communist, he would become one if that seemed to be "the only hope of getting rid of the present KMT Government."[97]

In March 1947, Chu Anping, founder and editor of *Guanchajia* magazine, a popular journal of political commentary in urban China during the late 1940s, summed up the drastically changed urban Chinese attitudes toward the KMT government. "The basis of the KMT Government's support was the urban population: government employees and teachers, intellectuals, and business and industrial circles," he wrote. "At present, however, few among these people have any positive feelings toward that regime." The KMT's "tyrannical behavior" triggered "deep hatred" among the urban Chinese, and the continuation of the civil war set off "waves of protests" everywhere in urban China.[98]

In October 1947, after the Democratic League was officially declared illegal by the KMT government, Chiang announced that elections would be held in late 1947 for delegates to the First National Assembly to choose China's president and vice president. From March 29 to April 29, 1948, more than 3,000 delegates gathered in Nanjing to hold China's first presidential election. Chiang won an overwhelming 2,430 votes. Li Zongren, an old opponent of Chiang's within the KMT, was elected vice president. The process of the election was "largely fair," acknowledged many delegates. The delegates were "very enthusiastic" in giving suggestions on how to improve China's domestic and international situations. A journalist remarked, "It is rare for any nation in the world to hold such a big National Assembly of more than 3,000 delegates. It is truly an achievement for those delegates to have such an orderly democratic election during such a critical time of our nation."[99]

The convention of the first National Assembly, however, did little to change most urban Chinese attitudes toward the KMT government. In November 1948, an editorial of the *Central Daily*, the KMT's official newspaper, entitled "Win the Hearts and Minds of the Chinese People," acknowledged that the "most painful reality" was the "giant gap between the rich and the poor." And "the poverty among the majority of the Chinese people" became "the major strength of the Communist rebellion." This was a fact "no one can deny anymore, no matter how much he wants to." The KMT must immediately adopt Otto von Bismarck's social policies of "state socialism" to "win back the hearts and minds of the Chinese people," particularly the urban population.[100]

By the end of 1948, it was indeed too late for the KMT government to win back the urban population. The traditional political polarization between the KMT government and the poor peasantry would soon send a poor peasant army, led by the CCP, into all the towns and cities of China.

In May 1946, Mao and the CCP Central Committee decided that land reform must be implemented in all CCP-controlled areas before the end of 1946.[101] Mao told the party, "If we can implement land reform immediately, we will win the strongest support of the peasants in our areas for a long time to come." By the end of 1946, more than 20 million peasants in Shanxi, Hebei, Shandong, and Henan provinces received new land, and more than 15 million peasants in Jiangsu and Anhui provinces received new land. Before the outbreak of the civil war, the century-old land-tax system was abolished in the CCP-controlled areas.[102]

Millions and millions of poor peasants now had their own land. They became staunch supporters of the CCP. As an editorial of *Jiefang ribao* (Liberation Daily) in Yanan declared on New Year's Day of 1947, "History will prove that our gallant peasant army will become the best guarantee of our final victory."[103]

For the newly elected National Assembly in Nanjing, the vital importance of land reform to the future of the KMT suddenly loomed large. The legislators urged the KMT government to implement land reform immediately.[104] The KMT government had neglected rural organization since 1927, however, and without the CCP's organizational networks in rural China, the KMT simply did not have any institutional mechanism to break up the landed elite's resistance. This dilemma was vividly illustrated in many field reports of KMT military officers. They found out that as soon as they drove out the Communists, the landlords came back and began their revenge against those poor peasants who had taken away their land under Communist rule. Colonel Liao Jiwu, for instance, reported to the KMT Defense Department from Anhui province that "in the areas we just took back from the Communist hands," the landlords not only stopped implementing the KMT Government's order of a "25% reduction of the poor peasants' tax," but also forced the poor peasants to pay back all the tax refunds they had received from the Communists. To return to the landlords all the benefits they had received from the Communists, some peasants had to "sell all their farming equipment," others simply "escaped from their homes and became bandits." He stated that these were not "isolated phenomena," but widely supported by the local governments. Most local officials who were supposed to take charge of the land reform were "either landlords themselves" or had "very close ties with the landlords."[105]

Song Qingling, widow of Sun Yat-sen, saw the grave danger inherent in the deepening polarization between the KMT government and the poor peasants. As she warned, with the villages on the side of the CCP, "very soon, we will wonder where the cities can obtain their resources, export commodities, and even get their food. The inflation rate, which already is swallowing up the cities, will continue to soar a thousand times. The KMT can never win such a civil war."[106]

The Marshall Mission: Unintended Consequences

On the eve of the First Chinese National Assembly meeting in February 1948, Truman proposed a China aid bill to Congress to help the "democratic transition" of the KMT government. Six major organizations of the Third Force, along with the Democratic League, immediately issued a joint statement to the Truman administration. It claimed, "The KMT government is currently engaged in the destruction of the Third Force, massive arrest of students, and a large-scale civil war. It can no longer represent the Chinese people. We therefore firmly oppose the China aid bill, which will greatly deepen the Chinese people's suffering."[107]

"The majority in the Third Force now believe that America does not want China to be a truly democratic country," remarked Ma Xulun, a prominent liberal scholar of the Third Force. "America only wants China to be controlled by the KMT, thus becoming an anti-Soviet base" in East Asia. Urban Chinese now felt "profoundly disillusioned" not only with the KMT government, but also with American China policy, he wrote. What the Third Force really wanted was "a genuine democratic polity" in China that would include the KMT, the CCP, and the Third Force. Such a China, he emphasized, would eventually become a "great friend" of America. But now most Third Force members were increasingly anti-American.[108] Or, as Zhang Dongsun wrote, "For us, a genuine coalition government including the KMT, the CCP, and the Third Forces, rather than a fake coalition government, which excludes the CCP and most members of the Third Force, should be true democracy for China." He asked: "Why did we fail to build such a genuine democratic polity in China?" His answer: "America had a very narrow concept of representative government in China." Indeed, "We knew from the start that the KMT had such narrow concepts of democracy. What we did not know was that Americans could not understand why the Third Party was committed to a different ideal of representative government in China."[109]

Something went "seriously wrong" with America's China policy, Luo Lungji told American diplomats in early 1947. The Democratic League observed two objectives of America's China policy in the postwar years, he said. One was "to establish a democratic, prosperous, and united China, which could be a good customer and a force for world peace." The other was "to establish a strong China that would, if necessary, fight with the U.S. against the USSR." And in the view of the Democratic League, "the past year has shown that U.S. concern is primarily with the second objective, and the first could be discarded under pressure." According to Luo, "Chiang sees that the U.S. is bound to support him no matter how his negotiations with the Reds go, and so he has pushed the negotiations ruthlessly." At the same time, the Democratic League and the CCP were increasingly convinced that Marshall's mediation was "tied to a partisan U.S. policy." Therefore, Marshall was "rapidly losing influence in liberal and Red circles in China." The

Marshall mediation could have succeeded, he argued, if Marshall had brought pressure upon Chiang for "real concessions."[110]

It is important to emphasize the Third Force's perception that in the United States' China policymaking, Washington's concern over its power struggle with the Soviet Union trumped its ideal of democracy in China was mistaken. The Truman administration, or more accurately, the president and the Far Eastern Bureau of the State Department, did intend to establish a representative government in China. The question is, Why did they fail to reach this desired policy outcome during the Marshall mission? As this chapter illustrates, what constituted a liberal solution in America's China policy took profoundly different forms in policy debates. At the core of those competing concepts was the issue of how to evaluate the nature of the CCP movement. Restated, the policymakers involved shared the strategic objective of decreasing Soviet power in Nationalist China, but differed sharply on how to analyze China's domestic development, particularly the sources of the CCP movement. If the Far Eastern Bureau's concept of "liberal solution" and its China policy proposal had ever prevailed, the outcome of the Marshall mission to China could have been very different. Unfortunately, the insights of John Carter Vincent and his colleagues were ignored, their concept of a liberal solution in China marginalized, and their China policy proposal for the Marshall mission rejected. In this sense, it was those mainstream American assumptions with respect to the political visions of urban Chinese middle class, the desires of Chinese poor peasants, and the nature of the CCP movement that fundamentally defined and conditioned America's China policy debates at the time. To a great extent, those widely accepted but rarely examined assumptions deeply penetrated most policymakers' interpretations of both power and ideology within the Truman administration. From this perspective, the apparent dichotomy between power and ideology ("power trumped ideology") in America's China policy debates was, at a deeper level, an illusory one.

Why did Truman's ideal of liberal democracy contribute to a political situation in China so contrary to America's China policy goals in the postwar years? Truman's concept of a liberal solution in China, no matter the lofty motivation, grew out of America's "exceptional historical experience." This vision of liberal democracy was not a sufficient basis for understanding the poor peasants' overriding demands for land reform and the urban middle class's alternative blueprint for democracy in China. During the Marshall mission, the majority of China's middle class aspired to establish a genuine coalition government among the KMT, the CCP, and the Third Force, so as to achieve a balance between the interests of urban and rural China in the post–World War II era. However, by identifying the political blueprint of the urban Chinese middle class with that of mainstream America, by neglecting the critical issue of land reform in China's democratic transition, and by attributing all social and political upheavals in China to Moscow's instigations, America's China policy became counterproductive. In addition to the traditional polarization between the Nationalist state and poor peasants, there was now polarization between the Nationalist state and the nascent civil society. This dual polarization in Nationalist China helped to pave the way for a rapid U.S.-China transition from an alliance to an adversarial relationship in the postwar years.

CHAPTER FOUR

New American Strategies

Debates over the Chinese
Communist Party and Taiwan
in the Truman Administration

From November 1950 to July 1953, the United States and the People's Republic fought a war in Korea. What was the underlying cause of the war? The recent American literature on the subject has increasingly emphasized the inevitable clash of security interests and ideologies in the origins of U.S.-China military confrontation in Korea. Some claim it was instigated by the Truman administration's confrontational policy against the PRC before the war; others claim it was generated by Beijing's confrontational policy against the United States in 1949–1950. From both these perspectives, U.S.-China direct military conflict in Korea was unavoidable.

However, based on recently declassified Chinese and Russian documents, the following chapters will argue that neither Washington nor Beijing had formulated a confrontational strategy in the critical year 1949–1950, before the onset of the Korean War. If the major concern of the Truman administration's China policy had been how to avoid driving the CCP further into Moscow's embrace, the primary preoccupation of the CCP's U.S. policy had been how to avoid driving Washington to rescue the Chiang Kai-shek government in Taipei at the eleventh hour. Thus, neither side had desired a military confrontation between China and the United States. It was fatal misjudgments of each other's intentions that contributed to direct military confrontation. And it was those deeply embedded policy postulates in both countries that underlay their fatal misjudgments in the time of crisis. The term *misjudgment* will be used, as Robert Jervis defines it, "to include inaccurate inferences, miscalculations of consequences, and misjudgments about how others will react to one's policies"; in short, "judgments and misjudgments of another state's intentions."[1]

U.S. Assumptions Regarding the Chinese Communist Party's Foreign-Policy Intentions

This chapter focuses on the Truman administration's China-policy debates in 1949–1950, before the onset of the Korean War. It examines different hypotheses underlying evaluations within the Truman administration of the CCP's intentions. In particular, it focuses on the formulation of a new China policy in that period. Why did Secretary of State Dean Acheson insist on a combination of new economic policy toward the CCP and new military strategy toward Taiwan in early 1950?[2] And why, in the course of its implementation, did this new China policy appear to be inconsistent, moving in "opposite directions" simultaneously?

By the end of 1948, two major international events generated fierce China policy debates in Washington. The first was the open split between the Communist Party of Yugoslavia (CPY) and the Soviet Union in June 1948; the second was the rapid collapse of the KMT government in Nationalist China. In November 1948, the U.S. Central Intelligence Agency (CIA) first predicted that the fall of the KMT Government might well occur in the following few months.[3] Ambassador John Leighton Stuart, a longtime supporter of Chiang Kai-shek's cause, warned, "Any effort to keep Chiang in power through American aid would not only be undemocratic but would also arouse greater sympathy for the Communist cause and create violent anti-American feeling."[4] In December 1948, General David Barr, the senior U.S. military representative in China, reported to the Department of Army that even "the formation of an American volunteer group can do little more than delay the eventual defeat of the Nationalist armed forces." In January 1949, he formally recommended that "no military aid and supplies be shipped to the Nationalist Government."[5]

Ten days after Truman's inauguration on January 20, 1949, all of China north of the Yangtze River was in the hands of the People's Liberation Army (PLA). If many in Washington were appalled by the demise of the KMT government, others were exhilarated at the open crack in the apparently monolithic Soviet bloc and thought the Yugoslav development important for America's future policy toward the Chinese Communists.

During the heated China policy debates, three different proposals emerged, which were, in turn, built upon three distinct assumptions with respect to the Chinese Communists' foreign-policy objectives.[6] One proposal was to defeat the CCP through continued military aid to the anticommunist forces in China.[7] Underlying this proposal was the assumption that the Chinese Communists were the puppets of the Soviet Union. It would indeed be naive to expect the split of Mao-Stalin alliance, since there were such "close ideological ties" between the Chinese Communists and the Soviet Union. As a National Security Council (NSC) memo commented, the CCP's "loyal parroting of the Cominform line on Tito," the communist leader of Yugoslavia, had dispelled "any lingering doubts" about the CCP's foreign-policy intentions. The United States had fought a war with Japan to prevent its predominance in China and East Asia. With the Chinese Communists in power, the memo warned, "the groundwork is now being laid for a Communist regime in North China in essential alignment with the global aims of the Soviet Union."[8]

This assessment of the Chinese Communists' foreign-policy goals led the NSC officers to recommend that the United States establish regional anti-Communist regimes in Xinjiang and Manchuria, particularly Manchuria. They insisted that the United States should provide military and economic aid in that "strategically important region," as it did in Greece, to build a pro-American regime to check the Soviet Union. This China-policy proposal, its authors claimed, received "enthusiastic support in a number of quarters of the administration."[9]

Another China policy proposal was just the opposite: it called for establishing a comprehensive trade relationship with the Chinese Communists. This proposal was based on an entirely different assumption with respect to the foreign-policy objectives of the Chinese Communists. As Paul Hoffman, director of the Economic Cooperative Administration (ECA), emphasized in his memo, the CCP leaders were by no means Soviet puppets, but "patriotic nationalists" and "social revolutionaries." This assumption was well articulated by a group of American diplomats at the U.S. Embassy in Nationalist China. These diplomats had been chosen by General Patrick Hurley in 1945 to replace the alleged "Communist sympathizers" in the embassy, such as John Stuart Service. Four years later, however, their opinions were much closer to Service's than to Hurley's. Their memo to the State Department in July 1949 argued that to understand the nature of the Chinese Communist movement, two "more important factors" in addition to Marxist doctrines must be taken into account. One was "the passionately nationalistic element of the CCP's teaching and practice," particularly among "its more liberal leaders and educated followers." The other factor was the Chinese common people's outcry for social and economic justice. Disillusionment with the KMT for having "neglected this feature of its avowed program" was, in their view, "one of the most potent influences in sending the idealistic over to the CCP, whose emphasis has been upon economic justice and amelioration for the masses rather than upon political liberty." Thus, they stressed that if America continued perceiving nationalism and communism in China as two antagonistic forces, America's China policy in the future might create even greater anti-American outrage among urban Chinese. "It is thus imperative that we bear constantly in mind the fact that Chinese intellectuals and progressive forces have been hostile to our policy," since they felt that through this single-minded anticommunist policy, "we sought to block Chinese national and social progress to our selfish advantage."[10]

The advocates of this policy proposal emphasized the importance of impressing the Chinese people as well as the CCP leadership with America's "sincere desire for help." In the words of Paul Hoffman, "One should not make the factor of Communism as such a completely controlling force in practical policy, particularly in the cases of China and Yugoslavia." With economic aid from the West, "powerful factions in the Chinese Communist Party" could recognize that "the cooperation of the U.S. and other non-Communist countries will be necessary in solving the vast economic problems facing China." Thus, "by evidencing a willingness to cooperate, the U.S. would strengthen the position of this group vis-à-vis loyal Moscow followers."[11]

However, in the view of the Division of Chinese Affairs at the State Department, neither the strategy of military confrontation nor that of comprehensive economic cooperation with the CCP would ever produce the desired policy results in China. They did not agree that the CCP was simply the puppet of the Soviet Union. Neither did they believe the Chinese Communists were "patriotic nationalists." Instead, they were convinced that although there were "some nationalistic sentiments" among the Chinese Communist leaders, the CCP was "currently subservient to Moscow." With this policy hypothesis, the third

China policy proposal called for promoting Titoism in China, which was designed to "induce" or "maneuver" the CCP leadership to detach gradually "from its current subservience to Moscow." Put another way, this policy aimed to create "the long-term possibility" that Mao's China, like Tito's Yugoslavia, would eventually break with the Soviet Union.[12]

As soon as Dean Acheson became secretary of state in February 1949, he turned down the proposal for continued military aid to anti-Communist forces in China. He also rejected the proposal for restoring comprehensive trade relations with the Chinese Communists. He agreed with the views of the Division of Chinese Affairs and decided to endorse the promotion of Titoism in China.

Formulating a New Economic Strategy toward the Chinese Communists

According to the officers at the Division of Chinese Affairs, to "induce" the Chinese Communists to break up with Moscow, two instruments could be employed. One was to have limited, rather than comprehensive, trade with the CCP, and the other was to grant diplomatic recognition to the Chinese Communists. Domestic politics surely made diplomatic recognition "out of the question," they acknowledged. Thus at a State Department meeting in late February 1949, the participants unanimously agreed: "the trade weapon" was the only and the best weapon available to promote Titoism in China.[13]

This new economic strategy toward the CCP, in the words of R. N. Magill, one of its principal architects at the China Desk, "involves a recognition that any orientation of the Chinese Communists away from the USSR must be motivated by 'self-interests.' " To speed up the CCP's awareness of its "self-interest," he said, the Truman administration should try "to maximize the *internal* pressures," rather than the "*external* pressures" upon the Chinese Communists.[14] The "essential problem" in China was no longer to drive out the Chinese Communists by outside forces, since the Chinese Communists took over "in such massive strength that there is patently no hope of driving them out by anything short of equally massive intervention." Such military interventions could never help the cause of the indigenous anti-Communist movements, which must be "purely Chinese" to be successful. "Unfortunately," he said, there was on the horizon no anti-Communist Chinese leader who was suited "by temperament or experience" to lead "a successful revolution against the Chinese Communists." And "any group, which must depend for its continued existence upon foreign aid, is unlikely to prove the savior of China." More important, as he and his colleagues agreed, an "overt support of subversive activities" could only "compel the Chinese Communists to eliminate any divergence of opinion within the party," to "drive them completely into the arms of the Soviet Union."[15]

To maximize the internal pressures, Magill argued, the United States must not restore a comprehensive trading relationship with China. "After we helped them over the hump," he stressed, the "internal pressures" upon the CCP would be gone, and "we should have to depend largely upon their gratitude to prevent them from turning upon us." In the words of W. W. Stuart at the China Desk, "Gratitude is perhaps the most ephemeral of all motivations in international relations."[16]

Then, how to maximize the internal pressures on the CCP? According to the officers of the China Desk, the focus should be the CCP's industrialization plan. Chinese Communists were faced with "the basic and fundamental poverty of China and their own promises of greater abundance." Once the land-reform campaigns were complete, the CCP would give priority to industrialization, which would require huge amounts of imports financed by current exports. The CCP would have to acquire the needed exports from the Chinese peasants and working people. To make the exports competitive, the CCP would have to hold Chinese people's wages down to the lowest possible level. The CCP would soon be faced, then, with three policy options. One was "to continue the harsh policies toward the very classes upon which they have relied and upon whose support they have ridden to power." The second was to drop their modernization plan. The third was to invite foreign investments and seek foreign loans and credits. It would be impossible for the CCP to give up its "grand plan for the rapid industrialization of China," they said. Neither could the CCP afford to continue to put pressure on its basic constituencies in China. Thus, they believed that to complete China's industrialization, the CCP would have to turn to the West and America.[17]

To maximize the internal pressures upon the CCP, the officers of the China desk suggested that the United States should not take the initiative in establishing economic relationships with the CCP. On the contrary, it should evince "restrained interest" even if approached by the CCP for economic aid. Important U.S. business and missionary interests in China should be "temporarily" moved out of China. With their withdrawal, the U.S. could make it even more "transparently clear" to the CCP leaders that "China needs intercourse with other countries, especially the U.S., more than the U.S. needs commercial and other relations with China."[18]

To further maximize the internal pressures upon the CCP, they also suggested that this limited trade should never help the CCP to consolidate its position in China. Instead, such controlled trade should function as an "inducement." It should allow the CCP to get something out of it or to draw some benefit from it, but it should never allow the CCP to get enough from it to enhance its power. Such a controlled trade should push the CCP to want more and to eventually develop its sense of dependence on American trade. By pushing the CCP to make the overtures and to develop its sense of dependence on America in China's industrialization, "we shall improve our bargaining position and create for ourselves a powerful psychological advantage."[19]

Therefore, they recommended that this new economic strategy should be designed to take two forms, "moderate restriction" and "severe restriction," with respect to Western and American trade with China, to demonstrate a "strategic flexibility of shifting to a tougher direction," to show "the hidden power, hidden strength of the United States."[20] "Moderate restriction" was a combination of "restricted export of certain important materials" and "non-restrictive control over other exports." Here, the restriction on "certain important materials" was less moderate than that on Western and United States trade with Eastern Europe.[21] And "severe restriction" was a combination of the uniform denial of "critical goods" to China and the restricted shipment of "important goods" according to specific criteria. This "severe restriction," however, could not be considered an embargo, which, they argued, because it was a form of "outward pressures," would only drive the CCP "more closely" into the arms of Moscow.[22]

According to the Division of Chinese Affairs, then, the key concept of the new economic strategy toward the Chinese Communists was neither a total embargo nor a comprehensive trade relationship but limited trade used as an "incentive" to pressure the CCP to develop the sense of "dependence" on the American economy. To achieve this objective, this new economic strategy was designed to take two different forms. The specific situation would determine which form would be used. "We should have to keep our hand on the pulse of Communist thinking and give doses of helpful cooperation" (moderate restriction) or of "calculated obstruction" (severe restriction), depending on both "the patient's reaction" and America's "global strategic needs."[23]

A New Military Strategy toward Taiwan

To make this new economic strategy work in the long run, Acheson believed, the precondition was America's military withdrawal from Taiwan. He did not come to this conclusion until late 1949. In early 1949, he had explored the possibility of Taiwan's independence through an indigenous Taiwanese movement, which, he hoped, with America's "covert support," could overthrow the KMT and declare Taiwan's independence from the mainland. Beginning in mid-1949, however, he began to realize that the various Taiwanese independence movements were still too weak to grow into a strong movement to overthrow the KMT.

In late 1949, when the CIA warned that the Chinese Communists were planning to launch their military campaign against Taiwan in the summer of 1950, and when the Pentagon reported that America's military force was not yet ready to defend the island, the State Department faced a dilemma: if the CCP's Taiwan campaign were to take place the following summer, what would the United States' policy be toward Taiwan? Should the United States try to deter the CCP by threatening military intervention, as recommended by the Pentagon? Or should the United States seize this opportunity to send a message to the Chinese Communists that the United States would not intervene in their Taiwan campaign, thereby undermining the ongoing Sino-Soviet alliance treaty negotiation in Moscow, as recommended by the Division of Chinese Affairs?

Of the two positions, Acheson believed that the latter was far better than the former. By late 1949, he had increasingly been convinced that only after the United States' military withdrawal from Taiwan could they point to Manchuria and North China and claim the Soviet Union was "the only nation" that tried to take away Chinese territories, threaten China's sovereignty, and oppose "the great nationalistic awakening" in China and Asia.[24] Thus America's military withdrawal from Taiwan, he asserted, could "effectively and powerfully" isolate the Soviet Union as the "only nation" that was "seeking territorial aggrandizement in Asia."[25]

Truman agreed with Acheson's recommendation. On January 5,

1950, he issued an official statement on America's policy toward Taiwan. He declared that America's traditional China policy, or the Open Door policy, "called for international respect for the territorial integrity of China." Then, he emphasized that Taiwan's legal status was part of China:

In the Joint Declaration at Cairo on December 1, 1943, the President of the United States, the British Prime Minister and the President of China stated that it was their purpose that territories Japan had stolen from China, such as 'Formosa,' should be restored to the Republic of China. The United States was a signatory to the Potsdam Declaration of July 26, 1945, which declared that the terms of the Cairo Declaration should be carried out. The provisions of this Declaration were accepted by Japan at the time of its surrender. In keeping with these declarations, Formosa was surrendered to Generalissimo Chiang Kai-shek and for the past four years the United States and the other Allied Powers have accepted the exercise of Chinese authority over the Island.[26]

In particular, Truman proclaimed,

The United States has no predatory designs on Formosa or on any other Chinese territory. The United States has no desire to obtain special rights or privileges or to establish military bases on Formosa at this time. Nor does it have any intention of utilizing its armed forces to interfere in the present situation. The United States Government will not pursue a course which will lead to involvement in the civil conflict in China.[27]

This statement was indeed the clearest indication that should the CCP's Taiwan campaign take place, the United States would not intervene.

On January 12, 1950, during his address at the National Press Club, Acheson further explained Truman's position and articulated a new military strategy toward Taiwan and East Asia. Acheson implied even more clearly that in the CCP's upcoming Taiwan campaign, America would not commit its military forces to the defense of Taiwan. Would America's national security or its vital strategic interests in the Western Pacific be seriously jeopardized by its loss of Taiwan? No, it would not, argued Acheson. He then introduced his new military security concept of the "defensive perimeter," or the "enclave military strategy" in East Asia.[28]

This defensive perimeter in the Western Pacific would run along the Aleutians to Japan, to the Ryukyu Islands, and to the Philippines, but would not include continental Asia and Taiwan. Acheson's position on South Korea seemed to be ambivalent. While he did not formally include South Korea in his defensive perimeter, he treated Taiwan and South Korea differently. Unlike Taiwan, he said, South Korea was highly important to America's position in the Western Pacific, because of its proximity to Japan. Thus, the continuation of U.S. military and economic aid to South Korea was imperative. If the United States were to stop defending South Korea, he said, it would be "the most utter defeatism and utter madness in our interests in Asia."

Why could such a perimeter, which would exclude Taiwan and Indochina, strengthen rather than weaken the United States' vital security interests in the Western Pacific and East Asia? For Acheson, the key was to "look at the big picture" in Asia. What was that "big picture"? A new age of "Asian consciousness" was dawning, based on two powerful forces. One was "a revulsion against poverty." The other was "the revulsion against foreign domination." These two revulsions tended to "fuse" in the minds of many Chinese and Asians, who believed that "if we could get rid of foreign domination, if we could gain independence, then the relief from poverty and misery would follow in due course." Thus "national independence has become the symbol both of freedom from foreign domination and freedom from the tyranny of poverty and misery," Acheson proclaimed. "Resignation is no longer the typical emotion of Asia. It has given way to hope, . . . and in many cases, to a real sense of anger."

What would be America's best security interests in the new age of "Asian consciousness"? It was to make the Chinese and Asian peoples realize that the Soviet Union, not the United States, intended to sabotage this "great nationalistic awakening." The fact that the Soviet Union tried to take away four northern provinces of China was, he claimed, "the single most significant, most important fact, in the relation of any foreign power with Asia."

"What does that mean for us?" Acheson asked. "It means something very, very significant. It means that nothing that we do and nothing that we say must be allowed to obscure the reality of this fact" of Moscow's "territorial ambition" in north China. And "the only thing that can obscure it is the folly of ill-conceived adventures on our part," or America's military presence in Taiwan or the Taiwan Strait. The Americans "must not seize the unenviable position which the Russians have carved out for themselves." In summation,

> I urge all who are thinking about those foolish adventures to remember that we must not undertake to deflect from the Russians to ourselves the righteous anger, the wrath, and the hatred of the Chinese people, which must develop. It would be folly to deflect it to ourselves. We must take

the position we have always taken that anyone who violates the "territorial integrity" of China is the enemy of China and is also acting contrary to America's own interest. This is the first and the greatest rule in regard to the formulation of American policy toward China.[29]

Acheson firmly believed, as he told his colleagues in private, that only after deflecting "the anger, the wrath, and the hatred of the Chinese people" from America to the Soviet Union, could the United States ever have a chance of using the trade weapon to detach the CCP from the Soviet Union in the long run.[30]

Implementation of the New U.S. China Policy

In the course of its implementation, the United States' new China policy—the new economic strategy toward the Chinese Communists and the new military strategy toward Taiwan—appeared to be moving in different directions simultaneously. The question is, under immense domestic and bureaucratic pressures, did Acheson and the State Department change their minds about the merits of their new policy?

At the end of February 1949, Acheson's report—"U.S. Policy Regarding Trade with Chinese Communists"—was transmitted to the executive secretary of the NSC for discussion. On March 3, 1949, Truman approved Acheson's report, NSC 41, and directed that it be "implemented by all appropriate Executive Departments and Agencies of the United States Government under the coordination of the Secretary of State."[31]

Louis Johnson, the secretary of defense, never liked NSC 41, which called for the use of trade as a lever to split the Sino-Soviet alliance. In September 1949, when Truman said that NSC 41 was "out of date and should be revised," Johnson saw his chance to change Acheson's economic strategy. In a draft of "NSC 48/2—U.S. Policy toward Asia," the Defense Department members of the NSC suggested giving up the basic ideas of NSC 41 in favor of economic warfare against the PRC.

The State Department immediately sent a memo to the NSC, arguing that "the basic revision" of NSC 41 was "unnecessary."[32] On November 17, 1949, Acheson summarized the policy debates and reported to Truman that "broadly speaking, there are two objectives of policy: one might be to oppose the Communist regime, harass it, needle it, and if an opportunity appeared, to attempt to overthrow it. Another objective of policy would be to attempt to detach it from subservience to Moscow and over a period of time, encourage those vigorous influences, which might modify it."[33]

Acheson told Truman the second policy alternative did not mean "a policy of appeasement any more than it had in the case of Tito." For Acheson, the basic question was "whether we believe that we should and could overthrow the regime, or whether we believe that the second course," to use trade as a weapon to promote Titoism in China, was "the wiser." He told the president that the State Department's consultants on China were "unanimous in their judgment that the second course was the preferable one."[34]

At the fiftieth meeting of the NSC in December 1949, with Truman's endorsement, Acheson won his victory over the Pentagon. In the final draft of "NSC 48/2: U.S. Policy toward Asia," the Defense Department's insistence on an economic embargo against the PRC was dropped. Instead, NSC 48/2 cleared the path for the State Department to continue to implement NSC 41, the new economic strategy toward the Chinese Communists.[35]

From mid-1949, the China lobby on Capitol Hill attempted to change the State Department's approach to Taiwan. The most effective way to do so, this contingent believed, was to threaten a reduction of Acheson's favored European programs. Thus, in August 1949, when Congress was considering an arms funding bill for Western Europe, Senator William Knowland (R-CA) asked the State Department to include in the bill a grant for the KMT government on Taiwan. When the State Department rejected this request, Knowland threatened to cut arms funds for Europe. One week before the Atlantic Pact Council was to meet in Washington, the State Department had to give in. A sum of $75 million was added to European military aid program for use in the "general China area."[36]

Worried about the impact this token aid to Taiwan might have on the new China policy, Acheson suggested that Truman give a public statement on January 5, 1950. As discussed above, this statement reaffirmed Taiwan's legal status as part of China and implied that the United States would not commit military force to defending Taiwan.

The China lobby in Congress was infuriated by Truman's statement. To retaliate, they voted against another bill favored by Acheson: the Korean aid bill. The opposition to Korean aid might be "a signal light as to what might happen," Knowland warned, if the needs of Taiwan were "ignored." To save the Korean bill, Acheson had to make another concession, proposing an additional $106 million for the Chiang Kai-shek government in Taiwan.[37]

Acheson's speech on America's new policy toward Taiwan at the National Press Club on January 12, 1950, triggered an even greater rage among the Republican conservatives on the Hill. The demise of the Nationalist government in China had been regarded as a historic defeat for the Pacific-oriented policies of the Republican Party. Up to that time, the Republican conservatives had been split over the Truman administration's European policy. Over Acheson's new China policy, however, they closed ranks. The debates over "who lost China" created a new political momentum within the Republican Party and within American domestic politics. The Republican conservatives were determined to seize the China issue as the best means not only of saving the Chiang Kai-shek government in Taipei, but also for defeating the Democrats and returning the Republican Party to political power in Washington, power they had lost since the Great Depression and the New Deal era.[38]

One week after Acheson's speech at the National Press Club, Senator Joseph McCarthy (R-WI) claimed that Nationalist China had fallen because of Communist influence exerted in or on the State Department. He announced that he had a list of 205 card-carrying members of the Communist party who were employed by the State Department to shape America's China policy.[39] Acheson in particular was under ferocious attack for his new policy toward Beijing and Taipei. As one of his critics bitterly charged: "The despised Secretary of State would not save Chiang Kai-shek, but refuses to turn his back on Alger Hiss." Acheson complained in private that the accusations of the "fervent McCarthyites" were indeed "the attack of the primitives." With the beginning of the McCarthy accusations and persecutions in Washington, a new orthodoxy was emerging in America's China policy debates before the outbreak of the Korean War. This new orthodoxy was the belief that there was a vast, effective international communist conspiratorial network headed by Moscow, the purpose of which was to destroy the free government of the United States.[40]

In spite of the political pressure from the Pentagon and Congress, the State Department stood firm. From March 1949 to March 1950, it worked hard to implement the new economic strategy of moderate restriction. The officers at the Division of Chinese Affairs had fully anticipated that the Chinese Communists would continue to show their ideological hostility toward the West and to express their loyalty to the Soviet Union. As Magill wrote on May 2, 1949, "We must be prepared to weather through a good many surface buffets, in the interest of supporting the long-run possibility for emergence of a relatively independent Chinese Communist regime."[41]

Thus, when General Claire Chennault, the commander of the "Flying Tiger" in wartime China, urged Washington to send military assistance to the anti-Communist Muslims in northwest China in the aftermath of Mao's public speech on "leaning to one side," the Division of Chinese Affairs quickly rejected his request. They told the general, "The U.S. should refrain from any kind of step that might . . . provoke a return to a more extreme policy that would be . . . a natural reaction to any outward form of foreign pressure."[42]

In October 1949, the officers at the China Desk again acknowledged, "The CCP's propaganda has continued to be hostile toward Western governments, particularly the United States, and has recently placed increased emphasis on identity of interest between China and Soviet Russia." Further, "The most reliable evidence suggests that the dominant faction in the party hierarchy is strongly pro-Soviet." However, they again insisted that "strategic and practical considerations" did not warrant a change of this new economic strategy toward the Chinese Communists.[43]

In mid-February 1950, with the signing of the Sino-Soviet alliance treaty, amidst condemnations of the PRC in Congress and in the media, Acheson continued to emphasize the wisdom of the new economic strategy of promoting Titoism in China. In his public lectures, he repeatedly stressed that the new Sino-Soviet treaty only proved China could never depend on the Soviet Union to carry out its industrialization programs. Moscow extended to China "only a credit of $45 million per year." Now the Chinese could "compare this with a grant, not a loan, of $400 million" from America to the Nationalist government in the single year of 1948.[44]

Acheson's long-term objective of promoting Titoism in China was well understood by Walter Lippmann: "The Acheson policy will have to be understood in a longer perspective than tomorrow's headlines. We must not wait tensely for news that Mao has defied Stalin, and is hurrying back to Peking to denounce Russian imperialism and the Cominform next week, next month, or next year."[45] In pursuing the long-term goal of this new economic strategy, the "great wisdom" of Acheson and the State Department was, Lippmann wrote, their determination to be "patient." Indeed, "the mills of the gods grind slowly, especially in Asia."[46]

In April 1950, all of a sudden, Acheson sent a letter to Louis Johnson, informing him that the State Department had just decided to shift from "moderate restriction" to "severe restriction" with regard to Western and U.S. trade with the Chinese Communists.[47] How did this apparently sudden change of policy take place?

This drastic shift was based on the State Department's overall changed strategic assessment of the Soviet military capability and its concern for U.S. security interests. A most ominous prospect was raised by a CIA report in early 1950 that the USSR was to launch an atomic attack on Western Europe or the United States by 1954. This frightening prediction was based on the CIA's estimates of the Soviet military capability of producing atomic bombs. It forecast that the Soviets would stockpile 120–200 atomic bombs by mid-1954. "If, after Soviet attainment of such a large atomic stockpile, U.S. defensive capability were to remain so limited . . . the USSR could make a decisive attack on the United States."[48]

This gloomy prediction was not shared by the Office of Naval Intelligence (ONI). "The fatal error" in this prediction, the ONI argued, was "its failure to mention Soviet intentions as well as its military capabilities. . . . Soviet intentions stem not just from the number of atomic bombs they [hold]."[49] George Kennan, a leading Soviet specialist, concurred with this assessment. As he clarified in a memo to Acheson, the CIA estimate "completely failed to take into account the fact that Russia has only recently been through a tremendously destructive war, and that the memory of that destruction is much more vivid in Soviet minds than it is in ours."[50]

Paul Nitze, who had just replaced Kennan as the new director of the Policy Planning Staff at the State Department, supported the CIA's estimate. He stressed, "It is a military maxim that one should not underestimate the enemy." Moreover, he argued that the ideological system of the Soviet Union, combined with its military capability, would constitute a "permanent threat" to America's national security. He recommended that from now on, the United States should make military buildup its top priority. This later became the core argument of NSC 68.[51]

Acheson was alarmed by the estimates that by the mid-1950s, the military capability of the Soviet Union could be superior to that of the United States. He thus agreed that military buildup was now crucial to America's national security.[52] As Henry Kissinger—who admired Acheson—subsequently remarked, the State Department's global strategy in early 1950 was "based on a flawed premise" that America's military capability was inferior to that of the Soviets. In fact, "we were stronger than they were."[53]

Although Truman did not ratify NSC 68 until the onset of the Korean War, a new set of policy premises was accepted in the State Department. In particular, the State Department's changed perception of the Soviet military threat had a significant impact on its Vietnam policy before the Korean War.[54] Given these new estimates of the Soviet threat, Vietnam suddenly became a critically important area to the Western military buildup, because of its impact on the French army, the "cornerstone" of NATO. As Robert Schuman, the French foreign minister, told Acheson, without U.S. support in its war in Vietnam, France would have to cut its military commitment for the defense of Europe. As a result, in March 1950 the State Department decided to abandon its policy of neutrality in Vietnam, and suggested to the Defense Department that it work out a program of direct military assistance to France.[55]

The change of America's policy regarding Vietnam, in turn, engendered a debate in the State Department over the policy of "moderate restriction" toward Beijing. Now the officers at the Division of Chinese Affairs feared that, in view of "the superior Soviet military capability," there was no way to guarantee "exports of important goods to China would not be transshipped to the Soviet Union." Moreover, given the close ties between Mao and Ho, they further argued, it would be "dangerous" to export "any goods important to the Chinese economy which would contribute to the military potential of the Vietminh." Therefore, they recommended a shift from the policy of "moderate restriction" to that of "severe restriction." Shipments of critical goods to Communist China should be now "uniformly denied," in contrast to the former rule of "presumptive denial." In contrast to the former rule of "quantitative controls," shipments of important goods to Communist China should be "handled according to the criteria used in approving or denying shipments of such goods to Eastern Europe."[56]

Could this severe restriction drive China into the arms of the Soviet Union? For the officers of the China Desk, the answer was no. Only an economic embargo, not severe restriction, they argued, could compel the Chinese Communists into complete dependence on the Soviet Union. Furthermore, the economic strategy of "severe restriction," in their view, "might highlight the fruitlessness of the alliance between China and the Soviet Union."[57]

With their recommendation, Dean Rusk, assistant secretary for Far Eastern affairs, sent Acheson a memorandum on April 20, 1950, which informed the Secretary of State that a consensus had been reached within the State Department. The policy of "moderate restriction" should be shifted to "severe restriction," because "Southeast Asia is in grave danger of Communist domination."[58] One difficulty Acheson perceived in implementing this new China policy was that the Sino-Soviet split was still a "long-range prospect." "If in taking a chance on the long future of China we affect the security of the United States at once, that is a bad bargain."[59]

Thus, by the end of April 1950, to counter what was considered the new challenge in Vietnam and Southeast Asia, the State Department upgraded the trade-restriction level. Nonetheless, to avoid driving the CCP entirely into the arms of the Soviet Union, it stopped short of being an economic embargo against the PRC.

Coherence of the American China Policy before the Korean War

Did the State Department formulate a coherent economic strategy toward China before the Korean War? Yes, it did. This new China policy was neither a policy of accommodation with the Chinese Communists nor a policy of supporting the KMT on Taiwan. Rather, it was a combination of deterrence and inducement, the mixture of an implicit threat of punishment and hope for future conciliation. The precondition for its success, according to Dean Acheson, was America's military withdrawal from Taiwan.

The basic assumption underlying the new China policy was that Chinese Communists were currently subservient to Moscow but that their nationalist sentiments could lead them to detach from Moscow in the long run. The key concept of this new China policy was that through maximizing the internal pressures on the CCP, the CCP would be compelled to concede that in China's struggle to industrialize, it would have to depend on the United States.

In the course of its implementation, however, this new China policy took on the appearance of being self-contradictory, apparently moving on several tracks at once. While Acheson publicly announced a hands-off policy toward the Chinese civil war in January 1950, he was also forced by Congress to give more aid to the KMT on Taiwan. While

Truman and Acheson implied that the United States would not commit military forces to the defense of Taiwan, American military equipment continued to flow to the island.

However, this apparent inconsistency did not represent a self-contradictory China policy desired by the State Department. Rather it was created through policy compromises Acheson and the State Department had to make to mollify strong domestic political pressures. What it indicated was not a change in the State Department's policy but the partial failure of the State Department to implement this new policy before the onset of the Korean War.

In summary, during America's China policy debates in this critical period, there were three distinct China policy assumptions with regard to the CCP's foreign-policy intentions or the relationship between nationalism and communism/internationalism in China. One view was that the CCP movement was manufactured by the Soviet Union and the CCP was the puppet of Moscow. Another view was that the CCP movement was an integral part of the broader nationalist and social revolutions in China and most of the CCP leaders were Chinese nationalists first. The third view was that the CCP movement was an "aberration" of the nationalistic awakening in modern China but that the CCP leaders had "some nationalist sentiment"; thus, the CCP could be eventually induced to detach from the Soviet Union. Among these three policy assumptions, the third one prevailed and became the foundation of America's new China policy before the Korean War.

CHAPTER FIVE

Two Sides of One Coin

*The CCP's Policies toward the
Soviet Union and the United States*

On June 28, 1948, when the Cominform expelled the Communist Party of Yugoslavia (CPY), it issued a communiqué pinpointing three major "incorrect lines" in the CPY's domestic and foreign policies. First, it charged, Tito's communist party put too much faith in the peasantry, instead of the working class, as "the most stable foundation of the Yugoslav state." Second, Tito's party continued its "united front" with the country's Third Force, whereas all other Eastern European countries had established one-party communist governments by mid-1948. Finally, and most important, it claimed that Tito's foreign policy, "contaminated" by the influences of the peasants and the Third Force, demonstrated "anti-Soviet bourgeois nationalism." The communiqué ended with a call for the CPY "to break with nationalism, return to internationalism."[1]

The Chinese Communist leadership had every reason to be deeply concerned about the Cominform's public denunciation of Tito. Like the CPY, the CCP had depended on the peasantry and its united front with the Third Force to win its national victory. Moreover, the Chinese Communist leaders were aware of Stalin's anxiety about their "nationalist," rather than "internationalist," foreign policy. "On the eve of our national victory, we knew there were widespread rumors in the socialist bloc that the Chinese Communists would follow the road of Yugoslavia," Mao said, "and that Mao Zedong would become the second Tito. . . . So we knew Stalin did not trust us at that time."[2]

From late 1948 to June 1950, when the Korean War began, the

Chinese Communist leadership's foreign policy had to respond to two concerns. On the one hand, it must eliminate Moscow's suspicion regarding the CCP's foreign-policy orientation. With Washington on the side of the KMT, and facing the paramount task of nation-state building on the eve of its national victory, the CCP could not afford to be regarded as a second Tito by the Soviet bloc. On the other hand, in responding to Acheson's new China policy, the CCP was anxious to seize this opportunity to show a flexible stance toward the United States. It could not afford, before its upcoming Taiwan campaign, to be regarded by Washington as confrontational. This, as Mao argued, could drive America to support Chiang on Taiwan.

To some extent, the CCP employed ideological rhetoric to "walk the tightrope."[3] That is, in public, the CCP repeatedly pledged its ideological loyalty to the socialist bloc, to distinguish itself from the CPY. But in private, the CCP made flexible gestures to Washington, trying to weaken the Taipei-Washington coalition and attempting to pave the way for eventual normalization of Sino-American diplomatic relations.

Thus deciphering the actual meanings of Chinese communist leaders' foreign-policy statements at that time requires going beyond the CCP's ideological rhetoric. The CCP's rhetoric in some cases reflected genuine expressions of its ideological beliefs, but it also served as a strategic instrument to win Moscow's trust and a means of achieving its domestic and foreign-policy agendas. This left room for the CCP's foreign-policy intentions to be misjudged.

CCP Conceptions of Nationalism and Internationalism: Domestic and International Milieus, 1948–1950

In the aftermath of the Cominform's denunciation of Tito, CCP leadership began to articulate a new theoretical framework for the party's foreign policy. To distinguish between the essence and the rhetoric of this new foreign-policy framework, one needs to recreate the domestic and international milieus in which the CCP leaders shaped their concepts of the vital interests of the party and the nation, as they perceived them at that time.

A major development domestically was the CCP's continued insistence on the system of New Democracy and, consequently, its continued united front with the Third Force after its nationwide victory. In March 1949, the CCP headquarters moved from Xibanpo village to Peiping (Beijing), the future capital. Mao evoked the name of Li

Zicheng, the peasant rebellion leader in the late Ming dynasty who triumphantly led his poor peasant army into the city but failed soon afterwards. Mao told his comrades, "As Li Zicheng did two hundred years ago, the new peasant rebellion army is marching into Peiping. I feel as if we are going to take a Grand National Exam there. Do you think we can pass the Exam?" Zhou smiled, and turned to Mao: "Yes, we surely can." However, the CCP did face unprecedented challenges. The most daunting of all was establishing the political legitimacy of the CCP's "new peasant army" in urban centers. To do this, the most critical test was the CCP's relationship with the Third Force, or the democratic parties, as they were called in China.[4]

In the heat of the civil war (1947–1949), some Chinese Third Force members had increasingly worried that such a large-scale military struggle might produce a one-party dictatorship in the end, no matter which party won the civil war. This result for them meant the probable demise of the nation. As an editorial in Shanghai's *Da Gong Bao* (Da Gong Daily) declared in February 1948, when a party became a highly disciplined political organization in the war, it would have to "sacrifice individual liberty." Such a party, which demanded "collective action," could not fit into "our taste as liberals." More important, "only when a nation has an opposition party in the parliament which can smite the table, scathingly denounce the government, and even hold demonstrations against it, can this nation be vigorous, full of vitality."[5]

In early 1949, with the CCP's sweeping military victory, some Third Force members became even more fearful that the CCP would be tempted to build a "proletarian dictatorship," as the Russian Bolsheviks had done after the October Revolution. In his "Respectful Address to the Chinese Communist Party," published in the *Da Gong Bao,* Liang Shumin, a leading member of the Democratic League, urged the CCP to build a coalition government after the civil war was over, as it had pledged to do at the start of the war. He emphasized that throughout Chinese history, it was never the military power, but the Chinese people's hearts and minds, that determined the success or failure of a political force in China. Why was the "moral prestige" of the CCP able to surpass that of the KMT in the war of resistance during World War II? It was because, he said, the CCP had given up its armed struggle with the KMT and "held high the banner of a united front against the Japanese invasion." At the end of World War II, however, "the KMT refused to listen to the democratic parties and the Chinese people," and "embarked on the road of civil war" with the CCP. That was why, he lamented, the KMT lost "the hearts and blessings of the Chinese people." Now that the civil war was almost over, "the overwhelming desires" of the Chinese people were "peace and economic reconstruction." And peace and economic reconstruction required that the CCP build a "coalition government," not a one-party Communist government in China, as the Bolsheviks had done after the Russian revolution.[6]

On the other hand, during the civil war, the CCP rank and file had increasingly resented the CCP's alliance with the Third Force, particularly "the three-three ratio governmental system," which mixed up the non-CCP and the CCP members in equal measure in all local governments in the communist areas.[7] On the battlefields of the civil war, a new slogan became popular among the rank and file: "The poor peasants have fought and won the military battles, and the poor peasants should be the sole masters of China."[8] A CCP Central Committee confidential circular of May 31, 1948, warned that many local party activists had "abused the non-party members in this system," and tried to change "the three-three ratio system" or the political system of the "united front." The CCP leadership was particularly concerned that "for such a vitally important political matter, no party organizations ever reported to the Central Committee before they made such decisions, or reported to the Central Committee afterwards."[9]

Obviously, the CCP Central Committee's position did not appeal to the rank and file. In early 1949, when the CCP leaders invited democratic parties' leaders to come to Beijing to discuss drafting a new constitution, the rank and file felt confused and angry. They complained, "Those folks in big cities never risked their lives in the revolution; they never shed their blood in the battlefields; they never fought side by side with us against the enemy. Why do they eat rice and pork, living comfortably in the best hotels, while we eat vegetables and live in small, shabby rooms?"[10]

Confronted with opposing political pressures, the CCP leaders decided to persuade the rank and file, so as to win the support of the Chinese democratic parties. In Mao's words, the CCP not only should let the democratic party leaders stay in the best hotels, the CCP should "beat drums and gongs to greet them, welcome them to join the new government." Why did the state of Shu in the *Romance of Three Kingdoms* collapse? It was because, Mao emphasized, one of its leaders, Guan Yunchang, had refused to unite with its allies and insisted on a closed-door policy. The CCP must not abandon its "magic weapon" of the "united front" with the democratic parties, which had helped the CCP to win its national victory.[11]

In this regard, the role of the Political Consultative Conference (PCC) of 1946 was, as Mao and Zhou argued, crucial for the political legitimacy of the CCP in urban China. The PCC had been recognized domestically and internationally as a "legitimate" political institution, "similar to the role of a parliament or a national assembly," they said. As discussed in Chapter 3, at the PCC, the Chinese Communists and the Third Force had proposed a coalition government in postwar China that would include the KMT, the CCP, and the Third Force. Since the PCC had done "many great things for China," it enjoyed "very high prestige among the urban Chinese,"[12] Mao emphasized.

In February 1949, the CCP Central Committee passed a resolution that it would support the reconvening of the PCC so it could continue its unfinished work from 1946. The PCC was to design the "Common Program," or the temporary constitution of the nation, and to elect the members of the first government of the PRC, which occurred on October 19, 1949.[13] One of the two vice presidents was Madam Sun Yatsen of the Third Force. Among the four deputy prime ministers, two were from the Third Force. Among twenty-one State Council members, eleven were from the Third Force. The "democratic personages," as they were called by the CCP, assumed the positions of ministers of culture, education, agriculture, transportation, publication, judiciary, post and communication, and the People's Legal Supervision Committee, among others. The Common Program called for women's liberation and the eradication of all Chinese legal codes that had perpetuated gender inequality. The "Marriage Law" of 1950 further legalized free marriage and abolished polygamy.[14]

"In name," Mao claimed, the new government was called the "people's democratic dictatorship"; yet "in nature, it is a coalition government." According to Mao, the new political system was based on the theory of New Democracy, or a coalition between the working class, the poor peasants, the intellectuals, and the private entrepreneurs or "national industrialists," led by the CCP. It was not "an old democratic political system" like that of the West, Mao said. He quoted Sun Yat-sen's critiques of Western democracy as largely "a system for the rich, not a system for the poor," to make his point. On the other hand, Mao also stressed that this "new democratic polity" in China was not a one-party communist government like that in the Soviet Union: "Russian history has shaped the Soviet system. . . . In the same way, Chinese history will shape the Chinese system. The system of New Democracy . . . will be entirely appropriate to the Chinese situation, and will be very different from the system of the Soviet Union."[15] Clearly, from Mao's 1945 work *On Coalition Government* to his 1949 work *On the People's Democratic Dictatorship*, the CCP's basic theme stayed the same: building a system of New Democracy in China while continuing the coalition between the CCP and the Third Force.

If the CCP's pledge of a continued united front with the Third Force won it political legitimacy in urban China, it immediately engendered anxieties in the Soviet bloc during the heightening of the Cold War.

When Yugoslavia was expelled, the Cominform accused Tito of refuting Stalin's key assumption in the Cold War: namely, that the world was divided into "two camps," with any Third Force only "a cover for capitalism." In the period between late 1947 and 1950, Eastern European countries had all abandoned coalition governments and established one-party communist governments.[16] Put differently, Stalin's major concern with the CCP's political blueprint was not about the Chinese coalition government per se, but about its foreign-policy implications in the bipolar world. In fact, to relieve Moscow's distrust during China's civil war, the CCP sent a letter to Stalin in late 1947 that said the CCP would follow the examples of Eastern European countries to establish a one-party communist government *after* it won the civil war. Stalin's reply showed that he understood the political necessity of the united front for the CCP's survival. He urged the CCP to continue this policy in the civil war.[17] By mid-1948, however, the CCP was no longer a party struggling for its survival, it was a party on the eve of its national victory. More important, with Tito's split from the Soviet bloc, and the formation of NATO in Western Europe, Stalin worried about how to prevent a triumphant Mao from becoming a second Tito on the Eastern front.

Stalin's apprehension was illustrated in the Cominform's "general guideline" to all communist parties, which stressed that the "Tito phenomenon" was not an isolated one. "The social and economic conditions in a peasant society," which nurtured "bourgeois nationalism" in Yugoslavia, also existed in other countries.[18] Meanwhile, Soviet specialists "confidentially" assessed Mao's theory of New Democracy and regarded it as "a deviation" from the key concept of Marxism-Leninism, or "the political hegemony of the proletariat," suggesting that Mao's "unorthodox" interpretations of Marxism might lead to an anti-Soviet foreign policy in China.[19]

With the Washington-Taipei alliance intact, the CCP needed the support of the Soviet bloc for the daunting task of nation-state building. If, three days after the PRC was established, no nation in the world granted diplomatic recognition, Mao said, "we would be in serious trouble." Moreover, Soviet economic aid was considered "crucial" for China's industrialization drive in urban centers, since the CCP did not believe that America would provide any. Third, to prepare for the upcoming Taiwan military campaign, the CCP needed Soviet help to build a navy and an air force. Finally, and most important of all, the CCP wanted to "replace" the existing Sino-Soviet Friendship and Alliance Treaty of 1945 with a new or "equal" one. The existing Sino-Soviet treaty, signed by Chiang, was widely regarded as an "unequal treaty" in urban China, since it had "compromised China's sovereignty in the Northeast" by preserving a Soviet naval base there.[20] "The Chinese people are now asking whether the Soviet Union will sign a new alliance treaty with the new China," Mao told Soviet leaders. Such a new treaty, which meant the Soviets' immediate withdrawal from Lushun naval base and the Dalian port, "could make the Chinese workers, peasants, intellectuals, and the left wing of the national bourgeoisie feel greatly inspired," Mao stressed. With this new treaty, "Internationally we can acquire much greater political power to end all unequal treaties between China and the imperialist powers."[21]

Clearly, to achieve all these important objectives, the CCP needed to mitigate Moscow's distrust. And the CCP had only two options available: one was to give up its alliance with the Third Force, thereby establishing a one-party communist government in China, as all Eastern European countries had done. The other was to continue its alliance with the Third Force, as Tito's Yugoslavia had, but declare the CCP's ideological loyalty to the Soviet Union in the Cold War, as Tito had not. The first option would ruin the CCP's political legitimacy in urban China, so the CCP leaders chose the second option.

On November 1, 1948, five months after the Cominform's denunciation of Tito, an article entitled "On Internationalism and Nationalism," written by Liu Shaoqi—the CCP's theoretician and second only to Mao in the CCP leadership—appeared in Yanan.[22] Liu claimed that on the ideological front of the Cold War, the CCP would stand by the side of "proletarian internationalism" and staunchly oppose "bourgeois nationalism." The CCP would become "the traitor of the proletariat," he said, should it ever "employ bourgeois nationalism to oppose the Socialist Soviet Union."

After the pledge of the CCP's ideological loyalty to the Soviet Union in the Cold War, Liu began to defend the CCP's political blueprint of New Democracy, or coalition government. He argued that China's national liberation movement took the "unique" form of a "united front," which included "workers, peasants, intellectuals, the petty-bourgeoisie, and the national bourgeoisie," led by the CCP. Was it possible to continue this front between the CCP and the democratic parties, or "the bourgeois nationalists," when "the worldwide struggles between the two camps are intensified?" It was precisely the question that was at the center of the theoretical dispute between Tito and Stalin. Yes, it was possible, emphasized Liu. While Sun Yat-sen's nationalism was "a form of bourgeois nationalism," its essence was "very progressive." He stressed that in the early 1920s, soon after Lenin announced his intention to abolish Russia's unequal treaties with China, Sun called for a "united front" between the KMT and the CCP, between the KMT and the Chinese workers and poor peasants, and between China and Lenin's Soviet Union. Sun was "a great example of the progressive character of revolutionary bourgeois nationalism in colonial and semi-colonial countries." Since a majority of the Chinese democratic parties supported Sun's three people's principles, Liu, by championing Sun Yat-sen, defended the "progressive character" of the Chinese democratic parties. The point was, in other words, that the continued union between the CCP and the Third Force would not push the CCP to adopt an anti-Soviet foreign policy during the Cold War.

More important, Liu argued, the "best embodiment" of "proletarian internationalism" in the Chinese revolution was "genuine patriotism," since China's national and social revolutions were aimed at the overthrow of colonial and imperialist rules in China. Thus to defend the Chinese revolution was to promote internationalism, or the worldwide struggle to end colonialism and imperialism. "Such patriotism," he said, had nothing to do with "selfish, anti-foreign biases and prejudices, or narrow-minded exclusivism, parochialism, and provincialism." In concluding, he quoted Mao as saying during World War II: "Our slogan is: 'Fight against aggression and defend our motherland'.... Patriotism is the application of internationalism."[23]

A few months later, Mao further emphasized that the key to an understanding of "proletarian internationalism" was "China's struggle for national independence and national equality." Obviously, Mao was eager to present the CCP's revolution not only as the "true defender" of Sun's revolution of 1911, but also Sun's interpretation of "internationalism": "From our twenty-eight years' experience we have drawn a conclusion similar to the one Sun Yat-sen drew in his testament from his 'experience of forty years'; that is, 'we are deeply convinced that to win victory,' as Sun Yat-sen said, 'we must arouse the masses of the people and unite in a common struggle with those nations of the world which treat us as equals.' "[24]

In sum, after the Cominform's denunciation of Tito, the CCP needed to articulate a new theoretical framework for its foreign policy. Within this new framework, the CCP pledged both its continued association with the urban middle class and its ideological loyalty to the Soviet Union, to maximize the CCP's political legitimacy in urban China and the Soviet bloc simultaneously. Moreover, with the CCP's distinctive interpretations of the relationship between nationalism and internationalism, making patriotism the core of internationalism, this new framework also provided conceptual space for a flexible policy toward the United States, so long as such an America policy could serve the ultimate goals of "promoting China's national independence and equality," as well as the CCP's political power in China. It was within this new conceptual framework that the CCP leaders formulated their foreign policies toward the Soviet Union and the United States from late 1948 to 1950.

The CCP's Pre–Korean War Policy toward the Soviet Union

During the Chinese civil war (1947–1949), although the CCP had frequently confirmed its ideological connection with Moscow, it had never publicly announced a pro-Soviet foreign policy. However, on June 30, 1949, when the CCP was on the eve of its national victory, Mao took the initiative to declare, loud and clear, a foreign policy of "leaning to one side." What was the motivation behind Mao's public announcement, or the relationship between the CCP's new foreign-policy framework and Mao's alignment with the Soviet bloc at that historical moment?

The CCP's political and strategic need for Moscow's full support was drastically increased in June 1949, when Taiwan installed a naval blockade of east China. Taiwan's blockade, along with its air strikes, caused severe damage to power and water plants in the coastal cities. As an American diplomat observed: "The Communists seemed unable to cope with Nationalist naval and air power, having little or none of their own." Mao had to cable Stalin to obtain Soviet air protection of Shanghai, the only financial center of China at the time. Taiwan's blockade and air strikes, apparently backed by U.S. naval and air force, inflamed anti-American sentiments in urban China. As the American Chamber of Commerce in Shanghai complained bitterly to the State Department, one result of Taiwan's "blockade of Chinese ports and aerial bombardment of Chinese cities," which was "made possible by American warships, planes, fuel, bombs, ammunition," was that American residents in China had to be "subjected to further hazards by mobs" in almost all Chinese cities.[25]

From the CCP's perspective, Taiwan's blockade demonstrated clearly the air and naval power superiority of the Washington-Taipei alliance. Meanwhile, Stalin maintained serious doubts about the CCP's foreign-policy orientation, regardless of Liu Shaoqi's article. As Ivan Kovalev, Stalin's envoy to Mao Zedong, wrote, "When I returned to Moscow in December 1948," two months after the publication of Liu's article, "I noticed that Stalin was still keenly interested in whose side the Chinese Communists took on the acute Yugoslav problem."[26]

In June 1949, in the midst of Taiwan's naval blockade, the CCP leadership made a critical decision: to declare publicly the CCP's foreign policy of "leaning to one side." The purpose of this public announcement was, as Deng Xiaoping told his comrades, "to add the Soviet power to our own," and "to force imperialism to give in." In his letter to the CCP Eastern Bureau in July 1949, two weeks after Mao's June 30 announcement, Deng quoted Mao as saying that the CCP's "leaning" at this moment was still "on our initiative," and that it was much better than being "forced to lean to one side in the future." Did this foreign-policy preference mean that the CCP was to give up its domestic policy of coalition government? Deng denied that would be the case. In the CCP's domestic policy, he wrote, "we emphasize self-reliance," which meant "the long-term construction of the New Democratic society," or the continued coalition of the CCP and the Third Force.[27]

According to Wu Xiuquan, director of the Soviet Affairs Bureau of the Foreign Ministry, it was exactly because of the CCP's desire to keep the united front that it felt compelled to declare ideological loyalty to the Soviet Union, to win the full support of the Soviet bloc. "When Chinese democratic parties joined the government, the Soviets wondered whether we would pursue a foreign policy oriented toward Great Britain and the United States." Mao's public announcement was "intended to relieve Stalin's anxiety, to win Stalin's full support for China's economic recovery and the final military battles against Chiang Kai-shek on Taiwan."[28]

Mao's announcement of the CCP's foreign policy of "leaning to one side" was carefully timed to occur just days before Liu Shaoqi left for Moscow to negotiate with Stalin on Soviet comprehensive support for China's industrial recovery and the CCP's upcoming Taiwan campaign, scheduled to take place the following summer. Also coinciding with a sweeping, popular anti-American ideological campaign in the CCP's newspapers,[29] Liu's visit to Moscow (July 8–August 14, 1949) was a "big success." Stalin apologized to Liu Shaoqi and the CCP delegation about the "serious mistakes" he had made at the most difficult time of the CCP movement and praised the "great significance" of the Chinese revolution. He spoke eloquently about a "division of labor" in the world revolutionary movement: while the Soviet Union would pay more attention to Europe, the CCP "should assume more responsibility in the Asian peoples' anti-colonial, anti-imperialist struggles." Significantly, he sent a clear message that Moscow would treat Beijing as an "equal partner." Liu pledged that "if the Chinese Communists and the Soviet Communists have controversies over some issues, after we explain our points of view, we will obey the Soviet Union's decisions," Stalin quickly differed. "We were surprised by the talk about 'obeying' the USSR's decisions. To ask one nation's party to obey the other nation's party is wrong, which should never be allowed to happen. Each party should only be responsible for its own people."

Finally, and most important of all, Stalin satisfied most of the CCP's requests in the negotiations. Regarding diplomatic recognition, Liu asked: "If all imperialist countries ignore us, can the Soviet Union and all Eastern European countries recognize the new Chinese government? And sooner rather than later?" Stalin replied, "As soon as the Chinese government is established, the Soviet bloc will recognize it."[30] Regarding Soviet economic aid, Stalin promised to offer China a loan of $300 million and send over 200 Soviet specialists to help China's industrialization. To promote Sino-Soviet trade, he also proposed that the Soviet Union help build a railroad to link Mongolia's Ulan Bator and China's Zhangjiakou, a city west of Beijing. Concerning the nature of the Chinese "coalition government," Stalin told Liu that the CCP's policy was a "correct" one, since the Chinese national bourgeoisie's attitudes toward colonialism and imperialism were "entirely different" from those of the Eastern European bourgeoisie. Thus the new political system in China should be "very different" from that in East Europe.[31]

With respect to the CCP's upcoming Taiwan campaign, however, Stalin declined Liu's request for Soviet participation, because the Soviet Union had suffered "tremendous losses" during World War II. "Soviet military support to an attack on Taiwan would mean a clash with the U.S. Air Force and Navy, which would provide a pretext for America to unleash a new world war." After Liu withdrew this request, Stalin pledged Soviet support for building a new Chinese naval and air force, which would be for the CCP's "coastal defense," if not for its upcoming Taiwan campaign.[32]

Stalin also agreed to negotiate the replacement of the existing Sino-Soviet treaty signed by the KMT in 1945 with a new, "equal" one. He candidly acknowledged, "The Sino-Soviet Friendship and Alliance Treaty of 1945 was not an equal treaty." "There were many American troops in Japan; and Chiang Kai-shek was allied with America," he said. "Soviet military presence in Lushun (Port Arthur) was to resist American-KMT joint military forces, to protect the Soviet Union, and to protect the interests of Chinese revolution" and "when we signed that treaty with the KMT, we had reached an internal decision," he told Liu. That is, after the signing of the Japanese Peace Treaty and the withdrawal of American military force from Japan, "the Soviet Union would consider its military withdrawal from Lushun of China" but "if the Chinese Communists want the Soviet military force to withdraw immediately from Lushun naval base to win more political capital in China, we may also consider doing so." Stalin expressed a preference for negotiating a new alliance treaty with Mao as soon as the new Chinese government was established.[33]

And so Mao's announcement on June 30, 1949, apparently relieved Moscow's suspicions. Even the CCP's domestic blueprint for a continued united front with the Third Force seemed no longer a problem for Moscow. The CCP seemed to have won Moscow's wholehearted support for the paramount task of industrialization drive and nation-state building in China.

On December 16, 1949, when Mao Zedong arrived in Moscow, he knew what his mission was: to negotiate a new treaty to replace the existing Sino-Soviet Friendship and Alliance Treaty between the KMT and Moscow, and to get back from the Soviet Union the Lushun naval base in northeast China.

On the eve of Mao's visit, however, Stalin had changed his mind about negotiating a new alliance treaty with the CCP. Mao wanted an immediate withdrawal of the Soviet force from Lushun, but Stalin preferred a transitional period. From Moscow's perspective, after its immense sacrifices in World War II, why should it give up its major strategic gains at Yalta, particularly before the signing of the Japanese Peace Treaty? Since it had agreed to withdraw from Lushun naval base *after* its peace treaty with Japan, why should it withdraw now?

At this juncture, Ivan Kovalev's memo to Stalin on December 24, one week after Mao's arrival, drastically deepened Stalin's distrust of Mao.[34] Kovalev complained that Mao wanted to gain diplomatic recognition from the United States and Great Britain and would try to use a new Sino-Soviet alliance treaty to achieve that goal. Kovalev told Stalin: "Mao urged the Soviet Union to abandon all its interests in China," and he quoted Mao as saying, "Relying on agreements with the Soviet Union, we would be able to revise and annul the unequal treaties concluded by the Chiang Kai-shek government with imperialist countries." The CCP's intentions in the Sino-Soviet alliance were, he claimed, "the direct result of pressures exerted on the Central Committee by the bourgeois democrats and other capitalist elements inside the country and the government," which had been "aspiring for the most rapid recognition of the new China by the United States and Great Britain."[35]

Kovalev's reports had "a chilling effect on Stalin," as Mao later recalled. After the first meeting, Stalin tried to avoid meeting with Mao. "Whenever I called Stalin at home, I was told he was not in. . . . I was very angry," Mao wrote. "I decided to stay home, doing nothing. . . . Kovalev suggested that I tour the Soviet Union. I declined. I replied: 'I would rather sleep all day long in this cottage.' " By the end of December 1949, "I felt more and more strongly that Stalin did not want to negotiate a new treaty with us."[36] Kovalev's account affirmed Mao's. Soon after Mao's arrival in Moscow, Mao "remained practically in isolation," wrote Kovalev. "Mao retaliated by declining to receive Roshchin, our ambassador to China." Kovalev told Stalin in his regular report that Mao was "upset and anxious." Stalin replied, "We have here many foreign visitors. Comrade Mao should not be singled out among them."[37]

On January 2, 1950, to Mao's pleasant surprise, Stalin announced that he was willing to negotiate a new treaty with the People's Republic. Stalin's change of heart was probably brought about, Mao speculated, by "the Indians and the British, who had just extended diplomatic recognition" to the PRC.[38]

On February 14, 1950, the Sino-Soviet Treaty of Friendship, Alliance, and Mutual Assistance was signed in Moscow. To distinguish between the new treaty and the old one, Zhou suggested that the words "mutual assistance" be added to the name of the original. This new treaty was a partial victory for Mao. The Soviet Union pledged to withdraw its military forces from Lushun naval base in 1952, rather than in 1975, as in the KMT's treaty. Put differently, the Soviet troops would withdraw *before* the signing of a Soviet-Japanese peace treaty. Apparently Stalin had abandoned the idea of acquiring an additional naval base in the Far East, which had been "his goal from the moment of the meeting at Yalta." But there were the "Additional Agreements" to the treaty, with secret protocols unknown to the public at the time, which granted special privileges to the Soviet Union in the northeast (Manchuria) and the northwest (Xinjiang). In these two regions, "only the Chinese and the Soviets could have residential rights."[39]

As Hu Qiaomu recalled, after Mao returned from Moscow, "the Central Committee asked him to give a talk about this trip, but he didn't want to say anything about it." So Zhou gave the report. "Chairman Mao was clearly upset by his first visit to the Soviet Union."[40] In Mao's mind, what Stalin had attempted to do was, in fact, to ask for "spheres of influence" in Manchuria and Xinjiang. With Stalin's insistence, Mao said, no third country's citizens could stay in these two areas. "It was very difficult for us to understand why Stalin imposed this on us, which could only provide the capitalist countries a tool to drive a wedge between the Sino-Soviet alliance," Mao told Soviet ambassador Pavel Yudin in 1956.[41] Mao also told Anastas Mikoyan—one of the top Soviet leaders—that the secret agreements on Xinjiang and Manchuria were "two bitter pills that Stalin forced us to swallow." In 1957, in a conversation with Andrei Gromyko, the Soviet foreign minister, Mao said, "Only imperialists would think of imposing such a deal on China."[42] In March 1958, at a CCP Central Committee meeting, Mao again talked about "two colonies" in China, where the people of third countries were "not permitted to settle down."[43]

From Mao's public announcement of "leaning to one side" in the summer of 1949 to the signing of the new Sino-Soviet alliance treaty in February 1950, what was the CCP's objective in its search for a new Sino-Soviet alliance? As Deng Xiaoping put it at that time, it was "to add the Soviet power to our own and to force imperialism to give in."

How did the Soviet leaders perceive or interpret the CCP's intention at that time? As Kovalev wrote, Mao made the CCP's intention crystal clear when he explained the "vital importance" of signing a new alliance treaty to replace the existing "unequal" one. He quoted Mao as saying that the CCP hoped to employ Soviet power to establish eventually "an equal relationship between China and the West." According to Kovalev, Stalin and other Soviet leaders were "fully aware" of the CCP's intention. Kovalev particularly emphasized that from Stalin's perspective, the CCP's objective in the Sino-Soviet alliance could be "potentially dangerous," since such a motivation might, eventually, "give Mao the grounds to reconsider all the secret agreements concluded with the Soviet Union," and "some of them were indeed humiliating for China."[44]

The CCP's Pre–Korean War Policy toward the United States

With Soviet power as the deterrent, the CCP began to send private messages of moderation to Washington. How flexible the CCP's messages to Washington should become, in Mao's view, would largely depend on America's intentions toward the CCP, as the CCP understood or interpreted them.

If the united front between the CCP and the Third Force was a thorny issue in Sino-Soviet relations, so it was also in Sino-American interactions. In late December 1948, Mao received information that, in his mind, indicated Washington might use the Chinese Third Force or democratic parties as a "Trojan horse" in the new coalition government, to defeat the CCP from within. According to Mao, the danger of America's direct military intervention in the Chinese civil war was diminishing rapidly, so long as the CCP could "continue to demonstrate its formidable power and strength in the battlefield."[45] However, based on the new information, Mao wondered if America would use trade as a lever "to split the united front."[46] Mao thus recommended that the CCP should not attempt to win America's diplomatic recognition until "the foundation of imperialism in China" was wiped clean. In his words, "We shall clean up our house first, before we invite our guests in."[47] What Mao meant was that only after the elimination of "imperialist infrastructures" in China would the CCP no longer need to worry about foreign powers' "plot" of using their "overwhelming prerogatives" to "beat the CCP from within."[48]

However, by the end of March 1949, when the PLA was poised to cross the Yangtze River, Mao began to change his mind, because of a letter he received from John Leighton Stuart.[49] The ambassador emphasized that America and the CCP "could become friends, and could cooperate with the Soviet Union to prevent the Third World War." He asked whether the CCP would regard America as its enemy, thus "increasing the danger of a Third World War." He also inquired whether the CCP would "abandon the non-Communist democratic parties and the idea of a coalition government," thus "embarking on the road of communizing China and Asia." If the CCP would refrain from doing these two things, he assured Mao that the American government would establish a "friendly relationship" with the CCP and would "help to build a new China."[50] On April 9, 1949, Mao asked Kovalev to inform Stalin that the CCP attempted to make "limited contacts" with Western countries, including the United States. Careful not to generate more suspicions in Moscow, Mao told Stalin that the CCP did not intend, at this point, to "legalize" this relationship.[51]

On April 28, 1949, five days after the PLA crossed the Yangtze River and occupied Nanjing—the capital of the KMT government—without direct military intervention from the United States, Mao began to emphasize the possibility that the United States and Great Britain might be willing to establish diplomatic relations with the CCP. In a letter to CCP leaders, Mao wrote,

> We must teach our troops to protect American and British citizens (and all foreign citizens), as well as foreign ambassadors, ministers, consuls and all diplomats in China, particularly American and British diplomats. Right now the American side has been trying to send us messages, which indicate its desire to establish a diplomatic relationship with us. Great Britain has also been trying to do business with us. If the United States and Great Britain could cut off their relationships with the KMT government on Taiwan, we would consider establishing diplomatic relations with them.[52]

On May 6 and May 7, 1949, when John Leighton Stuart told Huang Hua, his former student at Yenching University and the CCP's director of the Bureau of Foreign Affairs in Nanjing, that he would like to hold regular meetings with Huang, the CCP headquarters immediately agreed. Mao instructed that at the meetings his goal should be "to detect the ambassador's real *intention*," or the "real intention" of America's China policy.[53] Mao also emphasized that he should not ask for any American aid, but should urge America to cut off its relations with the KMT, and "never to intervene in Chinese domestic affairs." As for the ambassador's indication that he was "willing to re-negotiate the Commercial Treaty," Huang "should not decline such an offer."[54] The other motivation behind the Huang-Stuart meetings was, according to Huang, the CCP's strong desire to weaken the Washington-Taipei alliance. "If there could be a working relationship between the CCP and Washington, the public might be given "an impression the United States would soon abandon the KMT government," which could help crush "the morale of the resistance forces in South China." More important, in preparing for the upcoming Taiwan campaign, the CCP needed "to forestall a major American intervention that might rescue the KMT at the eleventh hour."[55]

One month later, in late May and early June 1949, when Taiwan began the naval blockade of East China, the CCP's suspicions about America's China policy quickly returned. However, given the American ambassador's conciliatory message prior to the naval blockade, the CCP did not want to adopt a confrontational policy toward the United States. While Mao was determined to employ Soviet power to reach "power equilibrium" with the Taipei-Washington alliance, he was also resolved not to do anything that would compel Washington to rescue Chiang Kai-shek on Taiwan.

The CCP's changing assessments of America's China policy intentions, mixed with fears, hopes, deep distrusts, and immense uncertainties, help to account for its seemingly inconsistent policies toward the United States before the Korean War.

According to Kovalev, while Stalin encouraged the CCP to develop economic relations with the Western countries, he was not "positive" about the development of diplomatic relations between the CCP and the West. "Stalin's attitude, to put it mildly, was not exactly positive toward the establishment of diplomatic relations between China and the imperialist powers," he wrote. "I do not mind admitting that any steps by the CCP in this direction brought about an overreaction." And, "This was only natural because the Cold War was at its peak."[56]

It was thus not surprising that Kovalev frequently complained of "a general impression that the Chinese were too soft toward the Americans." As he told Stalin, such an impression originated from the Ward spy case—which unfolded from November 1948 to mid-1949—when Mao Zedong did not agree to place Angus I. Ward, American Consul General in Shenyang (Mukden), under house arrest, as Kovalev had recommended.[57] This case illustrated the CCP's apparently self-contradictory stance toward Washington and disagreements between the CCP's headquarters and its Northeastern Regional Bureau, and between Mao and Stalin.

On November 9, 1948, the PLA entered Shenyang (Mukden), the capital of Liaoning province in Northeast China. The CCP had just won a decisive victory in the Liao–Shen (Liaoning-Shenyang) military campaign in Manchuria, and had just begun its major military campaign in the Ping (Beiping)–Jin (Tianjin) region. In a telegram of November 10, 1948, in responding to the question of how the Northeastern Bureau should treat the American, British, and the French consulates in the northeast, the CCP Central Committee suggested "squeezing them out": "Since the American, British, and the French governments refuse to recognize our government, we should not offer their consulates in Northeast China diplomatic status either. Thus, we should treat their consuls as ordinary foreign residents in China." As long as "we continue to do so, limiting their freedom of movements in Northeast China, those consulates will be forced to withdraw on their own." However, it also emphasized that the Northeastern Bureau's diplomacy toward the American, British, and the French consulates must show flexibility, thus to "leave room for a change of policies."[58]

On November 15, 1948, the PLA's military commission in Shenyang issued an order that all Chinese and foreign personnel turn in their transmitter-receivers within thirty-six hours. They would be returned after completion of the PLA's military deployment in that city. On November 16, one day after the order was issued, the Soviet consul general in Harbin called Gao Gang, the head of the CCP Northeastern Bureau, and recommended that the CCP confiscate all transmitter-receivers in American, British, and French consulates in Shenyang. He emphasized that such an action would be "very important" to Soviet "security interests" in the area.

On November 18, the PLA military commission informed Angus I. Ward, the consul general in Shenyang, that since he had missed the deadline for turning in the transmitter-receivers, the military commission was to confiscate the American consulate's radio station. Ward protested that the station was American government property and the consulate needed it to communicate with the State Department. Kovalev told the CCP Northeastern Bureau he had "reliable information" that the consulate had housed "a US–Chiang Kai-shek intelligence center." He thus proposed that "the American Consulate in Mukden should be blocked and its personnel should not be allowed to leave its territory."[59] The CCP Northeastern Bureau followed Kovalev's recommendation. On November 20, 1948, the PLA military commission in Shenyang confiscated the American consulate's transmitter-receiver and put all American diplomats in the consulate under house arrest, cutting off their electricity and telephone service as well as their running water.

The CCP headquarters, however, disagreed with Kovalev's recommendation and was dissatisfied with the Northeastern Bureau's decision. On November 23, 1948, Mao and Zhou sent a telegram to the Northeastern Bureau that said it was "possible" the CCP might establish diplomatic relations with the British and the French governments in the near future. It was also "possible," Mao and Zhou continued, that the CCP would establish diplomatic relationship with the United States eventually. Thus the Northeastern Bureau's policy toward the American consulate in Shenyang should "leave room for a change of policy in the future." Mao and Zhou thus asked the PLA military commission to inform the American diplomats that the consulate would retain "ownership" of the radio station but that the PLA military commission would "keep it for now" and "return it to the American government after the establishment of the Sino-American diplomatic relationship." One day after this telegram was sent, the CCP Northeastern Bureau sent in another report, which claimed that the U.S. consulate in Shenyang was the "center" of a "spy network" in Northeast China.[60]

Mao then sent a telegram to Stalin: "Comrade Kovalev had advised to isolate the consulate and seize the radio station" but "we hesitated." Mao stressed, "We are worried about the confiscation of the radio station," because that required "an entry into the consulate's territory." "We request your advice as to our further actions."[61]

Stalin asked Kovalev why he had recommended isolating the entire U.S. consulate, rather than just the radio station. Kovalev replied, "I have noticed a curious tendency with the Chinese comrades—they don't want to quarrel with the Americans, they want us to do the quarreling. As for me, if I were in their shoes, I would treat the consulate in Mukden the way the enemy HQ is treated in wartime. But I did not want to advise that to the Chinese, for they would later say that it was done on my advice." As Kovalev recalled, after his explanation, "Stalin laughed and approved of my stand. He did not answer Mao's cable."[62]

The Ward spy case dragged on throughout early 1949.[63] In June

1949, coinciding with his announcement of his alignment with the Soviet bloc, Mao published an article in the CCP's newspaper entitled "The British-American Diplomacy: The Spy Diplomacy," which denounced Angus I. Ward as an American spy. In the following months, Mao wrote five articles for the CCP's news agency sharply criticizing the State Department's white papers published in August 1949.[64]

Why did Mao change his mind about Kovalev's recommendation? In the summer of 1949, when Mao decided to make his pronouncement, he obviously realized that he must make political concessions to Moscow to eliminate all of Stalin's possible suspicions brought on at least in part by the Ward case. This did not mean, however, that Mao decided to implement a confrontational policy toward the United States. Such a rigid, antagonistic policy, Mao believed, would tip the United States toward Chiang Kai-shek, and so as Mao denounced Ward, the CCP was, in an apparently paradoxical move, sending private messages of flexibility and moderation to Washington.

In fact, on June 15, 1949, two weeks *before* his June 30 announcement, Mao gave another public announcement at the preparatory meeting for the new PCC on the CCP's domestic and foreign policies. The CCP was "willing to discuss with any foreign government the establishment of diplomatic relations on the basis of the principles of equality, mutual benefit and mutual respect for territorial integrity and sovereignty," proclaimed Mao, provided that the government was "willing to sever relations with" Taipei. He concluded, "The Chinese people wish to have friendly cooperation with the people of all countries and to resume and expand international trade in order to promote economic prosperity."[65]

On the same day, a new communication channel between Mao and Zhou and Stuart and Acheson was formally established. Different from the much-publicized Huang-Stuart talks, of which the CCP had regularly informed Moscow, this new channel was unknown either to the public or to the Soviet Union at that time. General Chen Mingshu and Lo Haisha—two prominent leaders of the Third Force—became the liaison. They both emphasized to the ambassador that the request to establish this new channel came directly from Zhou Enlai and that they were to report directly to Mao and Zhou.

On June 21, 1949, Chen told the ambassador that "Mr. Mao Zedong spoke personally to me, asking that Mr. Stuart read his statement of June 15, 1949, from which you would know his (Mao's) attitude." What Mao referred to, as Chen explained, was his "great hope" for the future relationship between China and the United States, and he pointed to Mao's concluding remarks that "China would like to open diplomatic and commercial relations with all countries on the basis of independence and equality."

On July 5, 1949, Chen told Stuart that Zhou had urged him "to explain to the ambassador the meaning of Mao's statement, to avoid any misconception of the Chinese Communists on the part of the United States." According to Chen, Zhou said, "On no account can 'leaning to one side' be misinterpreted as implying dependence on others. To understand the phrase in that way would be an insult to us. ... As regards our national independence, there can never be any question of dependence on others."[66]

Zhou also emphasized that Washington should not confuse the CCP's "sincere desires to develop good working relations with America" with the CCP's "political or ideological beliefs." The CCP's "national position and its ideology must not be identified with each other," Zhou told the ambassador. During World War II, Russia's ideology was "not the same as that of England and America," Zhou said. However, "from the point of view of national position, Russia could fight shoulder to shoulder with England and America."

In early August 1949, before Stuart left for the United States, Chen again told him that Mao and Zhou wanted to convey to the ambassador "the importance attached by the CCP to future Sino-American relations." Lo Haisha also conveyed that "Mao and Zhou wanted to send Mr. Stuart their most important hopes for the future. . . . These are the very great hopes for future Sino-American relations." Lo told the ambassador, "What Mao and Zhou mean by 'hopes' is of course not that the United States walk the road of the Soviet Union or enter the embrace of the Soviet Union, but they hope that hereafter the United States will be able to act and formulate policies in the manner of President Roosevelt, General Stilwell, and Mr. Wallace. If the United States can treat the future China like this, China will naturally treat the United States with similar friendship. This will of course depend upon Mr. Stuart's efforts after he returns to his country." As Chen and Lo told the ambassador, Mao and Zhou believed that to build China into a great nation, "China must have a long period of peaceful construction." China did not want to have a war with America.[67]

After Ward's public trial in the summer of 1949, the CCP leadership attempted to prevent spy charges being brought against Western missionaries in China. On August 3, 1949, one month after Mao's public denunciation of America's "spy diplomacy," the CCP Central Committee issued a confidential circular that said, "Since the land reform started, there have been grave problems in the local party organizations' treatment of foreign missionaries." In the village of Yang, Huailai county, West Chahar, for instance, "the alleged Catholic spy case involved 75 persons including foreign and native priests; among them, six were wrongly sentenced to death, six were sent to jail without proper reasons, eighteen died, and one French priest is still in prison without evidence against him at all; and all of the Church property was wrongly distributed among the poor peasants." This circular particularly criticized the party organizations in "the Northeast Liberated Zone," where "90 percent of 180 churches were wrongly confiscated or occupied, and more than one hundred foreign missionaries were wrongly implicated in spy cases without solid evidence against them."[68] In another confidential circular of September 27, 1949, the CCP Central Committee emphasized that the CCP "must respect freedom of religion" in the land-reform campaigns: "As long as those foreign missionaries observe Chinese laws, we must not intervene in their religious activities. It would be a dangerous, extremist policy for the CCP members to confiscate or destroy the churches. The land reform campaign is not equivalent to confiscation of all church properties. The anti-spy campaign is not equivalent to opposition to freedom of religion."[69]

However, while the CCP headquarters repeatedly asked the local organizations not to confiscate the Christian churches in the land revolution in late 1949, it was not hesitant to confiscate American barracks in Beijing in January 1950. What was the CCP's motivation behind its confiscation policy at a time when Mao was negotiating a new alliance treaty with Stalin in Moscow?

These American barracks in Beijing were seized in the aftermath of the Boxer uprising. In 1901, after the Boxer rebellion in China, twelve nations signed a treaty with the Qing dynasty, which was widely regarded in China as the most humiliating of all the unequal treaties. In addition to extraterritoriality and the control of Chinese customs, these twelve nations had the rights to build barracks and station troops in Beijing, Tianjin, and other surrounding Chinese cities.[70]

In July 1946, a KMT governmental committee recommended that all foreign barracks in China, particularly in Peiping (Beijing), should be confiscated: "The continued existence of foreign barracks in Peiping and other cities is an intolerable insult to the dignity of the Chinese people." It recommended "taking back all these foreign barracks in Peiping." The Chiang Kai-shek government was sympathetic but did not adopt the recommendation at that time.[71]

On the morning of January 6, 1950, a proclamation appeared in front of the American, British, French, and the Netherlands consulates in Beijing, issued by Nie Rongzhen, chair of Beijing's military commission, declaring the confiscation of those countries' barracks. Oliver Edmund Clubb, U.S. consul general in Beijing, protested against Nie's proclamation. "Based on the treaty of 1901, signed by 12 nations and China," he wrote, "the American government owns this piece of land and all its buildings." This treaty right was "reaffirmed in 1943" in the new treaty between the United States and the KMT government. He thus stressed: "The new Chinese government should not violate the treaty rights of the United States in China."[72] The Office for Foreign Affairs in Beijing refused to accept his letter, arguing that since the U.S. government did not recognize the new Chinese government, the American consul general would not be treated as a U.S. diplomat there. He thus had no right to represent the U.S. government in addressing the new Chinese government.

Four days later, on January 13, Clubb warned that should the CCP insist on the confiscation, the U.S. government would withdraw all its diplomats from China. The British consul general in Beijing delivered the letter, since the British government had just announced that it would grant diplomatic recognition to the new Chinese government. At his meeting with Huan Xiang, the director of Western European Affairs at the Chinese Foreign Ministry, Huan told the British diplomat, "The existence of such foreign barracks in China is not only the shame of China, but also the shame of those countries that sent troops to invade China in the past. Only when the foreign barracks are wiped out from the Chinese territory, can Sino-Western relations have a new beginning."

On the same day, Beijing's military commission and the Chinese Foreign Ministry reported to Mao, who was still in Moscow, asking for instruction on this matter. Mao replied, "Agree with your decision on confiscation of all foreign barracks. Prepare for America's withdrawal of its consulates in China."[73]

On January 14, 1950, American barracks in Beijing were confiscated. The CCP's confiscation policy generated uproar in American public opinion. Many Americans who had risked their careers to champion the normalization of U.S.-China diplomatic relations were dismayed at the CCP's decision to force the withdrawal of all American diplomats from China. In their view, such a decision was particularly appalling given that just two days earlier Acheson had delivered a speech in which he explained why the U.S. government should not send troops to rescue the Chiang government on Taiwan.[74]

In fact, Mao did not know about Acheson's speech until January 17, 1950, five days after the speech and three days after the CCP's confiscation of American barracks in Beijing, when V. M. Molotov, deputy premier under Stalin, showed Mao a copy. In this speech, Acheson reaffirmed Truman's implicit pledge of America's military withdrawal from Taiwan. Acheson also claimed that Moscow was trying to take away Manchuria, Xinjiang, and four provinces of north China, as it had taken Outer Mongolia from China in 1945. Molotov suggested that the Chinese government issue a statement to rebut Acheson's claims about Soviet "territorial ambitions" in China.

On January 21, 1950, the Soviet foreign minister, the Mongolian foreign minister, and Hu Qiaomu, the director of the Chinese News Agency, all issued statements to counter Acheson's speech. However, the Chinese statement, drafted by Mao himself but issued in Hu Qiaomu's name, was unsatisfactory to Stalin. Consequently, Stalin invited Mao and Zhou to the Kremlin for a "private conversation." On the Soviet side, there were only Stalin and Molotov, and on the Chinese side, Mao and Zhou, as well as Shi Zhe, the only interpreter at the talk.

According to Shi's record, Stalin and Molotov told Mao and Zhou that it was not enough for the CCP to issue a "personal," rather than a "governmental" statement to rebut Acheson's claims. "Any news reporter could voice his views," Stalin said, but such media views could never "represent the official position." He continued, "To issue a statement in the name of the director of the Chinese News Agency, no matter what he said, his statement meant nothing for the international community." Molotov concurred: "Both sides had initially agreed that China was to issue an official statement by the Chinese government." The CCP had not done what "we had initially agreed to do," and thus "violated our accord." Hu's "personal statement" did not produce "our anticipated result." Stalin further stressed, "Right now, we are not keeping in step. If each goes his way, our overall strengths will be weakened. We should stand by our agreements, keeping in step with each other. Only through unity can we become more powerful in the world." "This is a warning for us," Stalin said. "Let's learn our lesson from this incident. Even though it may not cause too much damage this time, the lesson is extremely important for us: should we fail to stick to our original plan, and not keep in step, we would leave loopholes for our enemies to exploit."

Mao looked "grave and angry," observed Shi. "Chairman Mao kept silent, and refused to explain, or to comment on Stalin's talks." Zhou made some explanations, such as that the CCP had always issued "personal statements" to express "official positions" in the past, such as the CCP's views on the State Department's white papers. Given Mao's "stubborn silence," Zhou did not explain much. The atmosphere in the room, in Shi's words, was "as heavy as lead."[75]

One can discern a major difference between the Chinese and the Soviet responses to Acheson's speech. The Chinese statement said nothing about two of Acheson's assertions that the Soviets took particular issue with. One was Acheson's assertion that Russia's ambition in Manchuria "long preceded Soviet communism"; the other was Acheson's contention that it was the Soviet Union that had pushed for Outer Mongolia's independence in 1945. Would the CCP issue a new "official statement"? No, it would not be necessary, Mao said. "Let's simply respect history."[76]

In October 1949, at Zhou's meeting with Chinese Third Force leaders, he talked about the "great importance" of building a "friendly relationship" between China and the United States. The CIA quickly reported this statement to Truman in early November 1949. Zhou "stated the following regarding the CCP's foreign policy in an interview with [the CIA's] source": "The Chinese Communist Party has to have allies, and if the KMT is allied with the United States, the CCP must ally with the Soviet Union. It would be a dream on the part of the American government to expect the CCP to split with the Soviets, but it can expect that the CCP will not always be anti-American. The Chinese Communists cannot afford two enemies at one time, but there is nothing to keep them from having more than two friends."[77]

In short, what was the objective of the CCP's America policy before the Korean War? Its objective was threefold. First, it did not intend to establish diplomatic relations at the time, but it intended to build a limited economic relationship with the United States. Second, its long-term goal was to normalize Sino-American relations. Third, before the upcoming Taiwan campaign, it was determined not to provoke Washington to change its Taiwan policy and to rescue Chiang Kai-shek at the eleventh hour.

The CCP's Soviet Policy and America Policy: Two Sides of One Coin

In the recent American literature, a widely accepted view of the CCP's foreign policy from 1948 to 1950, the critical period before the Korean War, has been that it was driven by Mao's confrontational position against the United States. According to this "confrontation thesis," "ideology's impact upon China's Cold War experience is reflected in Mao's 'continuous revolution' as his central theme in shaping Chinese foreign policy and security strategy." Thus "in the final analysis, the CCP's confrontation with the United States originated in the party's need to enhance the inner dynamics of the Chinese Revolution after its nationwide victory." In this regard, the Ward spy case of late 1948 was highlighted as a clear "turning point" in the CCP's foreign policy following its nationwide victory, or the beginning of its offensive strategy against Washington.[78]

Based on declassified Chinese and Russian documents, this chapter's argument is in clear disagreement with the above viewpoint. First, the confrontation thesis does not specify what it means for the CCP's domestic program "to enhance the inner dynamics of the Chinese Revolution after its nationwide victory." The concept of continuous revolution had its explicit meaning and definition in the CCP's ideological rhetoric at the time. The CCP divided the Chinese revolution into different stages of evolution, particularly the two stages of New Democracy and socialism, and the notion of continuous revolution refers to the transition from New Democracy to socialism, or according to Mao, from anti-imperialism and antifeudalism to anticapitalism. The latter, in turn, means that the CCP's political alliance with the urban Third Force might be terminated. There is no historical evidence to indicate, however, that in the two to three years before the Korean War the CCP had any intention of dismantling its relationship with the Third Force or advancing to the next stage of the revolution, anticapitalism, after its nationwide victory. To the contrary, from Liu's article "On Internationalism and Nationalism" to Deng Xiaoping's letter to the East China Party Bureau, and from Mao's report *On Coalition Government* of 1945 to his work *On the People's Democratic Dictatorship* of 1949, historical evidence points in one direction. Namely, the CCP insisted on the stage of New Democracy, and consequently, on its united front with the Third Force. It was precisely the CCP's emphasis on its New Democracy and its continued political alliance with the Third Force, before the Korean War, that encouraged Moscow's fears and worries with respect to the "bourgeois nature" of the CCP's domestic and foreign policies. Put differently, there is no historical evidence to indicate that there is a linkage, direct or indirect, between the CCP's domestic program of New Democracy and an "uncompromising hostility" against the United States in 1948–1950.

Second, and more important, like the notion of continuous revolution, the concept of revolutionary diplomacy also had its distinct interpretation in the CCP's ideological vocabulary during that time. It placed patriotism at the heart of proletarian internationalism, as shown in Liu's article "On Internationalism and Nationalism" and in Mao's works during that critical period. In particular, before the upcoming Taiwan campaign, and with Stalin's insistence that the Soviet Union not be involved, the CCP made strenuous efforts to avoid provoking Washington to intervene. A confrontational posture, according to Mao, could compel the Truman administration to change its new Taiwan policy, thus ruining the CCP's own chance of success and destroying the "revolutionary cause of national reunification." Put another way, there is no historical evidence to demonstrate that the CCP's concept of revolutionary diplomacy was designed as a confrontational strategy against the United States before its upcoming Taiwan campaign in 1949–50, before the outbreak of the Korean War.

Finally, with regard to the Ward spy case, what emerged from all declassified Chinese and Russian documents was a much more complex picture than the black-and-white one of the CCP's "confrontational strategy" against the United States.

According to the predominant view in the recent literature, the Ward spy case clearly showed the CCP's confrontational strategy: "When the Americans refused to hand over their radio equipment, the Communists, following Soviet advice, placed Angus Ward, the American consul, and his staff under house detention on 20 November."[79] Historical evidence illustrates, on the other hand, that it was the CCP Northeastern Bureau's policy, on the advice of Soviet diplomats, to put Angus Ward under house detention. That was why on November 23, in its telegram to the Northeastern Bureau, the CCP headquarters expressed its concern over the Bureau's policy. According to Mao and Zhou, "the CCP's decision not to recognize the KMT's diplomatic relations with the United States, Great Britain, and France does not mean that we will never establish diplomatic relations with these countries."

True, in the CCP headquarters' telegram of November 10, Mao and

Zhou had emphasized the necessity of squeezing out American, British, and French diplomats from the Northeastern region, on the grounds that they refused to "recognize the new China." True, also, that the CCP headquarters approved the Bureau's decision to confiscate the radio equipment of the American consulate in Shenyang. However, it was not true that the CCP headquarters' telegram of November 23 continued the same theme. To the contrary, it questioned the Northeastern Bureau's decision to put Angus Ward under house arrest. It particularly emphasized that the Northeastern Bureau must take into account the possibility that "even if we squeeze out American diplomats from the Northeast for now, we might normalize our diplomatic relationship with the United States in the future."

The differing instructions in these two telegrams from the CCP headquarters probably resulted from its drastically changed assessments on how soon it could win the national victory. As the Chinese scholar Yang Kuisong notes, the telegram of November 10, 1948, was based on the CCP headquarters' earlier assessment that it would take five years to reach that goal. But the telegram of November 23 was based on Mao's assessment that the CCP's recent military success might bring final victory in only one year. Based on this new assessment, Mao, in the telegram of November 23, obviously began to think seriously about the prospect of establishing diplomatic relations with Western countries in the future.[80] That was probably also why Mao himself sent a telegram to Stalin to inquire about the merit of Kovalev's advice regarding putting Angus Ward under house detention. It is interesting to note that while the confrontation thesis highlights the Ward spy case as the turning point of the CCP's confrontational strategy against the United States, Kovalev, in his memo to Stalin, singled out this case to underscore "the CCP's soft attitude toward Washington in the heightened Cold War."

The thesis of this chapter is that after its nationwide victory, the CCP's policy toward America was neither accommodation nor confrontation. Instead, it demonstrated a dual character: deterrence and moderation. While Beijing intended to deter the Washington-Taipei alliance through the Beijing-Moscow alliance, it also sent messages of flexibility and moderation to Washington, in its response to Acheson's new China and Taiwan policy. Meanwhile, the CCP's policy toward the Soviet Union aimed to strengthen Beijing's political, economic, and, in particular, military power, to prepare for the upcoming Taiwan campaign and for the paramount task of industrialization and nation-state building. Put differently, from Beijing's perspective, its foreign-policy objectives and Moscow's overlapped but were not identical. While Moscow's primary concern was Washington, Beijing's was the Taiwan question.

Such an apparent contradiction in the CCP's foreign policies toward Moscow and Washington cannot be simply interpreted as an expression of the CCP's ideological beliefs and rhetoric. Such a foreign-policy objective before the Korean War can be better explained by the CCP's new conceptual framework for its foreign policy, articulated after Tito was expelled from the Soviet bloc. To keep its coalition with the Third Force, as Tito did in Yugoslavia, while avoiding Tito's fate, the CCP decided to declare publicly the CCP's ideological loyalty to the Soviet bloc in the Cold War. However, beneath its ideological rhetoric, the essence of the new framework for the CCP's foreign policy was not about "exporting revolution." The "best embodiment" of "proletarian internationalism" in the Chinese revolution was, in Mao' words, "China's struggle for national independence and national equality."

At a fundamental level, such an apparent contradiction in the CCP's foreign policies was shaped by the powerful force of nationalism. This unique manifestation of Chinese nationalism was rooted in both rural China (through the CCP's land-reform program) and urban China (through the alliance between the CCP and the urban middle class) at that time. In retrospect, John King Fairbank, dean of China studies in the United States at that time, regretted that America neglected this distinctive expression of Chinese nationalism. "The epitaph for America's China policy in the 1940s should begin by noting the Americans' profound ignorance of the Chinese situation," he wrote. "The CCP side of the picture was almost entirely blank to the Americans." To this was added "the American preoccupation with anti-communism." This meant that most of the American public did not realize that a national and social revolution was going on in China that "had its roots in the past and would determine the future." He emphasized, "Seldom has a national posture been more ineffective and unproductive."[81]

It does not mean, however, that the entire U.S. foreign-policy establishment misread the CCP's foreign-policy intentions before the Korean War. If one compares the vastly differing China policy assumptions within the Truman administration, one may see clearly that the minority stance at the State Department, which argued that the CCP movement was an integral part of the broader nationalist and social revolutionary movements since the Opium War, could be widely embraced by the urban Chinese at the time. The other view—that the CCP movement was entirely manufactured by the Soviet Union and that the CCP was the puppet of Moscow—cannot be substantiated by Chinese and Russian documents as discussed in this chapter. And the third view, the mainstream one at the State Department, was only partly accurate.

Proponents of this view clearly saw the major historical trend in China and Asia as "nationalistic awakening," which aimed to achieve national independence and eradicate poverty. Yet they also believed that the CCP movement was an "aberration" of the nationalist movements in modern China and that the CCP leadership was currently "subservient" to Moscow, although there was the long-term possibility of splitting the Sino-Soviet alliance. While this view was unquestionably a drastic departure from the views on the Hill and in the media at the time, it nonetheless failed to see the rise of a unique form of Chinese nationalism. This distinctive manifestation of "national awakening" was founded on the political alliance between the CCP and the Third Force, or coalition between rural and urban China, aiming to achieve national independence through land or social revolutions and to continue China's historical quest for modernity and new identity in the post–World War II era.

CHAPTER SIX

From Adversaries to Enemies

Military Confrontation in Korea

Despite their opposing ideological rhetoric, the State Department's China policy and Beijing's America policy from 1949 to mid-1950, before the outbreak of the Korean War, bore amazing similarities. First, neither side attempted to establish a diplomatic relationship with the other in the short run. Second, neither side formulated a confrontational policy against the other. Third, and most important, both sides intended to build a limited working relationship, starting in the economic arena.

These policy similarities can be attributed to both sides' overriding objective: splitting the other's strategic partnership. Washington's goal was to break up the Sino-Soviet coalition, and Beijing's was to weaken the Washington-Taipei alliance. A war with Beijing, from Dean Acheson's viewpoint, could only drive China into the arms of the Soviet Union. A war with Washington, from Mao's perspective, could only compel Washington to rescue the Chiang Kai-shek government in Taipei at the eleventh hour.

By the end of 1950, however, China and America were at war in Korea. How could Beijing and Washington have become so rapidly engaged in military conflict, an outcome that was the opposite of both sides' initial strategic goals?[1] To answer this question, this chapter first examines why both sides failed to establish even a minimal working relationship in the summer of 1949, when there were secret communication channels available. It then addresses how both sides tried to assess each other's intentions in the time of crisis, when the Korean

War erupted on June 25, 1950. Finally, based on recently declassified Chinese and Russian documents, this chapter argues that fatal misjudgments of each other's intentions played a crucial role in the U.S.-China military conflict in Korea by the end of 1950.

CCP and U.S. Misjudgment before the Korean War

If both the State Department and CCP leaders attempted to use trade as a means of formulating a limited working relationship, why were both sides unable to do so? The following examines three cases of U.S.-China communications at that time to reveal both sides' underlying core assumptions and the effects of a mismatch in those assumptions, or the gap between both sides' deeply engrained policy postulates.

On June 3, 1949, Zhou Enlai had supposedly transmitted a message to the U.S. consul general in Beijing that said, "China is on the brink of complete economic collapse and desperately needs assistance from abroad, which the USSR cannot give and which therefore must come from the U.S. and the UK." According to the message, "Good working relations between the U.S. and China would have a definite softening effect on the Communist Party's attitude toward the Western countries."[2] This message was referred to as the "Zhou Enlai Demarche" in the State Department file.

Zhou's aides have since strenuously maintained that Zhou never sent this message.[3] The point, however, is that both Truman and Acheson did believe in the authenticity of Zhou's message and responded accordingly.

How should the State Department respond to the Zhou Enlai demarche? Acheson asked for comments from the American diplomats in China. O. Edmund Clubb, the U.S. consul general in Beijing, emphasized, "It is probably already clear to the Soviets and the Chinese Communists that the USSR will be unable to supply China's economic needs and both may be reconciled to China's dealing with the U.S. to avoid economic collapse." But, he warned, "It would be premature to accept the development of Titoism in the Chinese Communist Party before the party rank and file have really appreciated the gravity of their economic situation."[4] The U.S. consul general in Guanzhou (Canton) concurred: It would be "fatal" for Washington to "assist the Communists in their period of need" only to find that "they wanted our help only until they could get along without us."[5] In the view of

John Leighton Stuart, Zhou's message did not imply "any basic change in the theory or program of the Chinese Communists," but only "a struggle for power" between Zhou Enlai and Liu Shaoqi, "the two men next in line after Chinese Communist chief Mao Tse-tung." He continued, "The radical wing of the party," represented by Liu, "has been gaining ascendancy owing to anti-American sentiments, hence Zhou's appeal to the U.S." Stuart determined that America's reply should thus stress the following: "While we sincerely welcome Zhou's protestations of pro-Western sentiments, they must be translated into deeds in order to convince us that continued American support for China is justified."[6]

On June 15, 1949, the State Department drafted a response to Zhou's message: "While we welcome the expression of friendly sentiments, Zhou must realize that they cannot be expected to bear fruit until they have been translated into deeds." On June 16, Truman approved this draft and asked the State Department to be "most careful not to indicate any softening toward the Communists but to insist on judging their intentions by their actions." On the same day, the U.S. consul general in Beijing sent the message to Zhou.[7]

Clearly, this response was defined by the framework of the State Department's new China policy, as discussed in Chapter 4. This message conveyed both implicit deterrence and an implicit suggestion of future cooperation. In this sense, it embodied the core concept of the State Department's new China policy, that is, that Washington should be neither confrontational nor accommodating toward the CCP. Instead, the new China policy offered a means of waiting out the Chinese Communists, to ensure that Titoism could eventually develop in China.

In early June 1949, Philip Fugh, Stuart's Chinese secretary, asked Huang Hua if it would be possible for Stuart to travel to Peiping (Beijing) to visit Yenching University, as the ambassador had done in previous years on his birthday and for commencement ceremonies.[8]

On June 28, 1949, two days before Mao's announcement of "leaning to one side," Huang delivered a message from Mao and Zhou to the American ambassador. As Stuart later wrote to Acheson, "He [Huang] reported that he had received a message from Mao Tse-tung and Zhou Enlai assuring me that they would welcome me to Peiping if I wished to visit Yenching University." The ambassador concluded, "I can only regard Huang's message as *a veiled invitation* from Mao and Zhou to talk with them. I received the clear impression that Mao, Zhou and Huang are very much hoping that I make this trip."

The ambassador himself felt that his visit to Peiping would have both positive and negative effects on America's security interests in China. On the positive side, he said, to accept Mao's invitation "would give me a chance to describe American policy; its anxieties regarding Communism and world revolution; its desires for China's future; and would enable me to carry to Washington the most authoritative information regarding CCP intentions." Moreover, "such a trip would be a step toward better mutual understanding and should strengthen the more liberal anti-Soviet element in the CCP." Finally, his trip "would provide a unique opportunity for an American official to talk to top Chinese Communists in an informal manner, which may not again present itself. It would be an imaginative, adventurous indication of our open-minded attitude towards changing political trends in China and would probably have a beneficial effect on future Sino-American relations."

"On the negative side," the ambassador cautioned, his trip to Peiping "would probably be misunderstood by my colleagues in the Diplomatic Corps, who might feel that the U.S. representative was first to break the united front policy, which we have sponsored" toward the new CCP regime. Moreover, his visit would have to be followed, or balanced, by a similar trip to Canton (Guangzhou), which the KMT government had just established as its temporary capital after its retreat from Nanjing. And his visits to both capitals might appear as "unwarranted interference in China's internal affairs, and would probably be misunderstood by Chinese Communists, thus undoing any beneficial effects of a visit north." Finally, "a trip of the U.S. Ambassador to Peiping at this time would enhance greatly the prestige, national and international, of Chinese Communists and Mao himself and in a sense would be the second step on our part (the first having been my remaining in Nanking) toward recognition of the Communist regime."[9]

On July 1, 1949, Truman instructed the ambassador not to accept Mao's and Zhou's invitation to visit Peiping. On July 14, 1949, in his memo to Acheson, Ambassador Stuart noted that he had observed "a visible change" in the CCP's attitudes toward him, he wrote. He suspected such "hardened" attitudes had been brought about by his refusal of Mao's invitation to visit Peiping. "In retrospect, I can only interpret it [Mao's invitation] as the earnest desire that I take the initiative to travel to Peiping and be available for conversations with some of them." With respect to the CCP's new claim, after he declined Mao's invitation, that the CCP headquarters had never intended to invite him to visit Peiping, the ambassador argued this was just the CCP's way to "save face." "According to my friends in Peiping, Mao openly stated that I would be welcome in Peiping if I wished to visit my old university," he reported to Acheson. "From other sources I have received reports that Mao-Chou counted on entertaining me and talking to me during this ostensibly private visit to Peiping." After his refusal to make the trip, however, "the attitudes of Communist authorities from the top down have changed and hardened, including our personal relations locally," and "I am inclined to agree there has been a change but whether it comes from chagrin over my refusal to visit Peiping or is a general reflection of the orthodox line laid down in Mao's July 1 article I cannot say."[10]

In fact, Mao's public announcement of "leaning to one side" and Stuart's refusal to accept Mao's invitation both contributed to a hardening of the CCP's attitudes toward the ambassador. As discussed in Chapter 5, the CCP's Soviet policy and U.S. policy could be characterized as a desire to strengthen its power by winning the full support of the Soviet bloc and simultaneously reducing the KMT's by sending messages of moderation to Washington. Obviously, the CCP's foreign policy was shaped by the concept of national interest as it was interpreted by CCP leaders at that time. So how the CCP leaders perceived Washington's intentions did matter. Stuart's refusal to accept what was perceived to be Mao's invitation helped to deepen the CCP's distrust of America's China policy in the midst of Taiwan's blockade.

The ambassador himself seemed to have somewhat regretted the decision not to make the trip. Although he listed both the positive and the negative effects of this trip on America's security interests in China, the positive side focused more on America's long-term interests, and the negative, more on America's domestic politics. Why did Truman decide not to accept Mao's invitation? Some scholars suspected that his decision was brought about by anger over the "leaning-to-one-side" speech, which Mao gave on the same day he issued this instruction. Historical documents showed, however, that he had made his decision before reading Mao's public announcement.[11] Was his decision brought about by concern over domestic political repercussions? Yes, but only partially. While Truman did not leave a record of why he declined Mao's veiled invitation, his motivation could be discovered in his earlier decision regarding how to respond to the so-called Zhou Enlai demarche. Two weeks earlier he had told the State Department that it should be "most careful not to indicate any softening toward the Communists but to insist on judging their intentions by their actions."[12] Put another way, Truman's decisions were based on his deep belief about the nature of the CCP movement in China. That is, the CCP movement was largely manufactured by Moscow, and its leaders were currently "subservient" to the USSR, even though there was indeed the possibility of splitting the Sino-Soviet alliance eventually.

Although Stuart declined the invitation, the secret communication channel between him and Mao/Zhou through two Third Force leaders, Chen Mingshu and Lo Haisha, was still kept open. In July 1949, the ambassador asked Chen to send a message to Zhou, which said that to carry out China's industrialization, China could not depend on the Soviet Union but would have to depend on the American economy. Zhou should understand that "China needs America much more than America needs China," the ambassador emphasized. Zhou immediately asked Chen to deliver the following message to the ambassador: "Mr. Stuart is wrong in saying that China needs to depend upon the American economy and that America does not depend upon China." Zhou used the statistics of Sino-American trade from 1937 to 1947 to make his point. "He [Stuart] says the U.S. has no need at all for tung oil, raw silk, or pig's bristles, but in 1937, America's imports of these items from China amounted to $69,000,000. And in 1949, it reached $233,000,000." Moreover, China would not have to depend upon America's markets for these exports: "England and Russia want tung oil. England is the most important buyer of pig's bristles. Other countries also want our vegetable oil, eggs, handicrafts, tungsten ore." As for China's imports, Zhou said, only petroleum, machinery, automobiles, and photographic materials had to be imported from overseas. And in a few years, China could export petroleum products on a large scale, in exchange for machine goods.

Zhou's main point, of course, is not what the statistics could prove. What he meant to argue was that China would establish economic relations with America on the basis of "equality and mutual respect." While China did want to establish economic relations with America, Zhou made clear "the most important thing" for China: "*We must base ourselves on the principle of equal advantage. No special rights, no monopolies, equal advantage, when the tide is in flood, and the boat is high.*"[13]

This conversation underscored the disparity between the two sides' fundamental policy premises underlying their strategic gestures. The State Department assumed that the CCP was currently obedient to

Moscow and so must be pushed to realize that China's industrialization would have to depend on the U.S. economy. The CCP's basic policy premise, however, was that it must employ the Sino-Soviet alliance to achieve equality between China and the United States.

On August 2, 1949, Stuart left China for Washington. His departure left the CCP and the State Department without a direct channel of communication.

In the summer of 1949, when an anti-American ideological campaign was sweeping the CCP's news media, Acheson and China Desk officers chose to downplay the campaign's importance for their new economic-based strategy toward the CCP. Acheson instead paid attention to those private messages he had received from Mao and Zhou through the communication channel between Chen/Lo and Stuart in June, July, and early August 1949. As Acheson remarked in private in August 1949, American media made "too much noise" out of the Ward spy trial.[14] A China Desk memo calmly stated in October 1949 that while "the CCP's propaganda has continued to be hostile toward Western governments, particularly the United States," "strategic and practical considerations" did not warrant a change of the new economic strategy toward the CCP.[15] After all, the China Desk officers had astutely predicted months earlier that America must be prepared to "weather through a good many surface buffets," to pursue "the long-run possibility" of the Sino-Soviet split.[16]

If the CCP's anti-American ideological campaign in the summer of 1949 did not trigger a change in the State Department's new China policy, why could even a minimal working relationship not be wrought?

First, on the CCP's side, there was no knowledge of the policy debates between the State Department and the Pentagon, and there was deeply embedded suspicion of Washington's policy intentions toward the CCP. As Zhou Enlai's foreign-policy aides acknowledged decades later, they did not understand the United States at the time. Zhang Wenjin, Zhou's top foreign-policy aide, did not recall "anyone being able to pay much attention to subtleties" in the Truman administration's China policy statements. Thus when Mao and Zhou were responding to Acheson's new China policy, their primary concern was "to forestall a major American intervention which might rescue the Guomindang (KMT) at the eleventh hour." According to Huang Hua, before his meetings with the American ambassador, he was told to "be receptive to any American overtures and avoid any gratuitous affront to the Americans at the crucial moment in the military campaign." Since the CCP leaders were "unaware of the differences among American leaders," Beijing made no conscious efforts to "coordinate" with the State Department when Acheson's new China policy was subjected to increasing domestic political pressures in the media and on the Hill.[17]

Second, on the American side, while domestic politics was surely on Truman's mind, it was not the only concern. According to the new economic strategy toward the CCP, Washington should evince only "restrained interest" even if approached by the CCP for economic aid, to maximize the psychological power of the trade weapon. Its goal was to push the CCP to develop a sense of "dependence" on the American economy, to detach itself eventually from its "current dependence" on the Soviet Union. Because of this, it was not hard to understand why the State Department paid special attention to the following argument when deciding how to respond to the Zhou Enlai demarche: "Before the party rank and file have really appreciated the gravity of their economic situation," there would be no chance for the CCP to limit its relationship with Moscow and turn to Washington. For the same reason, neither was it hard to understand why Stuart's dialogue with Zhou so persistently focused on China's need to look to the American economy in its industrialization drive.

But while both sides had surprisingly similar strategic stances, characterized by neither accommodation nor confrontation, inherent in their strategies was a substantial mismatch in their core concepts: in the State Department's strategic design, the CCP must be pushed to develop a sense of "dependence" on the American economy, to break with Moscow eventually, whereas in the CCP's strategic planning, the goal of the Sino-Soviet alliance was to add the Soviet power to its own and to establish Sino-American relations "from the position of equality." The underlying issue here is that both sides had entirely different assumptions with respect to Beijing's motivation in the Sino-Soviet alliance or about the nature of the PRC's foreign policy. In the minds of the CCP and the Third Force, the new China would be an independent nation, with its own legitimate national interests to defend. It was not dependent on the Soviet Union now, and it would not depend on the United States in the future. In the minds of Acheson and his staff, the CCP was an "aberration" of "national awakening" in modern China and Asia, but with "some nationalist sentiments" in Beijing, the Sino-Soviet alliance might be split in the future.

In short, this critical divergence in both sides' fundamental assumptions regarding the basic nature of the Sino-Soviet alliance and Beijing's foreign-policy objectives would soon prove fatal.

The Question of the 38th Parallel in Beijing's Decision to Enter the War

Before the outbreak of the Korean War, the CCP's top military priority had been the Taiwan campaign, which, according to Mao's plan, would take place in the summer of 1950. Throughout 1949, Mao's concern in North Korea had been how to prevent South Korea's attack on the North after the Soviet military withdrawal from the peninsula. When South Korea moved 41,000 soldiers up to the 38th parallel, Mao quickly agreed to Pyongyang's requests to send back the Korean soldiers in the PLA, to strengthen North Korea's defense force. Mao was aware of the military reunification plan, espoused by Kim Il-Sung, then premier of North Korea, but he was in accord with Stalin throughout 1949 and early 1950 that North Korea should focus on how to defend itself, rather than how to achieve reunification with military power.[18]

By the end of January 1950, however, Stalin had changed his mind about Kim's plan. During the premier's visit to Moscow in April, he formally approved Kim's blueprint of achieving military reunification. Stalin did not explain his sudden about-face. Sergei Goncharov, John Lewis, and Xue Litai speculated that it probably had a great deal to do with Acheson's speech of January 12, 1950, wherein Acheson put South Korea outside America's "defense perimeter" and reaffirmed America's military withdrawal from Taiwan, which was, in Stalin's view, aimed at "driving a wedge between the Sino-Soviet alliance." To counter Acheson's wedge strategy, "Stalin was pursuing his goal of sharpening the divisions between Beijing and the West." If the CCP were to complete its Taiwan campaign in the summer of 1950, there would be no barrier to the normalization of Sino-American diplomatic relations. Could Stalin's sudden support for Kim's military unification plan have been aimed at postponing Mao's Taiwan campaign?[19] On the other hand, Chinese scholar Shen Zhihua argued that Stalin might aspire to get an alternative access route to the Pacific on the Korean peninsula. The new treaty between Moscow and Beijing, signed in February 1950, "threatened crucial Soviet privileges in the Far East" that Stalin gained at the Yalta conference and in the treaty with the Chiang Kai-shek government, including the Soviet naval base in Lushun. Thus, by the end of January 1950, "to retain Soviet control of warm-water ports" in the Western Pacific, Stalin began to change his attitude toward Kim's proposal with regard to "military reunification."[20] In any case, when Stalin approved Kim's plan he suggested that Kim visit Beijing to get the CCP's blessing.

On May 13, 1950, at a meeting with Kim Il-Sung in Beijing, Mao first learned about Stalin's approval of Kim's plan. When the meeting ended at nearly midnight, Mao sent Zhou to the Soviet Embassy, to inquire about Stalin's changed decision on Kim's military unification plan. As Soviet ambassador Nikolai Roshchin reported immediately to Stalin (identified as Filippov in all telegrams):

> Today on May 13, at 23 hours 30 minutes Chou En-lai paid a visit to me and, following the instructions of Mao Tse-tung, let me know the following:
>
> . . . In the evening comrade Mao Tse-tung has had a meeting with them (Kim Il Sung and minister of foreign affairs of North Korea). In the conversation with comrade Mao Tse-tung the Korean comrades informed about the directives of comrade Filippov that the present situation has changed from the situation in the past and, that North Korea can move toward actions; however, this question should be discussed with China and personally with comrade Mao Tse-tung.
>
> . . . In connection with the abovementioned, comrade Mao Tse-tung would like to have personal clarifications of comrade Filippov on this question.

The ambassador conveyed that "the Chinese comrades are requesting an urgent answer."[21]

On May 14, 1950, Roshchin delivered Stalin's message to Mao. Stalin confirmed that he had indeed approved Kim's plan, because of "the changed international situation," on which he did not elaborate. The "final decision," the message said, should be made between Kim and Mao. "If the Chinese comrades do not agree," Kim's unification plan should be changed.[22]

On the same day, Mao implied to Kim that his plan might need to be postponed, since the situation was not yet "ripe" for such a military campaign. Mao expressed concern that America might intervene in Kim's plan, since "South Korea is so close to Japan." Should 20,000 or 30,000 Japanese soldiers participate in the war, Mao said, the war would become "a protracted one," which would be detrimental to the interests of North Korea. Kim, however, assured Mao that the unification war could succeed in a very short time. Moreover, he stressed, Stalin was "confident" America would not intervene.[23] But Mao still thought it necessary "to take precautions." China might deploy three armies along the Yalu River, and if the United States did not intervene, "no damage would be done." If the United States intervened but decided not to cross the 38th parallel, Chinese troops would not cross the Yalu. Kim told Mao China did not need to take such precautions and that the North Koreans could fight the war of national reunification themselves.[24]

At Stalin's suggestion, Kim did not inform Mao of the specific schedule of Pyongyang's military campaign. Thus after Kim's departure on May 15, Beijing continued, or more accurately, accelerated, its preparation for the Taiwan campaign. By mid-May, with the completion of the military campaign in Hainan Island, Mao's next target was Taiwan. The KMT's loss of Hainan and its voluntary abandonment of Zhoushan island allowed the Chiang government to transfer an additional force of 200,000 KMT soldiers to Taiwan, bringing the numbers defending the island to over 400,000. On May 17, Su Yu, the CCP's commander in chief of the Taiwan campaign, suggested increasing the troops of the first attack echelon from four to six corps (*jun*). On June 23, 1950, he suggested increasing the total battle troops from twelve to sixteen corps. On the same day, Mao and the Central Military Commission approved transferring four corps to the Taiwan Strait region.[25]

On June 25, 1950, one day after Mao's deployment of four more corps to the Taiwan Strait,[26] North Korea launched its military campaign against the South. On June 27, Truman reversed his original Taiwan policy and sent the U.S. Seventh Fleet to the Taiwan Strait. On June 29, he instructed General Douglas MacArthur to employ the naval and air forces of his Far East Command to support South Korea. On June 30, Truman further ordered the use of American ground troops stationed in Japan for military campaigns in Korea.[27]

On July 2, at his meeting with Roshchin, Zhou stressed that at meetings with Kim two months earlier, Mao had warned of the possibility of America's military intervention. "Unfortunately," Zhou said, "the Korean comrades did not pay enough attention to this possibility." Zhou also pledged that since the war might become a protracted one, China planned to send nine divisions to the Sino-Korean border region, to prepare for all eventualities. "If the American troops do not cross the 38th parallel, the Chinese troops will not cross the Yalu River," emphasized Zhou. "However, should the American troops cross the 38th parallel, the Chinese troops would enter the Korean War."[28]

On July 8, 1950, MacArthur was appointed as the commander-in-chief of UN troops in Korea. This drastically increased, in Mao's mind, the possibility that UN troops would cross the parallel. He told his comrades that China must "repair the house before it rains," an arch principle in Sun Zi's classic *The Art of War*. The Chinese Northeast Border Defense Army (NEBDA) was established on the same day. China's major military forces also began transport from the Taiwan Strait to the Sino-Korean border, to prepare for the "worst scenario," namely, that MacArthur's troops would cross the 38th parallel.

After MacArthur's successful Inchon landing on September 15, Mao was certain that MacArthur's troops would cross the parallel. On September 17, Zhou sent a five-member team led by General Chai Chengwen to North Korea to map the land.[29] When the team passed by Shenyang, General Chai delivered Mao's letter to Gao Gang. It said, "It looks like we may have no other options but to send our troops across the Yalu."[30]

On the night of September 29, Mao received a report from Zhou that said Washington had decided to advance north of the 38th parallel. Zhou emphasized there was "no defense force north of the 38th parallel" and that MacArthur's troops could quickly occupy Pyongyang.[31] Mao drafted a public statement and asked Zhou to make it the following day: "Chinese people love peace. However, to defend peace, we have never feared, and will never fear waging wars of resistance against military invasions." It declared, "Chinese people will never tolerate military aggression. Neither will Chinese people allow imperialists to invade our neighbors."[32]

On October 1, 1950, South Korean troops crossed the 38th parallel. Intelligence from Beijing indicated that the first U.S. troops had begun to cross the parallel. Stalin sent Mao a telegram asking Beijing to send at least five to six divisions to help defend the 38th parallel. Meanwhile, Kim sent Mao a letter asking for China's direct, immediate military aid to North Korea.[33] In the early morning of October 2, Mao drafted a telegram to Stalin pledging that China would send its troops to North Korea if the Soviet Union would provide air protection for the Chinese troops.[34]

Mao's draft telegram of October 2 was, however, never sent out to Stalin. After he had composed it, he attended the Central Committee

Secretariat meeting, wherein most participants were against sending Chinese troops to North Korea. Lin Biao claimed that he could not be the commander-in-chief of the Chinese troops in Korea, due to "his poor health." Mao then recommended Peng Dehui as the commander in chief, and he asked Zhou to fly to Xian in northwest China to accompany Peng to Beijing. As Nie Rongzhen, army chief at the time, recalled, at that meeting, "most participants were inclined to the view that China should not fight this war in Korea, except that it is out of absolute necessity, that is, as the last resort."[35]

As soon as the meeting ended in the early morning of October 3, Zhou met with the Indian ambassador, K. M. Panikkar, asking him to send an urgent message to Indian prime minister Jawaharlal Nehru, knowing that the Indian government would immediately send this message to the Truman administration. "The American troops are trying to cross the 38th parallel, to expand the war to the north," Zhou said. If the South Korean troops crossed the parallel, the Chinese troops would not intervene, since it was still an "internal matter" in the Korean peninsula. However, "should American troops cross the parallel, we would not sit idle. We would intervene." He also told the Indian ambassador, "We need peace for economic constructions." But peace did not seem possible now. While there had been a pledge at the American, British, and French foreign ministers' meeting in September that without UN authorization, the UN troops were not to cross the 38th parallel,[36] China could no longer trust the pledges of the U.S. government. "We think that the American government will not be constrained by this agreement." Zhou repeatedly told Panikkar, "Should US troops cross the 38th parallel, China would send troops to North Korea."[37]

After Zhou's meeting with the Indian ambassador, Mao sent a telegram to Stalin saying that China would not send out its troops to North Korea at that time. Mao wrote, "We originally planned to send several divisions to North Korea to help the Korean comrades, when the enemy launches attacks on the north of the 38th parallel. However, after serious considerations, we now believe that such an action on our part might have extremely grave consequences."[38]

According to Mao, it was "almost impossible to reverse the situation in North Korea only through the force of several divisions," since the CCP's equipment was "very poor" and its soldiers had no experience fighting U.S. troops. More important, Mao said, if there was "an open confrontation between the United States and China," then "our entire plan of peaceful reconstruction would be totally disrupted, and many in China would be dissatisfied with us. (The deep wound of war in China has not yet been healed, and the Chinese people do need peace)." This was not Beijing's final decision, Mao told Stalin. The final decision would be made at the CCP Central Committee meeting.

Roshchin complained to Stalin that Mao's message "altered the Chinese leaders' initial position on the Korean situation." The Soviet ambassador believed there were two reasons that the CCP changed its attitude: "the deterioration of the international and the Korean situations," and that "the British and the Americans have co-conspired to use Nehru to urge the Chinese to restrain themselves, to avoid falling into disasters."[39]

On October 4, Stalin sent Mao a telegram, attempting once again to persuade him to send six Chinese divisions to North Korea. At this critical moment, Stalin did not employ any ideological rhetoric. He did not mention "a division of labor in revolutionary movements" between Beijing and Moscow. Stalin homed in on the future of Taiwan to persuade Mao. Should China not dare to engage in "a serious contest of strength" and "to demonstrate convincingly its power," Stalin stressed, "China would never take back Taiwan from the United States."[40]

At the enlarged Politburo meeting on October 4, the majority was still against China's participation in the war. In their view, China's top priority was, along with the Taiwan campaign, to restore the extremely shaky economy and to complete the nationwide land-reform campaigns, all of which were essential for the CCP's consolidation of power in China. Moreover, China did not have any air and naval forces, they said. Mao did not speak. Before the end of the meeting, he simply said, "When our neighbor faces such a national crisis, is it right for us to stand by and do nothing? No matter what we say, don't we feel sad in our hearts?"[41]

On the morning of October 5, Peng agreed to be the new commander in chief. Mao told him, "MacArthur's troops are advancing toward the 38th parallel. We should send our troops as soon as possible." At the enlarged Politburo meeting that afternoon, Peng in turn told his comrades, "Should the American troops settle down in both the Taiwan Strait and the Sino-Korean border, it would be easy for them to find an excuse to invade China in the near future."

On the same day, intelligence indicated that the U.S. troops were to cross the 38th parallel. The majority of the Politburo members quickly came to the conclusion that the Chinese troops must go to North Korea. Nie described the changed mood of the participants at that meeting: "MacArthur's troops are approaching our border. What else can we do but to fight back resolutely?"[42]

On October 7, 1950, when the U.S. troops crossed the 38th parallel, Mao formally informed both Kim and Stalin that China was going to send nine divisions to North Korea. On October 8, Mao ordered the establishment of the Chinese People's Volunteer Army to join the Korean War.[43] On October 8, 1950, Zhou and Lin secretly left Beijing for the Soviet Union to negotiate with Stalin about Soviet military aid, particularly Soviet air protection of the Chinese troops in North Korea. However, the negotiation did not go smoothly. Stalin was unwilling to commit the Soviet air force to the protection of Chinese troops in the Korean peninsula. He had been receiving intelligence reports that American warships—including one battleship, five aircraft carriers, six cruisers, and twelve destroyers—had appeared at sea near Pyongyang and the Sino-Korean border. The CCP leaders suspected Stalin's major fear: "Should the Soviet air force support the Chinese and the Chinese lose the war, the Soviet Union would be dragged in and engaged in a military confrontation with the United States."[44] After the severe devastation of the Soviet Union in World War II, Stalin had no desire for a direct military conflict with the United States. According to Zhou's account at a CCP Central Committee meeting, "We went to speak with Stalin. We asked him if he could help us with Soviet air force. He hesitated. He said, 'If China has difficulties, it will be all right that you don't send troops. If we lose North Korea, we still have China, we still have the socialist bloc.' "[45]

On October 11, Zhou sent a telegram to Mao informing him that Stalin had just recommended China not send its troops to North Korea right away, since the Soviet air force might not be ready for two and a half months.[46] At the same time, Stalin himself sent a telegram to Kim recommending that he withdraw all North Korean troops to Manchuria and establish a government-in-exile there. In Pyongyang, according to the Soviet ambassador, Kim "looked shocked" by Stalin's message. Kim said it was "very painful" for him to accept Stalin's recommendation. But "we will try to carry it out."[47] In Beijing, Mao was also "astounded" by the news that there would be no Soviet air protection for two and a half months. On October 12, Mao asked Peng to suspend military preparations and return to Beijing for "further consultations."[48]

On October 13, at the Politburo meeting in Beijing, the participants unanimously agreed that since MacArthur's troops were "advancing rapidly to the Chinese border," China must send its troops immediately, even with the delay in Soviet air protection. On the same day, Mao sent a telegram to Zhou in Moscow, informing him of this decision:

> If China does not immediately send its troops to North Korea, MacArthur's troops would rapidly press to the Yalu river, and the domestic and international enemies would be swollen with arrogance. Such a situation would be detrimental to all sides, but first of all it would be most dangerous to the Chinese Northeast region. Our Northeast Border Defense Army would be tied down indefinitely, and the electric power of South Manchuria would be permanently controlled by a hostile situation.
>
> Therefore, we believe that China should join the war, and China must join the war. . . . If we do not enter the war, the entire situation would become extremely perilous to us.[49]

Mao asked Zhou to stay in Moscow for a few more days, to negotiate with Stalin about two important matters. The first was whether China had to "purchase" Soviet weapons, or whether the Soviet Union could "rent" them to China. "As long as we don't take money out of the current budget on economic and cultural constructions or general military and administrative expenses," Mao wrote, "our troops could engage in sustained war in Korea, while preserving our national unity at home." The second and more pressing matter was whether the Soviet Union would actually provide Soviet air protection for the Chinese troops in two or three months.[50]

On October 14, Stalin replied that the Soviet air force would protect Chinese troops crossing the Yalu, but it would not go beyond the Yalu to protect the troops in North Korea. Mao considered Stalin's proposal to let a North Korean government-in-exile be established in Northeast China "a much worse option" than becoming engaged in the conflict. As Mao told his comrades, "If we don't fight now, China will never have a chance to reverse the situation south of the Yalu river." On October 16, Peng announced to all ranking officers of the Chinese Volunteer Army that Beijing had made the final decision: China was to join the war. However, once again, Mao hesitated. Without Soviet air protection in North Korea, he needed to change his initial battle plan. On October 17, once again, Mao asked Peng Dehui to fly to Beijing to devise a new plan.[51]

On October 18, at the Central Committee meeting, Mao said, "In a matter of a few days the U.S. troops will push to our border. We must enter the war now."[52] The participants at the meeting overwhelmingly supported this view. On October 19, 1950, under cover of nightfall, the first Chinese troops crossed the Yalu.

Two decades later, Mao and Zhou still remembered the anguish of their final decision to enter the Korean War, as they told Kim:

> *Mao:* Although we had placed five armies along the Yalu river, our Politburo could not make up its mind. . . . Because of China's wavering, Stalin was disheartened. He told us: "Forget it." . . .
>
> *Zhou:* We proposed two options, and let him choose. What we asked for was that if we joined the war, we would need the support of the Soviet air force.
>
> *Mao:* We only needed the help of the Soviet air force, but they turned it down.
>
> *Zhou:* At the beginning, Molotov had agreed to our request; but Stalin called him, telling him that the Soviet air force could only protect the Chinese troops in the Chinese territory, not beyond the Yalu river, not in North Korea.[53]

The agony of the final decision in Beijing, in fact, ran deeper than Mao and Zhou were willing to concede here. Hu Qiaomu, Mao's top aide from the early 1940s to the early 1960s, recalled, "It was extremely difficult for us to make the final decision to send our troops to North Korea. . . . At that time, the civil war had just ended, we had mountains of problems at home. We did not want a war with the United States. We did not incite North Korea to launch the Korean War." He said he had attended all the Central Committee meetings and Politburo meetings before Chinese troops crossed the Yalu. "It was crystal clear to us at those meetings that it was only with great reluctance that we finally decided to send our troops. In the end, we all felt there was no other alternative when MacArthur's troops were advancing to our border."[54]

After the outbreak of the Korean War, Beijing's top concern was the security of Manchuria—China's only industrial base at that time. Zhou repeatedly stressed the importance of Manchuria, particularly southern Manchuria, for China's industrialization: "Half of China's heavy industry is in the Northeast, and half of the industry in the Northeast is in its south." It was not accidental that in Mao's telegram to Zhou on October 13, 1950, he focused entirely on the security of Manchuria as the primary reason for China's participation in the war. In Mao's view, "even if US troops did not cross the Yalu after they took over North Korea, how could we ever have industrial reconstruction in the Northeast with such a constant security threat from the US military presence across the river?" According to Zhou, if U.S. troops were to stay in North Korea, "how many troops shall we deploy to defend the Sino-Korean border in the future? How could we ever have a secure environment for industrial production in the Northeast?"[55]

And should U.S. troops be stationed indefinitely in North Korea, it could mean the Soviet Union's indefinite occupation of the Lushun naval base. As Article 2 of the Sino-Soviet alliance treaty stipulated, there would be "the joint use of Lushun as a military base should either side be attacked by Japan or any countries aligned with it." In that case, the national resentment could build up quickly, particularly among the urban Chinese, and national unity could be lost.

Finally, and most important of all, a widely shared conviction in China in the post–World War II era held that when facing aggression, retreat and appeasement could only lead to national surrender, but resolute resistance could save the nation. To retain its patriotic credentials, the CCP could not afford to be perceived by the Chinese people as "appeasing" America when its troops were advancing to the Chinese border. Such "appeasement" could not win peace for China, Zhou proclaimed, but could only invite more attacks on China in the future.[56] According to Mao,

> America is trying to stick three daggers into our body: one into our head from Korea, another our waist from Taiwan, and the other our feet from Vietnam. . . . Should there be any change in the world situation, America could attack us from all three directions, and China would be placed in a most perilous situation. If we can beat off the punch resolutely in Korea this time, we can avoid ten thousand punches from all directions in the future.[57]

Thus from the beginning of the Korean War, Mao was preoccupied with the question of whether the U.S. troops would cross the 38th parallel. He often quoted a Chinese proverb: "When the lip is gone, the teeth will be very cold; when the gate is broken, the house will be in peril." When MacArthur's troops crossed the 38th parallel and approached the Chinese border, the delicate balance between nationalism/patriotism and internationalism/communism was quickly reached in Beijing's decision to enter the war. Peng Dehuai recalled in a private conversation with his aides in 1955, "It was not until American troops crossed the 38th parallel, did I become entirely certain that we would enter the war."[58] And as Mao told a Soviet Central Committee delegation in September 1956, "Our 'bottom line' in the Korean War was whether US troops would cross the 38th parallel. If the Americans intervened, but decided not to cross the 38th parallel, we would not join the Korean War. However, should US troops cross the 38th parallel, we would send our troops across the Yalu. That was the 'bottom line' in our final decision to enter the Korean War."[59]

Washington's Decision to Cross the 38th Parallel

Since the onset of the Korean War, the Truman administration had focused on the strategic objective of the UN intervention in Korea, specifically, whether the UN troops should cross the 38th parallel, or should stop south of the parallel, simply "to restore the status quo shattered by the North Korean attack." This decision in turn was based on the Truman administration's assessments of the Soviet and Chinese intentions in the Korean War.

The majority in the Truman administration was convinced that North Korea's attack on the South confirmed the ominous prediction of NSC 68; that is, that by the mid-1950s, the Soviet Union would launch a military attack on the West and the United States. The outbreak of the Korean War was, in their opinion, "the preliminary stage of Third World War," or the first step toward the Soviet military conquest of the world. By sending American troops across the parallel, they argued, future Soviet aggression would be deterred.[60] Furthermore, they argued, crossing the parallel was a matter of moral principle, which was to defend international law and morality. "When all legal and moral right is on our side, why should we hesitate?"[61]

On the other hand, in the view of George Kennan and a few others in the administration, who had been opposed to the basic assumptions of NSC 68,[62] the majority's assessment of Soviet intentions in the Korean War was wrong. Kennan argued that the Soviet Union "did not launch the Korean operation as a first step in a world war or as the first of a series of local operations designed to drain U.S. strength in peripheral theaters." The Soviets simply "saw what looked to them like a favorable set of circumstances" in which they could control South Korea. "They did not think it likely that we would intervene militarily."[63] Thus Kennan was against crossing the 38th parallel, which, he warned, could only invite intervention from the Soviets or the Chinese, "solidify the Moscow-Beijing axis," and deflect the United States' attention from Western Europe.[64]

When Kennan left the State Department in mid-August 1950, the majority's opinion prevailed in the Truman administration. They were aware of the dangers of crossing the parallel, but the attractions were too great. They wanted to have both: to cross the parallel and to avoid a military confrontation with the Soviets and the Chinese.[65] On September 11, 1950, with Truman's approval, NSC 81/1 formally authorized the UN occupation of North Korea, "*provided* there was not entry into North Korea of major Soviet or Chinese forces, no announcement of intended entry, and no threat to counter U.S./U.N. military operations."[66]

According to George C. Marshall, the new Defense Secretary, the United States must not become "involved in a general war in China with the Chinese Communists." To do this would be "to fall into a carefully laid Russian trap."[67] By that time, all the intelligence reports indicated that the Soviet Union would not join the war. And so assessing Chinese intentions in the war became the crucial point in Marshall's decision whether the U.S. troops should cross the 38th parallel.

On September 27, under Marshall's instruction, the Joint Chiefs of Staff directed MacArthur "to make a special effort to determine if the Chinese intended entering the war." MacArthur assured that "there was no present indication of the entry into North Korea by Chinese Communist forces." As a result, on September 29, Marshall instructed MacArthur: "We want you to feel unhampered tactically and strategically to proceed north of the 38th parallel."[68]

On October 3, 1950, Acheson received Zhou's urgent message through Panikkar, which warned that if American troops, not the South Korean troops, crossed the 38th parallel, "China would enter the war."[69] Some officers at the China desk believed that Zhou's warning "cannot safely be regarded as mere bluff." But, they argued, "If China and the USSR are prepared now to accept the danger of a clash with the UN in Korea, that means that they are prepared to risk the danger of World War III, and feel ready to meet that danger." They emphasized, "In such a case, we cannot avoid danger either by retreating from it or by surrendering to the Peiping threat. Either move would increase, not diminish, the danger inherent in the situation for us."[70]

Other officers at the China desk, however, argued that Zhou's warning was simply "bluffing." Panikkar's reports on China had always been "biased and misleading in the extreme," they claimed. It was "unfortunate" that he was "our principal foreign diplomatic source of information in Peiping." Walter McConaughy, former consul general at Shanghai who had known the Indian ambassador, stressed that Panikkar's biases were evident in his judgments about the fundamental nature of Beijing's domestic reconstruction and foreign-policy orientation since the founding of the PRC. He quoted Panikkar as saying that the Beijing Government was in effect "a coalition government," and it had accomplished "genuine reforms," which were "acclaimed by the Chinese people." Even worse, McConaughy said, the Indian ambassador believed that the Beijing government was "free from outside control" and could be expected "to exercise independent judgment." McConaughy thus suggested that the State Department should not trust Panikkar's message from Zhou. "We should exert great efforts to get more and better reports from the European representatives in Peiping," particularly the reports from the British diplomats, "whom we can trust." In conclusion, "it is my considered judgment that Panikkar's reports from Peiping should be taken with a large grain of salt." If Panikkar could not even understand the "subservient" nature of the CCP regime at home and abroad, if he had such "poor judgments" regarding the fundamental nature of the PRC, how could Washington trust his "urgent" message from Zhou concerning the importance of the 38th parallel for China's entry into the war?

> Panikkar's recent urgent message warning of the imminence of Chinese Communist intervention in Korea if UN forces crossed the 38th parallel may have been sent in good faith, but at best they show a poor sense of evaluation. . . . Far from identifying Zhou's message as a possible or probable *bluff*, Panikkar made the Chinese warning sound as alarmist as possible.[71]

Most analysts in the Truman administration agreed with his assessment, believing the Indian ambassador had not told the truth and that Zhou was in fact bluffing. Acheson was convinced that this message was a bluff and that the CCP was launching "a combined Sino-Soviet effort" "to save the North Korean regime."[72] Since the key vote on the UN resolution was to take place on October 4, Truman suspected that Zhou's warning could be part of the "desperate" Soviet attempt to "blackmail" the United Nations to save North Korea.[73] In the opinion of the CIA, if the Chinese had indeed intended to help the North Koreans, they "might have turned the tide at an early point, but that time had passed." Thus "the odds are that Communist China, like the USSR, will not openly intervene in North Korea." Even after the first clear sign of Chinese involvement in late October, the Truman administration still believed that Beijing was "acting at the Soviet behest, continuing the 'war-by-proxy' experiment."[74]

The president, however, did not want to ignore Zhou's warning entirely. At the strong recommendation of the China Desk, based on Oliver Edmund Clubb's analysis, he emphasized that MacArthur must "obtain authorization from Washington prior to taking any military action against objectives in Chinese territory."[75] To make sure that MacArthur would follow this instruction, Truman left for Wake Island to meet the general on October 9. In this meeting, Truman again asked the general about the possibility of Chinese intervention and MacArthur again assured Truman that the chance was "very little." In any case, the Chinese did not have any air force, he emphasized. Should the Chinese try "to get down to Pyongyang," there would be "the greatest slaughter in human history."[76] Truman stressed in particular the importance of not attacking Chinese territory. Military forces could not beat communism in China, he said. Rather, the solution was "a long-term one," which would come about when the CCP leaders could recognize that their best self-interests were not be served by being "subservient to the Soviet Union." Truman then reminded MacArthur that America must not forget its major commitment to Western Europe: "the United States must not become engaged in a major war in the Far East, and thereby dissipate its strength in a peripheral area."[77]

By the end of December 1950, Chinese and American troops were engaged in direct military confrontation in Korea. The casualties from this military conflict were the result of fatal misperceptions concerning one another's intentions. Neither China nor America had intended to have a military conflict with the other, but both sides were driven inexorably toward one in the time of crisis.

The Causes of U.S.-China Military Confrontation in Korea: The 38th Parallel Thesis Revisited

As early as 1960, Allen S. Whiting first pointed out that if the UN troops had not crossed the 38th parallel, the U.S.–China military confrontation in Korea might have been avoided. "Inadequate communication, or the failure to convey accurately to an opponent one's intentions and one's probable responses, played a pivotal role between August and October 1950 in precipitating war" between China and America. As he makes clear, in the time of crisis, "one obstacle to successful communication is the difficulty each side has in projecting itself into the frame of reference within which the other operates. Yet, this is necessary if one is to understand the opponent's interpretation of one's own signals, as well as the motives behind his."[78]

Years later, Hans Morgenthau made a similar point regarding how to assess the Chinese intentions: "It was not necessary in 1950 to have technical intelligence as to the intentions of China. One needed only to take a look at the map and another brief look at Chinese history in order to realize that no Chinese government able to help itself would countenance the approach of a potentially hostile army to the Yalu." In other words, he said, "the foreign policies which Mao Tse-tung has pursued in Asia since 1949 have been the foreign policies of China and not of communism."[79]

In the recent literature, there is an emerging consensus that rejects this thesis about the vital importance of the 38th parallel and the role of misjudgments of each other's intentions in the U.S.-China confrontation in Korea. It has been argued that Mao's national security concepts were deeply shaped by his communist ideology of continuous revolution and the Chinese cultural tradition of Sinocentrism, and that Beijing's major concern before and during the Korean War was how to help Kim promote revolution in the Korean peninsula. As a result, no matter whether the U.S. troops crossed the 38th parallel, the U.S.-China military confrontation would have taken place in Korea.

At the center of the emerging consensus are declassified CCP documents that apparently illustrate an inconsistency between Mao's draft telegram to Stalin on October 2, 1950, pledging to send Chinese troops to Korea, and Zhou's message to the Truman administration on October 3, pledging that if U.S. troops did not cross the 38th parallel, China would not join the war. According to this argument, when Zhou asked Panikkar to deliver his urgent message to Washington, Beijing had already made its decision to join the war. As a scholar writes in his rejection of the 38th parallel thesis:

> Why did Zhou send off this message after top CCP leaders had made the primary decision to enter the Korean War? In the past, without an understanding of the relationship between Beijing's decision to enter the war and Zhou's issuance of this warning, many scholars of the Korean War took this as evidence that Beijing did not want a direct military confrontation with the United States. This warning served as the last chance to avoid direct Chinese-American confrontation, scholars argue, and if

Washington had responded seriously to this warning and ordered the UN forces not to cross the 38th parallel, China's military intervention could have been averted. Zhou's warning has thus been taken by many scholars both in the West and in China as the single most important piece of evidence supporting the argument that the Beijing leadership sent Chinese troops to Korea only to protect the safety of the Sino-Korean border.[80]

So far, the above arguments, and in particular, the use and interpretation of Mao's draft telegram of October 2, 1950, have not yet been seriously challenged in the American literature on the origins of the Korean War.

As mentioned, Mao's draft telegram of October 2 was never sent to Moscow, because of strong opposition from the CCP leaders in their meeting that afternoon. In fact, there is no time stamp on the telegram.[81] Neither is there a copy of Mao's draft telegram of October 2 in Stalin's file. Instead, Stalin received Mao's telegram of October 3, which informed Stalin that Beijing was not going to send its troops to Korea immediately. Stalin's receipt of this telegram is reaffirmed by his message to Kim on October 7, 1950, which read,

> My reply has been delayed because of my consultation with the Chinese comrades, which took several days. On October 1, I sent a letter to Mao Zedong, inquiring whether he could dispatch to Korea immediately at least five or six divisions. . . . Mao Zedong replied with a refusal, saying that he did not want to draw the USSR into the war, that the Chinese army was weak in technical terms, and that the war could cause great dissatisfaction in China.[82]

On October 3, when Zhou asked Panikkar to deliver his urgent message concerning the crucial importance of the 38th parallel for China's participation in the war, he did so after Beijing's decision not to join the war right away. Not until October 7, 1950, when U.S. troops crossed the 38th parallel, did Mao send new messages to both Kim and Stalin, informing them of Beijing's decision to enter the war.

Furthermore, the emerging consensus emphasizes that Beijing began its "military and political preparations" to join the war as early as July 1950. As one scholar argues, "To my surprise, I found that early in August 1950, more than one month before the Inchon landing, Mao Zedong and the Beijing leadership had been inclined to send troops to Korea, and China's military and political preparations had begun even a month earlier."[83]

Judging from declassified CCP and Russian documents, Beijing's "military and political preparations" since early July were based on

Mao's assessment that U.S. troops might cross the 38th parallel. This assessment was illustrated in the exchange of telegrams between Beijing and Moscow. On July 5, 1950, after Zhou had informed Moscow of Beijing's decision concerning the critical importance of the 38th parallel in China's participation in the war, Stalin reaffirmed Beijing's decision: "We consider it correct to concentrate immediately nine Chinese divisions in the Chinese-Korean border region for volunteer actions in North Korea, *in case the enemy crosses the 38th parallel.*"[84]

More important, three times, according to Mao, in early July and late July, as well as early September 1950, he and Zhou "warned the North Korean comrades of the grave danger that MacArthur's troops could land on Inchon from the sea, to cut off the advancing North Korean army's retreat route, and then to cross the 38th parallel."[85] This demonstrates that Beijing's "military and political preparations" from the early July through September were not separate from but intimately tied to its primary concern about the possibility that U.S. troops would cross the 38th parallel.

Finally, the emerging consensus argues, "Mao and the CCP leadership emphasized the central role the Chinese revolution was to play in promoting the worldwide proletarian revolution." Thus China's participation in the Korean War was the direct result of such an ideological outlook.[86] However, as the Chinese and Russian documents indicate, it was Li Lisan, head of the CCP from 1931 to 1933, not Mao and his comrades, who had proposed that the Soviet Union send troops to China to help the Chinese revolution, and "use a successful Chinese revolution to promote the worldwide proletarian revolution." Ironically, this proposition was rejected immediately by Stalin, causing Li's downfall from the CCP's leadership.[87]

Did Mao intend to make China play the "central role" in "promoting the worldwide proletarian revolution?" If so, Mao probably would have sent Chinese troops to the Sino-Korean border region before the outbreak of the Korean War. Historical evidence shows that there was no concentration of Chinese troops along the Yalu at the time. Indeed, on June 23, 1950, one day before the outbreak of the Korean War, Mao had ordered four more corps to move from Eastern China to the Taiwan Strait, to prepare for the upcoming Taiwan campaign, to achieve "national reunification."

Based on historical evidence, this study thus suggests it is mistaken to argue that "there was little possibility that China's entrance into the Korean War could have been averted." To the contrary, declassified

Chinese and Russian documents reaffirm convincingly Whiting's thesis that the 38th parallel played a critical role in China's participation in the war. Moreover, this study suggests it is also incorrect to argue that Beijing and Washington had already regarded each other as "dangerous enemies" and the "stage for a military confrontation had already been set" before the Korean War.[88] To the contrary, before the Korean War, neither the State Department nor Beijing had formulated a confrontational policy. Finally, this study further suggests that there was a direct link between U.S.-China miscommunication in the time of peace, and fatal misjudgments of each other's intentions in the time of crisis. Both could be attributed to these essentially differing assumptions regarding the objectives of the PRC's foreign policy or the basic nature of the Sino-Soviet alliance. Was this alliance driven by communist ideology? Did Beijing attempt to use this alliance to achieve regional domination? These questions would continue to confound American strategic planners in the following administrations in Washington.

The Korean War suddenly erupted, and the Sino-American military confrontation became a tragic reality. It confirmed the worst fears of the Republican conservatives and crushed many liberals' faiths and hopes for the new China. Many State Department officers at the China Desk became the hapless prey of ruthless McCarthyism, because of their support of the new economic strategy toward the CCP and the new military strategy toward Taiwan. Unfortunately, their analytical paradigm underestimated the immense power of nationalism as the force driving the PRC's foreign policy and thus fell short of offering an accurate assessment of Beijing's intentions in the time of crisis. With China's entry into the war, the majority in Washington became convinced that Beijing was more ideological, more loyal to the Soviet Union than the State Department had ever supposed. Between these two major competing policy assumptions with respect to the PRC's intentions, the State Department's were further discredited and the Pentagon's apparently vindicated. The Korean War thus developed a momentum of its own, which was not desired by the Truman administration, but which greatly narrowed the range of its policy options with respect to the future of U.S.-China relations.

CHAPTER SEVEN

Inducement versus Containment
U.S. China Policy under Eisenhower

What were the origins of U.S.-China indirect military confrontation in the Vietnam War? Was it a "necessary war" that frustrated the "communist aggressions," particularly the PRC's call for "world revolutions" in the 1960s, as some scholars have emphasized? Or was it an unnecessary war that was based on misjudgments of "the geopolitical intentions" of Moscow, Beijing, and Hanoi in Southeast Asia, as argued by other scholars and by Robert McNamara, former defense secretary under the Kennedy and Johnson administrations?

To answer these questions, the following chapters will examine three critically important issues in the origins of U.S.-China confrontation in Vietnam, which have not yet been addressed in the recent literature.

First, America's drastically increased involvement in South Vietnam was directly tied to the installation of a "peripheral military containment strategy" toward the PRC in South Vietnam, reversing Acheson's strategy of maintaining a "defensive perimeter" or the "enclave strategy." How was this new strategy of peripheral military containment formulated in 1956? Why could it defeat a competing China policy proposal in the Eisenhower administration of relaxing the China embargo? What were the administration's different policy assumptions concerning the PRC's intentions in that period?

Second, why did Beijing change its Vietnam policy from "peaceful reunification" (1954–1959) to the support of guerrilla warfare in the South in early 1960? What propelled such a major shift in the PRC's Vietnam policy? What was the complex relationship between Beijing's changing domestic programs and its shifting foreign-policy agendas in the 1950s? More important, how was this dire move in early 1960 related to the CCP's foreign policies toward the Soviet Union and the United States, or its changing perceptions of China's international security environment at the time?[1]

Third, were the Eisenhower administration's policy hypotheses concerning Chinese domestic conditions and foreign-policy objectives consistent with the Chinese reality? In other words, what was the driving force behind the PRC's domestic and foreign policies during that period? Was it Soviet communist ideology, or was it Chinese nationalism? Regardless of the ideological rhetoric, were China's domestic and foreign policies, at a deeper level, shaped by China's historical quests for modernity and new identity? If this question is still the major focus of current debates on the origins of the Vietnam War, it was squarely at center stage of the Eisenhower administration's China policy debates in the 1950s.[2]

Formulation of the U.S. Strategy of Peripheral Military Containment, 1956

At a closed congressional hearing in March 1955, there was a brief yet important discussion about the PRC's intentions in the Sino-Soviet alliance: Were the Chinese Communists nationalists first? Or were they "real international communists?" Put another way, was Beijing's ideological loyalty to the Soviet Union rather than Chinese nationalism the primary driving force in the alliance?

> *Mrs. Frances Bolton (House member of the Committee on Foreign Affairs):* I wonder what you know about the attitude of the Chinese toward Asia for the Asians? . . . So the evolutionary processes will tend toward Asia for the Asians, Africa for the Africans?
> *Colonel Culley (military intelligence G-2 officer):* Yes. In that connection, this Africo-Asian Conference might have some interesting indications of that.
> *Mr. Walter Judd (House member of the Committee on Foreign Affairs):* Does your G-2 indicate that nationalism has a more powerful hold and produces more fanatic supporters than communism? Is your answer to Congresswoman Bolton quite the whole story? The impression that the loyalty of Chinese Communists to their color, their national origin, is greater than their loyalty to this doctrine of world revolution? I think the Chinese Communists

use and exploit nationalism. But the hard core is not made up of Chinese patriots, Korean patriots, or Viet Minh patriots; they are world revolutionists.

Mrs. Frances Bolton: But in the meantime they are building something in China, something that I think we have to try to understand a little better.[3]

This discussion highlights the competing American assumptions about the PRC's foreign-policy intentions, assumptions that formed the basis for all American China policy debates in Washington throughout the 1950s. Congresswoman Bolton's question was, in fact, raised again by Alexander Grantham, the British governor of Hong Kong, one month later. In his letter to the State Department in April 1955, Grantham suggested an in-depth debate about the assumptions underlying the entire Western strategy toward the PRC, specifically, about Beijing's intention in the Sino-Soviet alliance. The current China embargo was, he emphasized, based on the supposition that the PRC's motivation in the alliance was to serve the Soviet ambition of world domination. But there could be another possibility, he argued. The CCP might perceive a grave threat from the West and the United States and intend to use this alliance to defend China's national security. Should the latter hypothesis be true, he warned, the current Western strategy of embargo could be "utterly counterproductive."[4]

In this U.S. China policy debate, there were competing policy assumptions about the PRC's domestic conditions and foreign-policy intentions. President Eisenhower held views similar to Grantham's. In 1956, a new China policy proposal, which the president supported, urged relaxing the Western embargo and the U.S. embargo against the PRC in particular. At the last moment, however, the State Department, under Secretary of State John Foster Dulles, overturned the new China policy proposal, kept the total embargo, and further installed the strategy of peripheral military containment toward the PRC in South Vietnam.

Eisenhower did not believe that communist ideology was the foundation of the Sino-Soviet alliance. "Few individuals" in the United States understood "the intensity and force of the spirit of nationalism," the president claimed. "It is my personal conviction," he wrote in his diary, that "almost every one of the new-born states of the world would far rather embrace Communism or any other form of dictatorship" than accept "the political domination" of a foreign government, even if that foreign government might bring a higher living standard. Thus he questioned whether the PRC's ideological bond with the Soviet Union was in fact as strong and predominant as popularly believed. Americans should avoid doing anything to provoke Chinese "nationalist sentiments" further, he said, and "to push the Chinese more deeply into the Soviets' arms."[5] Eisenhower's perception of the nature of the Sino-Soviet alliance was shared and better articulated by the Council on Foreign Relations Study Group on Sino-Soviet Relations, which the State Department had invited to assess the nature of the Sino-Soviet alliance early in 1956.

In one of the working papers, "Some Ideological Aspects of Sino-Soviet Relations," Benjamin Schwartz—one of the Study Group members and a Harvard professor of Chinese history and politics—wrote that the Sino-Soviet alliance was not chiefly based on communist ideology, but rather was "an alliance between two independent centers of power." He concluded that "the Chinese Communist regime is not organizationally controlled by Moscow as are the States of Eastern Europe."

This assumption did not exclude, he noted, the importance of ideology in the alliance. It was still quite possible that both Chinese and Soviet leaders "genuinely believe" that because they were "committed to eradication of the private ownership of the means of production they embody the interests of the downtrodden masses," and that "the non-Communist world is doomed to destruction."

Schwartz considered this ideological bond to have been severely undermined, however, by the Chinese Communists' insistence on their "unique way to industrialization and socialism." As he wrote, after the Stalin-Tito split in 1948, Moscow's theory of people's democracy in Eastern Europe underwent substantial changes.[6] According to Stalin, in the Eastern Europeans' march to socialism, the Soviet path was to be followed. This meant that people's democracies in their later phases should be "in essence dictatorships of the proletariat," which would demand "the liquidation of the kulak and bourgeois classes" through violent revolution, as the Soviets had done. In Schwartz's view, when the Soviets talked about the East Europeans, they also had the Chinese Communists in mind, but the Chinese Communists insisted that they would take "a different, more peaceful path to socialism." The CCP would not physically "liquidate" the rich farmers and bourgeois in China. For Schwartz, it was precisely in this different theoretical emphasis that "an unclosed gap between Soviet and Chinese ideology" would continue to exist. He saw that the weakening of the fabric of ideology as a basis of solidarity could create a situation in which "power interests may ultimately come to assert themselves more strongly in shaping the course of events." With this in mind, he predicted that Titoism might emerge in China and that the Sino-Soviet alliance could be split in the near future.[7]

Robert Bowie, the assistant secretary of state for policy planning, and his staff also disagreed with some basic premises behind the containment strategy. As Robert McClintock, one of his staff members, wrote in a memo in December 1957, "The first fact to be evaluated is the degree of stability and public support of the People's Republic of China." There was possibly "a widespread element of discontent under the communist regime." But he stressed that "for many centuries there have been similar elements of discontent in China against any regime, which was incapable of fulfilling the almost limitless needs of the Chinese population." He believed that in spite of much discontent in China, the PRC had won solid support among the majority of Chinese people and that the best indication for the degree of public support within the PRC was actually the attitudes of the overseas Chinese. In the past, they had supported Chiang. Now they supported Mao. Such a shift in loyalty was brought about, in McClintock's view, by their "feeling of vicarious pride that there is in their estimation a strong government of Peking, dominated by no foreign influence." For the overseas Chinese, the PRC brought about "a recrudescence of Chinese power not witnessed in more than a hundred years, since the treaty which terminated the Opium War in 1842." Thus he emphasized that if the United States could change its policy from containment to a friendlier stance, there might be "the possibility of China evolving first, to become a power not beholden to the USSR, and eventually a power not dominated by Marxist doctrine."[8]

"The greatest defeat in the history of the West," Eisenhower said, was the emergence of the Sino-Soviet alliance in East Asia.[9] A weakening of the Sino-Soviet alliance, he believed, would fundamentally change the structure of the balance of power in favor of the United States. The alliance could split in the near future, but the best way to speed up the split was to ease the Western embargo against the PRC. If the United States assumed that the PRC was not driven by ideological fanaticism, then the PRC could be "induced" by practical economic gains. As he emphasized at a cabinet meeting in 1953, "How are you going to keep them interested in you? If you trade with them, you have got something pulling their interest your way. . . . You are not going to keep them looking toward us and trying to get out from under that umbrella, unless you give something in the way of inducement to come out. You just cannot preach abstraction to a man who has to turn for his daily living in some other direction." It was naïve, he said, to suppose that Chinese Communists could be defeated simply by the blocking of their trade. Instead, to the detriment of American security interests, it would only compel them to rely more on the Soviet Union. In fact, at Eisenhower's first cabinet meeting, he sharply criticized the notion of a "naval blockade" of China as proposed by Senator William Knowland (R-CA), despite his own rhetoric during the presidential election campaign about "releasing" Chiang. What a naval blockade might do, he remarked, was "force all these Communists . . . to depend on Moscow for the rest of their lives."[10]

According to Eisenhower, this strategy of economic inducement toward the PRC could also help America strengthen its allies' economies and save American taxpayers money. He did not believe that the Soviet military threat was imminent, as NSC 68 had assessed in early 1950.[11] He feared that the continuation of a high rate of federal spending on defense in excess of federal income, at a time of heavy taxation, would weaken and eventually destroy the American economy. He was particularly troubled by the federal budget deficit of 1953. To restore a balanced budget, Eisenhower favored cutting expenditures in "National Security," such as foreign-aid programs.[12] To reduce foreign aid, Eisenhower urged an end to American "donation diplomacy."[13] The United States must find "a substitute for the purely temporary business of bolstering the free nations through annual handouts." If, after $33 billion of foreign aid had been disbursed, "the central problem is as far from solution as it is today," something must have been "wrong in our thinking."[14]

The answer was a liberalization of world trade, Eisenhower proclaimed, including a relaxation of the China embargo.[15] In the case of Japan, as he understood it, the "long-term solution" for Japanese economic problems rested in trade between Japan and China. Eisenhower saw the alternative as endless subsidization of the Japanese economy by the American taxpayer.[16] He believed that "the effort to dam up permanently the natural currents of trade, particularly between such areas as Japan and the neighboring Asian mainland, would be defeated."[17] Moreover, some of the U.S. allies in Western Europe urgently needed more markets for their growing output.[18] By liberalizing world trade, especially the China trade, America could certainly get "more security with fewer dollars."[19] He acknowledged that a resumption of commerce between the West and China would provide certain advantages for both sides but posited that the United States should not keep its eye solely on that part of the trading that supported the Chinese Communists. Rather, American policy should be guided by a consideration of the net advantage: wherever trade in nonstrategic goods brought a net advantage to the United States, it must be allowed.[20]

For the majority at the State Department, led by Dulles, it was beyond the shadow of a doubt that Beijing was consumed by communist ideological fanaticism. If some in the State Department had shared Acheson's belief about the possibility of promoting Titoism in China, China's participation in the Korean War shattered their hope. As Walter Robertson, assistant secretary for Far Eastern Affairs, wrote, "The Chinese Communists and, for that matter, the other Asian Communists such as the Viet Minh," were all "real international communists," even though "they may have points of conspicuous physical difference from the Russians." He continued, "To true Communists, the international Communists, it is in terms of Communist doctrine alone that the world and all that goes on in it are to be regarded." All communists, from Moscow to Beijing to Hanoi, he stressed, were guided by the same Leninist principles. First, "the existence of the Soviet Republic side-by-side with imperialist states for a long time is unthinkable. One or the other must triumph in the end." Second, when the Communist Party encounters an obstacle, it must retreat by changing its methods of attack, just as a man who is ascending a steep mountain and reaches an obstacle, finding it impossible to proceed, must then "turn back, descend, seek another path, longer perhaps, but one which will enable him to reach the summit." Third, the "summit" was to eliminate American capitalism by stages: to take Eastern Europe first, then the masses of Asia. Then the United States would be surrounded, falling into communist hands like an "overripe fruit."[21]

Robertson thought the key to understanding the PRC's "true intention" in the Sino-Soviet alliance was whether the CCP had ever "wavered" in its "devotion" to the Leninist doctrine. The answer was no. He quoted Mao as saying in the early 1940s, "I am a Marxist, dedicated to communizing China and the world under the leadership of Moscow." Robertson also spoke with Zhou Enlai in Chongqing in

1945, and recorded Zhou as asking him why so many Americans had called the CCP "agrarian reformers." "With a flash in his eye, Zhou said, 'We are not agrarian reformers; we are Communists and we're proud of it.' " And he also quoted Liu Shaoqi, "the number-two man" in the CCP, as saying in May 1956, "The Soviet road is the road that all humanity must inevitably take." The "overwhelming evidence" proved that, as he quoted from a report of the National Intelligence Estimate in 1956, Beijing tried to "reorganize economic and social institutions and build military power along the lines of the Soviet model."[22]

In the economic arena, for instance, State Department officials stressed in November 1956 that the CCP attempted "to remold the entire economy to conform more closely to the Soviet pattern." Such a Soviet pattern of industrial development was to concentrate on "heavy industry and military weapons—not on goods and services for people," since heavy and defense industries could help the Communists "shift the balance of power in the world." This contributed to the belief that China's industrialization drive was aimed at building "a vast war-supporting industry."[23]

In the political arena, the CCP worked hard to create "a Soviet-style state" in China, although, according to the National Intelligence officers, the CCP's tactics were a somewhat modified form of the Soviet model, showing more "flexibility toward groups which they regard as basically hostile." However, the CCP's tactic of "tension and release" was still meant "to unnerve the populace and to destroy whatever cohesiveness and independent leadership the intellectuals, private entrepreneurs, and well-to-do peasants may have possessed." In this regard, Allen Dulles, director of the CIA, observed, "Students and intellectual unrest are a troublesome challenge to a dictatorship." The CCP had experimented briefly with "placating critics by liberalizing their thought-control system," the Hundred Flowers policy. But "in the face of the far-reaching criticism promptly voiced by Chinese intellectuals," the CCP "resumed the practice of publicly executing students who dared to suggest that China's ills result in part from flaws in the Communist system itself." As far as domestic public support was concerned, even during the period of the Hundred Flowers policy in 1956, the National Intelligence Estimate concluded that "much of the populace" felt "disillusioned or disaffected" with Beijing.[24]

The PRC's foreign-policy objective was, according to Walter Robertson, to drive out American influence from Asia, or, as stated in the National Intelligence Estimate, to create "an Asia ruled by Communist governments." And "this long run objective, derived from Communist doctrine, is reinforced by the traditional Chinese view of China as the center of civilization."[25] Robertson predicted that the PRC would soon be capable of taking over South Korea, Taiwan, Southeast Asia, and Japan by military force, "in the absence of extensive United States counteraction." "The indigenous Communist Parties and the 12,000,000 overseas Chinese in Southeast Asia," according to intelligence officers, could provide the PRC with "unique instruments for undermining non-Communist governments." Should all these goals be achieved, Robertson warned, "our Pacific frontiers might well be pushed back to the west coast and Lenin's dream of surrounding America would be well on its way to fulfillment."[26]

Were Robertson and State Department officials aware of the PRC's five principles of peaceful coexistence of 1954? Yes, they were. However, the majority of these officials understood the PRC's call for peace to be only the means, not the end, of PRC foreign policy. Beijing, following current Soviet strategy, they argued, had opted "political warfare" because "military conquest has for the moment at least proven impossible." The five principles of coexistence were "Communist tactics from the menacing military posture to the alluring and benevolent smile," techniques consistent with the second principle of Leninism. This "subtler threat" could be even "more dangerous" to American interests in Asia. As Robertson wrote in January 1955, "this siren song of coexistence is making some headway—among neutral nations, among some of our allies, and perhaps even with some Americans." Should China continue this course of "political rather than military action," according to the National Intelligence Estimate, "most non-Communist countries will probably have recognized Peiping and established normal economic relations with Communist China." And even worse, the PRC would have been accepted into the UN as "the major Asian power" by 1960.[27]

Such a gloomy prospect worried John Foster Dulles. Like the American pioneer naval strategist Captain Alfred Mahan, Dulles believed that it was of the greatest importance in American diplomacy "to face toward the East as well as the West." "The Western rim of the Pacific was," he argued, "extremely vital to the U.S."[28] And so "to keep the Western Pacific and East Asia out of Communist control is essential to the maintenance of the Pacific Ocean as a friendly body of water with our defenses far from and not close to the continental United States."[29]

If Secretary Dulles had had some ideas about the possibility of splitting the Sino-Soviet alliance, the first Taiwan Strait crisis (1954–55) changed his mind. He considered the motivation behind this crisis to be the CCP's belief that "the entire non-Communist position in the Western Pacific, extending from the Aleutians in the north down to Australia and New Zealand in the south," was "ripe to crumble under the impact of their successive thrusts." To him it was clear that the PRC was determined to become "the hegemonic power" in the Western Pacific and that the Chinese and the Soviet Communists had "the same ideological motivation," though their "manifestations" were different. The Soviet method of "coldly calculated and deliberate steps" might prove "more formidable" in the long run. In the short run, however, the CCP's method of "successive thrusts" became "more dangerous and provocative of war." He warned of the PRC emerging as the new Nazi Germany in East Asia, constituting "an acute and an imminent threat" to American security interests in the Western Pacific.[30]

Dulles urged changing the basic assumptions behind the United States' traditional Open Door China policy, or the principle of preserving China's national sovereignty and territorial integrity. "The territorial integrity of China became a shibboleth," he argued. "We finally got a territorially integrated China, but for whose benefit? The Communists."[31] Certainly, "This is something that cannot be in writing." But between a territorially united China, which was leaning toward communism and serving the Soviet ambition in Asia, and a breakup of China into geographical units, "I prefer the latter."[32]

Based on this assessment of the nature of the PRC and the Sino-Soviet alliance, Dulles insisted that nothing could appeal to the "real international Communists" in Beijing, except a show of a "position of strength." In Robertson's words, "Every basic Communist interest is predicated upon our progressive defeat and final destruction. The only way we can 'get at' them is through manifesting the power to defend our rights and interests."[33] Since the PRC was emerging as a new Nazi Germany in East Asia, posing a more direct or imminent challenge to American security interests, the United States saw the need to employ the strategy of containment to exert much greater pressures on China than on the Soviet Union.

Some U.S. cabinet members acknowledged that the China embargo could not prevent China from getting Western goods in the Soviet market. But they argued that the Chinese would have to transport these goods either through Eastern European vessels or overland via the Trans-Siberian Railway. Such transportation costs, according to their calculation, could represent an annual loss to China of roughly $200 million. If this $200 million were to become available to the PRC, "it would be sufficient to enable China to increase its imports of capital goods by as much as 50 percent, a considerable contribution to China's industrial growth."[34] With this loss to China's industrialization, they anticipated that Beijing would have to turn to the Soviets for more help, and consequently become a heavier burden for Moscow. The Naval Intelligence Agency reported that strained relations had already begun to emerge between the Soviets and the Chinese, "due to differences arising directly from foreign trade difficulties." Even with aid from the satellites, the Soviets had been "unable to satisfy these demands."[35] In the view of the Commerce Department, a failure of the Soviet Union or of China to meet its current and future commitment to the other for goods or services could become "a significant cause of Sino-Soviet friction."[36]

The primary value of the containment strategy, for John Foster Dulles, was not just its ability to impede China's industrial growth but its ability to undermine the PRC psychologically from within. "The sense of ostracism is the greatest pressure we can bring to bear" on the Communists, he believed—to make the Chinese feel that they were "inferior to the civilized world," that they were "not accepted, not respected by the civilized world." According to the psychological theory, there was simply no people, no nation in the world who could endure such "a sense of ostracism" for long. Sooner or later they would collapse from within psychologically. They would be anxious to conform to "the moral norms of the civilized world," striving to become "respectable in the civilized world." Although the nonrecognition policy and the strict economic embargo could retard China's industrialization, in the long run, the sense of "ostracism" was "much more important" for the collapse of the PRC.[37]

There was also another psychological function of the containment strategy, Dulles argued, which was to uphold the morale of the anticommunist governments in the offshore island chains in the Western Pacific, particularly Taiwan. Dulles predicted in August 1956 that it would take at least 100 years to achieve a final split in the Sino-Soviet alliance because of the intimate ideological bond and the CCP's "desperate needs" for Soviet military aid.[38] Given that, how could the United States rebuild the structure of the balance of power in the Western Pacific? He stressed the importance of the matter: "There would be no profit for the non-Communist world," he said, if differences finally emerged between the Soviet Union and Communist China "after our vital interests have already been impaired."[39] The best way to avoid such a situation was "to maintain the off-shore defense positions (Japan, Ryukyu, Taiwan, the Philippines, Australia, and New Zealand)." Taiwan was the "key link" in America's island defense system in the Western Pacific.[40] To the leaders of Taiwan, "the most disturbing and unacceptable" idea was that "Titoism might appear in Red China." Even Dulles's reported statement to Congress in 1953 that "the unholy alliance between Communist Russia and Communist China could not be tolerated" made the Taiwan officials "greatly discouraged." A high-ranking official in Taipei complained to the State Department: "I seemed to feel that the CCP regime would be tolerated once it broke with Soviet Russia. . . . An open declaration of this principle would have a grave effect here."[41]

In short, for the majority in the Eisenhower administration, the containment strategy in East Asia served as an important tool for slowing down China's industrial growth and a powerful psychological weapon for ostracizing the PRC and, conversely, boosting anticommunist morale in Taiwan.

In early 1956, Eisenhower asked the Committee of Foreign Economic Policy (CFEP) to study the issue of relaxing the China embargo. A subcommittee of the CFEP—the Economic Defense Advisory Committee (EDAC)—began to review U.S. embargo policy against the PRC at both multilateral and bilateral levels.[42]

On August 6, 1956, Zhou extended his formal invitation to American journalists to visit China. The timing was perfect. On August 23, 1956, EDAC's draft report "A New Look at U.S. Economic Security Policies and Actions" was completed, and it summarized the consensus within its executive committee. Except for the Department of State, all member agencies, including the Department of Defense and the CIA, had agreed that the United States should relax the China embargo at the multilateral level. They also agreed that the U.S. bilateral China embargo "should in general be reduced to the same level as the agreed multilateral level."

The EDAC executive committee asked the State Department to review this new China policy recommendation. Within the State Department, opinions were sharply divided. The policy planning staff, led by Robert Bowie, strongly supported it. The Office of Chinese Affairs and the Office of Far Eastern Affairs, however, were determined to defeat it. Walter McConaughy, now director of the Office of Chinese Affairs, told Tyson, deputy director of the Office of Far Eastern Affairs, that the United States must continue its total embargo against the PRC, which would have "the moral, psychological and political effect of setting Communist China apart from the rest of the Communist bloc."

Tyson agreed. On the same day, August 24, 1956, he sent a memo to Robertson emphasizing that this new China policy recommendation even tried to relax the U.S. embargo against the PRC. He proposed that the Office of Far Eastern Affairs support "to the fullest the position of the Office of the Chinese Affairs to oppose the EDAC paper."[43]

Robertson instantly approved this position, citing the Leninist principles behind the three major goals China wanted to achieve through the Sino-Soviet alliance. One goal was to control "the manpower of China," which had been achieved in 1949. Another was to control "the industrial capacity of Japan." The Chinese intention in the Korean War, in his view, was to conquer not South Korea but Japan's industrial resources. Third, and the most important goal for the Chinese, was to control "the raw materials and excess food of Southeast Asia," given the rapidly increasing population and food shortage in the PRC. Robertson saw the war in Vietnam, "sparked and supplied by the Red Chinese, as marking the beginning of the Communist bid for Southeast Asia." And the guerrilla warfare in Burma and the rest of Southeast Asia, he claimed, could be all traced to "Red China's instigation and support." It was therefore extremely dangerous, he argued, for Washington to embrace "the appealing idea of splitting Communist China off from the Soviet Union" through a strategy of relaxing the China embargo.[44]

Dulles stood resolutely by the side of Robertson, and Robertson, picking up on Dulles's estimation of how long it would take to dissolve the Sino-Soviet alliance, further explained that in 100 years or so, Beijing might be able to supply its military needs from its own economy. "Until that time comes," it would be "most unrealistic" to expect the CCP leaders to cut themselves off from "their only source of modern war materials."[45]

The year 1956 was particularly important for the United States, Dulles stated. According to the Geneva Agreement, it was the year in which the Vietnamese national election was scheduled, which, he warned, would make the Communist leader Ho Chi-minh the president of a unified Vietnam. After the end of the Geneva Conference of 1954, Ngo Dinh Diem was sent back from America to become the president of South Vietnam in 1955 to forestall such a development. In March 1956, Dulles and Robertson visited South Vietnam. They were "so struck," as Robertson put it, "at the progress Free Viet-Nam made toward stability, security, and strength." In Ngo Dinh Diem, Robertson claimed, "Asia has given us another great figure."[46] As Dulles saw it, the major threat to Ngo Dinh Diem and a free Vietnam, or the "source of all evil" in Southeast Asia, was not the Vietminh, not even the Soviet Union, but "an aggressive, militaristic, imperialist, Communist China."[47]

For Dulles, Southeast Asia was thus "the coming battleground" between the United States and China. He had lamented "the collapse of the morale in France" and its "unwillingness to carry on the struggle" in Indochina. Indeed, "Nothing in Indo-China from the national interest standpoint of the United States is particularly important," he said, "except as it may open the door to this other thing." What was "this other thing"? He meant that if the United States were to give up on South Vietnam after the Geneva Conference, communism would overwhelm all of Southeast Asia and intrude into the Western Pacific through Indonesia. By then, communism would occupy a position in which it could "flank all of our offshore island chain positions," and "cut in between the Philippines and Australia."[48]

That was why, Dulles further argued, America needed to continue its economic embargo against the PRC and also needed a new military strategy—the "periphery military containment strategy"—to build up South Vietnam to stop the PRC's ambition to occupy Southeast Asia through military means. That was also why "the largest expenditures" under the American mutual security program were no longer in Western Europe but in the Pacific and Far East.[49]

However, maintaining the China embargo and installing the new strategy of periphery military containment in South Vietnam were, to Dulles's mind, not just for American national interests. "National action should always reflect principles." Peace alone was not what America pursued. What America pursued was "the right of individuals to exercise their God-given capacity to think and to believe in accordance with the dictates of their mind and conscience."[50] Thus "craven purchase of peace at the expense of principle can result in destroying much of the human spirit on this planet." Neither was economic interest alone what America pursued. America was different: "We have a rather unique tradition. Our nation was founded as an experiment in human liberty." And so for Americans the success story of the United States should never be the "exclusive preserve" of the American people.

And "a central theme" in American diplomacy, he declared, was its "world mission" for universal liberty. Therefore, American leaders must make every effort to put "moral considerations above material considerations" in their China policy debates.[51]

On August 28, 1956, a State Department counterdraft was submitted to the EDAC executive committee.[52] With such strong opposition from the State Department led by Secretary Dulles, the EDAC had to back off from its recommendation to relax the China embargo at both multilateral and bilateral levels. By the end of August 1956, the State Department had successfully overturned the new China policy recommendation and begun to implement its strategy of periphery military containment in South Vietnam.

In sum, by the end of 1956, former Secretary of State Acheson's "enclave strategy," wherein America's "defensive perimeter" in the Western Pacific included only Japan and the Philippines, was reversed. South Vietnam, along with Taiwan, was now added to America's "defensive perimeter" in the Western Pacific. Dulles's policy was that from now on, America must do everything in its power to build up South Vietnam as the "beacon of freedom" and the military fortress against the PRC's "aggressive ambition in Asia."

The China Embargo: U.S. Allies' Opposition and the Eisenhower Administration's Responses, 1954–1958

In September 1952, in the heat of the Korean War, the Truman administration established a separate apparatus, the China Committee (CHINCOM), within the framework of the Consultative Group Coordinating Committee (COCOM). CHINCOM set up a much broader list of export controls for China and North Korea than for the Soviet Union, which came to be known as the China Differential. Moreover, a U.S.-Japan bilateral agreement, also signed in September 1952, required Japan to maintain export controls toward the PRC at a level even higher than the levels of the China Differential.

As the Korean War came to an end in 1953, U.S. allies began to urge the United States to relax the China embargo. Marshall Plan aid was also terminated in 1953, and the sanctions incorporated in this program for forcing compliance with the U.S. embargo ended with it. These developments led to negotiations in late 1953 and early 1954 among the United States and fourteen allies, resulting in a considerable easing of restrictions previously imposed on shipments of strategic goods to the Soviet Union. This relaxation, the U.S. representatives in the COCOM insisted, should not apply to the PRC. Japan and Great Britain in particular, however, were dissatisfied with Washington's insistence and started to press for relaxation on the China embargo.

Eisenhower's approach to the China embargo was very different from that of Secretary Dulles and many cabinet members. Because of his team style of leadership, the president did not impose his own ideas upon the administration. He accepted some of Dulles's arguments, compromised with his cabinet on the others, and formally approved all NSC decisions on the China embargo. It did not mean, though, that he gave up his own approach entirely. He was prepared to ease curbs on Western trade with China, when he had opportunities to do so. Such opportunities arose when America's major allies pushed to remove the restrictions on their trade with the PRC between 1954 and 1958.

Before World War II, Japan's trade with Asiatic countries accounted for 65 percent of its total trade volume, and over half of that was with China. Because of the international embargo policy toward the PRC in the 1950s, however, Japan was obliged to purchase iron ore, coking coal, and other essential raw materials in the U.S. and South American markets, shipped via the Panama Canal and the Pacific Ocean. Japan was also obliged to export manufactured products to non-dollar areas, since the high cost of importing raw materials made it almost impossible to bring the price of Japanese manufactured products down to a competitive dollar-market level. The new Japanese trade pattern thus caused essential difficulties in balancing Japan's dollar account. Indeed, the Korean War was the chief source of the fragile stability of the Japanese economy. And with the close of the Korean War, fear began to rise in Japan that a slump in Japan's economy might well follow. The end of the Korean War would oblige the Japanese to seek alternative outlets for the goods that bolstered the U.S. war efforts.[53]

The most natural source of alternative outlets was obviously the Asian mainland, with the traditional Chinese market the most desirable. The idea that "Japan must trade with Communist China—it is inevitable" was affirmed by such figures as Hisaakira Kano, spokesman for Japan's most powerful industrial group.[54] In industrial circles in Japan, as a Japanese newspaper described in 1953, "the call for China trade is desperate, the demand for China trade contains a sort of hysteria."[55] For the sake of the Japanese business community, Japan must oppose America's "imposition of stricter embargoes for Japan against trade with Communist China than for Western Europe."[56]

The Japanese government was reluctant to facilitate the expansion of Japanese trade with the PRC despite pressure from the business community. And thus the business community's demand for relaxation of China trade control spilled over into the 1953 election campaign and was intensified by the formation of a suprapartisan "Dietman's League for the Promotion of Sino-Japanese Trade." This league became the largest organization in the Diet, consisting of approximately seventy conservative liberals, forty progressives, and all members of the left-wing Socialist party, who pressed for reopening the China trade.[57]

When the new Ichiro Hatoyama cabinet was established in 1955, it immediately took the lead in encouraging China trade. Beyond economic considerations, the expansion of China trade was also considered an essential step toward a politically independent Japan. Prime Minister Hatoyama wanted Japan to adopt a "new approach" toward peace and security in the Cold War. It was possible to have peaceful coexistence among nations with different ideological systems, as long as "no nation tries to impose its own ideological system upon others," as long as every nation respected others' "national sovereignty." He thus proposed to "try his best to promote Sino-Japanese trade at non-governmental levels."[58] For the new foreign minister, Shigemitsu Mamoru, broader relations between the West and China were inevitable, and Japan was well qualified to act as a "bridge." He also believed that a more cooperative relationship between the United States and the PRC, with Japan as a mediator, "could effect a change in Communist China's alignment with the USSR." In the process of mediating between the United States and China, Japan could "reassert her leadership in Asia."[59] The Hatoyama government lost no time in pushing for elimination of the bilateral U.S.-Japanese agreement on the China embargo.

In Washington, State Department officials were suspicious of the political orientation of this demand, believing that the Japanese plan of serving as a go-between was "detrimental" to U.S. security interests in Asia. At the same time, however, they were worried about the deteriorating economic situation in Japan. Dulles stressed, "The Japanese are now running an adverse trade balance of some 1,000 million dollars. They have survived only because, due to the Korean War, we have made heavy purchases in Japan." Such a situation "could not go on for long without disaster." He called attention to "the extreme importance" of finding new markets for Japanese products.[60]

But to Dulles, the new markets for Japanese trade certainly did not include China. The alternative he recommended was the American domestic market. He conceded that Japanese imports might "disrupt U.S. domestic markets," but he insisted that the interests of individual industries that would be hurt by the import of Japanese goods "must be weighed against the overall national interests."[61] The American market had to absorb goods it might not need, unless it was willing "to put Japanese industry at the service of the USSR and Communist China to assist them to bring up their military strength."[62]

Commerce Department officials were deeply upset at the prospect of opening up American markets to Japanese goods. Some domestic industries had already been hurt "severely" by even limited importation of Japanese goods, they argued. "One fact is predominant" in this "unfair competition," Assistant Secretary of Commerce Loshair Teetor complained in a memo to the State Department. This was "the low wages paid in Japan" in comparison with "the high wages" enjoyed by American workers.[63]

Dulles had to admit that in the long run, "there is little future for Japanese products in the United States." He thus turned to Southeast Asia.[64] Why should the United States put 75 percent of its defense expenditure in that area? Because "one of the serious consequences of the loss of Southeast Asia would be its effect on Japan." "If we could salvage a substantial part of Southeast Asia there would be the possibility of developing Japanese trade with that area."[65] But this plan could not be carried out immediately, he said, since the Japanese had left "bad memories" there and "would not be welcomed back easily." In the short run, then, the United States had to buy more Japanese goods.[66]

While the Cabinet was deciding, the Japanese economy worsened. In March 1954, the American Embassy in Tokyo warned, "A serious economic crisis may develop as early as this summer as a result of the continuing deterioration in Japan's foreign exchange position."[67] At this juncture, Eisenhower intervened. He strongly advised his cabinet to offer concessions to Japan. As he commented at a cabinet meeting in August 1954, "It is an absolute fallacy to say that there should be no East–West trade. Instead, some Japanese trade with her Communist neighbors should be encouraged and would set up influences behind the iron curtain, which . . . would hurt Russia rather than help the Soviets because it would turn Peiping away from Moscow and create a friction between the Communist countries."[68] The cabinet members had to accept Eisenhower's proposal.[69] In the fall of 1954, the NSC agreed to release Japan from its obligation under the U.S.-Japanese bilateral agreement to maintain export controls with China at a higher level than the level of the China Differential in Western Europe.[70]

While the Japanese were pressing for relaxation of the bilateral U.S.-Japanese agreement on the China embargo, the British demanded total abolition of the China Differential. For the Labour Party, assessing the PRC's intention in the Sino-Soviet alliance was closely related to the assessment of the basic nature of the PRC. To some from Labour, the PRC was a great improvement over Nationalist China under the KMT. Regardless of whether the PRC was hostile to the West or represented an ideology alien to the British, they were willing to welcome it because they thought it a better alternative for the welfare of the Chinese people. Many others from the Labour Party, however, took the position that communism was not an entirely good thing for the Chinese at the time, although they conceded that communism in China and Asia might be "objectively a liberating force which may well provide the kind of authoritarian regime that in Western Europe was the immediate successor to feudalism and the necessary prelude to political democracy." Still others from Labour saw in the PRC two opposing tendencies: "On the one hand, rational thought, good administration and respect for the common man; on the other, unreasoning faith in dogma, bureaucracy and contempt for the individual." In their opinions, "the development of China is likely to take completely different paths according to which tendency predominates." It was thus their conviction that the West should try its best to see that the former tendency in China prevailed through a friendly China policy. Generally speaking, officials from Britain's Labour Party interpreted the nature of the PRC not in terms of communist power versus Western powers, but of nationalism versus imperialism.[71]

Accordingly, the predominant Labour view was that China, "if properly handled," could "in the long run" be separated from Moscow. In the words of British prime minister Clement Attlee, "There is a strong mixture of Chinese nationalism in their Communist attitudes." Therefore, "there is a chance of Titoism" in China.[72] According to British foreign minister Ernest Bevin, the Western countries should not cooperate to contain China, but should "cooperate to give China a chance."[73]

For the British Tories the nature of the PRC was viewed not in terms of nationalism versus imperialism, but in terms of power politics. In China they merely saw a vast shift in the world balance of power in favor of the Soviets. However, they advocated accommodation of the PRC. A hostile policy, in their view, meant a very unstable relationship between London and Beijing, which might lead to the nightmare of Western involvement in a land war with China and of Soviet moves in Europe and the Middle East to take advantage of this development. Indeed, Winston Churchill declared that nothing could be more foolish than for Western armies to be "swallowed up in the vast spaces" of the PRC. The position of the Tories was that, given the decline of British military and economic strength in the postwar era, British national priorities in world politics inevitably put Europe first, the Middle East second, and Southeast Asia and the Far East third. They thus believed that stability in the Far East could best serve British national interests. A stable relationship between the West and the PRC, in their view, could not be achieved by a containment policy against the PRC. As Churchill wrote to Eisenhower in 1954, "The problem of peace is to discover a means whereby differently minded nations can avoid war, not to invent a formula to which all nations to prove their right-mindedness must necessarily subscribe."[74]

Thus Labour and the Tories shared the idea that Titoism could grow in China and that lifting the China embargo could surely help to split the Sino-Soviet alliance. In the wake of the Korean War, the British Conservative government immediately tried to ease the China embargo. But unlike Labour, the Tories were more willing to keep in step with Washington to achieve that goal. It did not want to take drastic actions to abolish the China Differential until the pressure from Parliament became irresistible. "All eyes now turned to Peking," a French newspaper reported in London. Competition in the China market was indeed remarkable, as a Western German correspondent observed: "British, West German, French, Japanese . . . feel triumph when they manage to conclude a contract with Communist China," and "they feel jealous and worried, if somebody else manages to do the same." There was also widespread concern for Hong Kong, which depended on China for the bulk of its food.[75] A British businessman told the British governor of Hong Kong how he felt about the China embargo: "It is very much like a man would feel," he said, "if you were to give him a knife and tell him that it was in his interests to cut his own throat."[76]

The voices for easing the China embargo at Westminster were rapidly becoming louder and angrier. In the parliamentary debates, many members pointed out that export licenses were refused for the export to China even of pumps for coal mines, stationary engines, electric coal drills, and so forth, amounting to a total of 10 million pounds' worth of general industrial machinery.[77] The licenses were denied because the equipment was regarded as "strategic."[78] Members on either side of the political divide in Parliament were worried that "we have lost very heavily from these embargoes at a time when our economic situation is not bright . . . and when our export trade is vital to the existence of this country." Although Britain's China trade currently accounted for only a small part of the British foreign trade, in the long run, "the Chinese market would surely help to maintain the not too certain chances of full employment in this country."[79]

Members of Parliament from both the Labour and the Conservative parties thus strongly urged the Tory government to break free from America's China embargo policy. As Sir Walter Fletcher, a Conservative at Westminster, claimed, "So far the policy of the government has been one of willingness to listen too much to American requests for restriction and control and has engendered in our government suspicion of every move of the commercial community. On the issue of strategic trade controls, the policy must be that of Whitehall and not Washington."[80]

Prime Minister Anthony Eden's government had to take into account the possibility that if the British economic situation continued deteriorating while strategic trade controls still existed, the opposition party could seriously challenge the government's position. In 1954 it began to push the Eisenhower administration much harder than before to abolish the China Differential.

How did the Eisenhower administration respond to British pressure for the end of the China Differential? Since early 1953, the Senate Permanent Subcommittee on Investigations, headed by Senator Joseph McCarthy (R-WI), had begun to accuse the British of trading with China. McCarthy kept reminding the public that American soldiers were being killed in Korea with materials supplied by America's allies. A hostile public opinion against Sino-British trade quickly developed. In a poll taken by Representative Thomas Martin (R-IA), for instance, as many as 89.7 percent of his constituents urged stopping U.S. financial aid to the British should they continue their trade with the PRC.[81] Representative Walter Judd (R-MN) sent Eisenhower "the latest Minnesota poll," which, Judd said, would "give pause to any administration people who are inclined to be over-influenced by the Edens."[82]

Thus in preparing for the 1954 congressional elections, both parties were anxious to show a tough stance on the China embargo. Calvitt Clarke, chairman of the Richmond Republican Committee in Virginia, warned the Republican candidates that "any soft nod" on British-China trade could make the Republicans "lose their majority in the next election in both House and Senate," given "the grass roots sentiment as I see it here."[83] Senator Knowland openly asserted, "The United States must cut off military and economic assistance unless the British do what we want."[84] The *Manchester Guardian* was deeply concerned that the McCarthy hearings could so rouse the American public that the Eisenhower administration might be forced into a retreat.[85]

The president did not want to be forced into a retreat. In Eisenhower's view, congressional reactions to the China embargo reflected "a far greater concern for local political sentiment than for the welfare of the United States." He wrote in his diary, "Each of these Congressmen thinks of himself as intensely patriotic; but it does not take the average member long to conclude that his first duty to his country is to get himself re-elected." Particularly in the case of the China embargo, whenever there was a conflict between national and local priorities, "local priorities usually won out."[86]

Eisenhower therefore stressed the importance of "educating public opinion on the question of trade between the Free World and the Communist countries." He predicted that this question might become increasingly important for U.S. allies. When it did, he then predicted that "certain well-known elements in Congress" will open up with their "preposterous and demagogic" question: " 'Isn't it awful for our allies to trade with our enemies?' " For him, it would be "a great pity" not to anticipate this, rather than "get caught unprepared and have to fight a rear guard action with denials." In 1954, he took action, asking Henry Cabot Lodge Jr., U.S. ambassador to the UN, to send a letter to the State Department to set up certain standards for educating the public. Lodge's letter, based on Eisenhower's ideas, set up two standards. The first concerned the allies' heavy dependence on foreign trade. The second concerned the idea of "net advantage" for the United States in its allies' trade with China.[87]

The Office of Far East Affairs at the State Department complained that Lodge's letter was "misleading and contrary to NSC policy." Further, it could be taken by some Western nations as "encouragement to broaden their trade with Communist China," when the United States was "anxious to continue maximum feasible pressure on the Chinese Communists." The Office of Chinese Affairs also protested that McCarthy would interpret this letter as an open invitation to U.S. allies to expand trade in nonstrategic goods with Communist China.[88] Secretary Dulles made a noncommittal nod to Lodge's letter. He praised the president's idea, which, he said, was "absolutely right." However, he told Lodge that the State Department had already prepared some monographs on this topic and issued them to the public for education.[89] Lodge's letter was soon buried in the files of the State Department.

In 1954, in the aftermath of the McCarthy hearings, Eisenhower had to retreat because he needed to push Congress to pass the Mutual Security bill, which would continue American aid to the NATO countries. If Congress turned it down, he was afraid that the British and other allies would not get the necessary U.S. dollars to support their fragile economies and defense programs, which might endanger the whole collective defense system in Western Europe. Hence Harold Stassen, the director of the Mutual Security Administration, who was sympathetic to British trade with China, advised the British at the Dulles-Eden meeting in 1954 that the British must make concessions to the U.S. embargo policy to assist in "getting us out of the jam we were in."[90] The Eden government had to bow to these American domestic political pressures. In December 1955, however, Secretary Dulles informed the cabinet, "The British now present us with the prospect of total disintegration of the multilateral control system," with or without America's approval. The cabinet then agreed to discuss the China Differential at the forthcoming Eisenhower-Eden talks, to be held in early 1956.

In remarking on the British position, the Office of Chinese Affairs and the office of Far Eastern Affairs had persistently asked "to overcome the current trend within the administration of appeasing the Chinese Communists."[91] Commerce Department officials also called for continued pressure on the British to retain the China Differential. To permit Sino-British trade would constitute "discrimination against American businessmen," they argued, since "we maintained a complete embargo" against the PRC.[92] "From a strictly military point of view," the Defense Department and the Joint Chiefs of Staff (JCS) wrote, any relaxation of the China Differential would cause "the gravest probability that the Pacific offshore island chain will fall under Communist domination."[93]

However, U.S. military and diplomatic representatives in Europe were almost unanimous in their opinion that the United States should not exert more pressures on its allies to keep the China Differential. Joe Walstrom, director of the Office of Security Trade Controls, U.S. Mission to NATO, told Washington that the great majority of U.S. allies wanted to abolish the China Differential, "since they found it increasingly difficult to defend vis-à-vis public opinion in their own countries."[94] The Office of European Affairs at the State Department agreed. They argued that the allies' budget problems were "no longer being relieved" by the Marshall Plan. As a result, "some minor adjustments are inevitable" in order to maintain "the essentials" of the "China Differential."[95]

The cabinet agreed to make "some minor adjustments" on the China Differential. But it insisted that the United States would offer "to acquiesce only in a *minimum* adjustment whereby *19 items* would be dropped from the multilateral China embargo list."[96] The president began to show that he did not entirely agree with his cabinet. He told Eden that the nineteen items that his cabinet had approved for decontrol were indeed not sufficient to negotiate with the British government. When Deputy Undersecretary of State Herbert Prochnow tried to persuade Eden that "the net gain" in relaxing the China Differential "would be greater for the Chinese Communists," Eisenhower immediately disagreed. Secretary Dulles told Eden, "It would be very important to avoid any indication that there has been a change in policy." The president shook his head and said, "Surely we cannot say that we made a flat decision in 1952 that cannot be altered in any detail."[97] The Eisenhower-Eden communiqué, instead of calling for a maintenance of the China Differential, announced that "the restrictions on trade with Communist China are to be reviewed in the light of changing conditions" by both governments.[98]

The Eisenhower-Eden communiqué provoked nationwide opposition to any relaxation of the China Differential. Only a few newspapers, such as the *New York Herald Tribune,* the *Christian Science Monitor,* and the *Detroit Free Press,* were sympathetic to the president's decision to revisit the embargo. Most of the newspapers, scattered from New England to the Far West, expressed their uncompromising position.[99] "Why beef up a known and remorseless enemy?" asked the *New York Daily News,*[100] which had the nation's largest circulation at the time.

A nationwide poll, taken by the National Opinion Research Center in early February 1956, showed that 61 percent of the American public "disapproved of changing U.S. policy to permit Americans to trade with Communist China."[101]

In Congress, Senator John McClellan (D-AR) led the attack on the Eisenhower administration's China policy. McClellan's Government Operations Committee held hearings on the China embargo intermittently between February 15 and March 29. The committee objected that "in a recent visit of Prime Minister Eden to the United States, Great Britain asked that controls over shipments to Communist China be relaxed," and Eisenhower had indicated that "this proposal will be studied." The purpose of the hearings was to see "whether the Battle Act provisions will be invoked against this action."[102]

When the Democrat-controlled committee was investigating the Republican administration's activities on the China embargo, the Republicans in Congress were eager to join their efforts. Knowland, the Republican Minority Leader in the Senate, praised the McClellan committee's position. He claimed that the Communists were using the plea for peaceful co-existence and trade to gain time, so they could "take over country after country without risk." Beijing, he argued, would interpret every effort of the West to trade with it as "a sign of weakness." "To show weakness to the Communists," he warned, "inevitably invites further aggression."[103]

Like the McCarthy subcommittee, the McClellan committee tried to pressure the administration by threatening to reduce financial aid to the British. McClellan and other Democrats served notice in the Senate that they would not vote for the $49 billion asked for by the administration for aid to NATO, "unless the whole matter" on the China embargo was "satisfactorily cleared up."[104] An article in the *New York Herald Tribune* opined, "Plainly the administration is in for trouble in the Senate on the whole foreign aid program, because of what has been done . . . to satisfy allies' pressures for more trade with the enemy."[105]

Eisenhower attempted to resist this pressure from Congress. He told the legislative leaders "this country could not absorb more European products at the end of Korean War and did not want to keep giving cash grants to sustain Europe." Trade, including East–West trade, became "particularly necessary" to the health of the allies' economies.[106] He also warned that a publicized investigation of trade between the NATO governments and Russia and China could lead to serious problems for U.S. allies: if "the desperate economic straits" of some of the

Western countries were to become known, the Soviets and the Chinese could "take advantage of the situation." They could either "refuse to trade" or "exact more vigorous terms."[107]

The State Department decided to join the congressional efforts to persuade the president to change his mind. Robertson complained that he was "shocked" at Eden's position on the China embargo: "A position without principle," he said, "as illustrated by Eden's remark that 'nobody was ever hurt by trading and making a few dollars.' "[108] But Secretary Dulles had a better way to persuade the president. He stressed to Eisenhower "the difficulties being placed in the way of the passage of the Mutual Security Act" because of the McClellan hearings. He specifically referred to "the danger of possible restrictive amendments which would prohibit aid to countries trading with the Communist Bloc." Herbert Hoover Jr., undersecretary of state, also warned about the partisan politics of an election year: due to "the desire of certain committee members to engage in partisan politics" by using the "explosive" issue of China embargo, he said, it was indeed unwise for the administration "to engage in a formal high-level negotiation" aimed at relaxing the China Differential.[109]

In the election year of 1956, the administration faced a dilemma: "If we do not acquiesce in some substantial relaxation of the control system, we may jeopardize the entire multilateral control system." However, "if we do acquiesce in any substantial relaxation, such action may give rise to opposition in this country, particularly in Congress, which could affect the trade control system and jeopardize other programs contributing to the mutual defense effort."[110] The president could not solve this dilemma until after the election of 1956.

In December 1956, after the presidential election, EDAC suggested to the CFEP that the United States should exert pressure to bring about an overall tightening of multilateral trade control against China.[111] The president immediately made it clear to Clarence Randall, chairman of the CFEP, that he believed the China embargo should be "liberalized" rather than "tightened." He proposed that Washington make significant concessions to meet the British demands.[112]

The CFEP then announced that due to "the fact that the president's trade program as a whole contemplates gradual reduction of trade barriers everywhere," and due to "the likelihood that the entire control mechanism will disintegrate unless the U.S. makes a substantial concession to the wishes of its allies," the U.S. should provide for "a substantial reduction" in the CHINCOM list. The "new policy" would retain a "meaningful China Differential," but one much less than the existing China Differential.[113] In February 1957, the NSC approved the new policy.

Nevertheless, the new policy, as the London *Economist* analyzed, still fell far short of the desires and intentions of the British, Japanese, French, and others, and failed to meet their demand for complete elimination of the China Differential.[114] On May 15, 1957, Dulles received a letter from British foreign minister Selwyn Lloyd, making clear that London would "have to gain greater freedom with respect to China trade and do so quickly because of the Parliamentary situation." Lloyd told Dulles that in Britain, "there was rising criticism of the United States in areas where there was unemployment, which was ascribed, rightly or wrongly, to U.S. refusal to let them trade with China."[115]

Dulles suggested to Eisenhower that he send a letter to British prime minister Harold Macmillan to the effect that the United States could not go all the way to meet the British and that the British must go further to meet Washington. Eisenhower told Dulles, however, that "basically, the Chinese Communists and the Soviets should be treated alike in this matter."[116] Nonetheless, he sent a message on May 16, protesting against the proposed British move and asking Macmillan to reconsider this decision.

Knowing that Eisenhower's apprehensions were "chiefly caused by the strong feeling in the U.S. Congress," Macmillan replied, "This Chinese business has become almost as much an obsession with us as it appears to be with your Congress." On May 28, he emphasized to Eisenhower, "The commercial interests of our two countries are not at all alike. We live by exports—and by exports alone." His government could no longer maintain the China Differential and would make a statement to this effect to Parliament the following day.[117]

In his reply, Eisenhower wrote that "as an individual, I agree with you that there is very little of profit in the matter of China Differential either for your country or for any other. . . . We understand your predicament, even though we may be compelled, in the final result, to differ sharply in our official positions."[118] On May 29, the British government declared in Parliament that it had decided to abolish the China Differential.

The Defense Department and the JCS were outraged. They urged Eisenhower to retaliate.[119] For them, "limited sanctions" against the British were absolutely necessary, to keep up anti-Communist morale in the island chains of the Western Pacific.[120] However, Eisenhower stood firm in his support for the British decision. He held a news conference and appealed directly to the American people:

> Now there is a very great division of opinion in America, about the value of trade with Communists.
>
> There is one school of thought that thinks any trade with the Communist countries is bound to be to their benefit; whereas there is another school of thought that thinks that . . . trade in itself is the greatest weapon in the hands of a diplomat, and if skillfully used, it can be used as a very great instrument of governmental policy.

After outlining the opposing positions, the president said, "Frankly, I am personally of the school that believes that trade, in the long run, cannot be stopped. I don't see as much advantage in maintaining the Differential as some people do."[121] Macmillan wrote with relief that "largely due to the President's influence, this Chinese affair which had caused me much concern, was not elevated by the American government or press into a great issue."[122]

With Eisenhower's quiet yet firm support, American and British experts began talks over revision of the China embargo list. The talks were followed by five months of negotiations in Paris, within a fifteen-nation Consultative Group. In June 1958, the group declared that the West would drastically reduce the COCOM and the CHINCOM lists of strategic items and merge the two lists into one. The China Differential was now formally eliminated.[123]

American China Policy Debate, 1957–58

By mid-1958, significant changes in Western attitudes toward the China embargo made the prospects for increased trade between China and the West "take on their rosiest hue since the onset of the Cold War ten years ago," a *New York Times* editorial stated. The *Los Angeles Times* predicted that the Eisenhower administration might soon decide "to accept as inevitable the gradual breakdown" of trade barriers between the United States and the PRC. In fact, with the collapse of the China Differential at the multilateral level in 1957–58, a major argument for the China embargo—to bring maximum pressure to bear upon China—could no longer work. Washington was confronted with a China policy dilemma: Should the United States give up its bilateral China Differential?

At the president's request, CFEP again began to discuss what advantage the United States might accrue from a relaxation of bilateral trade control with China. In August 1957, its conclusion was that the "net advantage" was not in America's favor. The economic implication of a resumption of Sino-American trade for the American economy would be "insignificant." According to the CFEP and the Commerce Department, the increase in American exports after the relaxation would at best range from $40 to $70 million annually. Sales possibilities would exist mainly in iron and steel products, as well as fertilizers, but even so, American iron and steel products might not be "very competitive" in the China market, since Japanese goods had "a clear advantage." American imports from China might amount to a little more than American exports to China and would consist mainly of tung oil, tea, silk, hog bristles, cashmere, and handicrafts. While American consumer selection could be broadened for certain commodities, "sizable imports" of China's low-priced consumer goods could trigger "additional impetus to pressures for increased U.S. tariff or import restrictions." The problem of competition between very low-priced consumer goods and American domestic products could become "far more acute." The CFEP agreed that China "might well represent an important *potential* market for U.S. products." But while the Sino-Soviet alliance was still in place, the U.S. could not fully tap the potential. The CFEP concluded that a relaxation of the U.S. bilateral China embargo would have "no major impact on the American economy in terms of the balance of payments, providing employment, or supplying needed raw materials."

The CFEP also guaged that the impact of the resumption of Sino-American trade upon the Sino-Soviet alliance would also be "insignificant." After relaxation, China's gains from trading with the United States would be "modest," giving Beijing no substantial motivation to expand China's trade with the United States. As a result, the economic bond between the countries would not be so strong as to "materially affect China's dependence on the Soviet Union."

Finally, the impact of a resumption of Sino-American trade upon the Congress would be "disastrous." It would be almost "impossible" for the administration to overcome the resistance of Congress to appropriate any money for a mutual security program in Europe. Thus in August 1957, in the aftermath of the British abolition of the China Differential, the CFEP—which had been sympathetic to Eisenhower's position in the administration—recommended holding out on the U.S. bilateral China Differential.[124]

Following Zhou's invitation for American journalists to visit China in August 1956, and with the Hundred Flowers policy gathering momentum in China throughout the spring of 1957, American journalists increased pressure on the State Department to allow them to accept Zhou's invitation.

Robertson was deeply worried about such a development. America's opposition to the PRC was not based on "the disapproval of an ideology or an economic system, much as we abhor both," he argued in February 1957. Indeed, "we recognize many totalitarian governments" and "we have not been unwilling to meet with them in the world forum of the United Nations." Neither was America's opposition to the PRC based on an "emotional reaction" to the Korean War. Instead, America's China policy was based on a combination of American national interests and American principles.

First, there was the consideration of "the security interests of the United States and the free world's collective security." Taiwan and South Vietnam were "vital links" in the free world's island chain of defense in the Pacific. That was the reason the United States could establish diplomatic relations with the Soviet Union but not China. Second, there was the consideration of "the interest of Asian countries in escaping Communist enslavement." If the United States were to abandon Taiwan, "to placate the insatiable Red Chinese," no country in Asia would feel that they could "rely on the protection of the United States against the Communist threat." Third, there was the consideration of "the long-range interests of the Chinese people themselves." America must not recognize the PRC and must continue its embargo, since "the defiant Marxist impostors in Peiping" were supported by "only an infinitesimal fraction of the Chinese people." This regime was kept in power "by bloody purges and the liquidation of some 18 millions of Mainland Chinese in 7 years" from 1949 to 1956. The regime's foreign policy consisted of endorsing "the Communist puppet Viet Minh armies." Furthermore, the PRC refused to release "all Americans detained in China against their will." Indeed, "by every standard of national and international conduct," the PRC was "an outlaw nation." It was America's "sacred mission" to oppose "the defiant, real international communists" in the PRC.[125]

In the wake of the British abolition of the China Differential, Dulles made a highly publicized speech, "Our Policies toward Communism in China" in San Francisco, on June 28, 1957. He was sharply critical of all arguments for recognizing the PRC or relaxing the U.S. bilateral China Differential. He focused especially on the argument that "if we assist the Chinese Communists to wax strong, then they will eventually break with Soviet Russia and that is our best hope for the future."

"No doubt," he said, there were "basic power rivalries" between Russia and China in Asia. But the Russian and Chinese Communist parties were also bound together by "close ideological ties." Perhaps, if the "ambitions" of the Chinese Communists were "inflated" by successes, they might eventually clash with the Soviet Union. Perhaps, too, he said, "if the Axis Powers had won World War II, they would have fallen out among themselves." But "no one suggested that we should tolerate and even assist an Axis victory because in the end they would quarrel over the booty—of which we would be part." His conclusion was clear: "neither recognition, nor trade, nor cultural relations, nor all three, would favorably influence the evolution of affairs in China."[126]

In mid-1958, the second Taiwan Strait crisis further confirmed his assessment of the PRC's intention to become the new hegemon in East Asia. It was indeed "crucial," he said, "to appraise the Chinese Communists' intentions" in the shelling of Jinmen and Mazu—two tiny offshore islands near the mainland. He believed that because of the coming congressional elections, Soviet leader Nikita Khrushchev saw "a chance for the Soviets to show the strength of the Sino-Soviet alliance" in the Western Pacific. Beijing's intention was to help Moscow to probe "the firmness of the Western position in the Pacific." It was "apparent," he said, that "the trigger to this grave threat to the free world" was Khrushchev's visit to Beijing in early August 1958, one month before the shelling. For him, "the nature of the menace" was clearly not only to Taiwan, but "to the whole Southeast Asian position," and even "to Pearl Harbor itself." A White House statement thus placed this crisis in "a broad context" and affirmed the American determination "to keep Southeast Asia free."[127]

After the crisis was largely over in early October 1958, the secretary was more anxious to strengthen the KMT position on Taiwan. He often mentioned Pericles' speech to the Athenians at the time of Athens' dispute with Sparta. Pericles said that the little town of Megara was not the end in itself; rather its defense was "a symbol of the resolution of the two contending parties that they could not give up their positions piecemeal to avoid risk." He quoted Pericles as saying that "the psychological elements" in the situation were of "great importance" and that "the nature of the national character is not divisible." For Dulles, Taiwan was therefore to be judged not in terms of its size but in terms of its moral and psychological significance for Southeast Asia and the entire Western Pacific.

Dulles died on May 24, 1959. To the last days of his life, he was more convinced than ever that the United States must not repeat Britain's fatal mistakes of appeasing Hitler before World War II. It was time for the United States to draw a line in Vietnam and the Taiwan Strait, as the British should have in Munich, he insisted, to oppose the PRC's "fanatic communist expansionism" in Asia.[128]

In 1958, the president was particularly eager to have the Reciprocal Trade Act and Mutual Security bill passed in Congress. He wanted to give the Reciprocal Trade Act five years instead of a one-year provision, as a major part of his plan to free world trade, especially the trade between the United States and Western allies.[129] He also proposed an increase of $700–800 million in the mutual security program in the Mutual Security bill, though the president considered even this amount to be $600 million short of what was actually needed. Therefore, any cuts Congress might make in the bill, he said, would have "most unfortunate" effects on America's European allies and on America's national security itself.[130]

However, the situation in Congress in 1958 was not favorable for passage of these measures, because the majority of Democrats were not enthusiastic about either.[131] Eisenhower felt his chances of success would now lie in the hands of the Republicans. "Unfortunately," Eisenhower wrote in his diary, "political individualism has been developing among the Republican Congressmen," who were "eager to run for Congress only on their own individual platform, repudiating completely such administration programs as the Reciprocal Trade Act and the Mutual Security Bill." The president was worried that "the most vitally important" programs for the long-term security interests of the United States might be weakened or even defeated by such "political individualism of Republican Congressmen." To overcome such a trend, Eisenhower turned to the powerful Republican Right on the Hill, most of whom were staunch supporters of the KMT government on Taiwan.[132]

Eisenhower knew too well that any further move toward a major change in U.S. bilateral trade control with China, after his significant concessions to the Allies, would undoubtedly precipitate furious rows in Congress, particularly among the Republican conservatives. Such an outcome, as he wrote, might permanently damage other, more urgent programs in his administration's security agenda, such as the Mutual Security bill for NATO.

Congressional pressure, however, was not the only reason for Eisenhower's retreat on the U.S. bilateral China Differential in 1958. During the second Taiwan Straits crisis in the summer and fall of 1958, the president became increasingly resentful toward, as he called it, Beijing's "expansionist intentions" in the Western Pacific.

While Eisenhower understood the nature of the Sino-Soviet alliance differently in the early years of his term, he had not established a coherent strategy to combine his new approach to the China embargo with his policy toward Taiwan, as Acheson had done in 1949 and early 1950. Acheson thought that if the United States wanted to wean China away from the Soviet Union through the weapon of trade, it would have to withdraw eventually from Taiwan. As long as the American military force was in the Taiwan Strait, Acheson believed, Chinese nationalist resentments would always be directed toward America. In contrast, Eisenhower regarded his new approach to the China embargo and his policy toward Taiwan as two separate policies, rather than two parts of one integrated strategy. Eisenhower supported easing the U.S. China embargo to drive a wedge into the Sino-Soviet alliance but concluded that America must support Taiwan and its key position in the island defense system of the Western Pacific. As he wrote, before the French withdrawal from Vietnam, "we had both Chiang and a strong, well-equipped French Army to support the free world's position in Southeast Asia." But the French had left. This situation made it "clearer than ever that we cannot afford the loss of Chiang, unless all of us are to get completely out of that corner of the globe. This is unthinkable to us."[133]

In the aftermath of the second Taiwan Straits crisis in 1958, Eisenhower began to change his mind about the PRC's intentions and particularly its objectives in Southeast Asia and the Western Pacific. By the end of 1958, he had accepted Dulles's arguments that the United States must uphold its bilateral China Differential and continue its military containment of the PRC in South Vietnam. By the end of his term, the president began to wonder if China was indeed a "willing partner" in international communism.[134] He began to mention "the specter of the Yellow Peril." The United States had to keep "a sharp eye on the Chinese" because they were a "smart people, . . . tremendous in number, and their leaders seem absolutely indifferent to the prospect of losing millions of people." Dulles once told Wellington Koo, the Chiang Kai-shek government's ambassador to Washington, that "the oriental mind . . . was always more devious" than that of the occidental. And when being asked whether nuclear weapons could be used against the Chinese, Dillon Anderson, the administration's national security adviser, replied: "Good God, they can breed them faster in the interior zone than you can kill them in the combat zone."[135] As American historian Gordon H. Chang states, such sentiments were "not unusually vicious but typical of many in their generation" who "had grown to maturity during years when Asians tended to be identified as both inferior and insidious." Unfortunately, he emphasizes, "with such racial attitudes, the reasons for the administration's unresponsiveness to Chinese overtures take on an added dimension. Signs of flexibility on China's part could easily be dismissed as Asian trickery. On the other hand, Chinese hostility seemed to confirm Asian fanaticism."[136]

American China Policy Debates, 1959–60: The Herter Doctrine

By the end of the 1950s, this changed assessment of the PRC's intentions in the Sino-Soviet alliance generated a new strategy, called the Herter Doctrine. In May 1959, with the passing of John Foster Dulles, Christian Herter became secretary of state. With increased intelligence reports regarding the "Soviet thaw" and "widening differences" between Beijing and Moscow, the State Department tried to resist two "temptations": one was to return to the Acheson strategy of economic inducement, and the other was to leave Moscow alone and denounce only Beijing. Herter proposed that Washington should blame Moscow for every Beijing "misconduct." He believed that such a strategy would be most conducive to the breakdown of the Sino-Soviet alliance.[137]

According to Herter and the officers at the Far Eastern Bureau, this strategy was based on the "fact" that Beijing and Moscow were still "closely leagued by considerations of common ideology, goals, and many mutual interests." As they stressed, "The Chinese Communists have continually acknowledged and the Soviets have continually solicited Peiping's acceptance of Soviet leadership over the world Communist movement." For instance, "before the shooting broke out in the Taiwan Strait last year," Khrushchev visited Beijing and talked with Mao. "It is our intelligence assumption" that the second Taiwan Strait crisis could be attributed to "certain ground-rules laid down by Moscow." In light of "essential Sino-Soviet solidarity and Peiping's acceptance of Soviet leadership over the Bloc," it would be "advantageous" to hold Moscow "accountable" for Peiping's "intransigence." Thus "if Chinese Communists persist in their aggressive policies,"

Table 7.1 Comparison of Assumptions Underlying Competing China Policies

	Assumptions Underlying the Strategy of Inducement	Assumptions Underlying the Strategy of Containment
PRC	China might be searching for "its unique path to industrialization and socialism"	China was pursuing a Stalinist economy model of industrialization
Polity	The PRC might have solid domestic supports with the CCP among the Chinese people	Widespread disillusionment
Foreign policy	Largely nationalist goals	To communize Asia, to drive out American influence, and to make the PRC the hegemonic power in the Western Pacific and Asia
Nature of the Sino-Soviet Alliance	National security might be first on the agenda	An unholy ideological alliance that would not be split for 100 years at least

Khrushchev must not be allowed "to dissociate himself in the eyes of the world from Peiping's intransigence and to continue depicting himself as an apostle of peace." While Moscow might be irritated by Beijing's "excesses in Tibet and India and possibly elsewhere," these irritations would not be translated into pressure from Moscow on Beijing, unless Moscow was held "accountable" before the world. Indeed, "the only really effective way of keeping Red China from some dangerous adventure at this critical, dynamic, expansionist stage" was through "moderating counsels strongly applied from Moscow."[138]

The "central point" of the Herter Doctrine was, according to the secretary and his staff, that Moscow would be "more irritated" with the PRC if responsibility for Beijing's "excessive actions must be partly borne by Moscow." "This irritation should widen the rift further."[139] In December 1960, the State Department portrayed an ominous picture of the PRC's foreign-policy intentions: "All of the classical elements which traditionally lead to expansionism are found in Communist China," particularly the combination of a "totalitarian regime" and an "explosive population." That is, "A totalitarian regime, fired by fanatic ideology in its early pristine fervor, emphasis upon military power and military solutions, an ethno-patricentric sense of mission in the world (riding an international dogma as its vehicle)." Furthermore, the PRC had "an explosive population problem with food surplus areas on the periphery." Thus Beijing had "sufficient domestic difficulties to make outside adventure attractive not only because of possible fruits *per se,* but as a diversion from domestic dissatisfactions."[140] This frightening portrait of the PRC's foreign-policy objectives was soon to compel the administrations that followed to deepen America's military involvement in Southeast Asia.

In summary, from 1954 to 1960, two different China policy proposals emerged in the Eisenhower administration: the policy of economic inducement versus that of economic and military containment. These two different policy proposals were based on very different premises concerning the PRC's motivations in the Sino-Soviet alliance, which were, in turn, based on different postulates (see Table 7.1) regarding the PRC's economy, political system, and foreign-policy objectives. Among these different American assumptions concerning the PRC's economy, polity, and foreign-policy intentions in the 1950s, which were more consistent with the Chinese reality?

CHAPTER EIGHT

The Foundation of New China

Conflicting CCP Visions of
Industrialization in the 1950s

From 1927 to 1949, the CCP's base area was in rural China, but this was only a "temporary home"; its major challenge, Mao emphasized in February 1948, was "to industrialize China." The "foundation" of New China, he said, must be "large-scale industry, not agriculture or handicraft manufacturing."[1] Without China's industrialization, as Zhou Enlai argued, China's political independence would soon be lost: "Only when China is industrialized can China truly stand up, tall and proud, in the world."[2] It was also a matter of political survival for the CCP after the revolution. "The real criterion for judging a political party's role—good or bad—in Chinese history," Mao stressed, was "to see whether it would promote or fetter China's industrialization."[3]

Throughout the 1950s, if there was a consensus on the paramount importance of China's industrialization in Beijing, there was no agreement on the best way to achieve that goal. In particular, two conflicting economic blueprints of how to achieve a balance between rapid growth and economic equality emerged in Beijing. What are the contents of these different economic blueprints? What are the relationships between these different blueprints and the Stalinist model of a command economy?[4]

The Gradualist Economic Blueprint (1949–1956)

In 1940, in "*On New Democracy*," Mao envisioned a long transitional stage of New Democracy in China before its eventual socialist transformation. The New Democracy projected a mixed economy, incorporating five economic components: the private, the cooperative, the individual farmer and artisan, the state capitalist, and the public, with the public sector as the leading one.[5] The "spirit" of a mixed economy, as Zhou explained, was "to take into account both the public and private interest, benefit both labor and capital, encourage mutual assistance between urban and rural, and promote domestic and foreign trade."[6]

Before the establishment of the PRC, this became the economic system in CCP areas. During the civil war, particularly in the land-reform campaigns (1947–1949), however, this system of mixed economy had encountered major challenges. Many poor peasants needed capital to develop the land they had just received. They went to nearby towns to confiscate private enterprises to get the capital; and they often had the sympathy and support of workers and local party cadres. In May 1947, Bo Yibo—who was in charge of industrial production in the communist areas and became a high-ranking CCP Politburo member in the 1950s and 1960s—bowed to these pressures and approved the local demand to revise the CCP's economic policy of protecting private enterprises. But in less than a year, as Bo reported to the Central Committee, 75 percent of towns and cities in the CCP's areas were in severe recession, brought about by this policy change.[7] In April 1948, Bo urged the CCP Central Committee to reaffirm the mixed economy system of New Democracy. The CCP must teach poor peasants and party members "to distinguish between feudalism and capitalism" in land reform and guide the labor movement toward "the goal of labor-capital mutual cooperation."[8]

Ten days later, Mao sent Bo's report to all party organizations. "Such extremist economic policy toward private enterprises is the reflection of the utopian notions of agrarian socialism, which is reactionary, backward, and which we must strongly oppose."[9] In May 1948, the CCP's North China Finance and Trade Conference formally restored the system of mixed economy in the CCP's areas.[10]

On the eve of the establishment of the PRC, Mao restated that the CCP's vision of a mixed economy was neither a Soviet planned economy nor a capitalist free-market economy but "similar to the economic doctrine laid down by Dr. Sun Yat-sen, the doctrine of People's Livelihood."[11] This vision of a mixed economy, with enthusiastic support from the Third Force in urban China, was upheld in the *Common Program* at the People's Consultative Conference of 1949, the temporary Constitution of the People's Republic of China. From 1949 to 1955 it became the principal economic blueprint of China's industrialization.[12]

The most daunting task in building a system of mixed economy was how to achieve a balance between apparently opposing poles in every major relationship in the economy, such as that between public and private enterprise, between poor peasants and rich farmers, and between workers and industrialists.

In the course of implementation, many serious problems emerged. Concerning the relationship between public and private enterprise, for instance, both sectors engaged in intense competition for limited economic resources. And the competition was further compounded by many cadres' preference for public enterprise. As Chen Yun, who was in charge of economic construction, said in December 1954, although "our economy, according to the Common Program, is a mixed economy, many of our cadres have often forgotten about the private sector." Indeed, "in the short run, it might be much more difficult to focus on both public and private enterprises." In the long run, however, he said at the State Council meeting, "we will face much greater difficulties in the economy, if we do not take good care of private industries."[13]

Moreover, there were enormous problems in reaching a balance between workers and industrialists in the private sector. With workers in public enterprise enjoying comprehensive welfare benefits, workers in the private sector demanded an increase in their salaries immediately. "The capitalists used to treat us badly," they said. "It is our turn to get even." Some workers began to seize the factories and divide the properties among themselves. Chen acknowledged that "many of our workers are eager to punish the capitalists, and demand to 'enter socialism right away.' They are angry when we do not support their demands." On the other hand, the industrialists and merchants were pessimistic and scared. Huang Jing, the mayor of Tianjin, reported in March 1949 that after the CCP entered the city, "three fears" were widespread among entrepreneurs: one was that their factories would soon be confiscated, another was that the CCP would install a pro-worker's policy in dividend distributions, and the other was that they would no longer be able to maintain discipline among workers. Many industrialists wondered if they should continue to expand production at all. A general manager of a big cement company complained bitterly:

"If I build more factories, shall I be regarded as a bigger capitalist with bigger crimes and be sentenced to death by the workers?" Some decided to abandon their factories and flee China.[14]

To achieve harmony between workers and industrialists in the private enterprise, and to calm the fears of the entrepreneurs, the CCP leadership tried to persuade the workers and the local party organizations to improve their relationship, to make the mixed economy work. In Liu Shaoqi's highly publicized trip to Tianjin from April 10 to May 7, 1949, he told the party cadres and trade union leaders that in the long run, the best policy for workers was the policy of "benefits to both workers and capitalists." He ask them to remember, "The national bourgeoisie is not our enemy, but our friend." The working class should "fight against capitalists' exploitative behaviors," but "the major aspect" of this relationship in the mixed economy was "unity, not struggle." Thus "we must persuade our workers not to bankrupt the capitalists. We must not pursue the short-term interests of workers at the expense of the long-term interests of the working class and the Chinese people." Liu urged the party, the city government, the public enterprises, and the trade unions to "take the initiative to cooperate with private enterprise, to work patiently with the capitalists to find a mutually beneficial solution for both sides."[15]

If it was hard enough to achieve a balance between workers and industrialists in the private sector, it was even harder to achieve equilibrium between the welfare of poor peasants and rich farmers. While many poor peasants received land in the land reform, they did not have the capital and the equipment to exploit it. Many rich farmers quickly took advantage of this situation, either by issuing high-interest loans, or by directly purchasing the land from the poor peasants, who had been the CCP's most important allies in the revolution. How should the CCP deal with this new class differentiation in the mixed economy?

For some in the CCP leadership, the best way was to help both poor peasants and rich farmers, respectively, to do better in different sectors: poor peasants in the cooperative sector, and rich farmers in the private sector. Deng Zihui, the deputy premier and minister of agriculture, stressed in February 1953: "We must protect two different kinds of rural initiative and enthusiasm." One was the "poor peasants' enthusiasm for mutual aid and cooperatives," and the other was the "individual farmers' enthusiasm for individual farming and private land ownership."[16]

To help the peasants do better in the cooperative sector, Deng proposed a production responsibility system, to connect the individual's performance directly to his rewards in the cooperative.[17] Liu Shaoqi further suggested that peasants should organize commercial cooperatives instead of production cooperatives, which could help establish processing factories and set up transportation and storage companies. Urban industries could provide industrial commodities such as machines and fertilizer to the commercial cooperatives at a better price.[18]

To help the rich farmers do better in the private sector, Deng recommended the policy of "Four Freedoms," that is, "freedom of employment of wage labor, freedom of private loans, freedom of tenancy and freedom of private commerce."[19] Liu explained that the purpose of the land reform was "not just to rescue poor peasants," but also "to liberate the agricultural production forces from the yoke of premodern feudal ownership." Moreover, to help individual farmers, Liu urged that "one third of the leaders in peasants' associations should be chosen from the middle peasants or rich farmers," to avoid "the abuse of power" by poor peasants and local party cadres.[20]

Clearly, in the mixed economy both the peasants and the workers wanted to expand the public realm to "enter socialism" immediately. On the other hand, entrepreneurs and rich farmers sought the protection of the private sector in order to develop the economy more rapidly. The CCP faced a political dilemma: it must ensure the continued loyalty of its basic constituencies while protecting industrialists, merchants, and rich farmers—its important allies in China's incipient industrialization. In the broadest sense, it was also the dilemma encountered by all modern Chinese reformers: how to strike a balance between fast development and social justice in China's search for a modern economy.

To address this dilemma in the mixed economy, Beijing began to consider a "socialist transformation" from individual farming to cooperatives in rural areas, and from the private to the public-private joint enterprise in urban centers. The major approach in this transformation, Zhou emphasized, was gradualism, which had three major components.

The first was peaceful redemption of all private enterprises, not violent confiscation. There could be three ways to transform Chinese private enterprise, Zhou said. One was to use public enterprise to squeeze out the private in the market; another was to confiscate private enterprises to force them to join; and the third was to encourage them to join voluntarily, and when they did, to redeem their private factories.

"We must adopt the measure of peaceful redemption, peaceful transformation."[21] In Zhou's words, through the policy of peaceful redemption, the Chinese industrialists' "great progressive role" in the industrialization could be "enhanced" and their "negative side of exploiting workers" could be "contained" in the public-private joint enterprise.

Mao conceived of this policy applying not only to the middle and small entrepreneurs but, more important, to the big industrialists. It was wrong, he argued, for the Ministry of the United Front to regard the big capitalists as "bad folks." The big capitalists were the "treasures" of China's industrialization, and their cooperation in this transition was "crucial" to the CCP's success. He acknowledged that many workers were "strongly opposed to our new policy," as were the middle and small capitalists. They were "angry with us," complaining that "we conceded too much." To protect China's industrialization drive, "we must persuade workers not to damage the interests of the big capitalists." The CCP's policy toward the private entrepreneurs must be "fundamentally different from that toward the landlords" in the land revolution.[22]

The second major component in this gradualist approach was the idea that the rural cooperative movement should be divided into two distinct stages. The first stage was the "elementary cooperative," in which distribution was according to one's labor and the amount of land contributed. Land and other property still belonged to the individual peasants. The second stage was the "advanced cooperative," in which the distribution was according to one's labor, but the land would be owned by the co-ops. As Deng Zihui emphasized, before the first stage was *fully* consolidated, the second one must not be introduced. And in both stages, the individual production responsibility system must be installed, to ensure that the individual's self-interests and the public interests be directly connected to each other.[23]

The third component in this gradualist approach was "voluntarism" in the transition. As Chen Yun recommended, "pilot projects" should be established first. Not until their production could "far surpass" that of the individual farming or the private enterprise should the rich farmers and industrialists be encouraged to join.[24] The CCP must be "very patient," allowing "a great deal of time" for the individual farmers and entrepreneurs "to experience the benefits and advantages" of these new organizations. In October 1953, after local newspapers reported that some village activists had forced the rich farmers to join their cooperatives through "physical violence,"[25] the Central Committee immediately criticized the "left-adventurism" in rural China. In January 1955, it further urged activists to cease organizing new cooperatives, "to protect the alliance between poor peasants, middle peasants, and rich farmers."[26]

Zhou kept repeating that the focus during the transition should be on creating the "conditions"; namely, raising the productivity of the pilot projects or existing joint enterprises and rural cooperatives. "When the melon is ripe, it will fall from the stem; where water flows, a channel is formed. That is to say, we must wait patiently for the conditions to ripen: When conditions are ripe, success will come."[27] Thus, according to Zhou, in pursuing this gradualist approach, the principal danger in the party was "impetuosity and premature advance." This transition would involve so many different classes' different interests that a "premature advance" could only bring about "disastrous consequences" for the Chinese economy. Since "rash advance" was "apparently consistent with our goal," "supported by masses' enthusiasm and activism," and had "the revolutionary flavors and appearances," it could be "much more difficult" to oppose in the transition. Therefore, he persistently reminded the party cadres: "To oppose rash advance and to insist on gradualism in this transition demands that we must be extraordinarily sober-minded, command incomparable willpower, display much deeper insight, and master much greater courage."[28]

By the end of 1955, the pressures from medium- and small-sized private enterprises to speed up the transition were building up rapidly. After large companies had joined the public-private enterprise, increases in state investments allowed them to become much more competitive in the market. As a result, private enterprises of small and medium size found it even harder to compete. Chen Shutong, the president of the Chinese Manufacturing Association, complained to Xue Muqiao, the director of the private enterprise bureau under the State Council, "The state has now taken in all the fat meat, and left the thin bones around." Indeed, he asked, "Would the state throw them away into the garbage pail?" He recommended transforming *all* private enterprises without delay.[29] The State Council decided to change its original plan of a more gradualist type to accommodate the new demand. In March 1956, the transition from the private enterprise to the public-private joint enterprise was completed in urban China, well ahead of the original schedule. Meanwhile, the rural transition was also completed, with direct encouragement from Mao himself. (Mao's ideas will be discussed later in this chapter.)

On September 15, 1956, the Eighth Party Congress was convened in Beijing. Its resolution formally declared that after the completion of the "socialist transformation" in rural and urban China, the "major contradiction" was no longer class warfare between workers and capitalists, between poor peasants and rich farmers. Instead, "the major contradiction is between the Chinese people's demands for material and cultural satisfactions and the inability of the currently backward Chinese economy to meet people's demands." The top priority of the nation was therefore to mobilize all Chinese people to speed up China's industrialization drive. Many deputies also pointed out that with the disappearance of the private sector and market mechanism, "bureaucratic orders now stifled and frustrated the activism and enthusiasm of workers and peasants" and caused "a sharp decline" in the quality and variety of consumer goods.[30]

To address these problems, Zhou, Chen, and Liu suggested reinstallation of part of the private and market sector, to restore a balance between the public and the private, and between planning and market mechanism. As Chen emphasized, the pursuit of a "pure socialist economy" or a "pure public sector" was hurting the economy. Instead of "purity," the Chinese economy should have more "diversity." He also suggested that while many small and medium private enterprises were regarded as public-private joint enterprise in name, in reality, they should continue to operate as private enterprises, to respond to consumers' diverse needs.[31] For Zhou and Liu, in particular, the Polish and Hungarian uprisings at the end of 1956 demonstrated that an enforced expansion of the public domain before the society could provide solid material conditions could only cause decreased living standards and increased resentment among the people. Since China's economy was more backward than those of Eastern European countries, Liu said, it would probably take even longer for China to lay down the material conditions for an eventual socialist transformation. It might be a mistake to attempt to abolish the private sector so soon. From now on, if Chinese entrepreneurs wanted to establish their own factories, they should be encouraged to do so. If individual citizens wanted to establish private schools, kindergartens, or clinics, the state should not impose any tax on them, since their private institutions delivered an important community service.[32] Zhou further suggested that it might be much better "to have more private enterprises and market competition in industry, agriculture, and handicraft industry and in every part of the Chinese economy, probably except railroads."[33]

By the end of 1956, the private sector quickly reemerged in China. Was it a contradiction to the mass campaign of "socialist transformation"? No, it was not, argued an editorial of the *People's Daily*.[34] In Mao Zedong's conversations with the leaders of the Chinese Association of Industrialists and Merchants in December 1956, he said the government now wanted to "encourage private investment in large-scale factories." For overseas Chinese investment, the Chinese government was to pledge that "their private enterprises here would not be confiscated for at least one hundred years." Mao said, "We have abolished capitalism, but we now may need to reintroduce capitalism into our industrialization drive." He emphasized that a mixed economy— "socialist and capitalist economy co-existing in the Chinese economy"— probably could meet people's needs much better than a "pure" socialist economy.[35]

The impact of this gradualist blueprint on the Chinese economy is reflected in the following statistics: from June 1937 to May 1949, the Chinese inflation rate increased several thousand times. By 1949, the currency was worth almost nothing. But by the end of May 1950, the galloping Chinese inflation was stopped and the price of Chinese consumer goods was stabilized. From 1949 to 1952, China's industrial production increased by 145 percent, agricultural production by 53.4 percent. And in a period of seven years, from 1949 to 1956, the average life expectancy in China increased 66 percent, from thirty-seven years to fifty-six years.

The Populist Economic Blueprint (1958–1960)

On the eve of the establishment of the PRC, there was a consensus within the CCP that the system of a mixed economy or the economy of New Democracy should be a long transitional stage, leading to a socialist economy in the distant future.[36] How did Mao and other CCP leaders come to change their minds about this gradualist economic blueprint in 1958?

By the middle of the 1950s, Mao felt increasingly uneasy about the reemergence of the gap between rich and poor in the aftermath of the land revolution. According to a local report, for instance, in the Xisu village of Jiangsu province, only five years after the land reform, thirty-nine households in this village had sold their land, and fifty-seven households had to obtain high-interest loans from rich farmers. The reporter quoted poor peasants as saying, "If we continue to go down this road, shall we go back to the old days before the revolution?" For Mao, the worker-peasant alliance was becoming "very shaky." It was land reform that had forged the alliance. But now, "for want of means of production, many poor peasants still live in poverty."

Mao argued, "The Chinese working class needs two allies in the industrialization, the poor peasants and the national bourgeoisie." Of the two, the first was "the more important," because without it, the cooperation of the national bourgeoisie would be "unstable or unde-pendable." He concluded that, the poor peasants' welfare should be protected first in China's industrialization. In Mao's mind, economic growth alone might not mean political stability in the PRC. If the peas-ants had to sell their land, "the poor peasants would abandon the party, they would say: 'why should we follow the Communists? With or without the land reform, we are still poor.' " The basic political base of the CCP would be eroded despite the industrial growth.[37]

For Mao, the best way to protect poor peasants' interests was to organize them into rural cooperatives. However, he was concerned that a rapid transition might reduce agricultural production. He was thus searching for examples of rural cooperatives that helped the poor peas-ants and increased agricultural production simultaneously. He found many such examples. According to a local report, for instance, when the Wang Guofan agricultural cooperative in Hepei province was first established, it only had twenty-three poor peasants, without any agri-cultural equipment. They cut tons of trees, sold them in the market, and bought fertilizer and agricultural equipment. They shared these limited resources to increase agricultural output. Their cooperative con-tinued to yield bumper harvests from 1953 to 1955. The whole county, inspired by them, established hundreds of cooperatives. Within three years, without borrowing one cent from local governments, grain yields in this county were increased by 76 percent, fruit trees by 62.9 percent, and sheep by 463.1 percent.[38] Mao was so impressed, he wrote that the Wang Guofan cooperative, "the poor folks' cooperative," repre-sented "the new image of the new China." With many similar exam-ples, Mao proudly declared: "The poor, the underprivileged, will have their glory now. The old system is dying. The new system is emerging in the People's Republic."[39]

Mao was angry, therefore, at the Central Committee's campaigns against "rash advance" in organizing rural cooperatives. Mao's speech "On the Question of Agricultural Cooperatives" of July 31, 1955, delivered at a meeting of the Central Committee and attended by secretaries of the provincial and municipal party committees, signified his decision to begin a faster "socialist transformation" in rural China. He asked his comrades, who had been the CCP's most staunch supporters in the revolution? For Mao, the worker-peasant alliance was, first of all, "an alliance between workers and poor peasants, not upper-middle class peasant or rich farmers."[40] And so the carefully preserved equilibrium in the gradualist blueprint between the interests of poor peasants and middle-class peasants, as well as rich farmers, was now tipped toward the poor peasants, in Mao's blueprint of rural development in China.

The rural cooperative campaigns, Mao was confident, could soon generate a much greater increase in agricultural production. He predicted that after the first couple of years, these cooperatives should be able to increase agricultural production by 20 percent to 30 percent. He thus began to push for an increase in the industrial production targets, to match the projected increase of agricultural productivity. However, Zhou and Chen disagreed. For them, a single-minded focus on a high rate of growth could upset many economic and social balances in the industrialization drive. They both urged: "We should resolutely cut down the industrial and agricultural targets in the second Five-Year Plan." From late 1955 to September 1957, their arguments won the support of the majority in the Politburo, the Central Committee, the third session of the First People's National Congress in June 1956, and the Eighth Party Congress in September 1956.

In this period, Mao obeyed the majority's decision. But deep down, he still believed that Zhou and Chen were wrong. "Why did John Foster Dulles dare to humiliate China, and refuse to recognize one quarter of humanity?" Mao often raised this question at the CCP Central Committee meetings. For him, it was simply because China was poor. "If you are poor, you are not industrialized, you will be beaten. Isn't this the lesson we have learned from our history of the past two hundred years?"[41]

In October 1957, at the Third Plenum of the Eighth Central Committee, Mao again raised the issue of the apparent "slow tempo" in China's industrialization. By now, in the wake of the antirightist campaign in the summer, a different atmosphere, one of left extremism, dominated the party debates. Mao won the majority vote this time.[42]

In the winter of 1957, local reports indicated that the economic predicament of poor peasants had worsened. The radical approach to socialist transformation in rural China had only generated strong resistance from upper-middle-class peasants and rich farmers, which resulted in the decrease of agricultural production that year. Mao's People's Liberation Army guards showed him steamed corn bread, hard and black. "This was the first time we had seen Chairman Mao in tears," his guards recalled. Even when his son was killed in the Korean War, "we did not see him cry." Mao could not understand: "We are a socialist country now, the forces of production should have been liberated. Life shouldn't have been so hard in the countryside." By the end of 1957, he was more anxious than ever to find new ways to achieve faster industrial growth and to elevate poor peasants from poverty at once. He claimed at the Central Committee meeting in early 1958, "We cannot afford to walk step by step, we must run, must jump!"[43]

In May 1958, the second session of the Eighth Party Congress was convened in Beijing, and it overturned the gradualist economic blueprint at the Eighth Party Congress of 1956, along with its concept of socialism without class warfare in China's economic development. The new resolution claimed that the "major contradiction" was the ideological struggle "between proletarian collectivism and bourgeois individualism" in China's industrialization. Why did the "socialist transformation," or the radical expansion of the public realm, not bring about faster economic growth? It was because, Mao believed, "bourgeois ideology of individualism destroyed unity between the party and the people." The CCP had been "so poor" in the revolution, but it won the national victory. Why? "Because we had the spirit of collectivism, we had equality and unity between the party and the people." But now "we have different clothes and different meals according to different official ranks." How could ordinary workers and poor peasants pour their hearts into the industrialization drive? A change of property ownership alone, he argued, could not guarantee the abolition of "bourgeois corruption." "The obsession with prestige and rankings among the party cadres and military officers . . . [and] the wage system in which the intellectuals can earn much more than the manual laborers," all "stifled" the enthusiasm of workers and peasants in the industrialization. He thus praised the system of "payment in kind"[44] as practiced in revolutionary years, and wondered if part of it could be restored to create a "new unity" in China. He knew that the economists would consider such a system "a sheer violation of the principle of 'material incentives,' or as the old saying goes: 'Money, and money only, can buy everything, even gods.' " For Mao, however, in the decades of revolution, so many heroes and heroines had sacrificed their lives, without anything in return. Why? Because they were inspired by noble ideals, not by "material incentives."[45] Only by fighting against "bourgeois ideology," he argued, could a new unity between the party and the people be reestablished, the creative energy of workers and peasants be "fully liberated," and a much faster industrialization drive be achieved.[46]

If the Eighth Party Congress of 1956 championed the concept of socialism *without* class warfare and the principle of "an overall balanced, steady development," the second session of the Eighth Party Congress in 1958, in contrast, advocated the concept of socialism *with* class warfare on the ideological front, and the principle of "achieving greater, faster, better, and more economic development," with "faster" being at the center.

In 1958, the Great Leap Forward and the commune campaigns seemed to have won enthusiastic support from the poor peasants. For many of them, the commune could "kill two birds with one stone." Not only could it concentrate more personnel and resources on big projects such as irrigation, it could "obliterate the differences between rural and urban ways of life."[47] For Mao, if Chinese workers' productivity in public enterprise was raised dramatically in the early years of the PRC, "thanks to the comprehensive welfare security," why could not the poor peasants also enjoy an expanded welfare in the commune to increase agricultural productivity?[48]

However, Mao soon acknowledged that such a system might not raise agricultural productivity. According to local reports, many poor and lower-middle-class peasants—the CCP's basic constituency—were now secretly hiding away their labor products instead of giving them up to the communes. He feared that to replace the system of distribution according to one's labor with that of distribution according to social needs, or to "fan the 'communizing wind,' " as he called it, might "substantially undermine the peasantry's supports" for the CCP. Indeed, "if we refused to deprive capitalists of their properties, if we purchased their enterprises rather than confiscating them, how can we now deprive the peasants?"[49] He quoted Dulles as saying that the CCP might well endure in the PRC if it were not for this commune system they had implemented. "Don't regard such comments as nonsense; what they have said makes sense," Mao warned. "If we mess up in the commune system, we might collapse." He began to push the restoration of the distribution system of elementary cooperatives, or the system of distribution according to one's labor, rather than according to one's social needs.[50]

Nonetheless, during this period, Mao continued to defend public institutions in the rural commune, particularly the public dining halls that provided free meals to commune members, public kindergartens for preschool-age village children, and public nursing homes for the village elderly. It was in this context that the Lushan Conference was convened. Between July 2 and August 16, 1959, the meeting of the enlarged Politburo and the Eighth Plenum of the Eighth Central Committee was held in the mountain resort of Lushan. Its theme was how to correct the "left adventurism" in the Great Leap Forward and commune campaigns. For Marshal Zhu De, the system of payment in kind was communism: could the Chinese peasants welcome communism? "I doubt it, I don't believe it." The "family-centered social structure" must be strengthened in the villages. The party must do everything to ensure that "the peasants get rich." This was "the most important issue concerning political and social stability among 500 million people in China."[51] Zhu De's comments had Zhou's endorsement. "Our nation is still too poor to provide public dining halls. If each takes one *jin* more every day, how many more grains should China produce annually?" Mao conceded: "I miss Chen Yun. China's economy should be run by Chen Yun."

For Peng Dehui, the defense minister, however, many party leaders had not yet fully realized the causes and disastrous consequences of this "leftist adventurism." He argued that many leaders had departed from the party's tradition of the mass line, that is, "listening to people's opinions carefully before formulating policies and constantly getting feedback from the people to revise the original policies." Such a departure from the "mass line" in the revolutionary era was, in his view, caused by "petty bourgeois fanaticism" in the party leadership. This fanaticism, he wrote, expressed itself in "the desires and attempts to march into communism in one giant step."[52]

For Mao and many party leaders, on the other hand, the people's commune, like the Paris Commune, was "the expression of the people's great spirit."[53] Mao argued that Marx had been against the uprising of the Paris Commune at the beginning, but when it broke out, he supported it, even though he knew it was to fail. "For Marx, even if the Paris Commune could exist for three months, it would be worthwhile." Of course, "if we only focus on the economic aspect of the Paris Commune, then it might not be worthwhile." For Mao, hundreds of thousands of peasants and local cadres had traveled to Hebei, Henan, and Shandon provinces to visit those "pilot communes." They made all those trips on their own, because they were "so eager to learn how to quickly get rid of poverty." How should the party view such "spontaneous socialist enthusiasm"? Was it petty bourgeois fanaticism? "Some fanaticism, but certainly not all." "These local cadres led hundreds of millions of people in the mass campaigns last year, among them at least 30 percent were genuine in their efforts." How many was 30 percent? They were 150 million of our people. "You describe all their efforts as petty bourgeois fanaticism? They are not petty bourgeoisie, they are poor and lower-middle-class peasants." Mao concluded: "All the rightists within China are against the commune. The Soviet Union and the whole world are also against it." The party leadership should unite to support these poor peasants' activism. But instead, "some among us seem to be influenced by the 'rightist trend' in China and the world." For Mao, Peng's problem, like Deng Zihui's, was that "he stood on the side of the middle-class peasants," "only 30 miles from the right wing's stand." He should stand firmly "on the side of the poor peasants and the working class."[54]

With the launching of the Anti-Right Opportunist Campaigns in that fateful month of August 1959, "left extremism" further took hold among party leaders, local cadres, and activists.[55] The second Great Leap "failed with a vengeance." "Agricultural output in 1960 was only 75.5 percent of that in 1958." In 1960, "light industrial output decreased by 9.8 percent. It then declined by 21.6 percent in 1961 and by another 8.4 percent in 1962." "Heavy industrial output also declined sharply, going down 46.6 percent in 1961 compared with 1960, and another 22.2 percent in 1962 over 1961."[56]

In early 1960, Mao began to reemphasize the danger of left adventurism in the economy, as on the eve of the Lushan Conference.[57] By mid-1960, the production and distribution system of elementary cooperatives was restored, though not in name. However, he continued to reject the system of individual production responsibility. Such a system, he argued, might "hurt the welfare of CCP's basic constituency—the poor peasants."[58]

In summary, the evolution of Mao's concept of China's economic development during the 1950s seemed to go full circle. It began with the blueprint of a mixed economy and the concept of socialism without class warfare but evolved into its opposite in late 1950s: a single-minded emphasis on the concept of socialism, with class warfare on the ideological front. It returned to its original emphasis on an overall plan of balanced, steady development in 1960. Yet this was not entirely a full circle: Mao did not again come to embrace the concept of socialism without class warfare as championed by Zhou, Chen, and the Eighth Party Congress of 1956.

The Stalinist Model of the Command Economy

In the formulation of the two different blueprints in the 1950s—the gradualist and the populist—the CCP leaders conscientiously studied the Soviet model of industrialization. What, then, was the relationship between the conflicting CCP economic blueprints and the Stalinist model of the command economy?[59]

The redemption policy in the transition from private enterprise to public-private joint enterprise was, Zhou said, a departure from the Soviet policy. "To confiscate all capitalists' enterprises," rather than purchasing them, was "the violent measure" taken by the Soviet Union and Eastern European countries in their socialist industrialization. However, because of China's "very different situation," "China should not, must not, adopt the same violent measure in its industrialization drive."[60]

More important, profoundly different key concepts separated the gradualist economic blueprint and the Stalinist command economy. The command economy was based on "pure" public ownership, a total dependence on national planning, and class warfare. In contrast, the mixed economy in the gradualist blueprint was based on balance and harmony between public, cooperative, and private sectors, between national planning and local activism, between workers and industrialists, and between poor peasants, middle-class peasants, and rich farmers.

In fact, the principal differences between the CCP's gradualist economic blueprint and the Stalinist command economy became a source of friction between Beijing and Moscow in the early years of the PRC. Gao Gang, the first party secretary of the Northeast region and the chair of the National Planning Commission (1952–1954), opposed the CCP's gradualist economic blueprint, particularly the concept of "balance and harmony between workers and capitalists." He was outraged by Liu's Tianjin speech of 1949 on the importance of the CCP's "united front with the national bourgeoisie to develop the private economy." As he complained to the Soviet envoy, Ivan V. Kovalev, Liu's speech was a "shocking betrayal of the Chinese working class." He was also annoyed by the CCP's redemption policy of purchasing all private enterprises. He preferred to wage class wars to confiscate them. As he told Li Weihan, the minister of the United Front, such a policy was simply "Bukharin bourgeois notion of 'peaceful growing into socialism.'" Gao thought that because Bukharin had been denounced in the 1930s as a "traitor to socialism," the CCP was wrong to now adopt a policy similar to that of Bukharin. He urged the party to think more carefully about the redemption policy. At a Central Committee meeting in June 1953, Gao openly criticized some party leaders' "right opportunism toward the Chinese capitalists."[61]

In October 1955, in the aftermath of Gao's exclusion from the CCP leadership, the Soviet leaders began to emphasize publicly "the paramount importance of accepting the principles of class struggle and the dictatorship of the proletariat in socialist industrialization."[62] Among the slogans issued in *Pravda* for the 38th Anniversary of the October Revolution that year was one conveying greetings to the lands of people's democracy including Albania and Mongolia, which were "constructing socialism." Another slogan conveyed greetings to the PRC, which was constructing "the foundations of socialism" rather than socialism itself. The different greetings conveyed to Mongolia and China became the subject of many foreign correspondents' speculations, since the difference between "constructing socialism" and "constructing the foundation of socialism" did not lie, they argued, in Mongolia's more advanced state of industrial development.[63]

In the same month in 1955, an article that appeared in the CCP's official journal *Xinhua Yuebao* (Monthly Gazette) in Beijing openly acknowledged the differences between Chinese and Soviet industrialization and defended vigorously the "Marxist nature" of the Chinese policy of "peaceful redemption" of private industry.[64] In April 1956, Mao further emphasized that there were "two different attitudes" about learning from the Soviet experiences to complete China's industrialization: one was "to copy them without thinking," and the other was "to combine thoughtful learning with one's own creation." Moreover, Mao called on Chinese intellectuals to learn from both socialist and capitalist countries' experiences in industrialization. He complained that "many scholars who know English no longer want to study it, and scholars' works are no longer translated into English, French, German, and Japanese to engage in academic exchanges." Such an attitude, he said, would do "great damage" to China's industrialization drive.[65]

In particular, Mao made special efforts to distinguish between the Stalinist command economy and the Chinese alternatives. He argued that the Soviet emphasis on central planning was achieved at the expense of local activism. "Too much centralization, too many disciplines," he said, "can only stifle local creativity." There should be "two kinds of activism—both the activism of the government and the activism of the people."[66] Furthermore, the Soviet development of defense and heavy industries was achieved "at the expense of light industry and agriculture." That was why, he said, Soviet grain production had not yet reached the highest level of the prerevolutionary era. That was also why, he stressed, in the Soviet markets consumer goods were "very inadequate." For Mao, the Stalinist economic model put too much emphasis on long-term public interests at the expense of individuals' short-term interests. The Chinese alternative was "to satisfy people's needs in their daily lives first, thus to make the foundation of developing heavy industry more stable, more enduring."[67] According to Zhou, if the "unbalanced" economic policies in the Soviet Union and Eastern Europe were to continue, the people there would rebel sooner or later. "The Soviet and Eastern European peoples' rebellions could be just a matter of time."[68]

Mao reminded his comrades that in the revolutionary era, the CCP had worked hard to "seek truth from facts," rather than from Marxist books or the Soviet model of revolution, and to make policies "consistent with Chinese indigenous situations." However, since 1949, many Chinese had "blindly copied the Soviet model of industrialization." Indeed, "in recent years the Soviets have exposed their shortcomings in their socialist economic constructions." He asked, "Do you still want to take the roundabout course they took? Don't you want to avoid the detours?" And he urged them "to search for a unique Chinese path to socialism and industrialization."[69]

In early 1958, when Mao shifted from the gradualist to the radical economic blueprint, he again emphasized the "flaws" in the Stalinist model of industrialization, from a different angle, and for a different reason. From 1949 to 1952, Stalin had repeatedly warned against any "rash advance" in China's industrialization. In July 1949, in his meetings with Liu, Stalin warned that China should not try to make "a giant jump" in its industrialization. A giant jump could give "false impressions of grand results" in the short run but would eventually "disrupt and ruin the industrial economy in the long run." In his discussions with Zhou about China's First Five-Year Plan in September 1952, Stalin suggested reducing the planned Chinese annual industrial growth from 20 percent to 15 percent. "When drawing up a plan, it is better to leave some leeway, to allow for unforeseen circumstances. If you can over-fulfill the targets, it can only increase people's confidence." The most important principle in industrial development, he stressed, was "to make progress step by step." Thus when Mao sharply criticized Zhou's policy against rash advances in 1958, Mao also strongly criticized Stalin.[70]

If Mao rejected Stalin's model of economic development, what was his major source of inspiration in shifting from the gradualist economic blueprint to the populist one? At the CCP's Sixth Plenum in 1958, in launching the commune campaign, Mao asked all party leaders to read "the biography of Zhang Lu" from the classic series of the *Comprehensive History of 24 Dynasties*. Zhang had led a rebellion of poor peasants and had established a peasant regime in Shanxi province (220–265 AD). He designed an economic system of public sharing that required all local authorities to set up public housing for the poor and to provide free meals to everyone. This peasant regime lasted for over thirty years. Written in the aftermath of the regime's collapse, the biography emphasized how "extremely popular" the system had been with the poor peasants. For Mao, Zhang's community medical service was similar to the "free medical service of the people's commune," and Zhang's free meal program was the "pioneer" of the free dining hall in the villages in 1958. Mao further pointed out that Zhang's system in Shanxi province was similar to that of the Huang Jin peasant rebellion in other parts of northern China at the same time. It was also similar to that of the rest of the poor peasants' rebellions in Chinese history. Mao proclaimed that the "great similarity" of all these economic systems in the peasant rebellions demonstrated "the persistent pursuit of poor Chinese peasants of equality, liberty, and prosperity," which had "such strong primitive socialist flavors."[71]

Indeed, 100 years earlier, in the 1850s, Hong Xiuquan—the leader of the Taiping peasant rebellion—wrote: "The distribution of land should be based on social needs: no matter male or female, if there are more heads in the family, it should receive more land. . . . Wherever there is land, let's work together to grow crops, wherever there is meal, let's share it with the hungry, wherever there is cloth, let's share it with the needy, and wherever there is money, let's share it with the poor. Let every place have equal distribution of wealth, let everyone on earth have warm clothes and delicious meals."[72]

In the commune campaign in the late 1950s, many party activists and poor peasants embraced the same dream, the same ideal. With professional managers being squeezed out of the middle-tier organizations and many poor peasants moving rapidly upward in officialdom, there was a "greater concentration of peasant cadres at the provincial through commune levels." The radical economic blueprint was not only warmly embraced but wildly expanded by many party cadres and poor peasants.[73]

By the end of 1958, however, to address the outcries of party activists and poor peasants for a system of distribution according to one's social needs rather than one's labor, Mao began to reread Stalin's *On Socialist Economy.* Stalin wrote that the destiny of the commercial economy was intimately tied to the level of economic development. The more backward the economy, the more important development of the commercial exchange should be. Mao agreed. Since China's economy was much more backward than those of Japan and Eastern European countries and of India and Brazil, China needed to develop commercial production and exchange, or to have a system of distribution according to one's labor, for a much longer time to come. Mao urged party activists to read Stalin's work. Mao's purpose, as he conceded, was "to use Stalin's work to stop the party cadres' and poor peasants' efforts to install a system of distribution according to one's social needs right away" in the commune campaigns.[74]

The relationship between the conflicting CCP's economic blueprints and the Stalinist model of industrialization in the 1950s was therefore much more complex than it appeared. If it is hard to argue that the gradualist economic blueprint was a copy of the Stalinist command economy, it is equally hard to conclude that Mao's shift to the radical economic blueprint represented his determination to embrace the Stalinist model in China's industrialization.

Concepts of Socialism in China's Industrialization:
Social and Cultural Underpinnings

How could there be such divergent interpretations of socialist industrialization in Beijing in the 1950s? What shaped such profoundly different understandings of the official ideology of socialism in China's
economic development?

First of all, for champions of the gradualist economic blueprint, the
birth of any new society, including a socialist one, depends on the level
of economic development in the society. Thus "to change political systems ahead of time could jeopardize the economy," which would eventually "prolong" the birth of the new society. Zhang Wentian, one of
the party theoreticians and a ranking member of the CCP Politburo,
emphasized, it was particularly dangerous to make constant changes
in the political system in the aftermath of revolution.[75] In Zhou's
words, after the revolution, "economic reconstruction should be the
basis of every other reconstruction in China." Therefore, "the final test
or judgment" of any new policy, including the transition from individual farming to cooperatives, from private to public-private joint enterprises, was "whether it could actually promote China's economic
development and improve people's living standards." If not, instead of
imposing the new policy, the policy itself must be "revised" or "recon-
sidered."[76]

Advocates of the populist economic blueprint believed, on the other
hand, that constant, sweeping political and ideological changes could
definitely bring about much faster economic growth. Mao believed that
public or socialist, ownership alone might not fully guarantee economic
growth, if "bourgeois ideology" built a wall between the party and the
people after the revolution. That was why, Mao believed, "politics
must take command in the economy."

Second, the champions of the gradualist economic blueprint held that
there should be balance and harmony in the relationships between
workers and industrialists and between poor peasants, middle-class
peasants, and rich farmers in China's economic growth. As Deng Zihui
elaborated, "If they cooperate, they would both benefit; if they separate, they would both suffer." For instance, the production of the rural
cooperatives was, in his words, dependent on "the combination of poor
peasants' manual labor and the agricultural equipment of middle-class
peasants and rich farmers." Thus, the best way to protect poor peas-

ants' interests was to create a mutually beneficial situation for both sides in China's industrialization.

The advocates of the populist economic blueprint, however, believed that capitalists, rich farmers, and even middle-class peasants could never be satisfied with the CCP's economic policy, since it would not give them a free hand to develop capitalism in China. Thus, the CCP should stand resolutely with the workers and poor peasants in China's industrialization. Otherwise, the CCP might lose everyone in the end, despite China's economic growth. As Mao argued, only by defending the interests of workers and poor peasants first could the CCP mobilize its basic constituencies and, through its increased strengths, win over the national bourgeoisie and its intellectuals.[77]

Finally, these two interpretations of socialism at work in China's industrialization were drawn from two opposing philosophical frameworks concerning how to construct a relationship between the private and public realms. According to the advocates of the populist economic blueprint, this relationship is defined in terms of confrontational contradictions. In their view, the CCP must defend the supremacy of the public realm and eventually eliminate the private sector. For the champions of the gradualist economic blueprint, it was vitally important to achieve a balance between the individual and the common good. At the Eighth Party Congress in 1956, Zhou said, "In economic construction, it is crucial to take into account both the public welfare and the individuals', both long-term interests and short-term ones, to achieve balance and harmony between the public and the private realms."[78] Clearly, Zhou's repeated emphasis on balance and harmony between the public and the private realms was shaped by the Confucian/Taoist philosophical assumption of harmony between opposites.

Differing from Zhou and other champions of the gradualist economic blueprint, Mao and many CCP leaders were deeply influenced by the Mohist philosophical assumption of antagonistic duality between the individual and the common good. Mao's shift from the gradualist to the populist economic blueprint had much to do with a change in his underlying philosophical assumptions, with his identification of the CCP's cause with rebellions of Chinese poor peasants, and with his reactions within his altered philosophical framework to both the reemergence of class differentiation in rural China and the perceived slow pace of China's industrialization.

In the Eisenhower administration, the advocates of the containment strategy believed that Beijing was attempting to remold the Chinese economy according to the Stalinist model. In 1956, when Beijing apparently speeded up the rural cooperative campaign and rapidly completed the transformation of private enterprise, the Eisenhower administration was further convinced that Beijing had decided to connect the entire Chinese economy to the Soviet "communist machine of world domination." In contrast, some leading champions of the economic-inducement strategy in Washington focused on the CCP's redemption policy in the transformation of private enterprise and focused on the CCP's desire to search for "a unique Chinese path to socialism and industrialization." However, the depth, scope, and intensity of China's quest for its identity in building a modern economy went far beyond U.S. analyses and observations during that time. In Beijing, these two conflicting economic blueprints, in turn, shaped two conflicting political blueprints in the 1950s.

CHAPTER NINE

Mao's Magic Weapon

From a Gradualist Political Program to the Hundred Flowers Policy

As a result of the nationwide land revolution in the late 1940s, the majority of the CCP officials were from rural villages. When they entered the cities in 1949, the major political challenge for the CCP was how to continue to strengthen the "united front" among "workers, peasants, petty-bourgeoisie, and national bourgeoisie" that Mao had referred to as the CCP's "magic weapon" and that had brought the CCP rapidly to its national victory. As Zhou put it, after the CCP entered the cities, its principal political task was to create "a new great partnership" among workers, peasants, and intellectuals in China's political reconstruction and address the challenge of mitigating the political tensions between rural and urban China in the aftermath of the land revolution.[1]

Directly related to these different economic blueprints were the two different political blueprints that emerged in the CCP leadership in the 1950s. What are the contents of these conflicting political blueprints? What caused the rise and fall of the Hundred Flowers policy in 1956 and 1957, which called for "letting one hundred flowers blossom, and letting one hundred schools of thought compete"? Why was the Khrushchev leadership so worried about Beijing's Hundred Flowers policy, when it had started its own domestic liberalization experiment?

The Gradualist Political Blueprint

The gradualist political blueprint focused on how to mobilize all Chinese people, particularly Chinese intellectuals, to participate in China's industrialization. It included the following major components:

1. Nurturing the complementarity of intellectuals and the workers/peasants
2. Constructing unlimited space for intellectuals' individual creativity
3. Fostering coexistence between the CCP and the Third Force, or the democratic parties
4. Teaching the vital importance of constitutional law and people's congresses in the polity
5. Condoning supplemental measures: strikes and demonstrations

During the revolutionary era, a powerful trend within the CCP was the regarding of intellectuals as "part of the bourgeoisie." After the collapse of the Communist-Nationalist united front in 1927, many in the CCP accepted the conclusion of the Comintern in Moscow that the failure of the Chinese land revolution (1924–1927) could be attributed to "the betrayal of bourgeoisie, petty bourgeoisie and their intellectuals." As a CCP resolution in August 1927 argued, the Chinese revolution should "only rely on the workers and peasants."[2] In early 1931, the party formally adopted an anti-intelligentsia policy, combined with a witch-hunt to eliminate all "potential spies and traitors" in the CCP. Many party members from academic or scholarly backgrounds were subject to investigations, and some were wrongly executed as counterrevolutionaries or special agents of the KMT government.[3]

Other CCP leaders, however, disagreed with the Comintern's view of Chinese intellectuals. For instance, in his letter to the Central Committee in November 1928, Zhou Enlai wrote, it was "highly detrimental" to the revolution to wage "an anti-intelligentsia campaign" in the party and to continue creating "serious divisions" between the CCP and the intellectuals. He called attention to the fact that, while some of the intellectuals had run away from the land revolution in 1927, many more were still fighting "courageously" on the side of the Chinese working people.[4]

Mao agreed with Zhou's arguments at this time. With the onset of the War of Resistance and Mao's rise to CCP leadership in 1935, the

CCP began to emphasize the importance of Chinese intellectuals in the revolution. It adopted the policy of "going all out to recruit the intellectuals into the party, going all out to promote them within the party."[5] At the end of the war, intellectuals constituted 85 percent of the middle-level leadership within the CCP.[6]

From 1947 to 1952, the greatest land revolution in Chinese history swept over all China. It brought millions of poor peasants into the CCP and its officialdom. The relationship among workers, peasants, and intellectuals once again became a central issue in the CCP's relations with Chinese intellectuals.

Zhou believed that although China's revolution needed the intellectuals, China's industrialization needed them even more.[7] Chen Yi—the young poet in the May 4th movement of 1919, a worker-student in France in the 1920s, vice premier for cultural affairs from 1954, and foreign minister from 1958 to 1966—agreed with Zhou's analysis. "Ignorance" was now China's new enemy, he said. How, then, could the CCP call China's "national treasures" "bourgeois intellectuals"? Party leaders from rural villages must respect the intellectuals.

To the intellectuals, on the other hand, Zhou and Chen conveyed the great importance of their respecting the workers and peasants. As members of the tiny community of intellectuals within the CCP leadership, Zhou and Chen had many experiences of their own in common with the Chinese intellectuals. As Chen told a group of Chinese scientists and writers, in the revolutionary era he had repeatedly been regarded by his peasant colleagues as a "people's enemy." But with perseverance, he forged lifelong friendships with most of them. For instance, he told them, at the beginning of the War of Resistance, he was assigned to organize peasant guerrilla forces into the New Fourth Army, to be affiliated with the KMT government, the CCP's "declared enemy" since the breakup of the CCP-KMT united front in 1927. But upon arriving at a CCP base area, he was arrested and accused of being a spy for the KMT. "You intellectuals like to use big words, but I don't believe one word you told me," the peasant guerrilla leader told Chen. "We believe in class struggle, but you talk about class reconciliation. . . . Just tell me who gave you the money to do this!" As Chen recalled, his hands and feet were tied up, and he was called "a counterrevolutionary pig." However, he was determined to find common ground, which was resistance of the Japanese invasion. When the guerrilla leader and solders realized that they had mistreated Chen, they cried, asking for his forgiveness. After that time, the peasant leader and his guerrilla force were among the best soldiers in Chen's troops, and also among his best friends.

The message Zhou and Chen sent to the intellectuals was clear. As Chen said, "If we urge workers, peasants, and party cadres from rural China to respect scientists and writers, if we urge the whole party to protect the intellectuals as national treasures," Chinese intellectuals should in turn "respect the ideals, feelings, and dignity of ordinary Chinese people." Otherwise, there could be "a new civil war," as Chen warned, among workers, peasants, and intellectuals. That would be the "greatest tragedy" in China's modernization drive.

Nonetheless, in the political tensions between the CCP cadres and the intellectuals, Zhou and Chen clearly saw that the major fault, the major responsibility, lay with the CCP. "The major danger in this relationship," Zhou stressed, was not that the intellectuals tried to "poison" the CCP with their "bourgeois individualism" but that many party officials intruded into the intellectuals' "private realm," or their "individual creativity."[8]

A centerpiece of the gradualist political blueprint was to train a new generation of party cadres from rural villages with a new attitude toward the intellectuals, and to allow unlimited space for intellectuals' individual creativity. The former was regarded as the means, and the latter the goal in China's political reconstruction.

Mao acknowledged that many CCP cadres believed that "we are the revolutionaries, we don't need the intellectuals." But he stressed that in China's industrialization, the CCP was "only 30 percent competent, 70 percent incompetent." Without intellectuals, "only depending on ignorant us, how can we ever accomplish anything?" The CCP cadres must learn a "new working style" with regard to the intellectuals. In the revolutionary era, in dealing with the "class enemy," many party cadres had been accustomed to "the crude methods of coercion." But the CCP was now dealing with problems among the people, particularly "the democratic parties, nonparty democratic personages, the national bourgeoisie, university professors, and doctors." The new working style, he emphasized, must allow "free discussions and competitions among different schools of thought." For Mao, many party cadres were unable to say anything "very convincing, very persuasive" in public debates. If the CCP could only use "coercion and suppression" to treat different opinions, "we are wrong in the first place, and we will lose," he warned at the Politburo meetings. Even when their ideas were wrong or "poisonous weeds," the party cadres must learn how to debate. After all, "crude methods of suppression cannot address any of the deep-seated beliefs, beliefs in people's hearts and minds, such as religion, Marxism-Leninism, the bourgeois and the proletarian world outlooks." If party cadres continued to use suppression and prohibition, rather than discussion and persuasion, to suppress different opinions and ideas, they would be "sapped of their vitality," their minds would be "rigid," and they would collapse the moment they were in touch with the "poison ivy."[9]

A major difficulty here, for Zhou, was that many party cadres were from rural backgrounds and came to maturity at a time of revolutionary warfare. They were not aware that there was "a substantial difference" between "the law of intellectuals' cultural creations" and "the way of life in the revolutionary war." Zhou told party cadres in August 1950 that while many CCP members' way of life had been founded on collectivism fostered in the revolutionary war years, intellectuals' cultural production was based on "individual efforts and individual initiatives." That was why, he said, many CCP cadres "resented the intellectuals' demand for individual freedom" in their professional work.

Moreover, Zhou understood CCP cadres' "ruthless intervention" in the private realm to have been brought about by the "impact of premodern feudalism as well." Chen thought many party cadres only had the notion that "I alone lay down the rules."[10] Such cadres could not even be called "bourgeois officials," he said, since "capitalism has some democracy." Indeed, "Only feudal lords have such a mentality toward the intellectuals: 'I am the remolder, you are the one to be totally remolded; I am the victor, you are my captive.'" Such a feudal mentality, he warned, could "ruin the new China." In China's new polity, Zhou emphasized, no one should "monopolize opinions," no one should "monopolize ideology." What had contributed to "such a monopoly of opinions and monopoly of ideology" in the PRC? It was "the ideology of premodern feudalism within the party." Many CCP cadres did not have "any democratic spirit and concepts" when working with intellectuals. They behaved just like "feudal gangsters."[11]

The goal of cultivating the new working style among the CCP cadres, Zhou maintained, was to construct unlimited space for intellectuals' individual creativity and, in the private realm, as Chen put it, to follow the Taoist teaching and "do doing nothing." This was different from "doing nothing," he said. "Do doing nothing" meant that the party cadres should consciously avoid intervening in the private realm, fully respecting the autonomy of every intellectual's "cultural productions." "Cultural production has its unique characteristics," the process of which "solely depended on the deliberations and brewing of ideas in the mind of the individual intellectual." For instance, he said, a playwright or a novelist must have "his own characteristic style and his specific personality," his works must express "his own ideas, his own emotions, demonstrate what he felt most deeply in his heart." And "the most ridiculous slogan" in the field of literature and art, for Chen, was that "the party cadre provides ideas, the masses provide experience of life, and the author provides skills." He sharply remarked, "Does the individual author not have any ideas? Only the party cadre does? Does the individual author not have his own experience of life? Are they all dead? Does the individual author only possess skills, nothing else?" He complained that he really did not know from where this "evil wind" came. "The individual genius, the individual effort," he emphasized, would be the "great spring fountain" of cultural and scientific creations in China.[12]

Zhou and Chen believed there must be a political structure in place to ensure enduring cooperation between the party cadres and urban intellectuals as China industrialized. To build such a political structure, Mao and Zhou proposed the concept of "long-term coexistence and mutual supervision" between the CCP and the Third Force or democratic parties. The democratic parties, in Zhou's words, had "important social constituencies among the intellectuals as well as industrialists." The Democratic League's constituency was intellectuals in the humanities field, the September 3 Association had scientists as its constituency, the Democratic Promotion Association had many followers among the industrialists and merchants, and the People's Advancement Association had as its major constituency elementary and secondary school teachers. Zhou believed all these intellectuals' different interests should be represented through the different democratic parties in the new political system. This political structure, in other words, should institutionalize the political alliance between the CCP and Chinese intellectuals and entrepreneurs.

From 1949 to 1954, the Political Consultative Conference (PCC), a coalition between the CCP and democratic parties, played a prominent role in the political system. According to the "Common Program" of 1949, the PCC was the equivalent of a parliament. In 1954, with the new constitution and the establishment of the National People's Congress (NPC), however, the PCC was turned into a consultative, or advisory, political body. After the first NPC's election in September 1954, the importance of democratic parties in the government further declined. Between 1949 and 1954, among four vice premiers, two were from the democratic parties. By the end of 1954, the democratic parties were no longer represented among the vice premiers. And among eighteen ministers under the State Council, only three were from the democratic parties. This new composition of the central government and the State Council generated complaints far and wide from the democratic parties.[13]

In December 1954, Zhou suggested enhancing the PCC's political power. The PCC should have the power to recommend candidates to the People's Congress for appointments, to make policy proposals to the State Council, and to advise and supervise government works. The "life expectancies" of both sides, in Mao's words, should be "exactly the same." The CCP and the democratic parties should "vanish together in the future when there is no need for any kind of political party in China." Moreover, since the CCP was the leading party and had many more members than all the democratic parties combined, as Zhou reminded his party's leaders, the CCP needed more supervision from the democratic parties to check its "arrogance of power" in the political system.[14]

The gradualist political blueprint emphasized the great importance of a legal framework and institutional opposition in the polity. Zhou claimed that while in theory the "people's democratic dictatorship" should be based on democracy, the power was, in reality, so "concentrated" in the CCP that it would easily corrupt the party. For Zhou it was imperative to "learn from the Western parliamentary system," which, he said, was based on the rule of law and "constructive opposition" within the political system.

The NPC, according to Liu Shaoqi, must not be the parallel of the CCP and the central government. It should be superior to both.[15] "Without such checks and supervision," insisted Zhou, "good party cadres may easily become bad." In addition, the local county and provincial people's congresses should also be constructed as institutional opponents to the CCP and the central government. They had more direct contact with the people, Zhou said, and therefore better understood the people's immediate interests. "Their strength is precisely the weakness of the central government." "Such mutual supervision," he asserted, "should strike a necessary balance between the emphasis on the people's long-term interests and their short-term interests."[16]

Furthermore, Zhou stressed the importance of autonomous social organizations in supervising the CCP. Concerning the role of labor unions in the state enterprise, for instance, there were debates on whether it should always support the party position. For Gao Gang, the answer was yes; for Mao and Zhou, no. The labor unions, Mao wrote in 1950, should "protect workers' interests in their daily lives," and "criticize the abuse of power by the party cadres or administrators," rather than "blindly following the party positions."[17]

To legalize all this "constructive institutional opposition," in Zhou's view, the CCP and the government at all levels must take great pains to develop a comprehensive legal system in China. At his insistence, "political education courses" at secondary schools began to focus on constitutional law rather than Marxist-Leninist ideology. He insisted that it was constitutional law, not anything else, that should be regarded as the supreme law in the People's Republic.[18]

If the CCP cadres were to continue to abuse their power, despite educational, legal, and institutional checks and balances, Mao maintained that "workers, peasants, students, and professors should be encouraged to take further actions such as strikes and demonstrations." These strikes and demonstrations should be regarded as "supplementary measures" to oppose the CCP's "arrogance of power."

"In some factories, some rural cooperatives, some schools, some department stores, and some government agencies, people now have no democracy whatsoever," Mao said at a meeting of provincial and municipal party secretaries in January 1957. "There is only centralized bureaucracy, not democracy." To oppose the CCP's abuse of power, he argued that the CCP must not fear strikes and demonstrations, unrest, and chaos. If the complaints of the demonstrators were justified, the CCP should correct the mistakes immediately. If their complaints were not justified, the CCP could criticize them through "free discussions and convincing persuasions." He emphasized that college students' activism in demonstrations must be protected: "Some have complained that the Communists are worse than the Kuomintang in expelling demonstrating students." If students wanted to demonstrate, "let them do it, and let them do it as long as they want to." It was "absolutely wrong to expel and even arrest the student activists in the demonstrations."

He warned, "The KMT was digging its own grave by suppressing the students; we must not learn from the KMT." During the time of students' demonstrations and chaos, "never use guns, never pull triggers, no matter what happens, never shoot."[19]

The Radical Populist Political Blueprint

In sharp contrast to the gradualist political blueprint, the radical populist blueprint had an entirely different theoretical premise about the role of Chinese intellectuals. At the second session of the Eighth Party Congress in 1958, Mao announced that China had two "exploiting classes," which included not only the former landlords but "the national bourgeoisie and its intellectuals," and two "working classes," which included only workers and poor and lower-middle-class peasants. This was the first time since the War of Resistance that Mao formally described Chinese intellectuals as "part of the national bourgeoisie."

This did not mean that the CCP wanted to alienate Chinese intellectuals. In Mao's words, indeed, they were "too important for China's industrialization to push to the enemy's side." However, the CCP could not win them over without consolidating its alliance with the poor peasantry first. The antirightist campaign demonstrated, he argued, that the intellectuals stood in the middle between the CCP and the bourgeoisie and would follow whichever had "the greater power."[20]

Since the intellectuals' attitudes had been "improving" toward the workers and poor peasants, Mao said, and since their achievements and mistakes might be now divided at the 70 to 30 ratio—"70 percent achievements and 30 percent mistakes"—the key issue in the ideological struggle between socialism and capitalism was how to further "transform the bourgeois intellectuals into proletarian intellectuals." He urged Chinese intellectuals to "surrender wholeheartedly to the workers and poor peasants."[21] Since private ownership was changed, he stressed, the intellectuals had "lost their social and economic base." They were now like "the barrels in the sky, unable to stand on solid ground with the ordinary people." The CCP, the workers, and the poor peasants should "enthusiastically hold out their hands to encourage the intellectuals to fall from the sky," and "to help them fall on solid ground, standing together with ordinary Chinese people."[22]

In September 1957, in the aftermath of the antirightist campaign at the Third Plenum of the Eighth Central Committee (September 20–

October 9, 1957), Mao first suggested that the major challenge in China's political reconstruction was "the ideological struggle between proletariat and bourgeoisie or between socialism and capitalism." He argued that while "capitalist private ownership" had disappeared in China, "the capitalist ideology" still existed. Therefore, "we must reemphasize the theme of class struggle between socialism and capitalism on the ideological front."

There were no agreements over Mao's new argument at the Third Plenum. Advocates for the gradualist political blueprint argued that the CCP must not abandon the concept of socialism without class warfare. To frame as the major challenge the ideological divide between the proletariat and the bourgeoisie, was, as Zhou stated it, "not consistent with the Chinese reality." As Zhou, Chen Yun, and Chen Yi argued, the major challenge in the new era was clearly to develop the economy and to raise Chinese people's standard of living, as emphasized by the Resolution of the Eighth Party Congress of 1956. With their dissenting opinions, the Third Plenum could not produce a new resolution. In May 1958, at the Second Session of the Eighth Party Congress, however, the situation changed. By then, the majority had shifted to the side of Mao. In his report on behalf of the Central Committee, Liu publicly declared that the major divide in postrevolutionary China was "the ideological struggle between proletariat and bourgeoisie" in China's political reconstruction.[23]

Thus, according to the populist political blueprint, to forge a new unity between the intelligentsia and poor peasantry in the political system no longer required educating the CCP cadres to respect intellectuals' demands for unlimited space for individual creations or educating both sides to work together, but transforming "the bourgeois intellectuals" into "the proletarian intellectuals." It was in this context of the CCP's conflicting political blueprints that the rise and fall of the Hundred Flowers policy could be better interpreted.

The Rise and Fall of the Hundred Flowers Policy (1956–57)

From late 1955 to the summer of 1957, the PRC implemented the Hundred Flowers policy. Two different interpretations of the rise and fall of this policy have existed in the U.S. literature. One sees it as Mao's "conspiracy" or calculated decision to take out his political enemies after the Hungarian uprising in October 1956. The other interpretation, presented by Roderick MacFarquhar, places more importance on the social tensions between new cadres from rural China and urban intellectuals in the aftermath of land revolution in the early years of the PRC.[24]

The following discussion concurs with MacFarquhar's thesis. It further argues, however, for the importance of competing, underlying assumptions: socialism *without* class warfare vis-à-vis that of socialism *with* class warfare.

By the end of 1955, or one year before the Hungarian uprising, Beijing decided to implement a Hundred Flowers policy, to encourage different schools of thought to compete and contend with each other in China's modernization drive. The CCP leadership had become increasingly optimistic about the political attitudes of Chinese intellectuals. Moreover, the urgent need for economic and cultural construction prompted the CCP's increasing support for a lively intellectual environment in the new polity. Mao expressed his admiration for the "extremely lively intellectual life in the period of the Spring and Autumn and Warring States (500 BC) when Confucianism, Taoism, Mohism, Legalism, and many other schools of thought were "freely debating and contending with each other."[25]

In January 1956, at a highly publicized national conference on the CCP's policy toward intellectuals, which Mao himself attended, Zhou proclaimed that it was "dangerous" for many CCP cadres to believe "we can depend on factory workers for production, and depend on Soviet experts for advanced technology." It was "ridiculous" to think that China should depend indefinitely on the Soviet specialists rather than on China's own intellectuals. The key to China's industrialization was "the modernization of science and technology" and "the creation of world-class cultural products." The most recent achievements in science and technology in the world had further demonstrated, he stressed, that mankind was now "on the eve of a new scientific and technological revolution." China had already been left behind. If China could not modernize its science and technology faster than other countries, China might never realize its industrial dream in the next century.[26] "Let the brain workers and the manual workers unite together," he declared, "to bring about the high tide of China's economic and cultural construction."[27]

On April 28, 1956, at the enlarged Politburo meeting, Mao formally proposed the Hundred Flowers policy: "The general guideline in developing artistic, scientific, and academic works in China is to let one hundred flowers blossom, let one hundred schools of thought contend."[28] In February 1957, at the Supreme State Council's Conference, he further proposed the concept of "nonconfrontational contradiction between working class and national bourgeoisie" in China. "The contradiction between exploitation and the exploited in the worker-capitalist relationship," he said, was originally a "confrontational contradiction" in the Soviet experiment. However, in China's "unique environment," it could be transformed into "a nonconfrontational duality" and solved by "peaceful means."[29]

Mao explained the essence of the Hundred Flowers policy as being to open up not to close up the new polity:

> To open up is to go all out to create a political environment wherein people can freely express their different opinions, dare to criticize and to contend, and wherein people do not fear incorrect opinions, or poisonous weeds, but to learn how to argue with them, to convince them with reason, not with prohibition and suppression.
>
> To close up is to prohibit people to express their different opinions, not to allow them to have incorrect views, and whenever they do, to punish them with big sticks. This is not the right way to solve the nonconfrontational contradictions among the people, but to expand them.
>
> We have now chosen to open up, because it is the only way to strengthen our nation and to promote rapid cultural and scientific development in China.[30]

Chinese intellectuals responded warmly to the Hundred Flowers policy. As Luo Longji said at the Third Plenum of the PCC in March 1957, for Chinese intellectuals, nothing was more important than "trust and understanding." No political order could ever force them to serve, and the "unique character" and treatment of Chinese intellectuals throughout Chinese history should be honored.[31]

However, many intellectuals also knew that the majority of the CCP cadres did not like the Hundred Flowers policy at all. As Fei Xiaotong—an internationally known Chinese sociologist and anthropologist—described in the *People's Daily* in March 1957, since the establishment of the People's Republic, the intellectuals had been "eager to contribute to their beloved motherland," but they soon found out that many CCP cadres from rural China did not trust them. In a sense, he wrote, the Hundred Flowers policy was "the second liberation" for Chinese intellectuals. But they did not yet feel it was a spring in full bloom. Instead, it was more like an early spring, when the weather was sometimes warm, sometimes chilly. Why? Because many CCP cadres did not intend to implement this policy "faithfully" or "entirely." As soon as they saw that different schools of thought were indeed circulating, they complained that "the bourgeois demons" were "cropping up." They thought they had been working hard to "keep the devils down," but the "stone tablet" was again thrown open, and the devils were now all "rushing out." In the words of Fei Xiaotong, while the intellectuals "so warmly welcomed" the Hundred Flowers policy, many CCP cadres, "to say the least," were "not enthusiastic" about its implementation.[32]

Mao was aware of this dilemma. In the spring of 1957, he left Beijing, beginning his nationwide tour from the north to the south to persuade party cadres everywhere of the great importance of this policy for the new polity. The situation seemed to be changing for the better, and intellectuals increasingly felt the arrival of spring in full bloom. The democratic parties' new policy recommendations began to pour in.

Ma Yingchu, a nonparty democratic personage and the president of Beijing University, for instance, decided to resubmit his proposal on population control and family planning to the NPC. By 1955, he had concluded that to have a birth-control policy was crucial to the success of China's industrialization and peaceful foreign-policy goals. While China had one of the smallest averages of arable land per capita in the world, its annual population growth rate of 2–3 percent had been among the highest in the world from 1949 to 1955. Even with a growth rate of 2 percent China would have a population of 1.6 billion by 2000. With the peasants' traditional belief in "more children, more fortune," more than half of the limited national revenue each year had been and would continue to be consumed in maintaining the people at subsistence levels. In 1955, when Ma first submitted his report, he was severely criticized by many CCP cadres. At the height of the Hundred Flowers period, he decided to reintroduce his "Theory on Population Control" to the Supreme State Council Conference. This time he received enthusiastic support from Zhou and Chen Yun. He gave public lectures at Beijing University on the importance of family planning and received spirited applause from the faculty and students.[33]

Zhang Bojun—the vice president of the Democratic League—suggested forming a "Political Designers' Academy," made up of the PCC, the NPC, the democratic parties, and the autonomous social organizations. All major policy proposals should first be submitted to this academy for in-depth debates and discussions. His real goal here, he said, was to explore new ways to "combine democracy with socialism" in the PRC.[34]

Chu Anping—a leading member of the Democratic League and general editor of the *Guangming Daily*—recommended restoration of the type of coalition government that had existed between 1949 and 1954. In that period, he said, there had been many representatives of the democratic parties and nonparty democratic personages in key positions of the Central Government and the State Council. But since 1954, most of these positions were taken by CCP members. In all levels of political organizations, there was always a CCP member as the head who usually had the final say in policy debates. While Chinese intellectuals were willing to contribute, they had not yet been given the full opportunity to do so.

In May 1957, when two British reporters visited Luo Longji for his opinions on the Hundred Flowers policy, he praised the new policy highly. No matter how many complaints intellectuals and democratic parties had made about the CCP, he said, the bottom line was that they did respect the CCP and love the new China "deeply and passionately." He quoted a leader of the democratic parties as saying, "The blossom spring has arrived; now you can hear the songs of the birds everywhere." [35]

On January 7, 1957, an article that appeared in the *People's Daily* sharply criticized the "bourgeois direction" in China's academics since the implementation of the Hundred Flowers policy. Many Chinese writers no longer talked about "serving the needs of ordinary workers, peasants, and soldiers," it warned. The "most visible works" in 1956 were no longer "directly" connected with "ordinary Chinese people's new lives" in the People's Republic. [36] This article struck a sympathetic chord among many CCP cadres. All major newspapers in northeast China, for instance, published either editorials or commentaries in support of this article. The *Liaoning Daily* stressed that this article demonstrated a "battle cry" for defending "the proletarian principle of the party," which, like a "tocsin," sounded an alarm, "loud and clear." The *Jilin Daily* emphasized that "we must insist upon the principle of serving the needs of workers, peasants, and soldiers in all literary works." [37] Meanwhile, the *People's Daily* kept "strange silence," as Mao put it, concerning the widespread criticism of the Hundred Flowers policy in many CCP newspapers. [38]

In March and April of 1957, in Mao's many talks with local party officials about the Hundred Flowers policy, he acknowledged that this policy had not received "a full endorsement" from the Central Committee: "Only Zhou Enlai and a few others are on my side in Beijing." He told the municipal and provincial party cadres that he now turned to them for their full support.[39]

During the Hungarian uprising in late 1956, in which a communist regime had been overthrown, the CCP leaders convened fourteen meetings in eighteen days, to discuss its implication for the CCP in China.[40] There was no consensus in the CCP leadership on what lessons the CCP should learn from the Hungarian uprising. According to Zhou, Chen Yun, and Chen Yi, the champions of the gradualist blueprints, the major lesson was the vital importance of improving people's standard of living and expanding democracy. However, for other CCP leaders, the major lesson was that the intelligentsia in Poland and Hungary had never given up their "bourgeois ideology," never given up their attempt to establish a "bourgeois republic" at the expense of working people's welfare. Indeed, even some loyal supporters of the Hundred Flowers policy agreed in part to such a warning. Deng Xiaoping, a strong supporter of Zhou's policy, for instance, remarked that an important lesson was that "Hungary never engaged in ideological reform of the intellectuals." For him, in the Hungarian intellectuals' clubs and salons, which had organized the uprising, "there were many highly talented intellectuals," and if the Hungarian communists had ever "helped them to engage in ideological reform," they could have done many "great things" for Hungary.[41]

In Mao's view, the root causes of the Hungarian uprising included a communist party that was "cut off from the people," an economic strategy that had sacrificed the production of consumer goods, and the "predominant influence of intellectuals' bourgeois ideology."[42] For those CCP leaders who felt bitter that they had fought through all the hard years of the revolution only to "defer to the intellectuals," Mao's theme was now that the CCP had to learn from the intellectuals in the new age of industrialization. "Until such time as new proletarian intellectuals emerge," the CCP cadres would have to "toughen their scalps." The intellectuals might "lift their tails high"; the CCP, however, had to "kowtow to them, at least for a while."[43] This does not mean, however, that after the Hungarian uprising, Mao treated the Hundred Flowers policy as a sort of political expediency. Mao still believed in the wisdom of this policy. Thus, in February 1957, he decided to leave Beijing to campaign for the Hundred Flowers policy himself among local party officials.

*   *   *

In May 1957, Mao and other CCP leaders began to frown over the confidential reports about some intellectuals' "vicious attacks" on the CCP. According to a report, a student at Qinghua University in Beijing claimed, "China has the dictatorship of peasant cadres. . . . We must adopt the Hungarian method to overthrow the current government, to shoot all those ignorant party cadres."[44] Upon receiving similar reports, Mao wondered whether some in the democratic parties and universities were, after all, trying "to stir up a violent, force 7 typhoon" to overthrow the CCP. He also wondered whether their strategy was "to first take over the leadership in the fields of journalism, education, art, and science," since they knew those fields were the CCP's "weakest points." He began to stress that the CCP must "pull back" those middle-of-the-roaders in the intellectuals' community, since China's economic and cultural reconstruction "desperately" needed them. He regarded smashing the rightists' attack on the CCP as the only way to pull them back. To his mind, the Hungarian uprising must have given the rightists' illusions about the possibility of "overthrowing" the CCP,[45] and the antirightist campaign would be like warfare for the CCP. Without winning this war, "a revolt similar to that in Hungary might occur in China." From that time on, Mao believed employing military strategies was necessary to deal with this group. It was a strategy, he said, "to lure the snake out of its hiding place" and "to seduce the enemy into a trap."[46]

At the start of the antirightist campaign, Mao was convinced that the number of the rightists nationwide was "very small," no more than 4,000.[47] One month later, by July 8, the number had doubled to 8,000.[48] By the end of August, local party leadership further increased the number to 60,000. In September and October 1957, the Central Committee twice issued circulars, to stop "the tendency to dramatically increase the number of the rightists."[49] But many party cadres chose to ignore these orders.[50] By early 1958, at the end of the antirightist campaign, 550,000 intellectuals all over China were designated bourgeois rightists.[51] These designated rightists were deprived of their opportunity to serve the nation and to play the role of outspoken critics of the status quo in Chinese society. China missed a golden opportunity for creating millions of new citizens who had "a higher order of loyalty."[52] Ma Yingchu, for example, was labeled because of his insistence on population control and family planning.[53] If his proposal had been implemented after 1957, China's population could have been well below 1 billion by the end of the twentieth century. If Zhang Bojun's proposal for a "Political Designers' Academy" had been followed through on, a new type of institutional mechanism for negotiations and compromises between urban and rural China might have been established in the early years of the PRC.

In August 1959, Yang Shangqui, the party secretary of Jiangxi province, wrote to Mao and Liu Shaoqi about the "urgency of correcting the dangerous mistake of magnifying the scope of rightists." Mao agreed. He proposed to Liu that it would be possible to "reeducate" at least 70 percent of these rightists in seven years, taking off their "rightist caps" in that period, or 10 percent each year, beginning in October 1959.

Zhou reiterated his support for Chinese intellectuals. Zhou asserted that the major points in his report on Chinese intellectuals in 1956 were still "fully valid." Some provincial and municipal party cadres had refused to distribute his report since the antirightist campaign. "If you have different views, you are welcome to argue with me." But the reason "I have felt sad" was that there had been "no response whatsoever" from these party cadres. "My report on Chinese intellectuals has simply been consigned to limbo."[54] He encouraged treating intellectuals as "national treasures": "There is no doubt that Chinese intellectuals belong to the working people. We should trust them, care for them. They are our 'national treasures.' It is wrong to continue to regard them as bourgeois intellectuals. . . . This basic assessment should be the foundation of all our policies toward Chinese intellectuals."[55]

Chen Yi joined Zhou in pinpointing the CCP's "horrible mistake" in mistreating the intellectual class. Since late 1957, he said, many Chinese intellectuals could only praise what the CCP had done. Very soon the CCP would be surrounded only by "eulogy," which would be "the most dangerous moment" for the new China. In the new political system, he emphasized, "everyone should be happy and have peace of mind, everyone should be able to say all he knows and say it without reserve, everyone should be able to contribute his talents and wisdom to China's modernization drive." The new China should be this kind of "open society." However, the situation had become "very different." With all those "regulations and restrictions, ideological labels, censorship and prohibitions in newspapers and publications," which had been "imposed by party cadres themselves," and most of which even he himself did not know, how could the CCP expect the intellectuals to speak their minds? How could the CCP expect the intellectuals to "share their hearts with us?" How could the CCP expect them "to contribute their knowledge and expertise to the common cause?" "I am crying and warning all of you," as he told the party cadres at numerous meetings, it would be "disastrous for our great country" if the party cadres did not change "such antidemocratic, anti-intelligentsia mentality." And he told the intellectuals that he knew they had been hurting. "You have loved the party and the new China. But the party has not trusted you in return." On behalf of the CCP, he said, he wanted to "apologize" to the intellectuals.[56] However, in the summer of 1962, both Zhou and Chen were criticized by other party leaders at a Central Committee meeting in Beidaihe for their rightist evaluation of the nature of Chinese intellectuals.[57]

The Hundred Flowers Policy and the Soviet Union

Before the Korean War, the participation of the democratic parties in the Chinese government and the possible impact of these groups on the CCP's foreign policy had been a thorny issue in Sino-Soviet relations. In the mid-1950s, the concept of "a multiparty system under proletarian leadership," particularly the Hundred Flowers policy in Beijing, caused greater concern in Moscow. As Mikhail Zimyanin, the head of the Soviet Foreign Ministry's Far Eastern Department, reported: "Since the start of the Hundred Flowers policy, the Chinese press has begun, with increasing frequency, to criticize Soviet authors' works in the fields of philosophy, history, literature, and art." Such criticism, in turn, gave "strong impetus to hostile statements by rightist forces who denounced the Soviet Union." In his words, these "rightist forces" charged that "Soviet assistance was self-interested and of inferior quality" and claimed that "the Soviet Union was extracting money from China in return for weapons supplied to Korea, which were already paid for with the blood of Chinese volunteers."[58]

In his memoir, Khrushchev stressed that he did not agree with the CCP's Hundred Flowers policy from the start. As he wrote, to let one hundred flowers blossom meant that "the socialist countries would allow all kinds of flowers to grow: not only pretty flowers, but also ugly flowers, even poisonous weeds." He told Mao during the Hundred Flowers period, "We certainly cannot allow those poisonous weeds to blossom. We must destroy them before they can even grow." Khrushchev himself admitted that it was because of his direct intervention that no Soviet newspaper ever reported on the Hundred Flowers policy in China and that the Hundred Flowers policy brought about "a big downturn" in Sino-Soviet relations throughout 1956.[59]

Mao told his Chinese comrades that the Soviet communists had stayed in the "greenhouse" for too long. They would not have any immunity from the poison ivy, since they had never had a chance to encounter the poison ivy and develop immunity. "Should the poison ivy ever enter their 'greenhouse,' " he predicted, "they might collapse very quickly."[60] Nonetheless, in his conversations with the Soviet ambassador in June 1956, he said it was fine if the Soviet newspapers and magazines did not report on the Hundred Flowers policy, because the CCP's policy might not be "appropriate" for the Soviet Union. "Situations in your country are surely different from ours. We all should formulate our policies according to our different domestic situations."[61]

In private, the CCP leaders were, however, very worried about the Soviet criticism of the supposedly antisocialist nature of the Hundred Flowers policy. In preparing for the Central Committee's political report to the Eighth Party Congress to be held in September 1956, Mao and the advocates of the gradualist political blueprint decided to add a discussion of "universality and particularity" in building socialist political systems, to defend the CCP's new political plan of action. Here is a selection from the final draft of the Central Committee's political report:

> Whether a one-party system as in the Soviet Union, or a multiparty system under the proletarian leadership as in China, the choice of these different socialist polities should be based on different political and economic conditions. While it was wrong to deny universality and to emphasize only particularity, it was equally wrong to deny particularity and to emphasize only universality in constructing China's socialist polity. It is impossible to imagine that there should be only one universal form of the socialist political system. As an eastern country, and as a big country, China not only had many unique characteristics in its revolution, it also will have many unique characteristics in its socialist construction. Even after the completion of China's socialist construction, China will continue to have many unique characteristics of its own in its political system.[62]

In the spring of 1957, with better implementation of the Hundred Flowers policy in local areas, thanks to Mao's personal campaign among local party cadres, the Khrushchev leadership's worry was heightened. Khrushchev twice sent Mao's personal friend Marshall

K. Y. Voroshilov to visit China, to persuade Mao to change the Hundred Flowers policy.

In Beijing, Voroshilov told Mao, "I brought with me the Soviet Communist Central Committee's serious concern over your Hundred Flowers policy." The Hungarian revolt had taught the Soviets "an important lesson." "Our enemies can seize just one mistake in our work to create a public opinion hostile to us, and to fan people's resentment toward us." If a secret report on Stalin could generate a national uprising in Hungary, "what about these openly published rightist opinions in your newspapers?" Indeed, "some of the speeches and writings in your newspapers are no longer criticism. They are intended to overthrow the Communist government, to deny socialism, and to break up the Sino-Soviet alliance." He asked Mao, "What is your purpose in proposing this policy? How can you ever agree to publish those anti-socialist speeches and articles in the Chinese Communist Party's official newspapers?" He was clear on the point: "Rightist speeches and writings must not be published in socialist countries. Is there any doubt on this question?"

On May 6, 1957, Voroshilov left China. But two weeks later, Khrushchev sent him back to Beijing. He warned Mao, "Your newspapers are continuing to paint the socialist world in black color, which has made all socialist countries very nervous." In Moscow, Marshal G. K. Zhukov, the defense minister, openly declared, "If any socialist country suffers from any capitalist country's attack, the Soviet Union will immediately launch a counterattack." Mao asked Khrushchev if this speech implied that the Soviet Union had "the right to send troops into any socialist country whenever the Soviet leaders believe that country is in great danger." Mao felt that the CCP could take care of these rightists in China and that the Soviet Union had no right to intervene in any socialist country's domestic affairs. But Khrushchev told Mao, "Zhukov made this statement on behalf of the collective decision of the Central Committee of the Soviet Communist Party."[63]

The Khrushchev leadership also indicated its interest in supporting China's nuclear program. Such crucial help, however, Moscow emphasized, would "depend on the development of the Chinese political situation." In a way, Khrushchev presented Mao with an unprecedented incentive to end the Hundred Flowers policy: the possibility of receiving Soviet support for China's nuclear program. It is still not clear to what extent Mao's final decision on the antirightist campaign was related to such an incentive, but the connection was hard to dismiss. In October 1957, in the wake of the antirightist campaign, the Sino-Soviet agreement on Soviet aid for China's nuclear program was signed in Moscow.[64]

Concepts of Socialism in China's Political Reconstruction: Social and Cultural Underpinnings

In building a modern Chinese polity in the wake of the social revolution, the greatest challenge was how to design a political mechanism for compromise and negotiation in forging a new coalition between rural and urban China. This new polity must incorporate the peasantry into the political process, so that it would represent not just the urban elite but the majority of the Chinese people. However, this new polity must also be able to create "unlimited space" for intellectuals' individual creativity, to protect the private realm from compulsive intrusions by "revolutionary populism and premodern feudalism" in the aftermath of the land revolution. To meet this formidable challenge, two different political blueprints emerged in China in the 1950s, shaped by different underlying assumptions.

First, to advocates of the radical political blueprint, Chinese intellectuals were part of the Chinese bourgeoisie. In contrast, to champions of the gradualist political blueprint, Chinese intellectuals were part of the Chinese working class and were valuable to China.

In his reflection on this party debate, Bo Yibo asked, "Why has our party's policy toward intellectuals shifted back and forth for decades since the establishment of the PRC?" The reason, he said, was "anti-intellectualism" in the party. The CCP did not quickly recognize the importance of intellectuals for China's modernization. "The majority of our party leaders and cadres were from a worker or peasant background and just went through revolutionary war." Their educational levels were "not high," and their direct contacts with intellectuals had been "rare." They were thus "not familiar with the intellectuals' characteristics, mentalities, and working styles," which further heightened their sense of "distrust or suspicion" of the intellectuals. In the time of the Hundred Flowers policy, as he recalled, intellectuals were "so happy, so supportive, so spirited, and so eager to contribute to China's modernization." During the antirightist campaign and the Cultural Revolution (1966–1976), however, "the intellectuals' great activism was immensely frustrated, particularly the intellectuals in the field of the humanities and social sciences." Certainly, the intellectuals were "not perfect," and they should not be. What was most important for the CCP was "to protect Chinese intellectuals' individual creative vitality." Once this was sapped, it would not easily be regenerated for a long period of time. "This lesson was so vitally important that the party must never forget."[65]

It was thus not accidental that after the Cultural Revolution, when Deng Xiaoping returned to power, he immediately reinstated Chinese intellectuals as "part of Chinese working class, not part of bourgeoisie." The united front between the CCP and the urban intelligentsia, or the coalition between villages and colleges would soon be resumed in the Deng reform era.

Second, in the populist political blueprint, the essence of the ideological transformation of Chinese intellectuals was the struggle between "socialist collectivism" and "bourgeois individualism."[66] After the antirightist campaign, Mao increasingly emphasized the creation of millions of "selfless socialist men" in China's polity. Even the slogan "Everyone serves me, and I serve everyone" was not a good one, since it could not forget "the small me." When some CCP leaders reminded Mao that it had been proposed by Karl Marx himself, Mao replied, "Let's not mention this was Marx's slogan, but let's not use the entire slogan either." In other words, the relationship between the individual and the common good was perceived in terms of antagonistic oppositions, which were obviously different from Marx's own interpretations, and surely more radical than the Soviet concept of collectivism.[67]

On the other hand, champions of the gradualist political blueprint did not perceive the freedom of the intellectuals to be in conflict with the ideal of the common good. Chen Yi argued, "When we emphasize the common good, why should some people believe it implies the denial of individual creativity or individuality? When we stress individuality, unlimited space for individuals' cultural production, why should some people think it contradicts the spirit of the common good?" The relationship between unfettered individual creativity and the common good of the Chinese people could be like Yin and Yang, mutually beneficial and complementary.[68]

While Mao supported the moderate/gradualist blueprints, he shared the deep-seated philosophical assumptions of Yin-Yang balance and criticized the Soviet leaders' "metaphysics" in their concept of socialism. As he commented in January 1957, "Stalin made many errors of metaphysics and taught many others in the Soviet Union to make similar errors. A most striking example was the Soviet interpretation of the philosophical concept of 'identity' or 'unity' in socialism." To Stalin, Mao said, the concept of identity or unity in socialist economies and polities should never be applied to essentially opposite categories, such as workers and capitalists, fragrant flowers and poisonous ivies, and the private and public realms. Mao argued that the relationships between these categories should not be defined in terms of "mutual exclusions." While they are profoundly different from each other, struggling against each other, they can also be unified in the same "identity."[69]

Clearly, the gradualist political blueprint aimed to create cooperation between rural and urban China, or a new political unity between poor peasants and intellectuals. In this regard, it was similar to the spirit of Sun Yat-sen's political blueprint. The CCP-led multiparty system was, in particular, similar to Sun's plan for tutelage rule in his theory of three-stage democratic evolution.

Unlike Sun's plan, however, this gradualist political blueprint did not articulate whether the role of the CCP would change in the future. When the urban population caught up with the rural population in the course of industrialization, when economic development produced a much larger middle class as the social foundation of the democratic parties, would there come a time when the CCP could both compete and cooperate with the democratic parties on an equal footing in national elections? This was an issue the gradualist political blueprint did not explore. One may also question whether in the international milieu of the time it was possible to explore that far.

The launching of the antirightist campaign stemmed from Mao's fatal misjudgment of Chinese intellectuals in the summer of 1957. Mao did not have a most nuanced understanding of Chinese intellectuals and the democratic parties, as he did of the poor peasants in the Chinese revolution. Unlike Zhou and Chen Yi, the seeds of distrust or suspicion of the intelligentsia and the democratic parties did exist in Mao's mind. When the seeds were dormant, Mao stood firmly with Zhou and Chen Yi. He demonstrated great wisdom in proposing the Hundred Flowers policy at the end of 1955 and enthusiastically led the campaign for this policy throughout 1956 and early 1957. With Soviet pressure—especially the lure of the nuclear program—mounting rapidly, and with memories of the Hungarian uprising quite fresh, the external environment was indeed conducive to Mao's change of mind. The doubt began to grow, and it grew quickly, substantially distorting

Mao's perceptions of the intellectuals' intentions and, consequently, the Chinese political situation.

It is also clear that Mao's decision alone could not account for the demise of the gradualist political blueprint. In the wake of the land revolution, the party, made up of peasants and workers who were recently peasants, was ruralized. If the state penetrated society by mobilizing people from below, by incorporating them into the state, the people in some sense defined what that state was.[70] They did not formulate general policies, but they were in a position to interpret them and to redefine or reshape them in the course of implementation. In this sense, the failure of the Hundred Flowers policy represented, according to John King Fairbank, a "class struggle between intellectuals and new party cadres" who were "from peasant ranks."[71]

The assumptions underlying the radical populist political blueprint—anti-intellectualism and peasant collectivism—were deeply embedded in peasant rebels' political visions in Chinese history. During the Taiping Poor Peasant Rebellion in the 1850s, for example, after the Taiping peasant rebels established their government in Nanjing, the gentry-scholars were quickly expelled from all local governments. Some of them were hired only occasionally as "copy clerks." As some gentry-scholars recorded with a sour tone, peasant rebels treated the poor people like "their own big brothers." But they called wealthy gentry-scholars "demons." Once the rich gentry-scholars were driven out of officialdom, the poor, "even the 'shrews,' " they bitterly complained, all "rushed in" and became the new officials in local governments.[72] Moreover, the Taiping government imposed a collectivist ideology upon the entire society. The Taiping's official ideology or religion was Christianity. But the way they interpreted Christianity followed the Mohist interpretations of public-private relationships. The Taiping rebels' political blueprint was thus to create "coordinated efforts" in the government to abolish "all individuals' selfish thoughts, which may harm the common good."[73]

A major weakness in Chinese discourse from the beginning of the modern era was that many modern reformers were not always fully or consciously aware of the vital importance of different philosophical constructions of the private-public relationship to China's long march toward modernity. So when the situation demanded national unity or social mobilization, they could be propelled by the urgency of the moment and subconsciously dragged into an absolutist philosophical framework. The relationship between the individual and the common good was construed as mutually contradictory, a radical populist legacy of Chinese peasant rebellions. This principal weakness illustrated itself vividly in the CCP debates of the 1950s.

One may argue that Mao based his policy shift on a calculation of political power that could be attributed to his personality. Such an interpretation, however, cannot explain how Mao's policy could be so counterproductive to his proposed goal: to strengthen the political alliance between the CCP and the intelligentsia through a method other than the Hundred Flowers policy. How could his new method of waging ideological warfare to eradicate "bourgeois individualism" produce the opposite policy outcome in China? To explain why there was a shift from the Hundred Flowers policy to the ideological warfare policy, or why the CCP's political power was drastically reduced rather than increased in urban China after the antirightist campaign, one must examine how Mao and his populist supporters redefined the concept of power and socialism—a concept that is intimately tied to their new construction of the relationship between the private and the public realms.

In short, if the Hundred Flowers policy and the gradualist political blueprint could not be categorized as a liberalization program of the American type, neither could the antirightist campaign and the populist political blueprint be categorized as the brainchild of Soviet communism. To some extent, they can be attributed to competing social and cultural assumptions in Chinese historical heritage.

In the 1950s, advocates of the containment strategy in Washington saw the Chinese political system as a "perpetual struggle" between a "unified, repressive communist state" above and "suffering individuals" at the bottom. In reality, as the rise and fall of the Hundred Flowers policy illustrated, neither the Chinese state nor the society was monolithic. The political reconstruction during the PRC's first decade manifested two opposite ways of addressing the political tensions between rural China and urban China, or between poor peasantry and urban intelligentsia, in the aftermath of the nationwide land revolution. To what extent did these conflicting visions for China's economic and political reconstruction influence the PRC's foreign-policy orientations in the 1950s?

CHAPTER TEN

Becoming First-Class Citizens of the World

China's Diplomacy of
Peaceful Coexistence

In the aftermath of the Korean War, Beijing proposed peaceful coexistence as the guiding principle of the PRC's diplomacy. However, despite its affirmations to that effect, Beijing's foreign policy demonstrated two different patterns in the 1950s. After 1954, the principle of peaceful coexistence was first applied to the PRC's relations with its Asian neighbors. After the Polish and Hungarian uprisings in 1956, Beijing also began to apply this principle to relations within the Soviet bloc. In August 1956, Beijing launched its peace initiative further afield toward Washington by inviting American journalists to visit China. And in January 1957, Beijing formally suggested to Moscow a new global strategy of détente, or reconciliation between the two blocs in the Cold War. In vivid contrast, from 1958 to 1960, the PRC's diplomacy suffered a series of severe setbacks: the Sino-Indian friendship came to an end, the Sino-Soviet alliance was on the brink of collapse, and Beijing stopped its overtures of peace toward Washington.

The apparent coincidence between the CCP's radical economic and political blueprints and China's foreign-policy setbacks raises an important question: what was the relationship between the CCP's domestic blueprints and its diplomatic behaviors in the 1950s? Was this relationship a direct one? More particularly, did advocates of the radical blueprints have a different foreign-policy agenda? Or was this relationship an indirect one? That is, were Beijing's diplomatic setbacks related instead to China's changed international security environment in the late 1950s? In other words, was the relationship between Beijing's domestic blueprints and its foreign-policy behaviors much more complex than it appeared to be at the time?[1]

Peaceful Coexistence: The Guiding Principle of the PRC's Diplomacy

In 1953, in the aftermath of the Korean War, Mao told his comrades that if there were new wars, China would have to feed many more soldiers, which could jeopardize China's economic recovery. He emphasized, "It will be in China's best interests to concentrate on its industrialization drive." Zhou concurred: "China desperately needs peace. The longer we can have peace, the better for improving the Chinese people's living standards."[2]

To create a peaceful international environment for China's economic development, Zhou stressed, China's diplomacy must not focus on the tensions between the Soviet and the American blocs. "The major contradiction in China's foreign policy is not the struggle between the socialist and capitalist countries but the contest between war and peace." He expanded on this in 1956: "If nations in the two blocs are turned into two iron plates, refusing to have exchanges with each other and continuing to attack each other, China will never be able to create a peaceful international environment for its domestic reconstructions."[3]

As soon as the Korean War ended, Zhou first proposed the five principles of peaceful coexistence during his conversation with the Indian delegation over the Tibetan question in December 1953. These five principles were: "Mutual respect for each other's national sovereignty and territorial integrity; nonaggression; noninterference in each other's internal affairs; equality and mutual benefits; and peaceful coexistence." Indian prime minister Jawaharlal Nehru warmly endorsed these principles. In April 1954, these five principles appeared in the text of the "Agreement on Commerce and Transportation between India and Tibet of China."[4] In June 1954, during Zhou's state visit to India and Burma, these principles were further highlighted in both the Nehru-Zhou and U Nu (the Burmese prime minister)–Zhou joint declarations.

The philosophical foundation of peaceful coexistence was recognition of the "extremely rich cultural and political plurality of the world." Zhou argued, "Social systems, moral values, ways of life, religious beliefs, and cultural traditions in the human world differ from place to place in thousands of different ways." How could countries live in peace in such a world? The best way, he said, was not to try to impose one's own standards upon everyone else but "to search for common ground" while preserving differences. He liked to quote Lao Zi—the founder of Taoism—as saying that the fundamental law of humanity, like that of the universe, was "the unity of the opposites." The major challenge to humanity was therefore not to eliminate differences but to find common ground between apparently opposite human values and interests in the world.[5] Mao also often quoted Mencius—Confucius' major disciple—as saying that "the nature of the world is the immense variety of things." As Mao argued in 1954, "Marx recognized the rich variety of things in the human world, as Mencius did, only metaphysics denies it."[6]

The first precondition for peaceful coexistence, Zhou said, was to respect every country's national sovereignty and territorial integrity. The implications for China's diplomacy was that it must not try to "export revolutions" or interfere in other countries' domestic affairs. As he emphasized in 1955, "the American people have chosen their present way of life and political and economic systems. We must respect their choice." Zhang Wentian, the deputy minister of foreign affairs (1954–1958), told a Chinese ambassadors' meeting in March 1956, "Whether a nation wants to have a revolution, or how it wages a revolution, is entirely a matter of its own people's choices." After all, "different political systems and ideological outlooks should not become the source of antagonism among nations and peoples."[7]

The second precondition for peaceful coexistence was, Zhou said, to practice the principle of mutual benefit. In negotiations, as Zhang explained, "we should take into account our own national interests, but we also should take into account the other side's national interests." If one side tries to maximize its advantages, Zhou often said, the agreement would not last long. In Chinese economic exchanges with other developing countries in particular, Zhou set down "Eight Principles for Chinese Foreign Economic Aid," and the guiding principle was that China must not try to gain any privilege from the country to which it provides aid. Economic aid should not result in that country's dependency on China; for example, in providing technological support, China should ensure that the native technicians master the technology.[8]

The third precondition for peaceful coexistence was to regard other nations as equals, regardless of the nation's power, wealth, race, and ideology. At the first PRC Foreign Ministry meeting in November 1949, Zhou emphasized this point: "From the Empress Dowager, Yuan

Shikai, to Chiang Kai-shek, who among them ever dared to stand up to the imperialist powers? None of them did. They all kneeled down to the ground to conduct China's diplomacy. The history of China's diplomacy in the past 100 years was the history of national humiliation. The diplomacy of the new China must be the diplomacy of national dignity, national independence, striving for national equality."[9]

China's diplomacy must not be "submissive" to the great powers' pressures. China's diplomacy must not be arrogant toward smaller or poorer countries. Just like the colored metals, Mao often said, the colored people were as "precious" as the white people. Both should be regarded as "first-class citizens" in the world.[10]

Would China become arrogant and expansive toward its neighbors *after* China's industrialization? H. S. Suhrawardy, the prime minister of Pakistan, thought the answer was yes. As he told Zhou in 1955, "China would soon be able to occupy Pakistan easily, as the Mongols did in the thirteenth century." Zhou said that before the Mongols invaded Pakistan, they had occupied China first. Both Pakistan and China were victims of the Mongols' invasions and devastations, and since the nineteenth century, "we suffered enough from colonial powers' repeated military invasions. We also witnessed their eventual defeats. How could we ever follow their footsteps to invade our neighbors?" He maintained that in Chinese cultural heritage and historical memory, "Military conquest is always identified with profound immorality, unavoidable downfall, and the deadly disease of imperialism."[11] Chen Yi declared, "It would be the greatest national shame, should China ever become a new 'colonial hegemon' in Asia and the world."[12]

However, Clement Attlee, the former British prime minister and the leader of the Labour Party, argued that though China was peaceful at the time, it could become aggressive by the end of the twentieth century, when China's "population pressures" would compel it to expand into Southeast Asia. Zhou told him in 1956, "An important reason we consider adopting a population control and family planning policy is precisely because we want our production level and the population growth to go hand-in-hand, so that China would be always able to take care of its people's needs."[13]

This does not mean Beijing did not worry about the possibility that China might commit "the fatal mistake of great power chauvinism" after its industrialization drive. Mao was deeply concerned about such a possibility. China now had a "modest attitude," he said, because it was still a developing country. Even if some Chinese wanted to "get cocky," their tails could only "stick up for one or two meters." After China's industrialization, even if China would not send troops to occupy new territories, it could still commit "the fatal mistake of arrogance of power." In Mao's words, "Big power chauvinism, the fatal mistake all other great powers have made in world history, China could make as well after its industrialization." This prompted him to tell his comrades often that China should let the entire world "supervise" China's growth. "Should China ever get cocky in the future, should China ever be infected by the deadly disease of great power chauvinism, everyone in the world must criticize China, denounce China." He accordingly insisted that all Chinese students should receive an education in "anti–great power chauvinism" starting in elementary school. The new China after its industrialization should be a "great nation," he often quoted Lao Zi as saying, that would "stand tall and proud, but not arrogant," that would be "strong and powerful, but loved, not feared by weaker and poorer nations in the world."[14]

Many foreign observers at the time perceived a dilemma for Beijing in its pursuit of a diplomacy of peaceful coexistence. As an American journalist pointed out in a question to Zhou, the PRC declared that it supported the Middle Eastern, African, and Asian countries' struggles for independence, but "if these countries' governments oppress their communist parties, deprive their peoples of the political rights to organize communist parties, will Beijing still support them?" China's support was, Zhou reiterated, based on the principle of peaceful coexistence and China's own historical sufferings. "Their domestic policies, good or not good, are matters of their own choices and judgments, in which we should not intervene. As long as they are fighting for peace, national independence, and their people's welfare, we will continue to support them."[15]

While Chinese diplomats should "faithfully implement these five principles," what should they do if conflicts occurred despite their desire for peaceful coexistence? Zhou articulated four guidelines on conflict management. First, be patient. With both sides in the heat of controversy, it could only worsen the situation "if we insist on our own views." A better way would be "to wait for the other side to come to the right solution on its own." Second, never shoot first. No matter how badly the other side treated China, "we must not treat them badly." Third, prepare to fight back, if the other side continued to bully China. Otherwise, "we would be looked upon as weaklings." Finally, in preparing for fighting back, "we should warn the other side twice before launching the attack." During the warning periods, two things might happen: the "farsighted" in the other nation might realize that China's retreat and warning was not a sign of weakness and would take caution not to intensify the conflict. The "shortsighted" might regard it as a "sign of weakness," and continue "to push China into a corner." Only then will we "definitely fight back." Zhou used the Korean War as an example: "Before we crossed the Yalu, we had warned the American government twice, but they did not listen. They pushed us to the corner. So we decided to fight back." Zhou emphasized that the "philosophical source" of these ideas came from "Chinese cultural traditions," rather than from "Marxist teachings."[16]

Thus, it was not "the export of revolution," not "the struggle between the socialist and the capitalist blocs," but the five principles of peaceful coexistence that became the declared guiding principles of China's diplomacy from 1954. As Zhou and Chen emphasized to Chinese Foreign Service officers, "Peaceful coexistence is not a temporary, tactical measure; it is the principal foundation of China's foreign policy."[17]

China's Diplomacy toward the Soviet Union: The 1950s

As both Chen Yi and Zhang Bojun wrote at the time, when they learned that the Soviet Union was willing to aid 143 industrial projects in China's first Five-Year Plan, they were "deeply moved." During Khrushchev's visit to China in 1954, he criticized Stalin's "insensitivity" toward the CCP's national feelings and returned Port Arthur and the Chinese-Eastern Railroad Company to Beijing. In April 1956, when Anastas Mikoyan visited Beijing, he signed two more Soviet economic aid agreements with the PRC.[18]

In October 1956, Zhou first suggested that the State Council reduce its expectation for Soviet economic aid. The Soviets had promised to grant additional aid to China without "careful consideration," when "they probably needed our support" after the twentieth Party Congress. "Now they might realize that they cannot afford this aid, but they cannot afford to tell us either. So they have to postpone many projects."[19] Zhou suggested that this delay might be a "blessing in disguise." "We must eliminate the notion of dependence" on the Soviet Union, he stressed. "If the Soviet comrades have their own difficulties, or in some respects they want to keep some advanced technology from us," it should be "understandable." "Let's remember," he reminded, that to achieve industrialization in China, "the decisive factor is the Chinese people, the Chinese intellectuals, not the Soviet aid."[20]

During the Hundred Flowers period in 1956, however, there was increased pressure in urban China to adopt a more neutral foreign policy, like Yugoslavia, so that China could learn from both the Soviet and the American experiences and speed up its industrialization drive. Mao acknowledged that "among democratic parties, nonpartisan democrats, and university professors, and in religious, industrial, and commercial circles, and also among part of the working class," there were "quite a number of people" who wanted to follow Yugoslavia's path, to take "a middle-ground position" between the United States and the Soviet Union in the Cold War.[21]

Because of Washington's repeated insistence on the China embargo, by the end of 1956, Mao started talking about the "illusion" that America would ever aid China's industrialization. As he said in December 1956, "Who has helped us to design and equip so many important factories in the past few years? Did the United States help us? Did Great Britain help us? None of them did." He conceded that China should find ways to do business with the Americans and the British, but "China should never have the illusion that America would help China develop its advanced technology and industry. America would never do such a thing for China." In today's world, Mao said, on the one side, there were "powerful imperialist countries," from which China "suffered enormously" in modern times. On the other, there were the Soviet Union and other socialist countries, which were willing to offer help, and which at least did not have an embargo against the PRC. "If we stand in the middle, it might appear to be more independent"; in reality, however, it could only subject China "to more humiliation by the imperialist powers." He concluded, "Since we still do not know how to design big factories, and the Soviet Union is still the only country willing to help us, China needs to lean to one side in its foreign policy. To achieve China's industrialization, China's national interest clearly lies in its continued unity with the Soviet Union and other socialist countries."[22]

In this period, the CCP and the Soviets did have ideological differences. Beijing did not agree with the method Khrushchev used to expose Stalin.[23] In spite of these differences, Mao praised Khrushchev's "great courage" in debunking the "Stalin myth." As he claimed in September 1956, "This is a war of liberation. Now everyone dares to talk, to think."[24] Beijing did not allow these ideological controversies to spill over and dominate the Sino-Soviet relationship. The CCP's placement of primary importance on economic development in the gradualist blueprint helped the CCP to submerge, rather than highlight, these ideological differences.

Beginning in 1956, Beijing began to apply these five principles to intra-Soviet-bloc relations. In June 1956, Zhou first declared at the Third Session of the First National People's Congress: "Equality, mutual benefit, and mutual respect for national sovereignty" should be the "guiding principles" among socialist countries.[25]

Three months later, at the CCP's Eighth Party Congress, Mao told Mikoyan—who headed the Soviet delegation—that to ask "a fraternal party" to follow Soviet orders, as in the case of the Chinese revolution in the Stalin era in the 1930s and the 1940s, was a "bad tradition." How could a party's own policy, based on its own "indigenous situations and specific interests," ever be subject to other parties' "orders and judgments," which worked in "very different situations, with very different priority of interests in mind?" The painful lessons of the Chinese revolution, which the CCP had learned with "the precious blood of its sons and daughters," proved that such a "father-son" relationship in the socialist bloc was "extremely dangerous." In his conversation with the Yugoslav party delegation, Mao was more explicit: " 'Freedom, equality, and fraternity' is a bourgeois slogan, but we are now fighting for it in the socialist bloc." "Thanks to Khrushchev," he said, the change from a father-son relationship to a fraternal relationship opposed "the feudal patriarchal system" in the socialist bloc. Indeed, "the ideological control" in the Soviet bloc had been "too tight," had even "surpassed feudal rule." In this regard, "the capitalist society is much better than feudal society." In the United States, for instance, "the two parties—the Republicans and the Democrats—at least can scold each other."[26]

In late 1956 and early 1957, during and after the Polish and Hungarian uprisings, Beijing intensified its efforts to champion the five principles of peaceful coexistence in the Soviet bloc. On October 19, 1956, the new Gomulka government in Poland decided to expel the pro-Soviet hardliners, to forestall nationwide anti-Soviet demonstrations. Khrushchev asked the CCP to support employing Soviet troops in Poland, to force the Gomulka government to change its mind.[27] On October 20, 1956, at an emergency Politburo meeting in Beijing, it was reported that Soviet warships were ready to enter the Polish port of Gdansk, Soviet troops were being transported from East Germany to the German-Polish border, and the Polish army and Warsaw workers were all mobilized to defend their country. "When the son does not follow the father's order," Mao remarked angrily, "the father wants to punish the son." A Soviet "armed intervention" in a sovereign socialist country would be "a sheer violation of even the minimal standard of international relations." "It must never, absolutely never be allowed to happen in the socialist bloc." The CCP leaders unanimously agreed. Mao immediately met with Soviet ambassador Yudin and informed him of the CCP's decision: "We most emphatically oppose the attempted Soviet military intervention in Poland." If the Soviet leaders decided to go ahead, the CCP would have no choice but to go public, "to condemn publicly the Soviet armed intervention in a sovereign socialist nation."[28]

The Khrushchev government decided against using military means to deal with the Polish situation. Instead, it invited a CCP delegation to mediate between Warsaw and Moscow.[29] In Liu Shaoqi's meetings with the Soviet leaders, he talked about Mao's recommendations on how to reconstruct Soviet–East European relations. First, the Soviet Union must stop intervening in Eastern European countries' domestic programs and let each of them formulate its own political and economic blueprints according to its indigenous situations. Second, the Soviet Union must consult with Warsaw Pact countries to see if they wanted Soviet troops to be stationed in their territories. If they did not, the Soviet troops should withdraw, to reduce anti-Soviet sentiment in Eastern Europe. Finally, the Soviet Union should engage in self-criticism in its relations with Eastern Europe and express its desire to build new relationships based on "sovereignty, equality, and mutual benefit." If the Soviet leaders would take the initiative, Liu insisted, the prestige of the Soviet Union might be "enormously enhanced," and the unity of the socialist bloc "greatly strengthened."[30]

On October 30, 1956, at the Soviet leaders' meeting, they were divided over Beijing's recommendations. To Lazar Kaganovich, the first deputy prime minister, it was "entirely inappropriate" to advocate "five principles of peaceful coexistence," instead of "proletarian internationalism," in the socialist bloc. Voroshilov, chairman of the Presidium of the Supreme Soviet, mildly dissented: "We must criticize ourselves—but justly." Foreign Minister Dmitrii Shepilov, however, felt that "anti-Soviet sentiments are widespread. . . . The underlying reasons must be revealed." On October 30, 1956, the Kremlin issued a statement acknowledging that in Soviet relations with Eastern Europe, Moscow had violated "the principle of equality." It pledged that the Soviet Union would "observe the full sovereignty of each socialist state" and reexamine the basis for its continued military presence in the Warsaw Pact countries, except for East Germany.[31]

While the Polish situation quickly returned to normal, an uprising was sweeping Budapest, the capital of Hungary. On October 30, Moscow decided to withdraw the Soviet troops from there. That evening, the news came that British-French troops had just invaded Egypt and that Hungarian prime minister Imre Nagy had called for Hungary's withdrawal from the Warsaw Pact. With this new development, on the morning of October 31, Khrushchev convened an emergency meeting in the Kremlin and proposed sending Soviet troops back to Budapest.[32] He informed Liu of this decision at the airport, before the CCP delegation left for Beijing. Liu assured him that Moscow could count on the CCP's "full support" in this matter.[33] Indeed, by the night of October 30, Beijing had come to the same conclusion. Because of the British-French invasion of Egypt, Mao regarded the Hungarian situation as "basically different" from the Polish one. In Poland, the major problem was Soviet "great power chauvinism." In Hungary, however, the major issue was not only Soviet "great power chauvinism" but also the "imperialist plot to undermine the socialist bloc from within."[34]

In January 1957, a CCP delegation led by Zhou visited the Soviet Union, Poland, and Hungary to help repair damaged relations in the Socialist bloc. In his first meeting with Khrushchev, Zhou emphasized that the initial Soviet decision to use military force to solve the Polish problem was an "incorrect" one. He suggested that the five principles of peaceful coexistence be the foundation of intrabloc relations in the future.[35] Khrushchev felt that Zhou was "lecturing" him on how to treat the Eastern Europeans. This meeting was quickly broken off.

Meanwhile, Beijing began to examine its own relationships with North Vietnam and North Korea. During his visit to North Vietnam in November 1956, Zhou issued a joint communiqué with Prime Minister Pham Van Dong, endorsing the principles of peaceful coexistence as the foundation of Sino-Vietnamese relations. In January 1957, Beijing decided to withdraw Chinese troops from North Korea. It also suggested that the Soviet Union withdraw its troops from East Germany as well as from other Eastern European nations, to minimize the anti-Soviet nationalist eruptions in Eastern Europe.[36]

As Russia specialists agree, "from the time of Peter the Great, when Russia's aspirations for naval power were born, the absence of icefree ports has often been cited as a motive for Russian expansion toward the Baltic and Black seas and toward the warmer waters of the Pacific Ocean." In particular, "in the Far East, Vladivostok is icebound for part of the year. . . . Only during the period when Port Arthur and Dairen were under Russian control was icefree passage to the Yellow Sea and the Pacific possible."[37] It was thus not surprising that Russia's persistent security concern over icefree ports reemerged in Soviet policy toward China. This was shown vividly in Stalin's efforts to regain control of Port Arthur and Dairen in the KMT-USSR Alliance Treaty of 1945, and in the negotiations of the CCP-USSR Alliance Treaty of 1950. In 1958, Russia's century-old security concern was, once again, in the forefront of the Khrushchev government's policy toward the PRC.

By early 1958, the Soviet Union could produce diesel and nuclear-powered submarines. On April 18, 1958, Marshal R. Malinovski, the Soviet defense minister, proposed establishing a joint long-wave radio station in China, to maintain Moscow's communications with its submarine fleet in the Pacific. On June 4, 1958, Peng Dehui suggested that the investment should be "China's sole responsibility," since China wanted to have "full sovereignty" over this station on Chinese territory. Mao agreed. He further suggested that "if the Soviet comrades try to force us to give in," Peng should simply "ignore this letter."[38]

At the same time, Soviet military consultants in China proposed that the Chinese navy request Soviet aid to build up its nuclear submarine fleet. In his reply to the Chinese request, Khrushchev proposed building a Sino-Soviet "joint nuclear-submarine fleet," instead of a Chinese fleet. As Yudin explained to Mao on July 21, 1958, in Khrushchev's view, since "the natural condition of the Soviet coast is not good for developing a nuclear-submarine fleet," Moscow would like to establish a Sino-Soviet joint fleet, "to take advantage of the excellent conditions along the Chinese Pacific coast." Yudin added that the purpose of the joint nuclear-submarine fleet was "to target the American Seventh fleet in the Taiwan Strait," or "to help China enhance its military power in its efforts to liberate Taiwan."[39]

Mao was angry and upset. The following day, he told the Soviet ambassador: "I have not been able to sleep, to eat, since you left yesterday." The Chinese navy's request for Soviet aid to build nuclear submarines would be "withdrawn." The Chinese navy had thought it would only ask for Soviet technological aid, and that it would still have "the sovereign right" over its own fleet, but that had not turned out to be the case. The "simple truth" was, he said, that the Soviet Union was the only nation in the bloc holding atomic secrets, and it wanted "to use this advanced technology to make China serve the Soviet interest." Khrushchev's request for a joint fleet, he told Yudin, reminded him of Stalin's requests for spheres of influence in the northeast and Xinjiang, programs Khrushchev had abolished in 1954. That was why, he said, the CCP was "so grateful to comrade Khrushchev." But why did Khrushchev now want to revive what Stalin had done to China? Even when Stalin was alive, "we never, never agreed, and argued hotly, very hotly, with Stalin about any indication of building a joint fleet in China."[40]

While the Soviets often complained that the Europeans looked down upon them, Mao conveyed that "we feel some Soviet comrades always look down upon the Chinese." All the talk about "fraternal relationships" in the socialist bloc was only lip service. In reality, it was a cat-and-mouse relationship. China needed Soviet aid in building its nuclear submarine fleet, he said, but if the Soviets asked Beijing "to compromise on China's sovereignty in return," "we would prefer not to receive Soviet aid, not in ten thousand years."

Then, after venting his anger, Mao softened: "The Soviet Union has helped us so much, yet we have made so many complaints; you must have felt sad at what I just said." He assured the ambassador that China would continue "to cooperate closely with the Soviet Union." He warned, though, "On the political issue of China's national sovereignty, we will never make any concession, not even half a finger's concession."[41]

In Moscow, Khrushchev was "shocked" by Yudin's report. The Soviet leaders urged him to go to Beijing immediately, to smooth things over. At a meeting on August 1, 1958, Khrushchev explained to Mao that the Soviets had never intended "to violate China's sovereignty, or damage its national pride." He also told Mao that Yudin misrepresented the issue of a joint fleet. What the Soviet Union actually wanted was a Soviet submarine base in China. "When I put this idea to Mao," Khrushchev recalled, "once again Mao became adamant." He rejected the suggestion "out of hand." Mao told him: "It would constitute an encroachment upon our sovereignty." Khrushchev asked Mao whether he would agree to a "reciprocal arrangement": the Chinese could have submarine bases in the Arctic Ocean along the Soviet coast in exchange for "our rights to your Pacific ports." "No," Mao said, "we won't agree to that either. Every country should keep its armed forces in its own homeland." Khrushchev returned to Moscow angry. He interpreted Mao's rejection of his personal request for a submarine base in China as "game playing," or "Asiatic cunning" and "treachery."[42]

Just before the controversy over the Soviet submarine base in China, the Sino-Soviet relationship had entered a honeymoon period. According to Khrushchev, if this relationship had gone downhill during most of 1956 due to the Hundred Flowers policy, the CCP's antirightist campaign in the summer of 1957 helped to bring it back.[43] On July 20, 1957, after Moscow expelled Molotov, Malenkov, and Bulganin from the Soviet leadership, the new Khrushchev government quickly offered to negotiate with the CCP for Soviet aid in China's defense industry. In early September 1957, in the aftermath of the antirightist campaign, a Chinese delegation, which included more than twenty leading Chinese specialists on missile and rocket technology, atomic energy, and the aviation industry, left Beijing. In mid-October 1957, the Sino-Soviet Agreement on Soviet Aid in Hi-Tech Defense Industry was signed in Moscow.[44]

Two weeks later, in early November 1957, when Mao led the CCP delegation to participate in the Moscow conference of world communist and workers' parties, he had every reason to support the new Khrushchev government. In spite of their theoretical differences over the possibility of peaceful evolution to socialism, Mao sided firmly with Khrushchev. He publicly supported the Soviet Union as the "head" or the "center" of the socialist bloc.

However, by mid-1958, when Beijing rejected the Soviet strategic proposals on a joint nuclear-submarine fleet and/or a Soviet submarine base in China, Khrushchev's resentments toward and suspicions of Mao and the CCP were drastically heightened. When the Soviets started launching satellites, which were better for maintaining radio contact with the Soviet submarines than a long-wave radio station in China would have been, even China's cooperation in the long-wave radio station was no longer needed.

On June 20, 1959, at Khrushchev's insistence, Moscow sent a letter to Beijing informing Mao that the Soviet Union would "terminate the deliveries of technical documentation and necessary materials for the production of atomic weapons." In other words, the Sino-Soviet agreement on Soviet aid to the Chinese defense industry of 1957 was now unilaterally canceled.

In late September 1959, during Khrushchev's visit to Washington, the new secretary of state, Christopher Herter, made a direct link between Moscow's China policy and Washington's Soviet policy. That is, if Moscow could cooperate with Washington on its positions over arms proliferation, Taiwan, and Tibet, Washington would cooperate with Moscow on its policy toward East Germany. Indeed, to Khrushchev, Mao's refusal to endorse his plan of building a joint fleet and a submarine base along China's Pacific coast represented sheer neglect of Soviet security interests. The PRC was now not only an undependable ally but a strategic liability for vital Soviet security interests in Europe. On October 1, 1959, during a visit to Beijing, Khrushchev told Mao that the Soviet Union was going to withdraw all Soviet atomic experts from China. He also urged Beijing to accept the status quo, rather than "provoking" a new world war in the Taiwan Strait, and to accept an independent Tibet as a "buffer zone" between China and India. He explained that the new Soviet policy was based mainly on the coming U.S.–Soviet conference on arms reduction.[45] As Deng Xiaoping put it at the time, the new Soviet policy toward China was made because Khrushchev wanted revenge for the CCP's rejection of a Soviet submarine base in China in the summer of 1958.[46]

Was Deng's perception right? Was the fallout from Sino-Soviet relations in late 1959 the direct result of China's refusal to give Moscow a submarine base in China? Or did the Sino-Soviet breakup in late 1959 originate from ideological differences? Actually, before the critical Mao-Khrushchev meeting in October 1959, ideological differences had not been regarded as the primary threat to the Sino-Soviet alliance. In a memo entitled "The Political, Economic, and International Standing of the PRC," completed on September 15, 1959, Mikhail Zimyanin, head of the Soviet Foreign Ministry's Far Eastern department, had downplayed the impact of the Great Leap Forward and the commune campaigns on the alliance.

However, *after* the Mao-Khrushchev October 1959 meeting, ideological differences, particularly the perceived flaws in the CCP's radical economic blueprint, loomed peculiarly large in Moscow's interpretation of the near collapse of the Sino-Soviet alliance. In December 1959, Mikhail Suslov, a senior member of the Soviet Politburo, explained at a plenum of the Central Committee of the Soviet Union's Communist Party that at the root of the downward spiral of Sino-Soviet relations was Mao's "cult of personality." It was similar to "the last years of Stalin's life," and it brought about disaster to China's domestic constructions as well as to the Sino-Soviet alliance.[47] The Soviet leaders' criticisms were right on target, but Mao's cult of personality did not directly produce an anti-Soviet policy. Zhou did not agree with Mao's radical blueprints, yet he obviously shared Mao's anger toward Khrushchev's requests for a joint fleet and a submarine base in China.[48]

In August 1960, all Soviet experts were withdrawn from China, 343 contracts were canceled, and 257 scientific and technological cooperative projects were abolished.[49] One month later, Deng Xiaoping told the Soviet leaders that nothing could defeat China's determination to modernize. He asked the Soviet comrades to think again: "On whom could you really depend when difficulties arise in the future?"[50]

How could there have been such a rapid deterioration of Sino-Soviet relations in the late 1950s? First, and most important, it was brought about by the widening gap between Beijing and Moscow on issues of national security. After the summer of 1958, when China had refused to allow a Soviet submarine base on Chinese land or to develop a joint Soviet-Chinese nuclear-submarine fleet in China, Khrushchev concluded that China's strategic importance in the alliance had drastically declined. Then, Khrushchev's refusal to support Beijing's position on Taiwan, along with his decision to end Sino-Soviet economic and military cooperation, brought Beijing to the same conclusion about the value of the Sino-Soviet alliance.

This does not mean, however, that the CCP's radical domestic blueprint had not had an impact on the Sino-Soviet alliance. Khrushchev recalled that in the first half of the 1950s, he thought "Mao might succeed in showing the world a Chinese economic miracle." While India had a "broader industrial base," China's standard of living was improving "faster." However, by the end of the 1950s, "famine broke out in the Chinese countryside," and Chinese industry was "totally disorganized." With the Chinese economy generally in shambles, he only had "contempt" for Mao.[51] The political language of the populist blueprints, particularly that about class warfare, further alienated the new generation of Soviet leaders, who had come to power with their passionate criticisms of Stalin's "personality cult" and their belief in Soviet economic constructions.

Since both parties sought to replace the moral code of religion and traditional philosophy, they both sensed that they must find a way to confer a legitimizing influence upon the arguments at stake. In the Sino-Soviet split, ideology thus became the sole vehicle through which the painful breakup could be expressed and justified, both in front of their peoples and in front of the world communist movement. Disguising the hard core of national security interests was not enough. They must also "glorify those interests and project them onto a universal plane." Thus the old ideological differences "between the comrades," such as the evaluation of Stalin, the issue of war and peace in the nuclear age, and the question of "peaceful transition to socialism," were now all re-articulated and reframed in terms of ideological orthodoxy, sparking spectacular emotional fireworks. However, neither these fireworks nor ideological rhetoric were the real origins of the Sino-Soviet split. Among all the Soviet charges against Mao and the CCP, some American scholars considered the "most accurate of all" of them to be those "accusing Mao of 'petty-bourgeois' nationalism." Indeed, Beijing's "passionate and shrill concern" for national sovereignty and national equality was, after all, "a feature of nationalism."[52]

China's Diplomacy toward Asia: The 1950s

In 1949, Ho Chi Minh asked the CCP to provide support for the Democratic Republic of Vietnam's (DRV) new war of resistance against the French reoccupation.[53] In December, Beijing decided to send a military advisory group to Vietnam. By the end of 1953, Ho Chi Minh's army took back the Sino-Vietnamese border region and began to prepare for its decisive battle on Dien Bien Phu, the French stronghold in North Vietnam. China increased its military aid to Ho's army, and the United States sent military aid to the French. On May 7, 1954, the French army surrendered in Dien Bien Phu. At the Geneva Conference, Zhou persuaded the new French government to withdraw from Vietnam. Meanwhile, to achieve a peace settlement, he also persuaded Ho to agree to a temporary administrative division of Vietnam along the 17th parallel, which would be abolished in 1956, when the Vietnamese national election was to take place.

In September 1954, after the Geneva Conference, the CCP suggested withdrawing its military advisory group from Hanoi. By early 1955, however, it was clear to Hanoi that the Eisenhower administration would not allow a national election in which Ho Chi Minh would be elected president of a unified Vietnam. Hanoi asked Beijing to postpone its withdrawal of the military advisory group. In July 1955, Liu and Deng Xiaoping persuaded Ho of the necessity of the withdrawal. By March 1956, the last CCP military advisory group members returned to Beijing.[54]

After the withdrawal, Beijing signed an economic aid agreement with Hanoi, pledging to help North Vietnam to "develop its industry, agriculture, forestry, irrigation, transportation, and postal service." In Beijing's view, although Washington had clearly violated the Geneva Agreement by making Ngo Dinh Diem the president of South Vietnam, Hanoi should continue focusing on its domestic constructions in the North, rather than on military struggles in the South. Zhou told Ho that by its successful economic development, North Vietnam could "point a new way to the Vietnamese people in the South and engage in political struggle to unify the nation through peaceful means."[55]

By the summer of 1958, Hanoi was increasingly frustrated by Washington's continued military support for the Diem regime and informed Beijing of its new plan to achieve national unification through guerrilla warfare in the South. Zhou again suggested that Hanoi focus on economic and political construction in the North and wait for a "better time" in the future to engage in struggles of "various types" in the South. In the joint communiqué between Mao and Ho in 1958, the CCP repeated its pledge to support Vietnamese national unification through "peaceful means."[56]

To the CCP leadership, following the deterioration of Sino-Soviet relations in late 1959, the United States' expanded military presence in South Vietnam looked more threatening than ever to China's security. According to Mao, the purpose of the U.S. military presence in South Vietnam was to prevent the unification of Vietnam under Ho and to serve as the centerpiece of America's new military containment strategy against the PRC. Should the Sino-Soviet alliance break down entirely, how could China counter such an "imminent national security threat" from South Vietnam?[57] In May 1960, Zhou and Deng Xiaoping informed Ho that Beijing was ready to support Hanoi in engaging in both "political and military struggles" in the South. In December 1960, when the Vietnamese National Liberation Front was established in the South, the PRC was the first to grant diplomatic recognition to it.[58] As

Hoang Van Hoan, former Hanoi ambassador to Beijing, wrote, "In 1960, after learning more about the new conditions in south Vietnam, the Chinese comrades expressed explicitly to the Vietnamese that they were not as well-informed as the Vietnamese comrades, for they had considered the time not ripe for revealing their strength. Now they agreed that the Vietnamese position for armed struggle in the south was correct and that they would fully support it."[59]

Clearly, in 1960, Beijing's change in its Vietnam policy was not directly brought about by its radical domestic blueprints. Rather, the change was part of its reaction to the worsened security environment; namely, the drastic decline of the Sino-Soviet alliance and the simultaneous expansion of the U.S. military presence in South Vietnam.

In the early years of the PRC, the Burmese government feared that because of the long border Burma shared with China's Yunnan province, it would be easy for the CCP to undermine the Burmese government. As U Nu, the Burmese prime minister, told Mao and Zhou in 1954, he had been deeply concerned that Beijing might use Yunnan as a base to support the Burmese guerrilla movements, which were led by a radical wing of the Burmese Communist Party. And he suggested that Beijing "send some objective Chinese researchers to observe the Burmese social conditions first hand, to see how the majority of the Burmese people really feel about those radical antigovernment guerrilla movements in Burma."[60]

Mao assured U Nu that it was an "arch principle" of the PRC's diplomacy that China only recognize the government "chosen by its own people." So it only recognized U Nu's government. Since the ethnic group was the same on both sides of the Sino-Burmese border, it was possible, he said, that people who were dissatisfied with their governments would run back and forth across the border. However, he pledged: "China would never use those people to do anything to undermine the Burmese government." He stated, "If we jeopardize each other's interests, we can never have enduring cooperation." It was indeed "very rare" in world history, he told U Nu, that a nation could ever win the victory of revolution by "depending on foreign countries' support." Eastern Europe was a "unique" case. The Soviet troops occupied those countries when they fought against Nazi Germany. "That is why we have declared that revolution should never be exported." True, there were "some radicals among the overseas Chinese in Burma," who had asked for the CCP's support. However, he said, "We have urged them not to intervene in Burma's domestic politics." Beijing's new policy in Southeast Asia, he told U Nu, was "to stop organizing the communist party branches among overseas Chinese," especially in those countries where there was a "large ethnic Chinese population." He stressed that the CCP branches, which had existed among the overseas Chinese, were now "all dismantled" according to the new policy.[61]

U Nu, however, still had a lingering fear, reflecting the speculation in foreign newspapers, that the establishment of a Tai (Dai) nationality autonomous district in Yunnan province indicated that China was indeed preparing to invade Burma and Thailand in the near future. There were 300,000 people of Thai nationality in Yunnan, Mao replied, who had wanted to organize an autonomous district there. For the same reason, he said, seven million of Zhuang nationality in Guangxi province, which shared a long border with North Vietnam, had also established an autonomous region. Would China use these autonomous regions as stepping-stones to invade Burma or Thailand? No, Mao replied. "We have never thought of it, we have never prepared for it, and we have never made such a policy." Beijing would like to invite both the Burmese and the Thai governments to establish consulates in Yunnan, he told U Nu, to see for themselves "whether the Chinese people are concentrating on domestic economic constructions, or preparing for invasions into neighboring countries."[62]

U Nu acknowledged that he had thought the CCP might be just like Hitler, determined to invade his country. By the mid-1950s, he conceded that his fears were "groundless." The Chinese treated the Burmese "with sincerity, like brothers."[63] It was U Nu who had first told Mao and Zhou about the preparations for the first Asian-African conference in history—the Bangdung Conference of 1955. And it was through the joint efforts of Burma, India, and Indonesia that China was invited to participate and to play an important role at this conference.

In the late 1950s, however, encouraged by the increased guerrilla warfare in South Vietnam, a Burmese minority group fled into China. They asked Beijing to arm them, send them back, and support their guerrilla struggle in the Sino-Burmese border region. Beijing immediately declined. At a meeting with Mao in September 1960, U Nu asked about their whereabouts. Mao said, "We told them that we could accept them, let them settle down in China to engage in agricultural production, but would never arm them to undermine the Burmese government, because China and Burma are good friends." U Nu was pleased to hear the news in Beijing. He made clear that "only on the basis of the five principles of peaceful coexistence can Burma and China have lasting friendship."[64]

In September 1958, Prince Sihanouk of Cambodia told the American ambassador that Zhou had emphasized to him that China was "prepared to accept the neutral states of Southeast Asia with their present regimes as buffers" between China and the West, and had "no intention of interfering in Cambodian affairs," or other countries' domestic affairs.[65] In January 1960, China signed a peace and nonaggression treaty with Burma; in April 1960, a peace and friendship treaty with Nepal; and in August 1960, a friendship and nonaggression treaty with Afghanistan. In short, in the late 1950s, Beijing continued its peace diplomacy toward most of its Asian neighbors, despite its implementation of radical blueprints at home.

When the PLA crossed the Tibetan border in October 1950, the Indian government was divided over Indian policy toward China. One view regarded a modernized China as India's "potential major enemy" in the future and asked to continue the British Tibetan policy; namely, to turn Tibet into an independent state, or a buffer state for India. The other view, led by Nehru, championed friendly ties with the PRC. His position was that both countries had suffered enough in the colonial era and both countries should cooperate to create a "new age" in Asia. India should respect China's suzerainty of Tibet, as he told the Indian parliament, since even London and Washington did not publicly raise any question about Tibet's legal status as part of China, following the establishment of the PRC.[66] On the other hand, he also emphasized that the PRC should respect the autonomy of Tibet. Beijing should not push its reform programs in Tibet as it had done in other provinces of China.[67]

On this crucial issue of Tibetan autonomy in Sino-Indian relations, Zhou agreed with Nehru. There had been two opposing approaches to the Tibetan reform in Beijing, Zhou said. One was the bottom-up approach, intended to mobilize the Tibetan serfs at the grassroots level. The other was the top-down approach, which was to wait patiently until most of "the upper strata of Tibet" would be willing to reform. The Dalai Lama expressed to Nehru his desire for reform but had recommended "taking it slowly"; that was why Beijing decided to take a gradualist approach to Tibetan reform. Mao related this to the CCP

Central Committee in 1954: "If the Tibetan government led by the Dalai Lama and the Panchen Lama feel that it is time to reform, we will begin the process a little bit. And we will not start the reform in Tibet until the Tibetan government believes it is the right moment."[68]

Nehru was satisfied with Beijing's "friendly approach" to Tibetan reform. In the "Agreement on Commerce and Transportation between India and Tibet of China" of 1954, India formally recognized China's sovereignty over Tibet and gave up all the privileges there it had inherited from Great Britain.[69]

In the winter of 1955–56, when advocates of the CCP's radical blueprint speeded up the rural cooperative campaigns, a Khamba (ethnic Tibetans who lived outside Tibet) uprising broke out in Western Szechuan. With the gradualist blueprint still predominant in Beijing, Zhou successfully persuaded the Dalai Lama and Nehru to continue their support for Beijing's Tibetan policy. In January 1957, during Zhou's visit to India, he delivered Mao's personal messages to Nehru and to the Dalai Lama, who had been visiting India. Mao assured both that there would be no mention of Tibetan reform in the second Five-Year plan. Whether there should be reform in Tibet in the future would "completely depend on the Dalai Lama's decision." Zhou also told the Dalai Lama that Beijing had sent a delegation to investigate "the mistakes and shortcomings" in the reform among the Khambas in Western Szechuan. If the Beijing government had made these mistakes, "we will correct them." If the local government made the mistakes, "we will help it to correct them." And he invited the government in Lhasa to send its own delegation to make separate investigations, "to help correct our mistakes" in Western Szechuan.[70] During this visit, Zhou also told Nehru that "American spies" had tried to keep the Dalai Lama in India, "to use the Dalai Lama to organize the Tibetan independence movement," "to break up China from within." Nehru assured Zhou that he would persuade the Dalai Lama to return to Tibet. Meanwhile he told the Dalai Lama that the Tibetan government "should accept Beijing's assurances in good faith and cooperate in maintaining that autonomy and bringing about certain reforms in Tibet."[71]

Although Mao emphasized that the new policy of the Great Leap Forward and the commune campaign must not be applied to Tibet,[72] it was implemented in Western Szechuan and Qinghai provinces, where the Khambas lived. The situation was further compounded by U.S.-China antagonism during the Cold War. Between October 1958 and February 1959, Allen Dulles's CIA dropped tons of weapons and supplies among the Khambas.[73] The Khamba uprising in December 1958 paved the way for the Lhasa uprising in March 1959. According to Jamyang Norbu, a leader of the Tibetan Guerrilla Force, which operated out of Nepal until 1974, two CIA agents—who were actually two Khambas from Western Szechuan—went to see the Dalai Lama's Chamberlain, Thubten Woyden Phala, and delivered a message, asking him to provide "an official request from the Tibetan Government for American military aid." Phala declined, since it was "impossible" to "trust the entire Cabinet or the Assembly with such a sensitive and potentially compromising message." He did agree "to keep the Americans informed of developments in the escape plan." Meanwhile, Mao was also kept informed by the local PLA officers concerning the Dalai Lama's departure from Lhasa to India. While the PLA officers recommended arresting the Dalai Lama, Mao's order was, "Let him go."[74]

The Lhasa uprising of 1959 won widespread sympathy in India, because many Indian nationals had originally come from Tibet and some Tibetan émigrés also lived in India. And as Nehru said, "all of them deeply respect the Dalai Lama." When news of the Lhasa uprising came to India, "there was immediately a strong and widespread reaction." He acknowledged that some people in India did seek to turn the popular reaction in "an undesirable direction." However, the basic fact was that "the reaction of the Indian people" was there. On April 1, 1959, at the Dalai Lama's request, the Nehru government granted him and thousands of refugees political asylum in India.[75]

In remarking on Zhou's gradualist approach to Tibetan reform, Nehru said, "It is not for us to say how much these friendly intentions and approaches materialized." The circumstances were "undoubtedly difficult." On the one side, he said, there was China, "a dynamic, rapidly moving society"; on the other, there was Tibet, "a static, unchanging society fearful of what might be done to it in the name of reform." The distance between the two was great, and there appeared to be "hardly any meeting point." For him, the cause of the Lhasa uprising could not be explained simplistically as a conspiracy of "a number of upper strata reactionaries in Tibet," as claimed by the CCP newspapers at the time. In Nehru's view, the Khamba revolt in December 1958 and "the ensuing flood of Khamba refugees pouring into Lhasa" had certainly created "a powerful impression in the minds of large numbers of Tibetans." Their fears might have been "unjustified." However, "such fears and strong feelings of nationalism could only be dealt with by gentler methods."[76]

In Beijing, the CCP leaders could not agree on how to assess Nehru's intention regarding Tibet. Some saw Nehru's plan as abandoning China to get economic aid from Washington. Indeed, as they argued, nothing seemed to be more revealing than America's aid package of $1.2 billion, which Washington immediately offered to India after it granted the Dalai Lama political asylum.[77] Mao and Zhou, however, had considered Nehru's India to be China's great friend and thought China must try hard to keep this friendship. On May 13, 1959, one month after Nehru had granted the Dalai Lama political asylum, Mao himself added the following to the Chinese Foreign Ministry's draft reply to the Indian Foreign Ministry: "India is China's great friend, it has been so in the past more than one thousand years, and it will continue to be so in the following one thousand and ten thousand years. This is our firm belief." He assured Nehru that the upcoming land reform in Tibet after the Dalai's departure would "never threaten the security of India." China's "major focus," he stressed, was on the Taiwan Strait: that is, on the United States. Even though the Philippines, Thailand, and Pakistan participated in the Southeast Asia Treaty Organization (SEATO), which had aimed to isolate China, China did not regard them as its enemies. India had never participated in SEATO, so how could China consider India as its enemy? No, India was "not our enemy, but our friend." "We cannot afford to have two enemies, and we cannot afford to regard our friend as our enemy. This is our national policy." Thus the quarrel between China and India in the past few months should be "just a small episode in the thousand and ten thousand years of friendly exchanges between our two countries." He appealed to Nehru: "Why don't you wait and see, as the Chinese saying goes: 'As distance tests a horse's strength, so time reveals a person's heart.' " He ended with a question: "Do you want to fight on two fronts? If not, then, the convergence of our two nations' interests will be here."[78]

By then, Nehru felt stung by CCP newspapers' attacks on his government, which had been called the "stooge" of London and Washington. For Nehru, these were "very serious charges against a country's leaders." It was especially sad, he wrote, because these charges were made by "the leaders of a people whom we have considered particularly advanced in culture and politeness and the gentler art of civilization. It has been a shock to me beyond measure."[79]

The situation along the Sino-Indian border rapidly worsened. Many incidents occurred between Indian and Chinese frontier troops, and in

November 1959, Mao and Zhou suggested to Nehru that both sides withdraw their frontier troops twenty kilometers from their respective sides of the border. Nehru declined. Mao ordered the Chinese troops to make a unilateral withdrawal of twenty kilometers.[80] In April 1960, in his visit to New Delhi, Zhou further proposed that China forgo its claims to Arunachal Pradesh in India's northeast and "broadly accept the McMahon Line," while expecting India to do likewise over the Aksai Chin plateau in the western sector. Nehru did not commit to this. An Indian scholar, Premen Addy, explained that Nehru had been the principal, if not the sole, architect of his country's China policy since 1954. In 1960, however, he was no longer prepared "to put his name singly to a second mortgage on Chinese goodwill." Any new Sino-Indian arrangement would have to "bear the collective signature of his ministers; without this there would be no deal. Zhou Enlai went home empty-handed."[81]

"The dissension in Tibet was," as CIA officers observed at the time, "insufficiently widespread to sustain a lengthy, open rebellion."[82] In Nehru's words, "vested interests joined the uprising and sought to profit by it." However, it was the CCP's radical populist blueprints that helped trigger the 1958 Khamba uprising in Western Szechuan, which, in turn, prepared the ground for the Lhasa uprising in March 1959. In this sense, the CCP's radical populist blueprints indirectly yet substantially contributed to the downfall of the Sino-Indian friendship by 1960.

With the establishment of Japan-Taiwan diplomatic relations in April 1952, Zhou decided to develop "people-to-people economic diplomacy," as he put it, or to promote nongovernmental economic and cultural exchanges between the PRC and Japan. The major obstacle to Beijing's brand of diplomacy, however, was not just the China embargo led by Washington. While many Japanese desired to "deepen their friendship with 600 million Chinese people," they had concerns about the PRC's foreign-policy intentions. They were particularly fearful that through the Sino-Soviet alliance, Beijing might try to expand its military at the expense of the Japanese people's welfare and to work with Moscow to dominate Asia and the world. As a result, when the first Sino-Japanese nongovernmental trade agreement of 1952 expired in sixteen months, Sino-Japanese trade had only reached 5 percent of the projected number in the agreement. The implementation of the second Sino-Japanese nongovernmental trade agreement of 1953 was better than with the first one, because of increased dialogue and cultural exchanges. By the time of its expiration in December 1954, actual Sino-Japanese trade reached 38.8 percent of the projected number.[83]

Zhou believed that the key to the success of people-to-people economic diplomacy was to help the Japanese understand the PRC's foreign-policy intentions. Since 1954, through his meetings with Japanese delegations, Zhou had emphasized that China and Japan had coexisted peacefully for more than two thousand years. Only during the sixty years since the late nineteenth century had Sino-Japanese relations been characterized by conflict, with the Japanese military repeatedly invading China. Zhou said, however, that "if our generation had to live through that period, our children, grandchildren, and future generations should not be influenced by that unfortunate period." Even during that period, he said, China had learned from Japan about Western cultures. Chinese people should be "grateful" for the Japanese cultural influence in China. He also revealed that more than 28,000 Japanese soldiers had stayed on in China after World War II, to "help the Chinese people's reconstruction." They worked "in our hospitals, factories, even armies, as our doctors, nurses, engineers." They were no longer the soldiers that "bullied us" and massacred the Chinese people—they had become "our friends." After China's industrialization, would China be in conflict with Japan? No, it would not, he asserted. Only an industrialized Japan and an agricultural China made the situation ripe for military conflicts between the two nations from the late nineteenth century to the mid-1940s. Only when China was industrialized, and the standard of living of Chinese people raised, could China import more from Japan and export more to Japan as well, leading to a genuine Sino-Japanese "coprosperity," which meant "equality, mutual benefits, and comparative advantage in economic exchanges."[84]

In early 1955, a high-ranking Japanese Diet delegation visited China, the purpose of which was to inquire directly about China's intentions toward Japan. For instance, would the Japanese Communist Party follow Beijing's orders to engage in sabotage activities within Japan? If so, did it mean that China would intervene in Japan's domestic politics, contrary to the declared policy of peaceful coexistence? Why did the Sino-Soviet alliance treaty of 1950 regard Japan as the "imaginary enemy" in the future? Would China seek revenge on Japan through its alliance with the Soviet Union? At Zhou's four-and-a-half-hour meeting with the delegation, he assured them that China would never export revolution to Japan or intervene in Japanese domestic politics. China would always stick to the principles of "noninterference, equality, and mutual benefit" in its relations with Japan. He also explained in detail why the Sino-Soviet alliance treaty was not designed to threaten Japan. "China will never seek revenge on the Japanese people, not in one thousand years. China looks forward to forging a new friendship with the Japanese people, which is vitally important for China's industrialization drive."[85]

When the Japanese Diet delegation returned to Tokyo, they reported "enthusiastically" to the new prime minister, Hatoyama, about the PRC's diplomacy. Two months later, in March 1955, the first PRC trade delegation was invited to visit Japan, even though these two nations did not have formal diplomatic relations. In April 1955, at the first Asian-African conference, Zhou again pledged that the five principles of peaceful coexistence would be the foundation of Sino-Japanese relations. When the Japanese people had chosen the Yoshida government, "we respected their choice." Now that the Japanese people had chosen the Hatoyama government, "we also respect their choice."[86]

The Hatoyama government responded warmly to Zhou's diplomacy. The third Sino-Japanese nongovernmental trade agreement was signed in Tokyo in May 1955. When it expired in May 1957, actual Sino-Japanese trade reached 77.67 percent of the number projected in the agreement. In March 1958, the fourth Sino-Japanese nongovernmental trade agreement was signed in Beijing. The new agreement stipulated an increase of more than 5 million pounds over previous trade agreements. It also endorsed scientific and technological exchanges. It even suggested establishing offices of nongovernmental commercial attachés in both countries, to build a "long-term" supply-demand relationship between China and Japan.[87]

In May 1958, just two months after the signing of the fourth Sino-Japanese trade agreement, Beijing suddenly announced the suspension of its implementation, the direct cause of which was the "Nagasaki national flag incident." Two Japanese residents had pulled down the PRC's national flag at the Chinese stamp exhibition in Nagasaki on May 2. Beijing regarded this incident as an insult to China and urged the Kishi Nobusuke cabinet (July 1957–July 1960) to punish these two offenders. Kishi rejected this request. In mid-May 1958, Beijing announced the suspension of all economic and cultural exchanges, to send a "political message" to the pro-Taiwan Kishi cabinet.[88]

In Japan, however, it was not the Kishi cabinet but the nongovernmental business community, the pro-PRC grassroots organizations, and the Diet members who had been pushing for more Sino-Japanese economic exchanges that were hit the hardest by Beijing's announcement. They considered Beijing's willingness to suspend the trade agreement over a "political incident" an overreaction. Their hopes for continued expansion of Sino-Japanese economic relations were dashed.[89] Although the Sino-Japanese nongovernmental trade relationship was reestablished in 1961, the momentum brought about by the fourth trade agreement had been lost.[90]

How did this change of policy in Beijing come about? While the CCP's radical blueprints did not directly produce a hostile policy toward Japan, the radical atmosphere in Beijing surely helped shape its reactions to the political incident. The emphasis on politics over economics in the radical vision had an implicit yet profound impact on the CCP's counterproductive reaction to the incident.

China's Diplomacy toward the United States: The 1950s

In May 1955, Mao stated that China was "willing to sign a long-term peace treaty with America, such as a 50-year peace treaty or a 100-year peace treaty, or longer. I just don't know if America would agree to sign it with us." Five months later, in his conversation with a Japanese delegation, Mao further stated that he wanted not just to visit Japan, "to show the Chinese people's friendship toward Japan," but to visit America, "to show the Chinese people's friendship toward the American people." "Unfortunately," he said, his desire "could not yet be realized." In December 1955 and February 1956, at his meetings with Thai delegations, Mao again stressed that "although America has created the greatest problems for us, we still want to be its friend. Only America doesn't want to be our friend. What can we do about it? We can only wait."[91]

When Mao's private peace initiative received no response from Washington, Zhou began to consider a different approach, which was to invite American journalists to visit China. In his view, many problems in Sino-American relations could be attributed to a lack of understanding between the two peoples. As he said at the Third Session of the First National People's Congress on June 28, 1956, China was a "newly risen nation." And a newly risen nation, particularly one that had the potential for becoming a great power, could frequently arouse "apprehensions." If to this fact were added "calculated slander and instigation by certain quarters," such a lack of understanding could even be "aggravated." However, he emphasized, slander would not stand "the test of facts," and lack of understanding could also be removed through "actual contact over a comparatively long period." In the contact between peoples across the Pacific, "we do not exaggerate our achievements, nor do we hide from them our shortcomings." By observing "the heroic and extraordinarily difficult process whereby the Chinese people are moving from backwardness to an advanced state," the Chinese simply hoped the world would understand that "China genuinely desires peace." It was possible, he said, that some people, who "originally harbored suspicions" about China, would retain their suspicions after their visits. The Chinese, however, would not be "disappointed." China wanted to extend an invitation to everyone in the world: "Come visit China, to see for yourselves what the Chinese people are doing and thinking." "In the long run, we are confident that through persistent contact and first-hand observation, more and more people in the world will understand China's desire for peace."[92]

On August 6, 1956, Zhou formally invited fifteen major American press agencies to visit China. One month later, he further urged Washington to sign several bilateral agreements, such as cultural exchanges between China and America. He emphasized that China wanted to "coexist peacefully with all countries, including the United States."[93] Was the purpose of Beijing's peace initiatives to get China into the UN? Or to get the American embargo lifted? If this was true, as President Sukarno of Indonesia told Mao, he and other Asian leaders wanted to help at the UN General Assemblies. No, Mao said, China was not eager to join the UN. China was still a poor country. With or without UN membership, America would "bully China." Neither would China "beg" to have the economic embargo relaxed. It would be even "better" if it could be eased a few years later. "Currently we don't have much to exchange with the Western countries, only apples, peanuts, pig's bristles, and beans. . . . We can wait for six more years, or ten more years. By then we can have much more to export or to exchange with the world." What China wanted from the United States was simply "a peaceful international environment for China's industrialization."[94]

American journalists' positive response to Zhou's invitation clearly encouraged Mao. On August 29, 1956, in reviewing the CCP Central Committee's political report to the Eighth Party Congress, Mao wrote the following: "For international peace and domestic constructions,

China is willing to establish friendly relations with all nations in the world, including the United States. We believe that we will eventually achieve this goal."[95]

The Hungarian uprising did cool the CCP's enthusiasm somewhat in its peace initiatives toward Washington. However, Beijing had no intention of abandoning them. In the aftermath of the Hungarian uprising, Mao recommended a "new global strategy" for the socialist bloc, which was to have détente in the world, and to have long-term defense at home. As Zhou explained to Khrushchev in Moscow in early 1957, socialist countries should "promote reconciliation between the two blocs." They should also strengthen their long-term cooperation, to concentrate on domestic constructions.

From the summer of 1955 to the summer of 1957, Beijing continued its peace initiatives toward Washington. Zhou made clear in the spring of 1957, "Chinese people are willing to have a friendly relationship with the American people. . . . To improve Sino-American relations, the Chinese side has made serious efforts." However, all these efforts had not yet received a "corresponding positive response from the American government."[96]

In Zhou's words, there was "no basic reason for antagonism" between China and America, "the only real problem being Taiwan."[97] By mid-1954, after the end of the Korean War and the settlement of the Indo-China War at the Geneva Conference, Beijing had proclaimed: "The Taiwan question will be at the center of our future relations with the United States."[98]

Many Chinese shed tears when the Cairo Declaration of 1943 announced that Taiwan was to return to its motherland. When the Chinese Nationalist government resumed sovereignty over Taiwan in 1945, many Chinese believed that their dreams of national reunification had finally come true. Zhou posited that the public statements of Truman and Acheson in January 1950 reaffirmed Taiwan's "legal status as part of China."[99]

In the summer of 1954, Beijing learned that Washington had been negotiating with Taipei for a mutual defense treaty. Mao proposed shelling Jinmen and Mazu, to prevent Washington from signing the treaty. There was also a separate agenda for the shelling, which was to take back Dachen Island, an island adjacent to Zhejiang province and still occupied by KMT troops. The shelling was not really intended to take back Jinmen and Mazu through military force.[100]

However, in Washington, the shelling was interpreted as a prelude to a CCP military attack, not only on Jinmen and Mazu, but on Taiwan itself. Thus, the shelling actually speeded up the signing of the mutual defense treaty between Washington and Taipei, and a war between China and America almost erupted over the crisis.[101]

How could Beijing defend its "one China policy" without provoking a war with the United States? In August 1955, in the aftermath of the first Taiwan Strait crisis, Zhou announced that the "precondition" for China's renunciation of the use of force in the Taiwan Strait was "America's military withdrawal from Taiwan and the Taiwan Strait." Both China and the United States should use "the means of peaceful negotiation, not the means of military forces or military threats, to address their major differences, including the Taiwan question." Among all the CCP's proposals on the Taiwan question, Zhou said, this one was "the most important." Without this "precondition," China would not renounce the use of military force "unilaterally." It did not mean that China intended to take Taiwan through military force, he told the Chinese Foreign Service officers. The point was the "principle of national sovereignty, national independence." Given the American military presence in Taiwan and the Taiwan Strait, "how could China ever bow to the American military pressures and give up China's rights to defend its sovereignty?"[102]

In Zhou's view, the reason that Dulles rejected his proposal was that Dulles never intended to discuss "when and how the American troops would withdraw from Taiwan and the Taiwan Straits." Dulles's motive in seeking China's "unilateral" renunciation of military force was not to solve the Taiwan question peacefully, but to "delay" its solution. Dulles's "hidden agenda," Zhou argued, was to bring "the pressure of world opinion" to bear on China, to force China to accept the existence of Taiwan as a separate, independent state in the future.[103]

How could Beijing end this impasse in the Taiwan Strait? During the Hundred Flowers period, democratic parties proposed "direct peace negotiations" between Beijing and Taipei. If class warfare was over on the mainland, or the "principal contradiction" was transformed from antagonistic to nonantagonistic, why could not the nature of the struggle between the CCP and the KMT also be transformed through peace negotiations?

In January 1956, Zhou announced that Beijing was willing to engage in negotiations with Taipei for "peaceful national unification."[104] Li Zongren—former acting president of the Nationalist government in

1949—immediately issued a statement from New York, where he lived, endorsing Zhou's call. Beijing was particularly interested in Li's endorsement. It had received a report that some in the U.S. Republican Party had been planning to replace Chiang with Li through a coup, because of their resentment of Chiang's prosecution of two high-ranking pro-American officials in his cabinet. Mao and Zhou agreed that should the American coup succeed, the situation in Taiwan could be "much more complicated." Thus, they hoped that Li could be persuaded to return to the mainland. In May 1956, through an arrangement by Li Jishen, a leading figure of the Third Force and former vice president of the PRC (1949–1954), Li Zongren's confidant Cheng Siyuan secretly visited Beijing from Hong Kong. In his dinner with Cheng, Zhou spoke highly of Li's policy proposal on peace negotiations. Zhou said he agreed with Li's recommendations, except for Taiwan's demilitarization. "After unification, Taiwan should continue to have its own military force for self-defense."[105]

In July 1956, Chiang Ching-kuo—Chiang Kai-shek's son—sent his former secretary, Cao Juren, to visit Beijing. Zhou reminded him that the CCP and the KMT had twice united against imperialism. "If the first united front ensured the victory of the Northern Expedition in the 1920s, and the second one guaranteed the triumph of the War of Resistance in the 1930s and the 1940s, why can we not have the third united front to achieve peaceful national unification?"[106] Chiang Kai-shek himself now tried to determine whether Zhou's call was genuine or a smokescreen for the CCP's military campaign against Taiwan. He decided to send someone he could trust to meet with Zhou. In April 1957, Song Yishan, Chiang's loyal student and former personnel chief of the KMT's Organization Department,[107] arrived in Beijing. Zhou told him that the call for a third united front was "not to summon the Nationalists to surrender." Rather, Taiwan and the mainland should achieve peaceful unification "on the basis of equality." After the unification, Taiwan would be an autonomous region and would continue to be under Chiang's leadership. The CCP would not send anyone to intervene in Chiang's governance. On the other hand, the KMT could send its representatives to Beijing to participate in the PRC's government. In May 1957, Song returned to Hong Kong and sent a detailed report to Chiang. His report warmly praised the "sincerity" of Zhou's call for a third united front and "the great national progress" the PRC had made in improving the standard of living of the Chinese people.[108]

At this critical juncture, the antirightist campaign was launched on the mainland, wherein many relatives and friends of the KMT on Taiwan were designated rightists, or people's enemies. Cheng Siyuan recalled in his memoir that during the Hundred Flowers period, he was "enthusiastically" planning Li's return to the mainland. But the anti-rightist campaign in the summer of 1957 changed his mind.[109]

In the aftermath of the antirightist campaign, Chiang revived his militant policy against the PRC. By the end of 1957, the United States had shipped Matador missiles to Taiwan and had begun to construct an airport with an extra-long runway that could accommodate B-52 strategic bombers.

America's drastic increase of its military presence on the island co-incided with the State Department's decision to suspend the U.S.-China ambassadorial talks in Warsaw in late 1957. While the State Department had persistently rejected Zhou's invitation for a year, since August 1956, it announced suddenly on August 22, 1957, that it would allow twenty-four American news organizations to send reporters to China for a seven-month trial period. This acceptance of Zhou's invitation was, the State Department claimed, both "conditional"—the American correspondents must be allowed to report on American prisoners in China—and "nonreciprocal"—there would be no arrangements for Chinese journalists to visit America.[110] Beijing quickly rejected Wash-ington's acceptance of Zhou's invitation because of these terms. On September 7, at his meeting with a group of young Americans touring China, Zhou rebuked the United States: "The State Department put an end to the matter by refusing reciprocal rights of coverage to Chinese reporters." Ambassador Alexis Johnson said he was "astounded" by the question of reciprocity, because when Zhou had invited American journalists to visit China one year earlier, the issue was never men-tioned.[111] He was right. When Zhou had extended his invitation the invitation itself had been unconditional. However, after Dulles's highly publicized June 1957 speech in San Francisco on the U.S. policy of "isolating, weakening, and containing" the PRC, which roughly coin-cided with Moscow's offer to help the PRC build its atomic bomb and Chinese scientists in high-tech and defense industries were preparing for their trip to Moscow, Beijing had no intention of allowing American journalists to visit China on a nonequal, nonreciprocal basis at that delicate political moment.[112]

Indeed, Dulles was infuriated by Zhou's new demand for reciprocity and further enraged by Mao's claim of Sino-Soviet unity in Moscow in late 1957. This prompted him to propose suspending the Sino-

American ambassadorial talks in Warsaw. He was convinced that Beijing did not want to honor any agreement, "major or minor." Beijing's only purpose was to exploit "the propaganda value" of the ambassadorial talks for "its sole advantage." The time had come, he argued, to take a break from the talks, "to warn Beijing, and await results." Meanwhile, a State Department spokesman openly asked, since there were two Koreas, two Vietnams, and two Germanys, why could there not be "two Chinas"? Kenneth Young, a senior State Department officer, immediately observed that Beijing evinced "great concern, disappointment, and even anger over the breakdown" of the Sino-American ambassadorial talks and Washington's public statements on "two Chinas."[113]

Mao's position was that there was never any international treaty that sanctioned two Chinas. Beijing was unanimous in its belief that "China must not appear to the Americans as weak or lacking in determination on the Taiwan question." In Zhou's words, "If we do not reply, others will think that we acquiesce in the legal status of 'two Chinas.' " Chen Yi, now the foreign minister, argued that China had been making conciliatory proposals to America throughout 1956 and the first half of 1957 but that China got nothing in return. Even worse, he said, Washington had intensified its efforts to create two separate Chinas. "We have not occupied any territory of the United States, we have not helped any of America's domestic groups to split the United States," he remarked angrily. "The American government is too arrogant." He told Chinese diplomats that it was time for China to "talk tough": "When the Americans wanted tensions, we advocated relaxation; and when the Americans continued increasing tensions, we continued advocating relaxation. However, if the Americans insist on increasing tensions, we have no other choice but to increase tensions to a much greater degree."[114]

It was within this broad context that the second Taiwan Strait crisis took place. In late June 1958, Mao suggested shelling Jinmen and Mazu a second time. The shelling, he said, was "to use our brinkmanship to deal with Dulles's brinkmanship, to force the Americans to return to the negotiation table," or to reopen the Sino-American ambassadorial talks. Furthermore, he said, the shelling also sent a message to Chiang, "to criticize his military cooperation with America."[115] The right time came in July 1958, when Washington sent troops to Lebanon to deal with the Iraqi uprising. The Taiwan question must not be perceived by the world as just a power struggle between the CCP and the

KMT, he emphasized. It should be directly tied to the anti-imperialist struggle in the Middle East, to demonstrate that there was a "direct connection" between the Chinese people's struggle for national unification and other people's struggles for national independence in the developing world. Besides, he said, "The Americans have bullied us for many years, now we have a chance, why don't we give them a hard time?"[116]

On the other hand, Mao was also extremely careful not to provoke a war with America over the shelling of Jinmen and Mazu. The shelling must not include Taiwan, he stressed. Jinmen and Mazu were not under America's "direct protection," according to the U.S.-Taiwan Mutual Defense Treaty of 1954,[117] so Washington would not fight a war with Beijing over shelling there. As he told the Supreme State Council meeting, "I always feel that America's military strategy is to occupy the 'middle area' between the two blocs first. Only if there would be real chaos in the socialist bloc, and only if the Americans would be certain that when they come, the Soviet Union and China would collapse, then they would come. Otherwise, I don't believe the Americans want to fight a war with the Chinese right now."[118] Thus, he was convinced that as long as China did not shell Taiwan, there would be no war between China and the United States.

Nonetheless, Mao gave the strictest orders to the PLA not to do anything to provoke the Americans. On September 7, 1958, heavily armed U.S. ships began to escort KMT's vessels on resupply missions to Jinmen. U.S. naval aircraft also were called into action to support the KMT's air force. Mao immediately issued an order that the shelling must not target the American escorts. Should the American ships open fire, the PLA would not fire back.[119]

Mao's initial plan was to take over Jinmen and Mazu through persistent shelling. In the middle of the shelling, however, he changed the plan, opting to leave Jinmen and Mazu in Chiang's hands. His change of heart was brought about by his realization that Dulles's new policy aimed to give up Jinmen and Mazu, thus forcing Chiang to accept "the reality of 'two Chinas.' "[120]

Should Beijing unite with Washington against Taipei by taking back Jinmen and Mazu? Or should Beijing unite with Taipei against Washington by leaving Jinmen and Mazu in the KMT's hands?[121] This was the question Mao posed for his comrades and the leaders of the democratic parties in Beijing in September 1958. "If we take back Jinmen and Mazu this time, we would actually speed up the creation of 'two

Chinas.' " To leave Jinmen and Mazu in Chiang's hands, on the other hand, could prevent Taiwan from falling into Dulles's hands. The original plan of taking back Jinmen and Mazu needed to be changed: Beijing decided to unite with Taipei against John Foster Dulles.[122]

On October 6, 1958, Beijing's shelling stopped. Defense Minister Peng Dehui issued a statement, written by Mao himself, that called for "direct peaceful negotiations" between the mainland and Taiwan. Moreover, Mao invited Zhang Shizhao, a prominent Third Force figure and Chiang's personal friend, to send a letter to Chiang. This letter stated that Chiang's mother's grave on the mainland had been well preserved. It also laid out the CCP's conditions for peace negotiations, both the minimal and the maximal ones. The minimal condition was that both sides were to establish limited contact, such as exchange of postal and phone services, direct flights, and shipping. The maximal condition was that Taiwan could have its own government, military force, party organizations, and the mainland could pay its expenses. Most important of all, Zhang's letter revealed the CCP's new policy of "uniting with the KMT against Dulles."[123]

"It is much better to have Chiang Kai-shek as the president on Taiwan," Mao emphasized at a Supreme State Council meeting in February 1959. "Let him experiment with the Three People's Doctrines there." According to Mao, Chiang understood that "sooner or later America would recognize the PRC." That was why Taipei agreed "to use secret channels to continue the dialogue." Chiang did not dare to do so openly, because he feared the U.S. response. But "we are not afraid of Americans." "The truth is," Mao emphasized, "Taiwan and the mainland are mutually dependent upon each other, and neither side could be separate from the other." After all, he said, both sides across the Taiwan Strait did support a "one China policy."[124]

The second Taiwan Strait crisis hardened Eisenhower's view of the CCP. If he had talked about an "inducement strategy" to split the Sino-Soviet alliance, he was now more inclined to agree with Dulles about a strategy of "punishment." By the end of 1959, Mao increasingly sensed that Washington was trying to split the Sino-Soviet alliance by hitting China harder than it did the Soviets, to isolate China first and to defeat the Soviet Union eventually. He was convinced that Washington's long-term number-one enemy was still Moscow. "We are an agricultural country, and we don't have any atomic bomb, not even a small one. So why should Americans fear us? Their major fear is still the Soviet Union." What Mao could not understand was why the Soviets did not believe it, and stood by the American side "to press China." To search for an answer, in November 1959, Mao invited a small group of CCP leaders to discuss Dulles's three speeches on the strategy of "peaceful evolution" in the Soviet bloc.[125]

Mao perceived Dulles to be a "thinker" who was interested in "long-term strategic perspectives." Mao wrote a brief commentary on each of Dulles's three speeches, focusing particularly on Dulles's new proposal of "encouraging internal changes" in the Soviet bloc. If "internal changes" could take place through America's persistent encouragement, according to Dulles, the Soviet bloc would change from within and would eventually be "concerned only with its own domestic affairs, without trying to realize its ambitions of global communism." In Mao's thinking, while America continued to base its foreign policy on military power, it now obviously was trying "to use the strategy of 'peaceful evolution' to complement it," to achieve "the goal of preserving itself (capitalism) and gradually destroying the enemy (socialism)." That was a goal, Mao said, that military means could never realize. Washington was "clearly trying to corrupt the Soviet Union to achieve its goal of capitalist restoration there." For Mao, this was a possible explanation for Khrushchev's behavior toward China. In such a "complicated international environment," he emphasized, "we will have to toughen our scalp to resist pressures from both Khrushchev and Eisenhower, to resist them for five to ten years."

Should the Soviet Union and the United States be treated alike now? No, Mao said. The "root cause" of the problems was not Moscow, but Washington's containment strategy against the PRC. He suggested, "We should not publicly criticize Khrushchev, neither should we criticize him by innuendo." The chief target of Beijing's criticism should continue to be Washington.[126]

However, when the PRC had to face pressure from two superpowers, was the policy of peaceful coexistence sufficient to bring about a peaceful international environment for China's industrialization? That was the question Mao repeatedly raised at various meetings in 1960. "We want to have peaceful coexistence with the Americans. But they obviously don't want to have peaceful coexistence with us," he said. If the United States' goal was not to maintain peaceful coexistence with China, if Moscow might fall under "the corrupting influence" of Washington, who else could China turn to in the world? In Mao's view, it was the Asian, African, and Latin American peoples who were struggling for national independence.[127]

Did Mao mean that China should no longer apply the principle of peaceful coexistence to Sino-American relations? He did think that Dulles's new strategy revealed his former strategy of brinkmanship could not best serve U.S. interests. It was still possible to "have détente with America." It was still possible for China "to win at least ten more years of peace." He emphasized that "China must not miss this opportunity." He proposed that China should continue pressing Washington to sign a convention of peace and mutual nonaggression, to send a clear message to America about "the Chinese people's desire for peace."[128]

China's diplomacy toward America must now have "two legs," Mao argued in May 1960. One was "the leg of big power negotiations and conferences, to talk about arms reductions at the table," or to champion the five principles of peaceful coexistence. The other was "the leg of the Asian, African, and Latin American people's struggles against colonialism and imperialism." "The best way to avoid a new world war and achieve world peace," he emphasized, was "to have all peoples stand up against the imperialist oppressors." To mobilize the peoples in Asia, Africa, and Latin America to oppose imperialism would, for Mao, be a significant addition to the policy of peaceful coexistence. With two legs, "one can stand up and walk." With only one leg, "one will fall down."[129]

Therefore, after the near collapse of the Sino-Soviet alliance by the end of the 1950s, China's diplomacy toward America began to shift from "one leg" to "two legs." Beijing clearly attempted to employ "people's power" to replace Soviet power, to redress the tremendous imbalance of power between Beijing and Washington.

Conflicting Domestic Blueprints, Nationalism, and China's Foreign Policy

The impact of the conflicting CCP's domestic blueprints on China's foreign policy was indirect. Advocates of the radical populist blueprints did not consciously intend to alter the Chinese foreign-policy objectives. Both Mao and Zhou agreed, as did most Chinese at the time, that the longer China could have peace, the better it would be for China's industrialization. The champions of the gradualist and the radical populist blueprints mainly differed on how to proceed with China's domestic reconstruction.

Although the impact of the conflicting domestic blueprints on China's diplomacy was indirect, it was profound and far-reaching: when the gradualist economic blueprint prevailed, the Chinese economy prospered, the Chinese people's standard of living improved, and China became a nation to be reckoned with in Asia and the Soviet bloc. When the radical economic blueprint ruined the Chinese economy, China's national power declined, and so did China's moral prestige in the world. In its reactions to the much harsher international security environments, advocates of the radical blueprints put politics, rather than economics, in command; a spillover, subconsciously as well as consciously, of their way of thinking on the domestic front. Their ideological rhetoric and radical political language could only further alienate China's former allies and friends.

Furthermore, when the gradualist political blueprint triumphed, when the Hundred Flowers were in blossom, the domestic united front was greatly expanded. It was this "broad domestic united front," as Zhou often emphasized, that was the "most solid foundation" of the united front across the Taiwan Strait, and the united front between the Chinese people and other peoples in the world. In his words, "Behind every individual Chinese we are working with, there are other individuals, different classes and social groups. The more Chinese people we can unite *within China,* the more Chinese people we can unite *across the Taiwan Strait,* and the more people we can unite *around the world.*"[130]

Finally, and most important, the philosophical foundation of peaceful coexistence is a recognition of the fundamental complementarity of different national interests and values in the world, or "harmony between opposites." Zhou reflected on the "major problem" in the Soviet philosophical approach to its neighbors in his memo to the CCP Politburo in January 1957:

The Soviet leaders perceived the relations between the interests of the Soviet Communist Party and those of the fraternal parties, between the interests of the Soviet Union and those of other countries, often in antagonistic terms, as opposing each other. Thus, if they are willing to correct one mistake, there is no guarantee that they would not make a new one. Even when they acknowledged that they did something wrong, they made such recognition often out of political expediency, rather than out of thorough self-criticism concerning their fundamental approach to those relationships.[131]

According to Zhou, within the philosophical framework of essential complementarity of divergent interests and beliefs, China's long-term national interests could not be best served if China tried to maximize its own national advantage at the expense of other nations.

In spite of the different patterns in China's diplomacy throughout the 1950s, a striking similarity persisted: the PRC's unrelenting emphasis on national sovereignty and equality. Thus, in Sino-American relations, the Taiwan question loomed large throughout the decade. In Sino-Soviet relations, in the period of the gradualist blueprints, the CCP vigorously opposed Soviet military intervention in Poland. In the summer of 1958, in the period of the radical populist blueprints, Beijing angrily rejected Khrushchev's requests for a joint submarine fleet or a submarine base in China.

From a historical perspective, the emphasis on national sovereignty and equality was not unique to China, India, Burma, and Vietnam, each of which had bitter historical memories of national disintegration and humiliation. It was also common to all newborn nation-states in Europe. During the seventeenth and eighteenth centuries, following the breakdown of medieval Christian universalism, a new international order emerged, founded on "national sovereignty and territorial impermeability." As Ishwer Ojha points out: "China, no less than other aspiring powers," illustrates that all its desires and aspirations in the period of nation-state building lie in the area of "nationalist goals." In comparison with rising nations in European history, "these nationalist goals would probably have been considered legitimate, if they had not been intermingled with Communist ideology and the tensions of the Cold War."[132]

This study further suggests that while China behaved like every other newborn nation in its passionate quest for national sovereignty and equality during its nation-state building stage, it also manifested its own unique form of foreign policy, as every other newborn nation had at different stages of development. From 1954 to late 1959, this distinctive feature of Chinese diplomacy was shown in China's new foreign policy of peaceful coexistence. Contrary to widespread expectations in Washington, Chinese revolutionaries, following their national victory, did not formulate a policy of exporting revolution. This dimension of the PRC's foreign policy was neglected in the United States' China policy debates throughout the 1950s. As Michael Hunt points out, two ideological interpretations of the CCP's foreign policy in the Cold War helped to close off "our vista" during that time. One interpretation "reduced the CCP's worldview to a function of an imported Marxist-Leninist ideology." The other emphasized "the tyranny of an indigenous tradition" of Sinocentrism. "Viewed in this way, the past became something of an embarrassment, a dead hand holding back China's accommodation to the contemporary international system." However, "a moment of meditation on the Chinese past suggests that if we look back beyond the revolutions of the twentieth century, or even past the 'middle kingdom' view of the nineteenth" during the Manchu dynasty, "we may find other, older styles of dealing with the world that have also persisted into the modern period." Most prominent among these is the Chinese tradition of cosmopolitanism, or the heritage of continuous economic and cultural exchanges with the rest of the world, which ran from the Han through the Ming dynasties. As he emphasizes, "any proper understanding of the genesis of the Chinese Communist foreign policy has as its logical starting point one basic proposition: China's approach to external relations has not been shaped by a single mold or imprisoned by a single tradition. We neglect its diversity and complexity at our own peril."[133]

U.S.-China Confrontation in Vietnam: Its Origins Revisited

In the Eisenhower administration, a China policy debate raged from 1954 to 1960, a debate similar to one that took place in the Truman administration from late 1948 to mid-1950. Only this time the outcome was different: the strategy of containment prevailed. By the end of 1960, the PRC was more isolated than ever. Not only had South Vietnam been built up as a military fortress to deter the PRC, the Sino-Soviet alliance was on the edge of a meltdown.

A more isolated China did not become a more tamed or submissive China, as predicted by Dulles. To the contrary, China became more militant. Beijing's perspective was that from 1954 to the end of 1959, China had walked with one leg, the leg of peaceful coexistence. Now China would have to walk with two legs. In addition to peaceful coexistence, China must also "actively support the oppressed peoples' struggles against colonialism and imperialism in Asia, Africa, the Middle East, and Latin America." By the end of 1959, Beijing's "peace initiative" toward Washington was dropped. In early 1960, Beijing abandoned its Vietnam policy of "peaceful unification" and adopted the policy of supporting Ho's guerrilla warfare in South Vietnam.

Underlying the Dulles strategy of peripheral military containment was the totalitarian model, by which the PRC's economy, polity, and foreign policy intentions were assessed in the 1950s. If an "illiberal" state was bad enough, an "authoritarian state" was worse, and a "postrevolutionary, totalitarian state" with an "embarrassing tradition" of Sinocentrism was the worst. It was much more repressive at home and much more expansionist abroad than all other types of illiberal regimes. According to this model, the state-society relationship in the PRC could be best understood in terms of a horizontal dichotomy, or the opposition between an overwhelming police state and repressed individuals in the society. Thus advocates of the containment strategy were convinced that the PRC's domestic programs were modeled after the Stalinist command economy and the Soviet police state, and its foreign policy objective was to communize all of Asia and become the predominant power in the Western Pacific, as Japan and Nazi Germany had tried to do in Asia and in Europe during World War II. They were further convinced that the first move in the PRC's war of conquest would be to conquer Southeast Asia through military force. In 1956, it was out of this intense fear that the State Department under Dulles defeated the new China policy proposal of relaxing the multilateral and bilateral China embargo and installed a strategy of peripheral military containment against the PRC in South Vietnam.

Across the Pacific, since the modern era, Chinese reformers perceived the major challenge to China's search for modernity as the vertical division between rural and urban China, as discussed in Chapter 1. In the 1950s, in the aftermath of the land revolution, the tensions between rural and urban China, or between the poor peasantry and the intelligentsia, intensified. The CCP's united front with the urban middle class underwent the most serious challenges. At the societal level, this tension between rural and urban China manifested itself, for instance, in the distrustful relationship between urban intellectuals and many new CCP cadres who had just come to cities. At the state level, it was highlighted in the competing blueprints for China's economic and political reconstruction. In spite of these two different patterns of Beijing's domestic policy, the PRC's diplomatic objective from 1954 to 1960 was not to export revolution. There is no evidence to show that Beijing had a plan to conquer Southeast Asia to solve "its pending food crisis due to the population pressures." Dulles's totalitarian model of analysis was, however, unable to comprehend the distinctive form of China's quest for modernity and new identity, which was further confounded by the difficult partnership between the poor peasants and the urban intellectuals after the nationwide land revolution.

It is important to note that this totalitarian model was by no means the monopoly of Dulles and the State Department under the Eisenhower administration. As Robert McNamara acknowledged candidly, in the Kennedy and Johnson administrations, "We—certainly I—badly misread China's objectives and mistook its bellicose rhetoric to imply a drive for regional hegemony. We also totally underestimated the nationalist aspect of Ho Chi Minh's movement. We saw him first as a Communist and only second as a Vietnamese nationalist." He particularly emphasized, "Such ill-founded judgments were accepted without debate by the Kennedy administration, as they had been by its Democratic and Republican predecessors. We failed to analyze our assumptions critically, then or later. The foundations of our decision making were gravely flawed." He bemoaned the loss of "the top East Asian and China experts in the State Department—John Paton Davies, Jr., John Stewart Service, and John Carter Vincent," who had been purged during the McCarthy inquisition of the 1950s. Otherwise, he wrote, they could have provided "sophisticated, nuanced insights" at that fateful moment in the Kennedy administration's decision on the escalation of the Vietnam War.[134]

According to Warren Cohen, the source of the liberal-conservative consensus on the Vietnam War was deeply rooted in America's intellectual undercurrents at the time. He points out that Acheson's "enclave strategy" was "rejected on moral grounds by Americans both left and right" at the beginning stage of the war:

> Conservatives wanted to oppose Communism everywhere because their wealth and power, as well as their principles, were being threatened. To the left, liberals, even many who considered themselves socialists, were offended by a strategy that seemed to abandon the developing nations, the weak and the poor. . . . Africans and Asians too were worthy of the blessings of democracy. In the 1960s, a conservative-liberal consensus was reached on the notion that the Third World constituted the new arena of the Cold War. . . . Liberal messianism eased the path to Vietnam.[135]

In the mid-1960s, at the full height of the Vietnam War, Hans Morgenthau first suggested that the war might have been based on a "fundamental misjudgment" of the PRC's foreign policy intentions. To understand the PRC's foreign policy, he argued, one needed to look beyond its ideological rhetoric and comprehend "the permanent aspiration of China," which, he argued, was to become a great economic and cultural power. "It is of great relevance for our policies in Southeast Asia that for a thousand years China has not tried to expand her influence and power west and southwestwards by military conquest and annexation." Instead, "it has relied, and history has shown it could rely, upon the enormous attractiveness which its powerful civilization has had upon the border states to the west and the southwest." It was thus "utterly mistaken," he wrote, to make an analogy between the PRC and Nazi Germany: "We have looked at China very much as we failed to look at Hitler's Germany—that is to say, as a power bent upon world conquest—and the spokesmen for successive administrations have time and again pointed to the similarity between Mao Tsetung and Hitler, Munich and Vietnam. . . . In truth, this analogy is utterly mistaken." He warned, in particular, that if China were not seeking "the physical conquest of additional territories" in Southeast Asia, the Vietnam War would become highly counterproductive to America's vital security interests in the Western Pacific.[136]

With historical hindsight, while there was still a containment component in Eisenhower's inducement strategy, it touched on, at least partially, some deeper historical and nationalistic undercurrents of the PRC's domestic and foreign policy agendas. If the inducement policy—no matter how imperfect—had been adopted, there might have been a relaxing of the China embargo and establishment of a limited trading relationship between Washington and Beijing, which might have led to a limited U.S.-China reconciliation sooner than through the Vietnam War, which cost the lives of 55,000 American troops and 4 million Vietnamese people. In other words, if Eisenhower's proposal to ease the China embargo and Mao's proposal for "détente with the West" had been given a chance in 1956, it was possible that the Vietnam War might have been avoided in the following decade.

According to the declassified CIA documents made public in 2004, regardless of the wedge strategy, "American intelligence agencies were slow to recognize the emergence of differences between the Soviet Union and China," wrote Douglas Jehl. In the words of Robert L. Suettinger, former deputy national intelligence officer for East Asia on the National Intelligence Council, a major shortcoming in America's China policymaking was "overestimating the importance of ideological solidarity . . . within the Communist Bloc at least during the 1950s."[137] In this regard, an increasingly rigid, ideological, or positivistic interpretation of Chinese domestic programs and foreign policy intentions, which neglected the deep historical undercurrents in China's long march toward modernity and new identity, did contribute to an increasingly counterproductive American policy toward China and Southeast Asia by the end of the 1950s.

In retrospect, if one studies the Vietnam War from its origins in the 1950s, rather than from the time when it was drastically expanded by Beijing and Washington in the 1960s, it is hard to conclude that the Vietnam War was a necessary war that "frustrated China's ambition to dominate Southeast Asia and the Western Pacific through military force." The Dulles strategy of peripheral military containment generated exactly the opposite of its projected policy objectives. In this sense, the Vietnam War was a tragic war of self-fulfilling prophecy in the origins of U.S.-China confrontation in Vietnam.

Conclusion

Ways of War and Peace

In *The Peloponnesian War*, Thucydides (c. 471–400 BC), the great Athenian historian, regarded in the West as the founder of international relations theory, identified the root cause of the war between Sparta and Athens as their struggle for power. He argued, "What made war inevitable was the growth of Athenian power and the fear which this caused in Sparta." In the first stage of the war, Sparta, the predominant power, decided to wage war against Athens; while in the second stage, Athens, the rising power, was determined to conquer Sparta. To mobilize their peoples, both sides defined the war in terms of conflicting moral values. However, according to Thucydides, moral ideals were invoked to mobilize their peoples for war: they were policy justifications, rather than the underlying reasons for the confrontation. "My work is not a piece of writing designed to win the applause of the moment," he proclaimed, "but was done to last forever." Thucydides said, "Human nature being what it is," given the same set of circumstances, "humans will react in much the same way." He deemed the perpetual struggles for power, or perpetual conflicts of vital interests, based on the rise and fall of state powers, the underlying cause for all military conflicts.[1]

This study takes the position that the origins and evolution of U.S.-China antagonism between 1945 and 1960 were more complex than the perpetual clash of vital interests Thucydides posited. The rapid transition from being allies to enemies was not the direct result of two sides' or even one side's determination to engage in confrontation. In-

stead, the drastic change of attitude toward America among the rising
Chinese middle class in the post–World War II years, and the origins
in the 1950s of the Korean War as well as the Vietnam War, to a great
extent, may be attributed to fatal misjudgments of each other's domestic conditions and foreign-policy objectives. In those tragic misas-
sessments, moral values were called upon not only to supply policy
justifications, as in the Peloponnesian War, but to form policy rationality for both China and the United States. Cultural visions of modernity and identity in each nation played a critical role in evaluating
the other's intentions and in defining interests and principles in their
interactions. In this sense, the underlying causes of U.S.-China military
conflicts were not real conflicts over vital interests, but the fallout from
illusory or perceived conflicts of vital interests across the Pacific.

In retrospect, there was a repeated pattern in U.S.-China diplomacy
from 1945 to 1960; that is, each side's foreign policies toward the other
were persistently counterproductive to its desired or anticipated policy
goals. It is clearly not enough to argue that each side simply tried to
defend its national interests or moral ideals. Should the investigation
stop here, one could never explain why policymakers and the general
public, who obviously did not intend to harm their vital interests and
moral principles, constantly endorsed foreign policies which, in reality,
jeopardized their best national interests and undermined their most
cherished ideals across the Pacific.

Barry Rubin once used the metaphor of a sailing boat to explain this
phenomenon. A nation's foreign policy is sometimes like a sailing boat,
he said; while it may intend to set off for the opposite shore of a river,
it can end up a hundred miles downstream. How could the intention
of the trip and its actual result become so different? It is because, he
emphasized, the people on the boat are ignorant of the unfathomable
undercurrents of the river.[2] Between 1945 and 1960, both China and
America, like the people on the boat, repeatedly failed to reach their
intended foreign policy objectives because they persistently failed to
understand the ocean of historical currents that deeply underlay the
other side's core policy assumptions or cultural visions of modernity
and identity.

U.S.-China interactions were taking place between countries whose
historical evolutions, cultural heritages, and social constituencies and
positions in the world economy were vastly divergent.

China's quest for modernity and a new identity did not begin with the Cold War. Regardless of the differences in ideology and rhetoric among them, Chinese blueprints for a modern economy and polity since the early twentieth century and throughout the Cold War have illustrated three major patterns. The first pattern centers on protection of poor peasants. Examples are the Taiping peasant rebellion in the 1850s, which claimed the imported religion of Christianity as its official ideology, and the CCP in the late 1950s, which moved toward a radical populist interpretation of socialism as its official ideology. The second pattern focuses on the needs and demands of urban centers, such as those of the Nationalist government in the 1930s and early 1940s, which held an elite-oriented interpretation of capitalism and republicanism as its official ideology. The third pattern aims to achieve a balance between the competing needs, demands, and aspirations in rural and urban China, or between impoverished villagers and an educated urban middle class. The best exemplar of the third approach is Sun Yat-sen's Three Principles of the People, but the CCP's gradualist blueprint in the early years of the PRC, and its moderate interpretation of socialism, also fits into this pattern of the search for modernity. It is important to clarify that these three different approaches to China's modernity share one goal in common: China's achievement of national freedom and equality in the world.

Underlying these different approaches to China's modern identity are two principal philosophical conceptions concerning how to draw the boundary between the private and the public realms. One is to construct this relationship in terms of mutual rivalry and animosity, as illustrated in the blueprints that exclusively favored either the poor peasantry or the urban elites. The other is to construct the private-public relationship in terms of mutual benefits and complementarity, as exemplified in the blueprints that envisioned building coalitions between villages and colleges, or achieving cooperation between poor peasants and intellectuals/entrepreneurs.

Among those different blueprints and philosophical foundations, the middle-ground approach that championed a coalition between rural and urban China, or between villages and colleges, consistently enjoyed the widest support among the Chinese people, including both peasants and the urban middle class, in the twentieth century. This moderate approach to China's modernity, and its unique philosophical construction of the private-public relationship—neither individualism nor collectivism—along with its distinctive manifestation of Chinese nationalism, and its projection of a world outlook of peaceful coexistence, however, defies simple categorization in the sweeping ideological dichotomy of the Cold War.

It is thus not surprising that between 1945 and 1960, even though these visions of moderate Chinese reformers generated distrust and suspicions in Moscow, Washington's foreign-policy agenda subsumed them into the Soviet model of domestic development and foreign policy objectives. Nor was it surprising that champions of dissenting China policy proposals that provided much more accurate assessments of Chinese domestic conditions and foreign-policy intentions were persistently marginalized, rejected, or persecuted in America's China policy debates during that period.

Across the Pacific, the danger of utilizing a single paradigm shaped in China's own mainstream parameters to analyze other nations' intentions is also shown vividly in China's counterproductive foreign policies of this period. Whenever discussions in Beijing employed a narrow approach to analyzing America's China policy intentions—for instance, framing the discussion as American imperialist ambition versus China's national independence—Beijing's foreign policy could not reach the hearts and minds of mainstream America and so could not quickly seize those limited opportunities for a more constructive relationship with the United States.

The impact of these divergent cultural visions of modernity and identity on U.S.-China diplomacy in this period was twofold. First, these deeply ingrained assumptions about modernity and identity generated, subconsciously as well as consciously, specific analytical categories or paradigms that functioned to select, filter, evaluate, and interpret the data, "evidence," or information with respect to the other nation's domestic developments and foreign-policy objectives. Cognitive psychologists uniformly agree that new evidence will always be interpreted to conform to those deep-seated analytical boxes in our heads. If it is consistent with them, we will accept it; if inconsistent or ambiguous, we will discredit, distort, or ignore it. In Richard Immerman's words, "this tendency is most pronounced when the belief is deeply felt and deeply held. Our values are hierarchically ordered, and our beliefs are interconnected to form a system; when incoming information is so discordant that we cannot ignore it, we will revise our least fundamental notions before even questioning our core assumptions. Our most highly valued beliefs are thus minimally disconfirmed" in the policymaking process.[3]

Second, different visions not only shaped deep-seated analytical boxes or filter systems, but also helped establish the different moral/political parameters of the mainstream foreign-policy debates on both sides. Such mainstream parameters in a society, as Emily S. Rosenberg casts it, are conceptual "spaces at which different systems of meaning and organizations intersect." Therefore depending on how one approaches these mainstream parameters, such "figurative borders," in her words, can engender opposite results in a nation's foreign-policy debates. "They may produce conflict, demoralization, fear, and oppression." And "they may generate hybridization, creativity, and liberation."[4] Unfortunately, on both sides of the Pacific in the historical period examined here, the mainstream parameters generated the former rather than the latter.

In the post–Cold War world, could the rapid transition from allies to enemies in the post–World War II and the early Cold War eras repeat itself in U.S.-China interactions? Yes, it could. By the end of the 1990s, America's China policy of "strategic partnership" was under siege. The image of the American ambassador standing behind a broken window in the U.S. embassy in Beijing after massive Chinese students' demonstrations protesting U.S. bombing of the Chinese Embassy in Belgrade, Yugoslavia, in 1999, combined with the image from ten years earlier of a Chinese youth standing in front of a People's Liberation Army tank on Tiananmen square, seemed to dissipate many Americans' good will toward the PRC. Frequent U.S. media reports on China's human-rights abuses perpetuated the image of a totalitarian regime that had rapidly growing economic and military power, apparently poised to challenge American power in the new century. Before the 9/11 tragedy in 2001, the champions of America's engagement strategy toward the PRC were increasingly subject to criticism, while the advocates of a new China policy of "strategic competition," or a strategy of implicit containment, seemed to have gained the upper hand in Washington. Joseph Nye gloomily predicted at the time that the widely accepted notion of the "China threat" in Washington may well bring about its own self-fulfilling prophecy in U.S.-China diplomacy.[5]

If China's quest for modernity did not start with the Cold War, neither did it end with the collapse of the Soviet Union. With China's entry into the World Trade Organization, both the content and rhetoric of mainstream Chinese discourse on China's modernity apparently changed. A fast-growing Chinese middle class is demanding more rapid political reform and greater investment in urban reconstruction. Meanwhile, village elections, which started in the mid-1980s and are now sweeping the Chinese countryside, seem to have produced uneven results: if many villages have derived benefits from direct elections at the grassroots levels, others have not, and in still other villages these elections apparently have sharpened the old divisions based on economic strata, ethnicity, or family clans. The "Go West Campaign," a developmental strategy to bridge the divide between coastal and inland China, has generated great enthusiasm in the Western region since the late 1990s; yet it has not progressed fast enough to reverse the flow of young talent from the inland regions to Eastern China. With the widening gap between urban and rural China, as well as within urban centers, there are rising demands for faster and greater investments in rural villages, mounting outcries to slow the pace of China's participation in globalization, and increasing warnings about new class warfare in the People's Republic. Meanwhile, opposing views, across a wide political and ideological spectrum, are hotly debated on Chinese Web sites, in students' dorms, and in intellectuals' gatherings, gradually shaping a new intellectual space for vigorous discussion of the government's domestic and foreign policies.

While reformers of different persuasions in the post–Cold War era may call themselves new liberals, new nationalists, or new left, their underlying concerns are remarkably similar to those in China throughout the twentieth century. Their ideas are, by and large, attuned to the needs and aspirations of urban China, to those of rural China, or to achieving a mutually beneficial situation for villagers and intelligentsia/entrepreneurs.

It is within the context of China's mainstream discourse that a new center has emerged, one that has appealed to both urban and rural reformers. This new center criticizes the bias toward efficiency and pushes for equilibrium between economic growth/efficiency and socioeconomic justice in China's developmental strategy. This new voice has also been sharply critical of a singleminded pursuit of high, rapid GDP growth rate based entirely on Western economic criteria. In the words of Pan Yue, the deputy minister of the Chinese environmental protection ministry, it is time for China to formulate a different growth criterion—the "green GDP growth rate," based on China's huge population and limited resources—to ensure China's sustainable development.[6] This new voice calls, too, for speeding up the CCP's political reform, by installing a comprehensive institutional mechanism of checks and balances within the party, holding direct elections of party officials among party rank and file through a "party congress system," and strengthening the supervisory power of political parties of the middle class over the CCP at all levels. More important, as Qin Xiaoying, the editor-in-chief of *China's Financial and Economic Daily*, emphasizes, Chinese reformers must be fully aware of the "fatal danger of tyranny of majority opinions" for China's intellectual creativity and national imagination. This new center cries out for "legal and institutional protection of minority views" in the Chinese constitution, to ensure that there will always be new ideas and new theories in Chinese communities of discourse, ones that may not be popular in mainstream discussions but that must be protected, preserved, and respected. Whenever the current mainstream views are proven by historical developments to be inadequate or incorrect, this would ensure that there are alternative concepts and theories to turn to, rather than a theoretical or philosophical vacuum. This new center calls for reinventing Chinese civilization by incorporating the best from the West and all other civilizations and making cultural pluralism, religious polytheism, and world peace and harmony the core of the new value system in China. In recent years, many of these proposals have begun to be incorporated into the PRC's domestic and foreign-policy agendas; for instance, the eradication of all rural taxes, drastically increased government investment in infrastructure in rural China, and free compulsory education in rural areas and the western region as guaranteed by national and provincial budgets. And the most outspoken champions of these views are now widely regarded as the "brain power" of the nation.[7]

Clearly, a major challenge to China's continued quest for modernity and identity, as in the twentieth century, is how to bring rural and urban China, or villagers and intellectuals/entrepreneurs together. Without integrating the liberal ideals of individual civil and political rights into the Chinese mainstream discourse, the knowledge and talents of urban China could never be fully released and China's search for modernity would never be complete. It is also clear, on the other hand, that without the enthusiastic participation of the rural population, which has demanded greater economic prosperity and social and economic justice, China's economic reform and political democratization could only be a facade, a sham. One may well predict that in the following decades, no matter what kind of ideological rhetoric Chinese reformers might use, those enduring social and economic challenges will continue to reassert themselves in China's modernization drive. In addressing those challenges, the middle-ground approach is likely to enjoy the widest measure of support among the Chinese people. It is not accidental that in articulating its philosophical foundation, the new center has increasingly turned to Sun Yat-sen's Three Principles of the People to transcend the ideological dichotomy between socialism and capitalism, or to rise above the boundary between the public and the private realms, and to make equality within China and among the other nations of the world the ultimate goal of China's modernization.[8]

It is ironic that while Chinese economic and political reforms have been progressing, before the 9/11 tragedy Chinese anxiety over America's China policy intentions was rising. At grassroots levels, Chinese increasingly wondered whether America's China policy would aim to slow down China's modernization drive or "those anti-China groups" in Washington would do anything "to prevent China's peaceful rise." After the embassy bombing in 1999 and the South China Sea incident of April 2001 involving a collision between a U.S. spy plane and a Chinese fighter, in China's journals and Web site chat rooms there was widespread resentment and disillusionment with America's China policy intentions, especially among the younger generation of the emerging Chinese middle class.[9] If the events of September 11, 2001, have dispelled much confrontational rhetoric in both countries, if U.S.-China diplomacy seems to have reached its peak since 1972, especially under the watch of former Secretary of State Colin Powell, there remains a strong undercurrent of mutual distrust and apprehension across the Pacific.

The rapid revival of antagonistic sentiments on both sides at the beginning of the twenty-first century has demonstrated, once again, how limited both sides' analytical boxes, categories, and mainstream boundaries still are in their foreign-policy debates. Each side continues debating its foreign-policy options within its own domestic parameters, employing its familiar categories and paradigms, without being fully aware of those of the other side. The danger still exists, then, that these two nations could be dragged into, as America's China scholars have warned, a "spiraling China-U.S. security dilemma dynamics."[10] That is why the problem of "fundamental attribution errors" may persist in U.S.-China diplomacy into the future. As Alexander George emphasizes, "Threat perception and threat assessment in the conduct of diplomacy" are influenced by one's basic belief about the "fundamental nature" of the other nation. In this sense, "intelligence indicators" of that nation's intentions, "both immediate and long-range, tend to be interpreted through the prism" of one's analytical frameworks.[11]

In this regard, it is particularly important to note that the United States and China's speedy transition from "strategic partners" to "strategic competitors" at the beginning of the twenty-first century demonstrates more clearly than ever how those core policy assumptions of the post–World War II and Cold War eras, as discussed in this study, could quickly reemerge under different names and continue operating in the background of U.S.-China diplomacy.

In his classic study *The Twenty Years' Crisis, 1919–1939*, Edward Carr, the founder of the English School of international relations theory, argues that the major condition for peaceful change in world politics is that there must be "a certain measure of common feeling as to what is just and reasonable in their mutual relations" in the world community, "so that a basis, no matter how imperfect, exists for discussing demands on grounds of justice recognized by both." The best way to do so, he further argues, is to engage in economic reconstruction, bridging the gap between the global north and south: "Here we have the same recurrent conflict between 'haves' and 'have-nots', between 'satisfied' and 'dissatisfied'; . . . the same appeals to 'law and order' by the satisfied group; and the same use, or threatened use, of violence by the dissatisfied in order to assert their claims." He finds that "ultimately, the best hope of progress toward international conciliation seems to lie along the path of economic reconstruction."[12]

Could economic reconstruction alone lay the foundation for peaceful change in world politics? This study suggests that it is not enough. When peoples use their own categories and paradigms to evaluate one another's domestic developments, to judge one another's intentions, and to engage in foreign-policy debates within their own domestic mainstream parameters, they talk past each other, even when they share the same goal of economic and political reconstruction.

In the post–Cold War world, concepts of modernity in the U.S. literature are still predominantly shaped by America's exceptional national experiences. The legacy of colonialism and yearning for national dignity and equality, the suffering of the poor and crying out for socioeconomic justice, and the agonizing difficulties of building a better relationship between the village or tribal societies and the urban elite in developing countries are still underappreciated or misconstrued in mainstream America's communities of discourse. From this perspective, an international intellectual space needs to be created wherein nations and regions, poor as well as rich, small as well as big, could discuss, debate, compare, and explore different meanings of modernity, different visions of identity, and different blueprints for economic and political reconstruction in their modernization drives. No governmental dialogues, no mutual visits among peoples at grassroots levels, can replace the creation of a global civil society. It is the rise of a globally inclusive intellectual forum for genuine, in-depth discussions and debates across racial and civilizational boundaries, along with economic reconstruction between the developed and developing countries, that might eventually build up "the embryonic character of this common feeling between nations."[13]

As the first step in constructing a global civil society, positivistic hypotheses and paradigms in current international relations theory must be tested and challenged, rather than being taken as the starting point. Positivism, in Richard Ashley's words, "treats the given order as the natural order" and consequently "limits rather than expands political discourse, negates or trivializes the significance of variety across time and space," and thereby "deprives political interaction of those practical capabilities which make social learning and creative change possible."[14] In this new century, international relations theory should become the tool for liberating the human imagination and the instrument for peoples achieving the freedom to make better choices.

Therefore nations and peoples are not doomed to perpetual struggles for power, not destined to repeated wars and confrontations. The underlying cause of military conflicts can be regarded as the failure to expand human capacity for finding better solutions to cope with clashing interests and principles. In this sense, to engage in dialogues between civil societies, peoples, and civilizations requires a depth of wisdom and compassion, unprecedented in human history. Between what is today and what ought to be tomorrow, there must be a bridge. This bridge is the long-term possibility of change. To build a world society, to enhance human civilization, and to achieve enduring peace on earth have been the most cherished, the most widely shared human ideals of all major religions and civilizations. The pursuit of this noble dream is the pursuit of the interest of all peoples, the conscience of every nation, and the heartbeat of humanity.

Notes
Primary Sources
Index

Notes

Introduction

1. Walter Lippmann, *Public Opinion* (New York: Harcourt, Brace, 1922), pp. 16–31; see also Ronald Steel, *Walter Lippmann and the American Century* (Boston: Little, Brown and Company, 1980), pp. 172, 181.
2. Ideally, this study should also include a systematic comparison between Chinese perceptions of America's domestic situations and foreign-policy intentions on the one hand and the reality in America on the other. Because of space limitations in this book, however, a comprehensive study of this subject has to be the focus of another volume.
3. The most recent study on U.S.-China Cold War history is Robert Ross and Jiang Changbin, eds., *Re-examining the Cold War: U.S.-China Diplomacy, 1954–1973* (Cambridge, MA: Harvard University Press, 2001). This excellent and important study does not cover the period between 1945 and 1954, because an earlier work covered that period: Harry Harding and Yuan Ming, eds., *Sino-American Relations, 1945–1955: A Joint Reassessment of a Critical Decade* (Wilmington, DE: SR Books, 1989). This pioneering study was based on research completed before 1987. Since its publication, there has been an explosion of archival materials made available in China and Russia, as well as in the United States. A result has been the renewal of heated debates concerning the People's Republic of China's objectives in the Korean War and the Vietnam War. Many previously accepted views on these topics have been challenged or rejected.
4. Michael H. Hunt and Steven I. Levine, "The Revolutionary Challenge to Early Cold War Policy in Asia," in Warren I. Cohen and Akira Iriye, eds., *The Great Powers in East Asia, 1953–1960* (New York: Columbia University Press, 1990), pp. 13–30.

5. Paul A. Cohen, *Discovering History in China* (New York: Columbia University Press, 1984), pp. 196–198.

6. Michael Schaller, *The U.S. Crusade in China, 1938–1945* (New York: Columbia University Press, 1979), p. xii.

7. Akira Iriye, "Culture and International History," in Michael Hogan and Thomas G. Paterson, eds., *Explaining the History of American Foreign Relations,* 2nd ed. (Cambridge: Cambridge University Press, 2004), p. 245, and *Cultural Internationalism and World Order* (Baltimore: Johns Hopkins University Press, 1997), pp. 180–183.

8. Gordon H. Chang, "Are There Other Ways to Think about the 'Great Interregnum'?" *Journal of American–East Asian Relations* 7 (Spring–Summer 1998): 120–122.

9. Robert Wuthnow, *Meaning and Moral Order: Explorations in Cultural Analysis* (Berkeley: University of California Press, 1989), pp. 109–110.

10. The importance of combining security and cultural studies is increasingly recognized in the field of international relations. See Joseph Nye Jr. and Sean M. Lynn-Jones, "International Security Studies: A Report of a Conference on the State of the Field," *International Security* 12, no. 4 (Spring 1988): 14. See also Peter J. Katzenstein, ed., *The Culture of National Security: Norms and Identity in World Politics* (New York: Columbia University Press, 1996).

    However, according to Akira Iriye, a major tension still exists between the school of security studies, which centers on "decision makers and geopolitical strategies," and the school of cultural studies, which focuses on the "decentered" or "local." He finds, "As yet, few convincing arguments or methodologies have been advanced" to integrate cultural and security studies. See Iriye, *Cultural Internationalism and World Order,* pp. 178–180.

11. *Complete Works of Sun Yat-sen,* vol. 2 (Taipei, Taiwan, 1956), p. 22.

12. Steven I. Levine, "Perception and Ideology in Chinese Foreign Policy," in Thomas W. Robinson and David Shambaugh, eds., *Chinese Foreign Policy: Theory and Practice* (Oxford: Clarendon Press, 1994), p. 34.

13. Michael H. Hunt, *Ideology and U.S. Foreign Policy* (New Haven, CT: Yale University Press, 1987), p. 12.

14. Robert Wuthnow, James Davison Hunter, Albert Bergesen, and Edith Kurl, *Cultural Analysis: The Works of Peter L. Berger, Mary Douglas, Michel Foucault and Jurgen Habermas* (London: Routledge and Kegan Paul, 1984), pp. 193–198, 224.

15. Alastair Iain Johnston, *Cultural Realism* (Princeton, NJ: Princeton University Press, 1995), p. vii.

16. Concerning cognitive psychologists' perspectives on the important role of values and beliefs in the policymaking process, see Robert Jervis, *Perception and Misperception in International Politics* (Princeton, NJ: Princeton University Press, 1976), pp. 283–284, and Richard Immerman, "Psychology," in Michael Hogan and Thomas G. Paterson, eds., *Explaining the*

History of American Foreign Relations, 2nd ed. (Cambridge: Cambridge University Press, 2004).

17. Scholars of contemporary cultural analysis include cultural sociologists, anthropologists, historians, philosophers, and political scientists who are interested in political culture and attempt to go beyond individuals' internalized worldviews and focus instead on cultural patterns, addressing the problems of hidden subjectivity in human society. Regarding the emerging school of contemporary cultural analysis, see Wuthnow, *Meaning and Moral Order.*

18. Clifford Geertz, *The Interpretation of Cultures* (New York: Basic Books, 1973), pp. 52–53.

19. Robert Jervis, "Political Decision-Making: Recent Contributions," *Political Psychology* 2 (Summer 1980): 85; see also Harold R. Isaacs, *Scratches on Our Minds: American Images of China and India* (New York: John Day Company, 1958), pp. 37–62.

20. Harold R. Isaacs, "Some Concluding Remarks: The Turning Mirrors," in Akira Iriye, ed., *Mutual Images: Essays in American-Japanese Relations* (Cambridge, MA: Harvard University Press, 1975), pp. 258–259.

21. Benjamin I. Schwartz, "Culture, Modernity, and Nationalism—Further Reflections," and Tu Wei-ming, "Introduction: Cultural Perspectives," in Tu Wei-ming, ed., *China in Transformation* (Cambridge, MA: Harvard University Press, 1994), pp. xi–xxv, 233–252; see also Benedict Anderson, *Imagined Communities: Reflections on the Origin and Spread of Nationalism* (London: Verso, 1991).

22. Isaacs, *Scratches on Our Minds,* p. 402.

23. Judith Goldstein and Robert O. Keohane, "Ideas and Foreign Policy," in Judith Goldstein and Robert O. Keohane, eds., *Ideas and Foreign Policy* (Ithaca, NY: Cornell University Press, 1993), pp. 8–12.

24. Gilbert Rozman, "Introduction: The East Asian Region in Comparative Perspective," in Gilbert Rozman, ed., *The East Asian Region* (Princeton, NJ: Princeton University Press, 1991), p. 19; Gilbert Rozman, ed., *The Modernization of China* (New York: The Free Press, 1981).

25. Jervis, *Perception and Misperception in International Politics,* p. 415.

26. Albert Einstein, *On Peace* (New York, 1954), p. 16.

27. Ernest R. May, foreword, to Ernest R. May and James C. Thomson, eds., *American East Asian Relations: A Survey* (Cambridge, MA: Harvard University Press, 1972), p. vii.

28. David M. Lampton, *Same Bed, Different Dreams* (Berkeley: University of California Press, 2000).

29. Warren I. Cohen, *America's Response to China,* 4th ed. (New York: Columbia University Press, 2000), p. ix.

30. Harry Harding, "The Legacy of the Decade for Later Years: An American Perspective," in Harding and Yuan, *Sino-American Relations, 1945–1955,* pp. 313–318.

31. Robert S. Ross, "Introduction," in Ross and Jiang, *Re-examining the Cold War*, p. 19.

1. Perceptions and Realities

1. For a comprehensive critique of cultural universalism, see Prasenjit Duara, *Rescuing History from the Nation: Questioning Narratives of Modern China* (Chicago: University of Chicago Press, 1995), pp. 5–6; for a thoughtful critique of cultural particularism, see Frank Ninkovich, "Culture, Power, and Civilization: The Place of Culture in the Study of International Relations," in Robert David Johnson, ed., *On Cultural Ground: Essays in International History* (Chicago: Imprint Publications, 1994), p. 9.
2. George Kennan, *American Diplomacy* (Chicago: University of Chicago Press, 1961), pp. 64–66.
3. Zhang Taiyan, "Sihuolun" (Four Confusing Theories), *Minbao* (People's Journal) no. 22 (Fall 1910).
4. Liang Qichao, "Xinminshuo" (The Theory of the New Citizen), in Liang, *Yinbingshi heji* (Works Written in Yinbin Study) (Shanghai: Datiandi tushu gongsi, 1936), pp. 54–57.
5. Liang Qichao, "Xinminyi" (Comments on the New Citizen), in Liang, *Yinbingshi heji* (Works Written in Yinbin Study), pp. 65–66.
6. Liang Qichao, "Xinshixue" (New History), in Liang, *Yinbingshi heji* (Works Written in Yinbin Study), pp. 122–127.
7. Ibid., p. 110.
8. Hu Shi, "Ibsen zhuyi" (On Ibsenism), *Xin Qingnian* (Journal of New Youth) 4, no. 6 (1918).
9. Ibid.
10. Hu Han-min, ed., *Zongli Quanji* (Complete Works of the Premier), vol. 2, (Nanjing: Minzhi Shuju, 1930), pp. 271, 311.
11. Thomas Jefferson, *Notes on the State of Virginia* (1781), in Henry Dethloff, ed., *Thomas Jefferson and American Democracy* (London: D.C. Heath and Company, 1971), pp. 11–12.
12. Richard Hofstadter, *The American Political Tradition and the Men Who Made It* (New York: Vintage Books, 1974), p. 12.
13. Ralph Waldo Emerson, *Complete Writings* (New York: William H. Wise, 1929), pp. 235–40.
14. Harry K. Girvetz, *The Evolution of Liberalism* (New York: Collier Books, 1963), p. 36.
15. Ibid., pp. 41–79.
16. Louis Hartz, *The Liberal Tradition in America: An Interpretation of American Political Thought since the Revolution* (San Diego: Harcourt Brace Jovanovich, 1991), pp. 5–6; J. David Greenstone, *The Lincoln Persuasion* (Princeton, NJ: Princeton University Press, 1991); Seymour Martin Lipset, *American Exceptionalism: A Double-Edged Sword* (New York: W. W. Norton, 1996), p. 20.

17. Daniel T. Rodgers, *Contested Truths—Keywords in American Politics since Independence* (New York: Basic Books, 1987), pp. 212–223.
18. Frank Ninkovich, *The Wilsonian Century: U.S. Foreign Policy since 1900* (Chicago: University of Chicago Press, 1999), p. 13; N. Gordon Levin Jr., *Woodrow Wilson and World Politics: America's Response to War and Revolution* (London: Oxford University Press, 1970), p. vii.
19. Benjamin Schwartz, "Some Polarities in Confucian Thought," in Arthur F. Wright, ed., *Confucianism and Chinese Civilization* (Stanford, CA: Stanford University Press, 1964), pp. 4–5.
20. Li Zehou, *Zhongguo xiandaisixiang shilun* (On the History of Ideas in Contemporary China) (Beijing: Dongfang chubanshe, 1987), pp. 32–33.
21. Lipset, *American Exceptionalism,* pp. 61–64.
22. Li Zehou, *Zhongguo jindaisixiang shilun* (On the History of Ideas in Modern China) (Taiwan: Fengyunshidai chubangongsi, 1990), pp. 16–19.
23. Mou Anshi, *Taiping tianguo shi* (History of the Taiping Peasant Rebellion) (Shanghai: Shanghai renmin chubanshe, 1962), pp. 124–177.
24. Liang Qichao, *Ouyou Xinyinglu Jielu* (Extract from a Trip to Europe) (Shanghai, 1907), p. 33; Liang Qichao, *Wang Jinggong Zhuan* (The Biography of Wang Anshi) (Tianjing, 1909), p. 79.
25. Kang Yuwei, *Lun Junpinfu* (On Fair Distribution of Wealth) (Shanghai, 1908), pp. 21–23.
26. Liang Qichao, *Ganshe yu Fangren* (State Intervention and Free Competition) (Tianjing, 1909).
27. Hsiao Kung-chuan, *A Modern China and a New World: Kang Yu-wei, Reformer and Utopian, 1858–1927* (Seattle: University of Washington Press, 1975), pp. 90–91, 125–130.
28. Zhou Jinsheng, *Sun Zhongshan xiansheng jingjisixiang* (Sun Zhongshan's Economic Thought) (Taipei: Zhengzhong shuju, 1968), pp. 389–399.
29. Ibid., pp. 3–29.
30. Drew R. McCoy, *The Elusive Republic: Political Economy in Jeffersonian America* (New York: W. W. Norton, 1982), pp. 20–26; Mario Einaudi, *The Early Rousseau* (Ithaca, NY: Cornell University Press, 1967); Bernard de Mandeville, *The Fable of the Bees: or, Private Vices, Public Benefits* (London, 1714); David Fate Norton, *David Hume* (Princeton, NJ: Princeton University Press, 1982).
31. Jefferson to Madison, October 28, 1785, in McCoy, *The Elusive Republic,* p. 126; Jeremy Bentham, *The Works of Jeremy Bentham,* ed. J. Bowring (Edinburgh: W. Tait, 1838–1843), vol. 3, p. 3; and McCoy, *The Elusive Republic,* pp. 173–179.
32. Wilson Carey McWilliams and Michael T. Gibbons, *The Federalists, the Antifederalists, and the American Political Tradition* (Westport, CT: Greenwood Press, 1992), p. 78.
33. Harry K. Girvetz, *The Evolution of Liberalism,* intro. Arthur Schlesinger Jr. (New York: Collier Books, 1963), pp. 68–70, 371–378.
34. Ibid., p. 287.

35. *Complete Works of Sun Zhongshan,* vol. 4, ed. Zhongguo Shehuike-xueyaun Jindaishi Yangiusuo (Beijing: Renmin chubanshe, 1983), pp. 98, 224–226.

36. Ibid., vol. 7, pp. 146–162.

37. Peng Ming, *History of the May 4 Movement* (Beijing: Renmin chubanshe, 1956), pp. 522–589. For a comprehensive study on anarchism in China, see Peter Zarrow, *Anarchism and Chinese Political Culture* (New York: Columbia University Press, 1990).

38. Shi Cuntong, *Huiyi wangshi* (Memoir) (Chongqing: Shangwu Yinshuguan, 1944), pp. 177–190.

39. Ibid.

40. Cai Hesen, "Cong wuzhengfuzhuyi dao shehuizhuyi" (From Anarchism to Socialism), *Xin Qingnian* (Journal of New Youth) (Winter 1920); Zhou Enlai, "Wo dui shehuizhuyi zhi sikao" (A Reflection on Socialism), *Xin Qingnian* (Journal of New Youth) (Spring 1921). Also see Gilbert Rozman, ed., *The Modernization of China* (New York: The Free Press, 1981), pp. 96, 98; Dwight Perkins, *Agricultural Development in China, 1368–1968* (Chicago: Aldine, 1969).

41. Zhou Enlai, "On the Issue of Intellectuals' Reform," in *Selected Works of Zhou Enlai,* vol. 2 (Beijing: Foreign Language Press, 1989), pp. 63–64.

42. Ibid., pp. 384, 479, 692, 723; Hu, *Zongli Quanji* (Complete Works of the Premier), pp. 509–510.

43. Patrick Cavendish, "The 'New China' of the Kuomintang," and Jack Gray: "Conclusions," in Jack Gray, ed., *Modern China's Search for a Political Form* (New York: Oxford University Press, 1969), pp. 138–186, 336.

44. Gray, "Conclusions," pp. 343–344.

45. Liang Qichao, *Xinmin lun* (On the New Citizenry) (Shanghai, 1902); Hu, *Zongli Quanji* (Complete Works of the Premier), vol. 1, p. 70.

46. Hu, *Zongli quanji* (Complete Works of the Premier), vol. 1, p. 70.

47. Girvetz, *Evolution of Liberalism,* pp. 33–38, 103; and Hofstadter, *American Political Tradition,* pp. 3–40.

48. Raymond Aron, *Main Currents in Sociological Thought,* vol. 1, trans. Richard Howard and Helen Weaver (New York: Basic Books, 1965), pp. 253–254, 256.

49. *The Federalist Papers,* ed. Clinton Rossiter (New York: Penguin Putnam, 1999), nos. 11 and 39; Alexander Hamilton, *Works,* vol. 2, ed. Henry Cabot Lodge (New York, 1904), pp. 67–74; Martin Marty, foreword to Mark G. Toulouse, *The Transformation of John Foster Dulles* (Macon, GA: Mercer University Press, 1985), pp. xi–xii; Hofstadter, *American Political Tradition,* p. 8; Adam Smith, *The Theory of Moral Sentiments* (Indianapolis: Liberty Classics, 1976), pp. 233–234.

50. Hsiao, *A Modern China and a New World,* pp. 155–179.

51. Liang Chi-chao, *Deyujian* (On Moral Education), (Guangzhou, 1905), pp. 76–78.

52. Sun Yat-sen, "The Principle of People's Livelihood," in Sun Yat-sen, *San*

Min Chu I: The Three Principles of the People, trans. Frank W. Price (Chungqing: Ministry of Information of the Republic of China, 1943), pp. 363–483.

53. Deng Xiaoping, "Building a Socialism with a Specifically Chinese Character," in *Selected Works of Deng Xiaoping,* vol. 3 (Beijing: Renmin chubanshe, 2000), pp. 62–66.

54. Benjamin I. Schwartz, "Culture, Modernity, and Nationalism—Further Reflections," in Tu Wei-ming, ed., *China in Transformation* (Cambridge, MA: Harvard University Press, 1994), pp. 241–242.

55. Ibid.; Fritjof Capra, *The Tao of Physics: An Exploration of the Parallels between Modern Physics and Eastern Mysticism,* 4th ed. (Boston: Shambhala, 2000); see also Wm. Theodore de Bary, *The Liberal Tradition in China* (New York: Columbia University Press, 1983) and *Nobility and Civility: Asian Ideals of Leadership and the Common Good* (Cambridge, MA: Harvard University Press, 2004); Donald J. Munro, *The Concept of Man in Early China* (Stanford, CA: Stanford University Press, 1969).

56. In *Moral Purity and Persecution in History,* Harrington Moore Jr. writes that "the main finding of this book, at least the one that most surprised its author, has been that the theory and practice of moral purity was limited to the three monotheistic religions, Judaism, Christianity, and Islam." He further argues that Confucianism is a polytheistic, rather than monotheistic, worldview ([Princeton, N.J.: Princeton University Press, 2000], p. 128). See also Tu Wei-ming, ed., *Confucian Traditions in East Asian Modernity* (Cambridge, MA: Harvard University Press, 1996).

2. Straining the Relationship

1. Memo re Treaty Negotiation, February 9, 1945, State Department Decimal File 611.9331/2–945, NA.

2. Minutes of the 31st National Foreign Trade Convention, New York City, October 9, 1944, NA; see also Memo from A. Viola Smith to E. F. Stanton, December 22, 1944, State Department Decimal File 611.9331/12–2244, NA.

3. Memo from A. Viola Smith to E. F. Stanton, December 22, 1944, State Department Decimal File 611.9331/12–2244, NA.

4. Memo re Treaty Negotiation, February 9, 1945, State Department Decimal File 611.9331/2–945, NA. On December 19, 1944, an identical memo was sent to H. H. Kung, the Chinese finance minister.

5. Minutes of the 31st National Foreign Trade Convention, New York City, October 9, 1944, NA; see also memo from A. Viola Smith to E. F. Stanton, December 22, 1944, State Department Decimal File 611.9331/12–2244, NA.

6. Memo, "United States Long-Range Economic Policy Objectives with Respect to China," October 9, 1946, CA, box 7, NA.

7. Letter from Mr. Willowby to Mr. Wood re Joint Memo submitted by the

National Foreign Trade Council and Far Eastern Council, September 16, 1947, State Department Decimal File 611.9331/8–2046, NA; see also Memo, "United States Long-Range Economic Policy Objectives with respect to China," October 9, 1946, CA, box 7, NA.

8. Chiang Kai-shek, *The Theory of China's Economy* (Nanking, 1943), pp. 4–26.

9. "The General Principles Regarding China's Postwar Industrialization," November 6, 1944, Supreme National Defense Council file, 43/203, SNAC.

10. "Industrial Reconstruction Program in Postwar China" by the Sixth Congress of Kuomintang, Central News Agency, English Service, Chungking, May 17, 1945.

11. Sun Fo, speech, May 20, 1945, Legislative Yuan file, 37/469, SNAC.

12. This association included, for instance, China's National Federation of Industries, China's Southwest Industrial Association, the Association of Factories Removed to Szechuan, and the Association for the Promotion of War Production. See Memo on Chinese Industrial Association, December 3, 1944, CA, box 10, NA.

13. "Our Proposal on China's Industrialization," by the Chinese Industrial Association, Chungking, July 2, 1945, Economic Ministry file, 45/209, SNAC.

14. Ibid.

15. Confidential order from Chiang Kai-shek to Wang Liangchou and Wu Danquen, the general secretaries of the Supreme National Defense Council, September 25, 1945, Supreme National Defense Council file, 43/82, SNAC.

16. Memo from the general secretaries of the Supreme National Defense Council to Chiang Kai-shek, October 17, 1945. Supreme National Defense Council File, 43/82, SNAC.

17. Memo from the Chinese Industrial Association to the Chinese Delegation at the Conference, "Some Views Concerning the Absorption of Foreign Capital and the Participation in the Free Trade System," April–May 1945, Economic Ministry file, SNAC; see also Remer Papers on the Chungking Meetings, CA, box 4, NA.

18. Conference record, "Postwar Economic Reconstruction in China," April–May 1945, Remer Papers, CA, box 4, NA.

19. Telegram from American Embassy, Nanking, to the Secretary of State, October 12, 1946, State Department Decimal File 711.932/10–1246, NA.

20. Conference record, "Postwar Economic Reconstruction in China," April–May, 1945, Chungking, Remer Papers, CA, box 4, NA.

21. Ibid.

22. Memo, Charles Remer to the State Department, May 6, 1945, Remer Papers, CA, box 5, NA.

23. Memo, State Department to Charles Remer, November 12, 1945, Remer Papers, CA, box 7, NA.

24. Memo, Charles Remer to the State Department, May 8, 1945, Remer Papers, CA, box 5, NA. As Remer put it, "Free enterprise in the United States

and the prospect of American investment in China has played a part in bringing about the current liberal trend. If this trend continues, it will have broad consequences for the international economic and political relations of the United States in the Far East and especially with China and Russia."

25. China Committee report, September 1946, State Department Decimal File 611.9331/91546, NA.

26. Memo, "Summary of Exploratory Discussions on American Proposal of a Draft Commercial Treaty," August 17, 1945, State Department Decimal File 611.9331/8–1745, NA.

27. "Minutes of Meetings Concerning the Draft Treaty of the Commerce, Navigation and Friendship between the United States and China," February 5, 1946, CA, box 1, NA.

28. "Notes of Conversation," July 9, 1945, CA, box 7, NA. Regarding the controversy over national treatment versus the most-favored-nation treatment, the following negotiation record may further illustrate both sides' points of view: "The Chinese negotiators said that American investors could rest assured that Chinese law would not discriminate against them. American negotiators raised the question of whether this meant non-discrimination as compared with other foreigners or as compared with Chinese investors in Chinese corporations. The Chinese pointed out that according to the wording of the counter-draft of the Chinese Government, nothing more than most-favored-nation treatment was conferred. However, they also pointed out that according to the Chinese company law, a corporation formed by foreigners in China would be considered as a Chinese corporation, and as such would be entitled to national treatment. . . . In further explanation of their proposal of most-favored-nation treatment instead of national treatment, the Chinese negotiators said that if Americans secured national treatment on land, other countries would expect it for their nationals." See "Minutes of Meetings," February 14, 1946, CA, box 1, NA.

29. "Minutes of Meetings," February 27–March 27, 1946, CA, box 1, NA.

30. Incoming telegram from American Embassy, Nanking, to State Department, March 27, 1946, State Department Decimal File 711.932/3–2746, NA.

31. Memo, "Removal of Legislative Discrimination against the Chinese, from the Standpoint of American National Interests," January 1945, CA, box 1, NA.

32. "End America's Closed Door Policy Now!" editorial, *Christianity and Crisis: A Biweekly Journal of Christian Opinion,* September 20, 1943.

33. Memo, "Removal of Legislative Discrimination against the Chinese from the Standpoint of American National Interests," January 1945, CA, box 1, NA.

34. Memo of conversation with Senate Foreign Relations Committee, May 23, 1946, State Department Decimal File 711.932/5–2346, NA.

35. Letter from Willard L. Thorp to Mr. Vincent of FE, March 29, 1946, CA,

box 2, NA; see also memo from FE to Secretary Marshall and Undersecretary Acheson, March 30, 1946, CA, box 2, NA.

36. Memo of conversation re the commercial treaty with China, December 10, 1946, State Department Decimal file 711.932/12–1046, NA.

37. Ibid.

38. *Da Gong Bao* (Shanghai), editorial, November 11, 1946.

39. *Hsin Wen Pao* (Shanghai), editorial, November 14, 1946.

40. *Chen Yen Pao* (Shanghai), editorial, November 12.

41. Incoming telegram from American Embassy to the State Department, November 15, 1946, State Department Decimal File 611.9331/11–1546, NA.

42. *Shang Wu Jih Pao* (Chungking), November 13 and November 18, 1946.

43. *Da Gong Bao* (Shanghai), November 8, 1946.

44. *Kuo Min Kung Pao* (Chungking), November 9, 1946.

45. *Shang Wu Jih Pao* (Chungking), November 15, 1946.

46. *Min Chu Pao* (Chungking), November 9, 1946.

47. *Min Chu Pao* (Chungking), November 11, 1946.

48. *Da Gong Bao* (Shanghai), November 8, 1946.

49. *Shang Wu Jih Pao* (Chungking), editorial, November 8, 1946.

50. Memo of conversation, February 28, 1947, CA, box 5, NA.

51. As Dean Acheson, then assistant secretary of state, stressed in 1944, "We cannot have full employment and prosperity in the United States without the foreign markets." Henry Wallace, vice president under the FDR administration (1941–45) and Secretary of Commerce under the FDR and Truman administrations (1945–46), also supported the idea that it was now the underdeveloped region that would offer America an "unlimited new frontier of opportunities." Henry A. Wallace, *The Price of Vision: The Diary of Henry A. Wallace, 1942–1946*, ed. John Morton Blum (Boston: Houghton Mifflin, 1973), p. 178. Dean Acheson, testimony at a congressional hearing on postwar economic policy, *Hearing before the Special Committee on Postwar Economic Policy and Planning*, House of Representatives, 78th Congress, 2nd session, 1944.

52. For a detailed discussion of Taiwan's intellectual debates over Taiwan's economic blueprints and Yin Chung-jun's economic theory in the 1950s, see Simei Qing, "Yin Chung-jun, Sun Yat-sen's Principle of People's Livelihood, and Taiwan's Quest for Modernity and Identity," in Hanchao Lu, ed., *Modernity and Cultural Identity in Taiwan (Taiwan de xiandaihua he wenhua rentong)* [in Chinese] (River Edge, NJ: Global Publishing Company, 2001), pp. 48–71.

53. Memo, Karl L. Rankin, ambassador to Taipei, to A. Guy Hope, Officer in Charge of Economic Affairs, Office of Chinese Affairs, State Department, January 14, 1955, CA, box 5, NA.

54. World Bank, *The Economic Miracle of Four Little Dragons in East Asia* (Washington, DC: World Bank, April 1991).

55. Zeng Minghui, dir. and ed., *Li Guoding—Forging an Economic Path* (DVD) (Taipei: Delta-Foundation, 2001).

3. Disillusionment and Polarization

1. For a thoughtful analysis of the American political context of the Marshall mission to China, see Michael Schaller, *The U.S. Crusade in China, 1938–1945* (New York: Columbia University Press, 1979). For a pioneer study on the CCP's political mobilization of poor peasants in the civil war, see Steven Levine, *Anvil of Victory: The Communist Revolution in Manchuria, 1945–1948* (New York: Columbia University Press, 1987). For an in-depth examination of the international context of the Marshall mission to China, see Odd Arne Westad, *Cold War and Revolution* (New York: Columbia University Press, 1993). For a more recent and comprehensive account of the Marshall mission to China, see Larry I. Bland, ed., *George C. Marshall's Mediation Mission to China* (Lexington, VA: George C. Marshall Foundation, 1998). For an excellent study of the Chinese civil war, see Suzanne Pepper, "The KMT-CCP Conflict, 1945–1949," in Lloyd E. Eastman et al., *The Nationalist Era in China, 1927–1949* (Cambridge: Cambridge University Press, 1991). See also Odd Arne Westad's revealing study *The Decisive Encounters: The Chinese Civil War, 1946–1950* (Stanford, CA: Stanford University Press, 2003).

2. Memorandum from the secretary of war and the secretary of the navy to the secretary of state re the situation in China, November 26, 1945, CA, box 12, NA; memorandum for General Marshall from Secretary of State J. F. Byrnes re U.S. Policy toward China, December 8, 1945, CA, box 12, NA.

3. Memorandum, the secretary of war and the secretary of the navy to the secretary of state re the situation in China, November 26, 1945, CA, box 12, NA.

4. Memorandum, George Marshall to Admiral Leahy, November 30, 1945, CA, box 12, NA.

5. Memorandum for General Marshall from Secretary of State J. F. Byrnes re U.S. Policy toward China, December 8, 1945, CA, box 12, NA; also, memorandum for record, December 10, 1945, CA, box 12, NA.

6. Memo for record re U.S. Policy toward China, from the Division of Chinese Affairs to the State Department, October 12, 1945, CA, box 10, NA.

7. Memorandum re China situation, John Carter Vincent to Dean Acheson, December 5, 1945, CA, box 11, NA. For a thoughtful study of John Carter Vincent, see Gary May, *China Scapegoat: The Diplomatic Ordeal of John Carter Vincent* (Washington, DC: New Republic Books, 1979).

8. Memorandum, "Policy and Information Statement," State Department, March 2, 1946, CA, box 12, NA.

9. Memo for record re the Marshall mission, Division of Chinese Affairs to the State Department, December 10, 1945, CA, box 12, NA.

10. Memo for record re U.S. Policy toward China, Division of Chinese Affairs to the State Department, October 12, 1945, CA, box 10, NA.
11. Memo, "U.S. Policy toward China," Division of Chinese Affairs, October 15, 1945, CA, box 12, NA.
12. Robert Donovan, *The Presidency of Harry S Truman, 1945–1948: Conflict and Crisis* (New York: W. W. Norton, 1977), pp. 150–151.
13. Harry S. Truman, *Memoirs,* vol. 2 (Garden City, NY: Doubleday, 1956), pp. 90–91.
14. David McCullough, *Truman* (New York: Simon & Schuster, 1992), pp. 548–549, 730.
15. George Marshall's notes on meeting with the president and undersecretary of state, December 14, 1945, CA, box 12, NA.
16. Patrick Cavendish, "The 'New China' of the Kuomintang," in Jack Gray, ed., *Modern China's Search for a Political Form* (New York: Oxford University Press, 1969), pp. 138–169; see also *Complete Works of Hu Hanmin,* vol. 8 (Taiwan, 1955), pp. 78–90.
17. Cavendish, "The 'New China' of the Kuomintang," pp. 163–164; see also the records of the KMT 5th Plenum, pp. 217–220, SNAC.
18. Hu Hanmin, "The Theory of the Kuomintang Mass Movements," July 1927, in *Ge-ming li-lun* (The Theory of Revolution), pp. 146–172; Dai Jitao, "Min-quan yun-dong de guo-qu ho he Jianglai" (The Past and the Future of the Mass Movements), *Zhong-yang Ban-yue-kan* (Journal of Central Fortnightly), 1 (n.d.): 9.
19. Jack Gray, "Conclusions," in Gray, *Modern China's Search for a Political Form,* pp. 334–337.
20. Sun Fo (Sun Ke), *China Looks Forward* (New York: John Day Company, 1944), p. 70.
21. Chiang Kai-shek, *China's Destiny* (Nanjing, 1943), pp. 225–229.
22. Chen Li-fu, *The Storm Clouds Clear over China: The Memoir of Che'n Li-fu, 1900–1993* (Stanford, CA: Hoover Institution Press, 1994), pp. 176–177. As the American Embassy in Chungking observed, even in the war of resistance, one of the major goals of the "C-C" faction was "to destroy Left Wing mass organizations and popularly elected local governments in the guerrilla areas." See memo, "Kuomintang-Communist Relations, 1937–1941" by G-2, December 27, 1941, CA, box 10, NA.
23. Jia Tingshi, Ma Tiangang, Chen Sanjing, and Chen Cungong, *Bei Chongxi xiansheng fangwenlu* (The Reminiscences of General Bai Chongxi), Oral History Series (4), vols. 1 and 2 (Taipei: Institute of Modern History, Academia Sinica, 1985), pp. 475–478, 847–848.
24. Sun Fo (Sun Ke), *China Looks Forward,* pp. 70–89.
25. Sun Fo (Sun Ke), "Speech at the Sino-American Cultural Institute," January 22, 1943, Chungking, State Department Decimal File 711.93/525, NA.
26. Zhonggong zhongyang wenxian yanjiushi, ed., *Zhou Enlai 1946 nian tanpan wenxuan* (A Selection of Zhou Enlai's Writings during His Negotiations with the KMT in 1946) (Beijing: Zhongyang wenxian chubanshe,

1996), pp. 418–419; see also *Chang Ch'un Memoir* (Taiwan, 1969); and Sun Qimin, *Hetan, Neizhan jiaoxiangqu* (The Symphony of Negotiation and Civil War) (Shanghai: Renmin chubanshe, 1992).

27. Jia Tingshi et al., eds., *Bai Chongxi xiansheng fangwen jilu* (The Reminiscences of General Bai Chongxi), vol. 2, p. 848.

28. Mao Zedong, speech at the Seventh Party Congress, May 31, 1945, quoted from Hu Qiaomu, *Hu Qiaomu huiyi Mao Zedong* (Hu Qiaomu Remembers Mao Zedong) (Beijing: Renmin chubanshe, 1995), p. 385; Zhongyan wenxian yanjiushi, ed., *Mao Zedong zai qida de baogao he jianghuaji* (Mao Zedong's Reports and Speeches at the CCP's Seventh Congress) (Beijing: Zhonggong zhongyang wenxian yanjiushi, 2000), pp. 54–56.

29. Mao Zedong, *On Coalition Government,* report to the Seventh Party Congress, *Jiefang Ribao (Liberation Daily,* Yanan), April 24, 1945. This paragraph did not appear in its edited version in the *Selected Works of Mao Zedong,* vol. 3 (Beijing: Foreign Language Press, 1965). See also Hu, *Hu Qiaomu huiyi Mao Zedong* (Hu Qiaomu Remembers Mao Zedong), p. 377.

30. Mao Zedong, *On Coalition Government,* in *Jiefang Ribao* (*Liberation Daily,* Yanan), April 24, 1945. Mao's optimistic prediction of British-U.S.-Soviet peace and cooperation was cut off in the edited version of *On Coalition Government* in the *Selected Works of Mao Zedong,* vol. 3.

31. Mao Zedong, comments on Zhou Enlai's report on coalition government at the CCP Central Committee meeting, which was convened to prepare for the Seventh Party Congress, February 18, 1945. Quoted from Hu, *Hu Qiaomu huiyi Mao Zedong* (Hu Qiaomu Remembers Mao Zedong), p. 371.

32. Ibid., p. 377.

33. Zhongyang wenxian yanjiushi, *Mao Zedong zai qida de baogao he jianghuaji* (Mao Zedong's Reports and Speeches at the CCP's Seventh Congress), pp. 70–74.

34. It is interesting to note that throughout 1945, both the CCP and the KMT were convinced that the United States, Great Britain, and the Soviet Union wanted to continue their cooperation in the post–World War II era. For KMT's optimistic analysis of the continuation of the Yalta international system in postwar years, see memorandum, "American, British, and Soviet Foreign Policies," November 1945, Foreign Ministry of Republic of China, File of Foreign Ministry of Republic of China, no. 18/3089, SNAC.

35. Frederic Wakeman Jr., *Policing Shanghai 1927–1937* (Berkeley: University of California Press, 1995), p. 123.

36. Ye Yonglie, *Guogong fengyun* (The KMT and the CCP in China) (Ulumuqi: Xinjiang renmin chubanshe, 2000), p. 47.

37. Hu, *Hu Qiaomu huiyi Mao Zedong* (Hu Qiaomu Remembers Mao Zedong), p. 76.

38. Department of State Bulletin, February 10, 1946, p. 201.

39. Hu, *Hu Qiaomu huiyi Mao Zedong* (Hu Qiaomu Remembers Mao Zedong), p. 74.

40. The CCP Central Committee's Confidential Circular of August 29, 1945. Central Archives of China, ed., *Zhonggong zhongyang wenjian xuanji* (Selected Documents of the CCP Central Committee), vol. 15 (Beijing: Zhonggong zhongyang dangxiao chubanshe, 1988), pp. 213, 243, 257–258.

41. Liu Shaoqi, "Yi zhuyaoliliang jianli dongbeiximan gejudi" (To Concentrate on the Creation of the Base Areas in the Northeast and North Manchuria), in *Liu Shaoqi xuanji* (The Selected Works of Liu Shaoqi), vol. 1 (Beijing: Renmin chubanshe, 1982), pp. 373–376.

42. *Chongqing tanpanjishi* (The Records of the Chungking Negotiation), (Chongqing: Renmin chubanshe, 1986), pp. 418–419.

43. *Da Gong Bao* (Shanghai), editorial, August 22, 1945.

44. *Chongqing tanpanjishi* (The Records of the Chongqing Negotiation), p. 313.

45. Ibid., p. 370.

46. Shi Fuliang, "Hewei zhongjianpai" (What Is the Third Force?), *Wenhuibao* (Wenhui Daily), July 14, 1946.

47. Zhang Dongsun, "Zhuishu women nulijianli 'lianhezhengfu' de yuanyin" (A Reflection on the Reasons Why We Wanted to Build a 'Coalition Government' in China), *Guanchajia* (The Observer) 2, no. 6 (April 5, 1947).

48. Shi, "Hewei zhongjianpai" (What Is the Third Force?).

49. Zhang, "Zhuishu women nulijianli 'lianhezhengfu' de yuanyin" (A Reflection on the Reasons Why We Wanted to Build a 'Coalition Government' in China).

50. Shi, "Hewei zhongjianpai" (What Is the Third Force?).

51. "Zhongguo nonggong minzhudan shengming" (Statement of the Chinese Peasant-Worker Party), *Guanchajio* (The Observer) 1, no. 4 (February 5, 1946).

52. Ruji Qing, *Zhanghou Jianguo wenti chuyi* (On Postwar National Reconstruction) (Nanjing, 1945), pp. 60–61, 78.

53. Ibid., pp. 93–94.

54. *Historical Documents of the Democratic League* (Beijing: Historical Achieves Press, 1983), pp. 88–93; see also Democracy Promotion Association, "Our View of China's Postwar Political System," *Huan Shang Bao* (Hua Shang Daily), May 15, 1946.

55. At the negotiation table, both sides pledged to make further concessions. Mao, on behalf of the CCP, agreed to discuss the reduction of the CCP's army before the establishment of the new coalition government. Chiang, on behalf of the KMT, promised to "consider the CCP's participation in the National Government before the dismantling of the CCP's army."

56. Chiang Kai-shek, conversation with the KMT delegates, Marshall Mission file, SNAC. The CCP conceded a KMT-CCP troop ratio of 7:1, which Mao

thought enough, since this was already a big reduction from the wartime ratio of 3.58:1. But Chiang Kai-shek still thought the CCP portion was "too high." He thought the CCP's aim was to retain its separate army and its separate local governments and that its proposal to withdraw its troops to the north of the Yellow River was intended to recreate the "Three Kingdoms" situation (AD 220–265) and make itself the master of one of them. In Chiang's words, such a situation could "never be accepted," the KMT would "never allow any new warlord to emerge in postwar China."

57. On September 20, in the middle of the negotiation deadlock, Chiang sent a secret order to the commanders of the KMT army, asking them to "successfully attack the CCP troops," so that the KMT negotiators would be "in a stronger position." On October 6, the news came to Chongqing that the CCP forces, under the command of Liu Bocheng-Deng Xiaoping, defeated eleven KMT divisions of 35,000. Public opinion in urban China overwhelmingly condemned the KMT's military attack on the CCP areas. Chiang had to make a public announcement that this military attack had been "independently" launched "without my knowledge in advance." To win back public support in urban centers, Chiang informed the CCP that the KMT delegation was "ready" to sign the Double Ten Agreement, also known as the Chiang-Mao agreement.

58. *Chongqing tanpanjishi* (The Records of the Chongqing Negotiation), pp. 313–326.

59. Li Wen, *Wang Rofei zhuan* (The Biography of Wang Rofei) (Shanghai: Renmin chubanshe, 1986), pp. 228–231. At first, Mao was so angry, that he sent a telegram to Zhou in Chongqing, urging him to take a "much tougher" position in the negotiation. Two days later, following the proposal of the CCP Southern Bureau in Shanghai, Mao agreed that the CCP could take this opportunity to wage a propaganda campaign to win the popular support of the urban Chinese.

60. "Welcome General Marshall," editorial, *Da Gong Bao* (Da Gong Daily) (Shanghai), December 16, 1945.

61. Memo, "The Major Differences between the KMT and the CCP in the Negotiations," Division of Chinese Affairs, State Department, March 2, 1946, CA, box 12, NA.

62. Minutes of the meetings of the Central Standing Committee of the KMT, February 2, 1946, KMT Central Committee file, SNAC.

63. "Information re Chiang Kai-shek's Response to the PCC Resolution," February 20, 1946, CCP file, 1945–1950, CAC.

64. *Zhou Enlai 1946 nian tanpan wenxuan* (A Selection of Zhou Enlai's Writings during His Negotiations with the KMT in 1946), p. 92.

65. Summary of Zhou Enlai's conversation with Marshall, January 31, 1946, in *Zhou Enlai 1946 nian tanpan wenxuan* (A Selection of Zhou Enlai's Writings during His Negotiations with the KMT in 1946), pp. 7–8.

66. Yang Kuisong, *Zouxiang polie* (Toward the Split: The Eventful Relationships between Mao Zedong and Moscow) (Hong Kong: Sanlian, 1999), p. 236.

67. Confidential letter, CCP Central Committee to CCP members, February 5, 1946, CCP file, 1945–1950, CAC.

68. Memo, "The Response to the PCC Resolution among Different KMT Factions," by CCP Intelligence Department, February 6, 1946; confidential circular: "Temporary Stopping of Propaganda Warfare against the KMT," CCP Central Committee to CCP members and organizations, February 7, 1946, the Marshall Mission file, CAC.

69. The KMT chief negotiator Zhang Zhizhong had first proposed a 6:1 ratio, while Zhou Enlai had proposed a 9:2 ratio. General Marshall initially proposed a 2:1 ratio in the army and further suggested that the CCP should occupy one-third of the navy and air force under the new coalition government. Chiang immediately ordered Zhang Zhizhong to turn it down before Zhou Enlai could learn about Marshall's draft proposal. In Marshall's new proposal, the CCP would not join the air and naval forces of the coalition government, and the KMT-CCP army ratio would be 5:1. KMT Central Committee file, 1945–1947, SNAC.

70. Zhang Baijia, "Zhou Enlai and the Marshall Mission," in Bland, *George C. Marshall's Mediation Mission to China*, pp. 201–234.

71. *Mao Zedong nianpu* (Chronological biography of Mao Zedong), vol. 3 (Beijing: Zhongyang wenxian chubanshe, 1993), p. 57; Zhang Baijia, "Zhou Enlai and the Marshall Mission," trans. Steven I. Levine, in Bland, *George C. Marshall's Mediation Mission to China*, p. 219.

72. Zhang, "Zhou Enlai and the Marshall Mission," p. 218; and *Zhou Enlai 1946 nian tanpan wenxuan* (A Selection of Zhou Enlai's Writings during His Negotiations with the KMT in 1946), pp. 111–113.

73. He Di, "Mao Zedong and the Marshall Mission," in Bland, *George C. Marshall's Mediation Mission to China*, pp. 173–200.

74. Liang Shumin, *Yiwang tanjiulu* (A Reflection on the Past) (Beijing: Zhongguo wenshi chubanshe, 1987), pp. 180.

75. *Zhonggong zhongyang wenjianxuanji* (Selected Documents of the CCP Central Committee), vol. 13 (Beijing: Zhonggong zhongyang dangxiao chubanshe, 1987), pp. 347–348.

76. Letter from Li Fuchen and Huang Kecheng to Mao Zedong, March 2, 1946, CCP file, 1945–1950, CAC.

77. He, "Mao Zedong and the Marshall Mission."

78. Zhang Qianhua, "Zhengxuexi zai dongbei jieshouwentishang de ruyi-suanpan" (The Political Intentions of the Political Science Group's Claim on the Nationalist Government's Sovereignty in the Northeast), in *Wenshi zilao xuanji* (Journal of Historical Documents) 42 (1988): 34–35.

79. Zhang, "Zhou Enlai and the Marshall Mission."

80. Memo, Marshall to Truman, May 6, 1946, CA, box 12, NA.

81. Ibid., June 5, 1946.

82. Chiang Kai-shek's speech at KMT Central Committee meeting, June 10, 1946, KMT Central Committee file, 1945–1949, SNAC.
83. Memo, Marshall to Truman, July 9, 1946, CA, box 14, NA.
84. Telegram, CCP Northeast Bureau to the CCP Central Committee, March 9, 1946, quoted from Yang, *Zouxiang polie* (Toward the Split), p. 238.
85. Hu, *Hu Qiaomu huiyi Mao Zedong* (Hu Qiaomu Remembers Mao Zedong), pp. 67–88, 431–432. Because Moscow's messages to Zhou Enlai all appear to have been oral, no written memos on Stalin's position have yet been found in Russian archives.
86. Jordan Baev, "The Greek Civil War Viewed from the North" (paper presented at international conference, King's College, London, April 1990). Based on a considerable number of newly declassified sources from Russian and Eastern European archives, Baev's work reinterprets Moscow's role in the development of the Greek civil war. According to this study, the Soviet Union, before the signing of the Paris Peace Treaties in January 1947, "kept its cautious political course in regard to the civil war in Greece."
87. Hu, *Hu Qiaomu huiyi Mao Zedong* (Hu Qiaomu Remembers Mao Zedong), pp. 91–92.
88. Liu Yalou, "Talks at the Meeting on the Writings of Fourth Field Army's History," December 13, 1962, Beijing, quoted from Liu Tong, "Guanyu kangzhanhou guogong neizhanzhong dongbei yezhanjun wuqi laiyuan de zhenglun" (On the Controversy over the Source of the Northeastern Field Army's Weapons in the Civil War), in *Dang de wenxian* (Archival Documents on Party History), no. 4 (Beijing: Zhongyang dangxiao chubanshe, 2000), pp. 18–19.
89. For more detailed information concerning U.S. military aid to the KMT government during this period, see *United States Relations with China* (White Paper), released by the State Department in August 1949.
      In 1948 both Moscow and Washington offered more aid to the CCP and the KMT forces respectively. According to Soviet sources, the Soviet Union transferred huge amounts of Japanese weapons it had taken to the CCP fourth field army in Manchuria. And according to State Department documents, in addition to the Economic Cooperation Act of 1948, $125 million more was appropriated for the KMT government. "As of February 28, 1949, $123,950,687.71 had been paid to the Chinese Government . . . from the $125,000,000 appropriated for additional aid to China through grants under Section 404 (b) of the China Aid Act of 1948." Moreover, "A considerable quantity of surplus military equipment has been made available to the Chinese armed forces through the Office of the Foreign Liquidation Commissioner. This material has consisted primarily small arms and artillery ammunition, aircraft and aircraft spare parts, and armament parts sold for a fraction of procurement cost." See Draft Memo, State Department to President Truman, February 28, 1949, box 8, CA, NA.
90. Hu, *Hu Qiaomu huiyi Mao Zedong* (Hu Qiaomu Remembers Mao Zedong), pp. 92, 425–436.

91. Ibid., p. 92.

92. Mao Zedong, "Talk with the American Correspondent Anna Louise Strong," August 1946, in *Selected Works of Mao Zedong,* vol. 4 (Beijing: Foreign Language Press, 1961), pp. 100–101.

93. *Chongqing Ribao* (Chongqing Daily), July 17, 1946.

94. Memo, Vincent to Acheson, August 21, 1946, CA, box 12, NA.

95. Memo, Marshall to Truman, November 8, 1946. Marshall declined Chiang Kai-shek's invitation to attend the Constitutional Assembly.

96. Memo re statement by Dr. Luo Longji (head of the Democratic League) to Robert S. Ward, January 21, 1947, CA, box 11, NA.

97. Memo, Robert S. Ward to Ludden, Esquire, First Secretary of the American Embassy, Nanking, re conversation with Dr. Luo Longji, December 6, 1946, CA, box 11, NA.

98. Chu Anping, "Zhongguo ti zhengju" (China's Political Situation), *Guanchajia* (The Observer), March 8, 1947, p. 3. Quoted from Suzanne Pepper, "The KMT-CCP Conflict, 1945–1949," in Lloyd Eastman, Jerome Ch'en, Suzanne Pepper, and Lyman Van Slyke, *The Nationalist Era in China, 1927–1949* (New York: Cambridge University Press, 1991), p. 306.

99. Zhu Wenguang, "On the First National Assembly," in *Dongfang zazhi* (The Orient Magazine) 44, no. 6 (June 1948).

100. "Win the Hearts and Minds of the Chinese People," editorial, *Zhongyiang ribao* (Central Daily, Nanjing), November 4, 1948.

101. According to the Nationalist government's statistics published in 1947, between 1912 and 1947 half of Chinese peasants did not own land. "Report on Chinese Agriculture," in Yan Zhongping ed., *Statistics of Modern Chinese Economic History* 5, no. 12 (Beijing: Kexue chubanshe, 1955), p. 276.

102. Central Archive of China, ed., *Jiefang zhangzheng shiqi tudigaige wenjianxuenbian* (Selected Documents of Land Reform in the Period of Liberation War, 1946–1949) (Beijing: Zhonggong zhongyiang dangxiao chubanshe, 1981), pp. 7–46. It is important to note that in the beginning phase of the land reform, the CCP leadership was very concerned about the attitudes of the Third Force, since many of its members came from the families of the landed elite. Zhou Enlai and Dong Biwu pledged, "We will not adopt the policy of confiscation." Instead, the CCP would "follow Dr. Sun Yat-sen's policy of purchasing the landlords' land." And those landlords who were on the side of the people in the war of resistance would be given "more benefits and privileges."

  With the onset of the large-scale civil war, however, little funding was available for the CCP to implement Dr. Sun's compensation policy. Moreover, as radical sentiments grew within the party, many CCP cadres campaigned for direct land redistribution. The property of both landlords and rich farmers was taken away. Even some top CCP leaders believed that these excesses might be necessary to mobilize poor peasants in the civil war, but Mao warned, "Nothing can hurt our party more in the civil war than such excessive policies toward rich farmers and ordinary landlords." See "Meetings between Zhou Enlai, Dong Biwu and the Representatives of the Democratic League," April 1, 1946, CCP file, 1945–1950, CAC; see also, *Selected Works of Mao Zedong*, vol. 4, pp. 48–71.

103. Yu Guangyuan, "Land Reform in the Liberated Region in the Past Year," *Jiefang ribao* (Liberation Daily, Yanan), January 1, 1947.

104. "Lifa weiyuan guanyu tudiwenti de zhixuan he Weng Wenhao neige de danfu" (Legislators Address Inquiries to Land Reform and the Weng Wenhao Cabinet's Reply), the minutes of meetings of the Legislative Yuan, July 3, 1948, file of Legislative Yuan (1948), SNAC.

105. Memo, Colonel Liou Jiwu to the National Defense Department, December 5, 1946. KMT Defense Department file, SNAC.

106. Madam Sun Yat-sen, "Against the Civil War!" *Da Gong Bao* (Da Gong Daily), April 3, 1946.

107. "Gemenzhudanpai shengming buchengren maiguotiaoyue" (Joint Statement of All the Democratic Parties in China), *Da Gong Bao* (Da Gong Daily), February 3, 1948.

108. Ma Xulun, "On the Third Force and the Democratic Front," *Qunzhong Magazine* (The Masses) 13, no. 10 (December 22, 1946).

109. Zhang Dongsun, "Zhuishu women nulijianli 'lianhezhengfu' de yuanyin" (A Reflection on the Reasons Why We Intended to Build a "Coalition Government" in China).

110. Memo re statement by Dr. Luo Longji (head of the Democratic League) to Robert S. Ward, January 21, 1947, Shanghai, CA, box 11, NA.

4. New American Strategies

1. Robert Jervis, "War and Misperception," *Journal of Interdisciplinary History* (Spring 1988).

2. Since Warren I. Cohen's pioneering study on Acheson's policy of generating "Titoism" in China, many studies have been done to explore America's "wedge strategy" toward the Sino-Soviet alliance. Among the most systematic of these studies are Nancy Bernkopf Tucker, *Patterns in the Dust: Chinese-American Relations and the Recognition Controversy* (New York: Columbia University Press, 1983) and David A. Mayers, *Cracking the Monolith: U.S. Policy Against the Sino-Soviet Alliance, 1949–1955* (Baton Rouge: Louisiana State University Press, 1986). So far, all of these studies have focused on the recognition controversy in Acheson's new China policy. No study has yet been made to explore the key concept of the new China policy, which centered not on diplomatic recognition of the People's Republic but on a new economic strategy toward the CCP and a new military strategy toward Taiwan.

3. "Possible Developments in China," November 3, 1948, CIA series, ORE reports, NA.

4. Memo, John Leighton Stuart to the State Department, December 1948, in

"Summary of Telegram," December 23, 1948, Naval Aide files, box 21, HST.

5. Memo, David F. Barr to the Department of Army for General Wedemeyer, December 2, 1948, and January 12, 1949, JCS files, 1948–50, NA.

6. The author would like to thank Professor John Coogan for pointing out an important institutional change at the State Department made in 1949. According to new procedures in the policymaking process, the career diplomats working at the country or area desks, such as those at the Office of Chinese Affairs, submit policy proposals to the assistant secretary of state meetings for discussion; then, the assistant secretary of state submits the new proposal to the secretary of state for final approval. These new procedures have made the desk files much more important than the decimal files (the secretary of state files), since the former can provide more insights into the competing policy hypotheses that surface during policy debates.

7. A National Security Council (NSC) memo argued that the United States should continue to support Chiang Kai-shek and that American policy should be "calculated to encourage resistance to communism and to weaken, and eventually eliminate, communist control" in China. NSC report, December 22, 1948, RG59, General Records of the Office of the Executive of Secretariat, box 16, NA.

8. Memo, Joe Agill and David Gordon to Dean Acheson, November 13, 1948, Papers of Dean Acheson, box 64, HST.

9. Ibid.

10. Memo, "Notes on a Future American China Policy," American Embassy, Nanjing, to the State Department, July 14, 1949, CA, box 18, NA.

11. Memo, Paul Hoffman to Dean Acheson, January 30, 1949, Papers of Dean Acheson, box 63, HST.

12. Memo, R. N. Magill to Butterworth, December 14, 1948; memo, S. C. Brown to Butterworth, January 5, 1949, CA, box 12, NA.

13. Position papers for the undersecretary meetings, February 24, 1949, General Records of the Office of the Executive Secretariat, box 15, NA.

14. Memo, S. C. Brown to Butterworth, January 5, 1949, CA, box 12, NA; telegram, American Embassy, Nanjing, to the State Department, January 21, 1949, CA box 12, NA.

15. Telegram, no. 1994, American Embassy, Nanjing, to the State Department, concerning General Chennaldt's request for U.S. aid to the anti-Communist Muslims in the Northwest of China, September 3, 1949, CA, box 14, NA; S. C. Brown, memo on China trade control, February 19, 1949, CA, box 18, NA.

16. Memo, R. N. Magill to Butterworth, December 14, 1948; memo, S. C. Brown to Butterworth, January 5, 1949, CA, box 12, NA; telegram, American Embassy, Nanjing, to the State Department, January 21, 1949, CA, box 12, NA.

17. Memo, "Summary of Discussion on China Trade Control," CA, box 15, RG59, NA. For the officers of CA, China trade offered more bargaining power than diplomatic recognition: "The unfortunate aspect of this

problem is that we are so tied to the defunct National Government that we are without positive inducements with which to bargain with the Chinese Communists on the matter of official representation."

18. Memo, J. M. Allison to Butterworth, January 20, 1949, Division of Chinese Affairs, box 20, NA; telegram, American Embassy, Nanjing, to State Department, April 23, 1949, Division of Chinese Affairs, box 22, 1949, NA.

19. Memo, W. W. Stuart to Butterworth, January 1949, box 19, RG59, NA. Position papers, undersecretary documents, box 1, RG59, General Records of the Office of the Executive Secretariat, NA.

20. Memo, W. W. Stuart to Butterworth, January 17, 1949, box 19, RG59, NA. Position papers, undersecretary documents, box 1, RG59, General Records of the Office of the Executive Secretariat, NA.

21. Position papers for the undersecretary meetings, "U.S. Policy regarding Trade with Chinese Communists," February 23, 1949, Records of the Office of the Executive Secretariat, box 15, NA.

22. Memo, "Summary of Discussion on China Trade Control," April 10, 1950, CA, box 20, NA.

23. Memo, W. W. Stuart to Butterworth, January 1949, box 19, RG59, NA. Position papers, undersecretary documents, box 1, RG59, General Records of the Office of the Executive Secretariat, NA.

24. Undersecretary documents, July 10, 1949, box 2, RG59, General Records of the Office of the Executive Secretariat, NA.

25. Dean Acheson, meeting at the National Security Council, December 29, 1949, NSC record, box 17, NA.

26. Statement by President Harry S. Truman, January 5, 1950, State Department Bulletin, NA.

27. Ibid. Truman also said, "The United States Government will not provide military aid or advice to Chinese forces on Formosa. In the view of the United States Government, the resources on Formosa are adequate to enable them to obtain the items which they might consider necessary for the defense of the Island."

28. For an excellent study of this new military strategy, see John Lewis Gaddis, "The Strategic Perspective: The Rise and Fall of the 'Defensive Perimeter' Concept, 1947–1951," in Dorothy Borg and Waldo Heinrichs, eds., *Uncertain Years: Chinese-American Relations, 1947–1950* (New York: Columbia University Press, 1980), pp. 61–118. This chapter further argues that this military strategy was intimately tied to, or an integral part of, the new economic strategy toward the CCP before the Korean War.

29. Dean Acheson, speech at National Press Club, January 12, 1950; State Department decimal file, NA.

30. Undersecretary documents, July 10, 1949, box 2, RG59, General Records of the Office of the Executive Secretariat, NA; Dean Acheson, meeting at the National Security Council, December 29, 1949, NSC record, box 17, NA.

31. Minutes of undersecretary's meetings, February 28, 1949, RG59, Records

of the Office of the Executive Secretariat, box 16, NA; NSC 41, CA, box 18, NA.

32. Papers of Dean Acheson, box 63, HST.

33. Memo of conversation with the president, November 1949, Papers of Dean Acheson, box 64, HST.

34. Ibid.

35. Defense draft of NSC 48/2, October 1949, JCS files, 1948–1950, NA; memo of conversation with the president, November 17, 1949, Papers of Dean Acheson, box 66, HST.

36. "Compromise Is Seen on China Token Aid," New York Times, September 9, 1949; also see "China Lobby and Its Intelligence," May 11, 1950, Papers of George Elsey, box 59, HST.

37. "Summary of Information on China Lobby," November 1949, Truman Papers, box 161, subject file—China Lobby.

38. Michael W. Miles, The Odyssey of the American Right (New York: Oxford University Press, 1980), pp. 23–78.

39. Warren I. Cohen, America in the Age of Soviet Power, 1945–1991 (New York: Cambridge University Press, 1993), p. 75.

40. O. Edmund Clubb, "McCarthyism and Our Asia Policy," Association for Asian Studies convention, Boston, March 29, 1969.

41. Memo re NSC 41, R. N. Magill to John Davis, May 2, 1949, CA, box 16, NA.

42. Memo, American Embassy, Nanjing, to the State Department, September 20, 1949, CA, box 19, RG59, NA; memo, S. C. Brown to Butterworth, September 24, 1949, CA, box 19, NA.

43. Memo, R. N. Magill to Philip Sprouse, director, Office of Chinese Affairs, October 24, 1949, CA, box 15, NA.

44. Acheson's testimony, congressional hearing, March 4, 1950; Papers of Dean Acheson, box 67, HST.

45. Walter Lippmann, "On Acheson's China Policy," New York Times, January 15, 1950.

46. Memo, R. N. Magill to Philip Sprouse, October 24, 1949, CA, box 19, RG59, NA; Dean Acheson, speech, March 13, 1950, Papers of Dean Acheson, box 58, HST; Walter Lippmann, "Acheson Takes Long View of the Revolution in Asia," New York Times, January 15, 1950.

47. Letter, Dean Acheson to Louis Johnson, April 18, 1950, Papers of Dean Acheson, box 71, HST.

48. CIA reports re the effect of the Soviet possession of atomic bombs on the security of the United States, January 16, 1950, ORE series, CIA records, NA; memo, the Military Liaison Commission to the Defense Department, January 24, 1950.

49. Memo, ONI to NSC, January 26, 1950, ORE series, CIA reports, NA.

50. Memo, George Kennan to Dean Acheson, February 3, 1950. Records of the Policy Planning Staff (PPS), country and area files, box 15, NA.

51. Memo, Paul Nitze to Acheson, February 28, 1950, PPS, subject files, box 6, NA.

52. Notes on cabinet meeting, February 28, 1950, Papers of Dean Acheson, box 65, HST.

53. Henry Kissinger, *The Necessity for Choice: Prospects of American Foreign Policy* (New York: Harper, 1961), p. 77.

54. During the first three years of the Indochina War (1946–1949), the Truman administration maintained a pro-French so-called neutrality. The State Department's Asian experts warned of the dangers of identifying with French colonialism, and American diplomats in Vietnam pointed out that Ho Chi Minh had established himself as "the symbol of nationalism and struggle for freedom to the overwhelming majority of the population." However, in the eyes of many in the Truman administration, Ho had remained loyal to Moscow throughout his career, and his lack of close ties with the Soviet Union meant that he was "trusted to carry out Stalin's plans without supervision." In early 1950, the southward advance of Mao Zedong's army raised the ominous possibility of the CCP's collaboration with the Vietminh and a prospect of French defeat in Indochina. Memo re Indochina situation, CA, box 7, NA.

55. Memo of conversation re French position in Indochina, March 6, 1950, Papers of Dean Acheson, box 65, HST.

56. Memorandum, "Summary of Discussion on China Trade Control," April 10, 1950, CA, box 20, NA.

57. Ibid.

58. Letter, Dean Rusk to Dean Acheson, April 20, 1950, Papers of Dean Acheson, box 65, HST.

59. Dean Acheson, speech, September 27, 1949, Papers of Dean Acheson, box 65, HST; letter, Acheson to Louis Johnson, April 28, 1950, Papers of Dean Acheson, box 65, HST.

5. Two Sides of One Coin

1. "Cominform Communiqué, 28 June 1948," *The Soviet-Yugoslav Dispute— Text of the Published Correspondence* (London: Royal Institute of International Affairs, 1948), pp. 61–70. As the communiqué claimed, "The Yugoslav leaders think that by making concessions they can curry favor with the Imperialist states. They think they will be able to bargain with them for Yugoslavia's independence and, gradually, get the people of Yugoslavia orientated on these states, that is, on capitalism."

2. Mao Zedong's conversation with Pavel Yudin, the Soviet ambassador to China, April 1956, Beijing; quoted from *Stalin wenti yanjiu* (Journal on Stalin Studies) (June 1997): 27–28; see also Mao Zedong, "Conversation with Soviet Ambassador Yudin," in Zhongyang wenxian yanjiushi, ed., *Mao Zedong waijiao wenxuan* (A Selection of Mao Zedong's Writings on Diplomacy) (Beijing: Zhongyang wenxian chubanshe, 1995), pp. 322–333.

3. This term was used by Shi Zhe, Mao Zedong's chief Russian interpreter from 1945 to 1953. Quoted from unpublished papers of Shi Zhe and kindly shown to me by Zhu Ruizhen, who was Mao's Russian interpreter

from 1953 to 1966 and the principal aide to Shi Zhe when Shi wrote his memoir.

4. For the complex relationship between the CCP and the Third Force in the post–World War II years, see Chapter 3.

5. "Zhengdang, heping, tiantu gongzuo" (Political Party, Peace, and the Work of Laying Foundation), editorial, *Da Gong Bao* (Da Gong Daily) (Shanghai), February 7, 1948.

6. Liang Shumin, "Jinggao gongchangdang" (Respectful Address to the Chinese Communist Party), *Da Gong Bao* (Da Gong Daily) (Shanghai), February 21, 1949.

7. Letters, Bo Yibo to Mao Zedong, May 2, 1948; Mao Zedong to Bo Yibo, May 10, 1948. CCP file, 1945–1950, CAC.

8. Mao Zedong, "On the Slogan 'The Poor Peasants Fought and Won the War, and the Poor Peasants Should Be the Sole Master of China,' " November 28, 1948; *Selected Works of Mao Zedong,* vol. 4 (Beijing: Foreign Language Press, 1961), pp. 198–199.

9. Confidential letter, CCP Central Committee to CCP members, May 31, 1948, CCP files, 1945–1950, CAC.

10. Bo Yibo, *Qishinian fendou yu sikao* (The Struggles and Reflections of Seventy Years), vol. 1 (Beijing: Zhonggong dangshi chubanshe, 1996), p. 523.

11. Ibid., pp. 518–520.

12. Regarding the PCC of 1946, see Chapter 3.

13. *Zhou Enlai nianpu, 1898–1949* (The Chronicles of Zhou Enlai, 1898–1949) (Beijing: Zhongyang wenxian chubanshe, 1989), p. 815.

14. *Zhou Enlai nianpu, 1949–1976* (The Chronicles of Zhou Enlai, 1949–1976), vol. 1 (Beijing: Zhongyang wenxian chubanshe, 1997), pp. 3–5.

15. Mao Zedong, "On the People's Democratic Dictatorship," in *Selected Works of Mao Zedong,* vol. 4 (Beijing: Foreign Language Press, 1961), pp. 411–424.

16. Walter LaFeber, *America, Russia, and the Cold War, 1945–1980,* 4th ed. (New York: John Wiley, 1980), pp. 76–77.

17. Telegram, CCP Central Committee to Stalin, November 1947; telegram, Stalin to CCP Central Committee, December 1947. These telegrams were first revealed by Anastas Mikoyan after the Sino-Soviet split. The originals have not yet been found in the CCP archives. Quoted from *Stalin wenti yenjiu* (Journal on Stalin Studies), (June 1997).

18. "Outline for Reporters on the Communist Information Bureau Resolution on Tito and Other Leaders of the Yugoslav Communist Party," issued by New York Education Department of the Communist Party of the United States, July 1948, Michigan State University library.

19. Sergei N. Goncharov, John W. Lewis, and Xue Litai, *Uncertain Partners: Stalin, Mao, and the Korean War* (Stanford, CA: Stanford University Press, 1993), p. 37.

20. Chiang Kai-shek's goal in signing this treaty in 1945 was to undermine Moscow's support for the CCP in the post–World War II era. For a more

detailed discussion of the impact of this alliance treaty between the KMT and the Soviet Union on the CCP's political and military agendas, see Chapter 3.

21. Wu Xiuquan, "The Process of Concluding the Sino-Soviet Treaty of Friendship, Alliance, and Mutual Assistance," in *Xin Zhongguo Waijiao Fengyun* (Main Diplomatic Events of New China) (Beijing: Shijie zhishi chubanshe, 1990), pp. 13–14. English translation from Goncharov, Lewis, and Xue, *Uncertain Partners,* pp. 94–95; Pavel Yudin, "Notes of Conversation with Mao Zedong," *Far Eastern Affairs,* no. 5 (1994).

22. Liu Shaoqi, *Internationalism and Nationalism* (Beijing: Foreign Language Press, 1951), pp. 1–51.

23. *Collected Works of Liu Shao Ch'I, 1945–1957* (Hong Kong: Union Research Institute, 1969), pp. 127–133.

24. Mao, "On the People's Democratic Dictatorship," pp. 412–415.

25. Edwin W. Martin, *Divided Counsel* (Lexington: University Press of Kentucky, 1986), pp. 55–59. Secretary of State Dean Acheson frowned on Taiwan's decision to install a naval blockade of China's east coast. But President Truman approved it, out of domestic political considerations. The British were strongly against Taiwan's naval blockade. Regarding the Anglo-American policy differences on Taiwan's blockade, see Martin's excellent account in chapter 11, "Blockade."

26. Sergei Goncharov, "The Stalin-Mao Dialogue," *Far Eastern Affairs,* no. 2 (1992): 104–105. This article features Goncharov's interview with Ivan Kovalev, Stalin's personal envoy to Mao Zedong.

27. Bo Yibo, *Ruogan zhongda juece yu shijian de huigu* (Reflections on Important Decisions and Events), vol. 1 (Beijing: Zhonggong zhongyang dangxiao chubanshe, 1991), pp. 87–90.

28. *Wu Xiuquan's Memoir, 1950–1958* (Beijing: Zhongyang wenxian chubanshe, 1983), pp. 5–15, 45.

29. For the reactions of urban Chinese, see the editorials and reports of *Da Gong Bao* in Shanghai and Hong Kong in the summer of 1949.

30. "Liu Shaoqi's Report to Stalin on Behalf of the CCP Central Committee," in *Jianguo yilai Liu Shaoqi wengao* (Liu Shaoqi Papers since the Founding of the PRC), vol. 1 (Beijing: Zhongyang wenxian chubanshe, 1998), pp. 17, 25–26.

31. At Liu's request, Stalin agreed to send over 200 professional experts to help China's industrial production. But Stalin proposed four conditions, one of which was, "If a Soviet expert committed a mistake or crime in China, this should be handled by the Soviet court, and China should not intervene in this matter." For the CCP delegation, Stalin was asking for the rights of extraterritoriality for the Soviet experts in China. In Liu's view, since the CCP had nowhere else to turn for experts and specialists, the CCP had to agree to Stalin's conditions. When Liu left Moscow in mid-August 1949, about 90 Soviet experts left with him, to help China's industrial recovery. Shi Zhe, *Zai lishi juren shenbian: Shi Zhe huiyilu* (At the

Side of History's Giants: The Memoirs of Shi Zhe), rev. ed. (Beijing: Zhongyang wenxian chubanshe, 1995), pp. 23–24, 419–426.

32. Liu's first meeting with Stalin, quoted from Goncharov, "The Stalin-Mao Dialogue," pp. 108–109; see similar account about this meeting in Shi Zhe), *Zai lishi juren shenbian: Shi Zhe huiyilu* (At the Side of History's Giants: The Memoirs of Shi Zhe), p. 109.

33. "Liu Shaoqi's Report to Stalin on Behalf of the CCP Central Committee," p. 25.

34. Yudin, "Notes of Conversation with Mao Zedong."

35. Kovalev, "The Stalin-Mao Dialogue," pp. 101–102; see also "Excerpts from Kovalev Report to Stalin, 'Some Policies of the CCP Central Leadership and Practical Problems,' " in Goncharov, Lewis, and Xue, *Uncertain Partners,* App., doc. 22, pp. 240–241.

36. Yudin, "Notes of Conversation with Mao Zedong." For a sophisticated and comprehensive account of Sino-Soviet treaty negotiations in late 1949 and early 1950, see Goncharov, Lewis, and Xue, *Uncertain Partners.*

37. Goncharov, "The Stalin-Mao Dialogue," pp. 109–110.

38. According to V. M. Molotov, second only to Stalin in the Kremlin at the time, his own suggestion might have been responsible for Stalin's change of mind. As he recalled, Stalin initially did not trust Mao: "Stalin told me, 'Go and see what sort of fellow he is.' " After his talks with Mao, Molotov tried to persuade Stalin to change his attitude: "Mao is a peasant leader, a kind of Chinese Pugachev. He is far from a Marxist, of course—he confessed to me that he had never read Marx's *Das Kapital.*" See *Molotov Remembers: Conversation with Felix Chuev,* edited and with an introduction by Albert Resis (Chicago: Evan R. Dee, 1993), p. 81. See also Yudin, "Notes of Conversation with Mao Zedong."

39. Goncharov, Lewis, and Xue, *Uncertain Partners,* pp. 121–127, 118–121.

40. Hu Qiaomu, *Hu Qiaomu huiyi Mao Zedong* (Hu Qiaomu Remembers Mao Zedong) (Beijing: Renmin chubanshe, 1995), p. 88.

41. Yudin, "Notes of Conversation with Mao Zedong."

42. From an interview with a senior Soviet diplomat stationed in Beijing during the 1950s, conducted in December 1990. Gancharov, Lewis, and Xue, *Uncertain Partners,* p. 122.

43. Mao Zedong, "Speech at the Chengdu Conference," *Jiangguoyilai Mao Zedong wengao,* vol. 7. English translation quoted from Goncharov, Lewis, and Xue, *Uncertain Partners,* p. 122.

44. Sergei Goncharov, "Soviet-Chinese Relations in 1948–1950: A Real History" (paper presented at the Workshop on Chinese Foreign Policy, Michigan State University, November 1–2, 1991).

45. Mao wrote in January 1949, "In all our military plans up to this point we have always taken into account the possibility of America's direct military occupation of Chinese coastal cities and engaging in warfare with us. We still need to take into account such a possibility in our future military plans, so that we will not be placed in a helpless situation of confusion, should

such an intervention occur. On the other hand, the more powerful, the more resolute Chinese revolutionary forces become, the less possible that American troops would directly intervene. . . . The hesitance and certain changes in American government's attitudes in the past year, particularly in the past three months, have proved this point. We therefore need to continue to overcome the incorrect views among the Chinese people and within our party, which overestimate the American power and strengths." Mao Zedong, "Yaoba meiguo zhijie chubing ganshe jisuan zainei" (To Take into Account America's Direct Military Intervention in Our Military Plans), in *Mao Zedong waijiao wenxuan* (A Selection of Mao Zedong's Writings on Diplomacy), p. 76.

46. "Zhongyang guanyu zhanzheng qijian jinzhi yiqie waiguojizhe caifang jie-fangqu de zhishi" (The CCP Central Committee's Instruction Concerning Refusing All Foreign Reporters to Visit the Liberated Areas), December 23, 1948. Many CCP leaders shared such a fear. They believed that "since the new coalition government would have many representatives of bour-geoisie and petty bourgeoisie," it would probably be easier for Wash-ington to beat the CCP by "political means." Bo, *Ruogan zhongda juece yu shijian de huigu* (Reflections on Important Decisions and Events), vol. 1, pp. 35–45.

47. Mao Zedong, "Zhongyang zhengzhi ju guanyu muqian xingshi he 1949 nian de renwu" (CCP Politburo on Current Situation and Our Task in 1949), in *Selected Works of Mao Zedong*, pp. 1435–1436.

48. Mao Zedong's conversation with Anastas Mikoyan, in Yanan, February 1949. Shi Zhe, *Zai lishi juren shenbian: Shi Zhe huiyilu* (At the Side of History's Giants: The Memoirs of Shi Zhe), p. 379.

49. Ambassador John Leighton Stuart sent this message to Mao through Gen-eral Chen Mingshu, a prominent Third Force leader in Shanghai.

50. "Mr. Chen Mingshu's Reports on American Ambassador's Two Secret Visits," March 26, 1949; in *Foreign Relations of the United States, 1949*, vol. 8: *The Far East: China* (Washington, DC: U.S. Government Printing Office, 1978), p. 174.

51. S. Tikhvinsky, "The Zhou Enlai 'Demarche' and the CCP's Informal Ne-gotiations with Americans in June 1949," *Far Eastern Affairs*, no. 3 (1994), Moscow. On April 19, Stalin wrote, "We believe that China's dem-ocratic government should not refuse to establish diplomatic relations with capitalist countries, including the United States, given that these countries formally abandon military, economic, and political supports to Chiang's government." Stalin also said that neither should the CCP "refuse to accept foreign loans or to do business with capitalist countries."

52. Mao Zedong, "Ruguo Meiying duanjue tong guomindang de guanxi ke kaolu he tamen jianli weijiao guanxi" (If America and Britain Cut Off Their Relations with KMT We May Consider Establishing Diplomatic Relationships with Them), draft for CCP Central Military Committee's telegram to Deng Xiaoping, Rao Shushi, Chen Yi, and Liu Bocheng,

April 28, 1949, in *Mao Zedong waijiao wenxuan* (A Selection of Mao Zedong's Writings on Diplomacy), p. 83. It is also important to note that the CCP's change of policy was not in direct conflict with Stalin's strategic thinking in this period. Kovalev, "The Stalin-Mao Dialogue," pp. 100–101.

53. Mao Zedong, "Huang Hua tong situleideng tanhua ying zhuyi de jige wenti" (Several Issues Huang Hua Should Keep in Mind in His Meetings with Ambassador Stuart), in *Mao Zedong waijiao wenxuan* (A Selection of Mao Zedong's Writings on Diplomacy), pp. 87–88.

54. The talk lasted about two months, from May to July of 1949. Chen Lisong, ed., *Situleideng Riji* (Stuart's Diary) (Hong Kong, 1976).

55. He Zhigong, "American Foreign Policy toward China, 1945–1949: An Assessment," *Jindaishi yanjiu* (Journal of Modern History) (January 1985).

56. Goncharov, "The Stalin-Mao Dialogue," pp. 100–103.

57. Ibid.

58. *Zhou Enlai nianpu, 1898–1949* (The Chronicles of Zhou Enlai, 1898–1949), pp. 794–796; Yang Kuisong, "Huade shijian yu xinzhongguo duimeizhengce de jueding" (The Ward Case and New China's America Policy), *Lishi Yanjiu* (Journal of Historical Research), no. 5 (1994). The CCP headquarters had sent an earlier telegram to the Northeastern Bureau, on November 1. In that telegram, drafted by Zhou Enlai, the CCP Central Committee instructed the Northeastern Bureau that during the time of the military control in the Northeast region, the PLA commission should "send troops to protect the American, British, and the French consulates," and after the military control period was over, the PLA commission should "send policemen to guard those consulates" but that neither the PLA troops nor the policemen should be allowed to "check on the foreign diplomats personally" or "inspect their consulate compounds." Moreover, regarding matters of diplomacy and international law, the Northeastern Bureau should "closely consult with the Soviet diplomats," whose recommendations should be used, however, only as "references." With respect to important foreign-policy issues in the region, the CCP Northeastern Bureau "must report to the Central Committee for instructions."

59. Goncharov, "The Stalin-Mao Dialogue," p. 102.

60. Yang, "Huade shijian yu xinzhongguo duimeizhengce de jueding" (The Ward Case and New China's America Policy).

61. Goncharov, "The Stalin-Mao Dialogue," p. 102.

62. Ibid.

63. According to the Northeastern Bureau's intelligence information and some KMT spies' testimonies, a KMT spy network did use the American consulate in Shenyang for some time. However, there has been no credible evidence to prove that Consul General Ward knew about its operation in the consulate or was responsible for it. See Yang, "Huade shijian yu xinzhongguo duimeizhengce de jueding" (The Ward Case and the Establishment of New China's America Policy), p. 110.

64. After a public trial in Shenyang, Consul General Ward was deported to the United States on December 11, 1949.

65. Mao Zedong, "Address to New Political Consultative Conference," in *Selected Works of Mao Zedong*, vol. 4, p. 408.

66. Memo, American Embassy, Nanjing, to the State Department, June 15–August 9, 1949, CA, box 19, RG59, NA.

67. Ibid.

68. Confidential circular, CCP Central Committee to the Regional Party Committees, August 3, 1949, CCP file, 1945–1950, CAC.

69. Confidential circular, CCP Central Committee to Regional Party Committees, September 27, 1949, CCP file, 1945–1950, CAC.

70. The twelve nations that signed the treaty with the Qing dynasty were Austria-Hungary, Belgium, France, Germany, Great Britain, Italy, Japan, the Netherlands, Russia, Spain, and the United States.

71. Memo, KMT shiguanjie qingli weiyuanhui (KMT Committee on Management of Foreign Embassy District) to KMT Executive Yuan, July 1946, Records of Executive Yuan, SNAC.

72. Ibid., pp. 83–84.

73. Nie Rongzhen Proclamation, no. 15, in Mao Chanbing, ed., *Diaoyutai Dangan* (Diaoyutai Archives), vol. 1 (Beijing: Hongqi chubanshe, 1998), pp. 78–85. In 1927, the KMT government decided to choose Nanjing as the capital of Nationalist China. From then until 1949, foreign embassies in Beijing were changed into consulates, but the buildings themselves were retained.

74. Stephen R. Mackinnon and Oris Friesen, eds., *China Reporting* (Berkeley: University of California Press, 1987), pp. 155–156.

75. Shi Zhe, *Zai lishi juren shenbian: Shi Zhe huiyilu* (At the Side of History's Giants: The Memoirs of Shi Zhe), pp. 455–457.

76. For the original texts of the Chinese and the Soviet statements, see *Xinhua Yuebao* (The New China Monthly) (February 1950); see also Liu Jiecheng, *Mao Zedong and Stalin* (Beijing: Zhonggong zhongyang dangxiao chubanshe, 1996), pp. 394–395. After this incident, as Shi Zhe noted, Stalin's attitude toward Mao actually changed for the better. Stalin began to make efforts to pay "more respect" to Mao's opinions in the remaining negotiations. Stalin never again mentioned the CCP's "personal statement" regarding Acheson's speech of January 12, 1950. Nonetheless, Mao felt that Stalin's "distrust" of him "lingered on." Throughout the treaty negotiation, he recalled, they had to bargain really hard with Stalin." As he told the Soviet ambassador Pavel Yudin in 1956, "It is not a pretty thing for us to admit that we had to bargain so hard with Stalin." However, "This fact itself could show that Stalin did not trust the Chinese Communists during that time." See Yudin, "Notes of Conversation with Mao Zedong."

77. Memo, the CIA to Truman, November 11, 1949, Truman Papers, box 128, HST. It is interesting to note that Kovalev also quickly reported to Stalin regarding this speech with anger and suspicion.

78. For a thoughtful presentation of this view, see Jian Chen, *Mao's China & the Cold War* (Chapel Hill: University of North Carolina Press, 2001), p. 7, and "The Myth of America's 'Lost Chance' in China," *Diplomatic History* 21, no. 1 (Winter 1997): 77.
79. Chen, "The Myth of America's 'Lost Chance' in China," p. 78.
80. Yang, "Huade shijian yu xinzhongguo duimeizhengce de queding" (The Ward Case and the Formulation of New China's Policy toward America).
81. John King Fairbank, *The Great Chinese Revolution, 1800–1985* (New York: Harper & Row, 1986), p. 268.

6. From Adversaries to Enemies

1. For in-depth studies of the origins of the Korean War from very different perspectives, see the following excellent works: Allen S. Whiting, *China Crosses the Yalu* (Stanford, CA: Stanford University Press, 1968); Bruce Cumings, *The Origins of the Korean War*, vols. 1 and 2 (Princeton, NJ: Princeton University Press, 1984, 1990); Rosemary Foot, *The Wrong War* (Ithaca, NY: Cornell University Press, 1985); Sergei N. Goncharov, John W. Lewis, and Xue Litai, *Uncertain Partners: Stalin, Mao, and the Korean War* (Stanford, CA: Stanford University Press, 1993); William W. Stueck, *Rethinking the Korean War: A New Diplomatic and Strategic History* (Princeton, NJ: Princeton University Press, 2002).
2. Summary of telegrams, June 3, 1949, Naval Aides files, box 21, HST.
3. Warren I. Cohen, "Conversations with Chinese Friends: Zhou Enlai's Associates Reflect on Chinese-American Relations in the 1940s and the Korean War," *Diplomatic History* 11, no. 3 (Summer 1987): 283–289.
4. Summary of telegrams, June 6, 1949, Naval Aides files, box 21, HST.
5. Ibid.
6. Summary of telegrams, June 8, 1949, Naval Aides files, box 21, HST.
7. Letter, Truman to the State Department, June 16, 1949, PPS, box 19, NA.
8. Memo, John Leighton Stuart to the Secretary of State, June 30, 1949, Nanking, quoted from Kenneth W. Rea and John C. Brewer, ed., *The Forgotten Ambassador: The Reports of John Leighton Stuart, 1946–1949* (Boulder, CO: Westview Press, 1981), pp. 333–334.
9. Ibid.
10. Memo, John Leighton Stuart to the Secretary of State, July 14, 1949, Nanjing, quoted from Rea and Brewer, *The Forgotten Ambassador*, pp. 337–338.
11. Truman's papers indicate clearly that the State Department received the intelligence briefing on Mao's "leaning to one side" speech, which appeared in the CCP newspaper on July 1, 1949, but that Truman did not read it until he had made the decision to decline Mao's invitation. Nor did he read Ambassador Stuart's full analysis of Mao's speech, which came on

July 6, 1949, or a week after he made his decision. See Summary of Telegrams, July 1, 1949, Naval Aides files, box 25, HST.

12. Memo, Truman to the State Department, June 16, 1949, PPS, box 19, NA.

13. Memo, American Embassy to the State Department, July 3, 1949. CA, box 19, NA. Emphasis in original.

14. Acheson, conversation with R. N. Magill and John Allison, August 22, 1949, Secretary's file, box 17, NA.

15. Memo, R. N. Magill to Philip Sprouse, October 24, 1949, CA, box 15, NA.

16. Memo re NSC 41, R. N. Magill to John Davis, May 2, 1949, CA, box 16, NA.

17. Cohen, "Conversations with Chinese Friends," pp. 285–287. In an example of the lack of understanding of the United States, Zhang Zai was "recruited on the basis of his study of English at Peking University." After the formal creation of the Ministry of Foreign Affairs, "he was assigned to the American desk, instantly becoming an American expert. Without guidance, he looked for books to read about the United States and discovered the usefulness of the *New York Times.*"

18. For a detailed discussion of Mao's motivation in sending back the Korean solders in the PLA to North Korea in 1949, see Shen Zhihua, "Mao's Approach to Kim's Military Unification Plan in 1949," in Shen, *Zhongsu tongmeng yu chaoxian zhanzheng yanjiu* (The Sino-Soviet Alliance and the Korean War) (Nanning, Guanxi: Guanxishifandaxue chubanshe, 1999). Shen's work is based on recently declassified Chinese and Russian documents as well as the author's extensive interviews with high-ranking PLA officers from that time.

19. Goncharov, Lewis, and Xue, *Uncertain Partners,* pp. 130–167.

20. Shen Zhihua, "Sino-Soviet Relations and the Origins of the Korean War: Stalin's Strategic Goals in the Far East," *Journal of Cold War Studies* 2, no. 2 (2000): 44–68.

21. Telegram, Roshchin to Stalin, May 13, 1950, Woodrow Wilson International Center for Scholars, Program on Cold War International History.

22. Qing Shi, "1950 nien jiefang taiwan jihua geqian de muhou" (Why the Taiwan Campaign Was Delayed in 1950), in Qiu Shi, ed., *Gongheguo zhongda shijian he juece neimu* (The Inside Stories of Important Policy Decisions in PRC History) (Beijing: Jingji ribao chubanshe, 1997), pp. 45–64; author's interview with Zhu Ruizhen, Mao's Russian interpreter, August 12, 2000, Beijing.

23. On March 31, 1956, during Mao's conversation with Pavel Yudin, Soviet ambassador to China, Mao again raised this issue. As Yudin recorded, "On the Korean question, when I [Mao Zedong] was in Moscow [in December 1949–January 1950] we came to an understanding about everything. The issue was not about the seizure of South Korea, but about the significant strengthening of North Korea. But subsequently Kim Il Sung was in

Moscow, where some kind of agreement was reached, about which no one considered it necessary to consult with us beforehand. It should be noted, said Mao Zedong, that there was a serious miscalculation in the Korean war about the supposed impossibility of intervention of international forces on the side of South Korea." Quoted from "Telegram, Excerpt from Cable from Soviet Ambassador to the PRC P. Yudin Regarding a Meeting with Mao Zedong," April 20, 1956; *Cold War International History Project: Virtual Archive, Collection: Korean War,* Cold War International History Project (CWIHP), www.CWIHP.org, by permission of the Woodrow Wilson International Center for Scholars.

24. Qing Shi, "Kim Il Sung zuzhi le Mao Zedong jinggong Taiwan de jihua" (Kim Il Sung Stopped Mao's Taiwan Military Campaign), *Mingbao yuekan* (Mingbao Monthly), no. 7 (1994): 81; Qing Yuan, "Hanzhang mimi dang an de gongkai" (The Opening Up of the Secret Archives of the Korean War), *Mingbao Yuekan* (Mingbao Monthly), no. 9 (1994): 68. Both sources quoted from Sheng Zhihua, "Zhongguo chubing chaoxian de juece guocheng" (The Decision-Making Process in China's Decision to Enter the Korean War), *Dangshi yanjiu ziliao* (Research Journal of Party History), no. 1 (1996): 3–4.

25. Liu Wen, *Su Yu Zhuan* (Biography of Su Yu) (Beijing: Dangdai zhongguo chubanshe, 2000), pp. 220–222.

26. According to Taiwan's intelligence assessment, the CCP's Taiwan campaign was to have taken place in early July 1950. See Gu Weijun, *Gu Weijun huiyilu* (Wellington Koo Memoir) (Beijing: Zhonghua Shuju, 1997). Koo was Taiwan's ambassador to the United States at the time.

27. On June 30, Zhou Enlai told Xiao Jinguang, the commander in chief of the naval force, that "the change of the situation has caused new difficulty for our Taiwan campaign, because now we have the American fleet out there in the Taiwan straits. . . . We will continue the demobilization of our army, concentrate on the construction of our naval and air forces, and temporarily postpone the schedule of the Taiwan campaign."

28. Yang Kuisong, *Zouxiang polie: Mao Zedong yu Moscow de enen yuanyuan* (The Road to Breakup: Grievances between Mao Zedong and Moscow) (Hong Kong: San Lian Shuchian, 1999), p. 300.

29. Goncharov, Lewis, and Xue, *Uncertain Partners,* p. 174.

30. Shen Zhihua, "The Sino-Soviet Alliance and China's Decision to Enter the Korean War," *Dangdai zhongguoshi yanjiu* (Study on Contemporary Chinese History), no. 5 (1996): 32.

31. Memo re North Korean military situation, Zhou Enlai to Mao Zedong, September 29, 1950; Pang Xianzhi and Li Jie, "Mao Zedong he kangmei yuanchao" (Mao Zedong and the Korean War), part 1, *Dang de wenxian* (Journal of Party Archival Documents) no. 4 (2000): 38. Pang Xianzhi was Mao's secretary.

32. Zhou Enlai's address to the National Committee of Political Consultative Conference, *People's Daily,* October 1, 1950.

33. Pang and Li, "Mao Zedong he kangmei yuanchao" (Mao Zedong and the Korean War), pp. 38–39.

34. Mao Zedong, "Guanyu pai jundui ruchao zuozhan gei Stalin de dianbao" (Telegram to Stalin Concerning Sending Chinese Troops to Korea), in *Jianguo yilai Mao Zedong wengao* (Mao Zedong Papers since the Establishment of the PRC), vol. 1 (Beijing: Zhongyang wenxian chubanshe, 1993), pp. 539–540.

35. Nie Rongzhen, *Nie Rongzhen huiyilu* (Nie Rongzhen Memoir), vol. 2 (Beijing: Jiefangjun chubanshe, 1984), p. 735.

36. The American, British, French foreign ministers' meeting was held between September 12 and September 18, 1950.

37. Zhou Enlai, "If American Troops Cross the 38th Parallel, We Would Intervene," in *Zhou Enlai waijiao wenxuan* (A Selection of Zhou Enlai's Writings on Diplomacy) (Beijing: Zhongyang wenxian chubanshe, 1986), p. 25.

38. "Telegram re Mao Zedong's Opinion That China Should Not Send Out Troops Immediately," in Shen Zhihua, ed., *Hanzhan eguo dangan* (The Korean War: Declassified Documents from Archives in Russia) (Taipei: Institute of Modern History, Academia Sinica, 2003), no. SD00316, p. 218. The telegram was sent by Roshchin to Stalin on October 3, 1950.

39. Ibid.

40. Telegram, Stalin to Kim Il-Sung, October 8, 1950, in which Stalin informed Kim about Mao's telegram of October 3, and his telegram to Mao the following day, Russian Presidential Archives, complete papers no. 45, catalogue no. 1, file no. 347, no. SD00322, pp. 65–67; Shen, *Hanzhan eguo dangan* (Russian Archival Documents on the Korean War), p. 222.

41. Peng Dehuai, *Peng Dehuai zishu* (The Autobiography of Peng Dehuai) (Beijing: Renmin chubanshe, 1981), p. 257.

42. *Nie Rongzhen huiyilu* (Nie Rongzhen Memoir), vol. 2, p. 735.

43. Mao Zedong, "Jianli zhongguo remin zhiyuanjun de mingling" (Order of Establishing the Chinese People's Volunteer Army), October 8, 1950, in *Mao Zedong Xuanji* (Selected Works of Mao Zedong), vol. 6 (Beijing: Renmin chubanshe, 1999), p. 100.

44. Hong Xuezhi, *Kangmei yuanchao zhanzheng huiyi* (Recollections of the War to Resist U.S. Aggression and Aid Korea) (Beijing: Jiefangjun wenyi chubanshe, 1991), pp. 25–26.

45. Zhou Enlai's talk at CCP Central Committee meeting in Baidahe, July 31, 1960; Jin Chongji, ed., *Zhou Enlai Zhuan* (Biography of Zhou Enlai) (Beijing: Zhongyang wenxian chubanshe, 1998), p. 1019.

46. Telegram, Stalin-Zhou Enlai to Mao Zedong, October 11, 1950; Pang Xianzhi and Li Jie, *Mao Zedong yu kangmei yuanchao* (Mao Zedong and the Korean War) (Beijing: Zhongyang wenxian chubanshe, 2000), p. 25.

47. Telegram, Terentii Shtykov, Soviet ambassador to Pyongyang, to Stalin, October 14, 1950, no. SD00330, Shen, *Hanzhan eguo dangan* (Russian Archival Documents on the Korean War), p. 225.

48. Telegram, Mao Zedong to Peng Dehui and Gao Gang, October 12, 1950. Pang and Li, *Mao Zedong yu kangmei yuanchao* (Mao Zedong and the Korean War), pp. 25–26.

49. Telegram, "Chinese Troops Should and Must Join the War," Mao to Zhou, October 13, 1950. *Mao Zedong waijiao wenxuan* (A Selection of Mao Zedong's Writings on Diplomacy) (Beijing: Zhongyang wenxian chubanshe, 1995), p. 144.

50. Pang and Li, *Mao Zedong yu kangmei yuanchao* (Mao Zedong and the Korean War), p. 28.

51. Ibid.

52. Du Ping, *Zai Zhiyuanjun zhongbu* (At the Headquarters of the Chinese Volunteer Army) (Beijing: Jiefangjun chubanshe, 1991), pp. 23–30.

53. Minutes of Mao Zedong–Kim Il Sung meeting, October 10, 1970; Pang and Li, *Mao Zedong yu kangmei yuanchao* (Mao Zedong and the Korean War), pp. 30–31. After the Chinese troops won the first victories in the battlefield in North Korea, Stalin changed his mind about Soviet air protection in North Korea, thus, the Soviet air force began to engage in direct fighting in the Korean War.

54. Hu Qiaomu, *Hu Qiaomu huiyi Mao Zedong* (Hu Qiaomu Remembers Mao Zedong) (Beijing: Renmin chubanshe, 1995), p. 87.

55. Zhang Min and Zhang Xiujuan, *Zhou Enlai yu kangmei yuanchao* (Zhou Enlai and the Korean War) (Shanghai: Shanghai renmin chubanshe, 2000), pp. 125–127.

56. Zhou Enlai's report to the Political Consultants' Conference, October 24, 1950, in *Zhou Enlai waijiao wenxuan* (A Selection of Zhou Enlai's Writings on Diplomacy), pp. 31–32.

57. Mao's conversation with Wang Jifan and Zhou Shizhou (Mao's close relatives and confidants), October 27, 1950; in Wang Yuqing, ed., *Wang Jifan papers* (Beijing: wenshiziliao chubanshe, 2002), p. 304.

58. "Minutes of Conversation between Peng Dehuai and Aides," February 11, 1955, in Pang and Li, *Mao Zedong yu kangmei yuanchao* (Mao Zedong and the Korean War), p. 11.

59. Mao Zedong's conversation with the Soviet Communist Party Central Committee Delegation, September 23, 1956, in Pang and Li, *Mao Zedong yu kangmei yuanchao* (Mao Zedong and the Korean War), pp. 7–8.

60. Memo, Oliver Edmund Clubb (CA) to Livingston Merchant (FE) re Chinese Communist Threat of Intervention in Korea, October 4, 1950, CA (1950), State Department file, NA.

61. *Foreign Relations of the United States, 1950*, vol. 7: *Korea* (Washington, DC: U.S. Government Printing Office, 1976), pp. 460–461.

62. For Kennan's analysis of NSC 68, see Chapter 4 of this book.

63. "Memorandum by the Counselor (Kennan) to the Secretary of State," August 8, 1950, in *Foreign Relations of the United States, 1950*, vol. 1: *National Security Affairs; Foreign Economic Policy* (Washington, DC: U.S. Government Printing Office, 1977), p. 361.

64. Memo, George Kennan to Dean Acheson, August 21, 1950, Papers of Dean

Acheson, box 65, HST, quoted from Bruce Cumings, *Origins of the Korean War*, vol. 2 (Princeton, NJ: Princeton University Press, 1990), p. 714.

65. Callum MacDonald, *Britain and the Korean War* (Oxford: Basil Blackwell, 1990), p. 29.

66. Foot, *The Wrong War*, p. 74. For a thoughtful discussion of America's perceptions of the Soviets' intentions in the Korean War, see pp. 74–75.

67. Goncharov, Lewis, and Xue, *Uncertain Partners*, p. 156.

68. Foot, *The Wrong War*, p. 199.

69. Memo, "Chou En-lai Demarche re Korea," Office of Chinese Affairs, October 3, 1950, CA, State Department Lot file, NA.

70. Memo, Oliver Edmund Clubb (CA) to Livingston Merchant (FE) re "Chinese Communist Threat of Intervention in Korea," October 4, 1950, CA, State Department Lot file, NA.

71. Memo, "Credibility of K. M. Panikkar, Indian Ambassador to Communist China," Walter P. McConaughy to Philip C. Jessup and Dean Rusk, October 12, 1950, CA, State Department Lot file, NA.

72. Dean Acheson, *The Korean War* (New York: W. W. Norton, 1969), p. 55.

73. Harry S. Truman, *Memoirs*, vol. 2 (Garden City, NY: Doubleday, 1956), p. 362.

74. Cumings, *The Origins of the Korean War*, vol. 2, pp. 734–735.

75. Ibid., p. 362.

76. James F. Schnabel, *The United States Army in the Korean War: Policy and Direction: The First Year* (Washington, DC: Center for Military History, United States Army, 1988), pp. 213–214.

77. John W. Spanier, *The Truman-MacArthur Controversy and the Korean War* (Cambridge, MA: Belknap Press of Harvard University Press, 1959), pp. 109–110.

78. Whiting, *China Crosses the Yalu*, pp. 168–171.

79. Hans Morgenthau, *U.S. Policy in the Far East* (New York: Council on Religion and International Affairs, 1968), p. 31.

80. Jian Chen, *China's Road to the Korean War* (New York: Columbia University Press, 1994), p. 180.

81. In the Chinese literature, Shen Zhihua points out that there was no time stamp on Mao's draft telegram. See Shen, *Stalin, Mao Zedong yu Chaoxian zhanzheng* (Stalin, Mao and the Origins of the Korean War) (Guangzhou: Guangdong renmin chubanshe, 2004), pp. 87–88.

82. Letter, Stalin to Kim Il Sung (via Terentii Shtykov), in Alexander Y. Mansourov, "Stalin, Mao, Kim, and China's Decision to Enter the Korean War, September 16–October 15, 1950: New Evidence from the Russian Archives," *Cold War International History Project*, no. 6–7 (Winter 1995/1996).

83. Chen, *China's Road to the Korean War*.

84. Telegram, Filippov (Stalin) to Chinese foreign minister Zhou Enali (via Soviet ambassador to the PRC N. V. Roshchin), ciphered telegram No. 3172; quoted from "New Russian Documents on the Korean War," p. 43. See also Woodrow Wilson Center virtual archive collection on the Korean War, Woodrow Wilson Center for Scholars, Washington, DC.

85. Mao Zedong, draft telegram to Stalin, October 2, 1950 (unsent); Pang Xianzhi and Li Jie, "Mao Zedong he Kangmei yuanchao" (Mao Zedong and the Korean War), part 1, p. 39.

86. Jian Chen, Introduction to *Mao's China and the Cold War* (Chapel Hill: University of North Carolina Press, 2001), p. 13; see also Chen, *China's Road to the Korean War.*

87. Hu, *Hu Qiaomu huiyi Mao Zedong* (Hu Qiaomu Remembers Mao Zedong), p. 87.

88. In the debates regarding whether there was a "lost chance" in U.S.-China diplomacy in 1949–1950, Thomas J. Christensen counters Jian Chen's view, arguing that "just because there was no chance for friendship does not mean that there was no chance for peace." Put another way, "The tightness of the Sino-Soviet alliance still may have depended in large part on American actions." With the most recently declassified Chinese as well as Russian documents, this study concurs with Christensen's argument. Thomas J. Christensen, *Useful Adversaries* (Princeton, NJ: Princeton University Press, 1996).

7. Inducement versus Containment

1. With regard to Chinese intentions in the Vietnam War, most studies in the recent literature have focused on Beijing's Vietnam policy in the 1960s, emphasizing the crucial role of communist ideology in China's participation in the war. See, for example, Qiang Zhai's solid and comprehensive study, *China and the Vietnam War, 1950–1975* (Chapel Hill: University of North Carolina Press, 2000), which is based on declassified CCP documents in recent years, and Jian Chen's provocative views and forceful, concise presentation, *Mao's China and the Cold War* (Chapel Hill: University of North Carolina Press, 2001).

2. For a foundational work on U.S. wedge strategy toward the Sino-Soviet alliance and the role of racism in choosing China as America's main enemy, see Gordon H. Chang, *Friends and Enemies: The United States, China, and the Soviet Union, 1948–1972* (Stanford, CA: Stanford University Press, 1990); see also David Mayers's comprehensive study, *Cracking the Monolith: U.S. Policy against the Sino-Soviet Alliance, 1949–1955* (Baton Rouge: Louisiana State University Press, 1986). For the Eisenhower administration's China and East Asia policy, see the different perspectives in Warren I. Cohen and Akira Iriye, eds., *Great Powers in East Asia* (New York: Columbia University Press, 1990), and Richard Immerman, ed., *John Foster Dulles and the Diplomacy of the Cold War: A Reappraisal* (Princeton, NJ: Princeton University Press, 1990). For an insider's thoughtful account, see Robert Bowie and Richard Immerman, *Waging Peace: How Eisenhower Shaped an Enduring Cold War Strategy* (New York: Oxford University Press, 1998); see also Nancy Tucker's thoughtful study, *China Confidential: American Diplomats and Sino-American Relations,*

1945–1996 (New York: Columbia University Press, 2001). For thoughtful analyses of U.S.-China diplomacy in this period, combining historical account and international relations theory, see Thomas Christensen, *Useful Adversaries: Grand Strategy, Domestic Mobilization, and Sino-American Conflict, 1947–1958* (Princeton, NJ: Princeton University Press, 1996), and Shu Guang Zhang, *Deterrence and Strategic Culture: Chinese-American Confrontations, 1949–1958* (Ithaca, NY: Cornell University Press, 1992) and *Economic Cold War: America's Embargo against China and the Sino-Soviet Alliance, 1949–1963* (Stanford, CA: Stanford University Press, 2001).

3. "Briefing on Military Buildup in the Far East," March 24, 1955; U.S. House of Representatives, Committee on Foreign Affairs, Subcommittee on the Far East and the Pacific, in Committee on Foreign Affairs, ed., *U.S. Policy in the Far East,* part 2 (Selected Executive Session Hearings of the Committee, 1951–56) (historical series), vol. 18, pp. 491–492.

4. Letter, British governor of Hong Kong to the Office of Chinese Affairs, State Department, April 15, 1955, CA, box 21, NA.

5. Dwight D. Eisenhower to George Humphrey, March 27, 1957, DDE Diary, box 13, DDE. He also speculated on whether Russia and China were natural allies at all, since Soviet interests lay primarily in Europe and the Middle East rather than in East Asia. See Robert Donovan, *Eisenhower: The Inside Story* (New York: Harper, 1956), p. 132.

6. As Schwartz observed, before the Tito split, "the theory of people's democracy had first been elaborated as a theoretical framework for the Soviet-imposed regimes in Eastern Europe. These regimes are presumably coalition regimes made up of bourgeois, peasant and proletarian elements under proletarian hegemony. Their forms of government differed from the Soviet form and they still had many 'bourgeois democratic tasks' to perform."

7. Benjamin Schwartz, "Some Ideological Aspects of Sino-Soviet Relations," State Department working paper, February 14, 1956, CA box 22, NA.

8. Memo, Robert McClintock, "Review U.S. China Policy: A Pacific Settlement?" December 31, 1957; *Foreign Relations of the United States, 1955–1957,* vol. 3: *China* (Washington, DC: U.S. Government Printing Office, 1986), pp. 662–663.

9. DDE Diary, May 1953; DDE.

10. Minutes of cabinet meetings, January 12, 1953; see also Minutes of cabinet meetings, March 10, 1953; April 2, 1954, microfilm, MSU Library.

11. DDE Diary, July 1953, DDE. Like George Marshall and George Kennan, he did not believe that the Soviet Union was going to launch an atomic attack against the West or the United States in the near future. He was convinced that the Soviets, just like the Americans, did not want war in the nuclear age. He was thus angry with the call from the Republican Right for a "preventive war" against the Soviet bloc.

12. National Security Council series, NSC 68, NA. To reduce defense expen-

ditures, Eisenhower focused on the military buildup of nuclear weaponry, or the capability of "massive retaliation," rather than on the military buildup of both nuclear and conventional forces.

13. JFD Papers, White House Memo Series, Dwight D. Eisenhower re U.S. foreign policy, April 30, 1953, box 8, DDE. After the outbreak of the Korean War, the emphasis on national security between 1950 and 1953 was directed toward building up the military strength of the United States and its allies at a rapid rate, "to a state of readiness on a specified D-day on the premise that at such time the West should be ready to meet the greatest threat of aggression by the Soviets." Truman's foreign economic policy was thus characterized in large part by programs giving huge amounts of U.S. financial aid to support the establishment of military strength in Western countries. It was assumed that the United States had no choice but to build up Western military defense around the Russian and Chinese land mass as quickly as possible, whatever the cost financially to the United States.

14. Eisenhower to John Foster Dulles, memo, September 8, 1953, Eisenhower Papers, Ann Whitman File, International Series, box 33, DDE.

15. DDE Diary, entry for July 2, 1953, Eisenhower Papers, Ann Whitman File, Eisenhower Diary Series, box 9, DDE.

16. Letter, Dwight D. Eisenhower to Walter Judd, March 6, 1955, DDE Papers, Diary Series, box 4, DDE; Donovan, *Eisenhower*, p. 131; letter, Dwight D. Eisenhower to John Foster Dulles, September 7, 1954; DDE Papers, Dulles series, box 8, DDE.

17. Letter, Dwight D. Eisenhower to John Foster Dulles, DDE Papers, Dulles series, box 8, September 7, 1954, DDE.

18. Conversation, Eisenhower with Randall, October 2, 1956, DDE Papers, White House Memo series, box 12, DDE.

19. Letter, Eisenhower to Dulles, September 20, 1953, Eisenhower Papers, Ann Whitman File, Dulles-Herter Series, box 1, DDE.

20. Donovan, *Eisenhower*, p. 89.

21. Walter S. Robertson, "The Problem of Peace in the Far East," address made before the Virginia Bar Association August 3, 1956, *Department of State Bulletin*, August 13, 1956, pp. 265–266.

22. Walter Robertson, "The Growing Partnership among Free Nations," speech at the Chamber of Commerce of Greater Philadelphia, PA, January 13, 1955, *Department of State Bulletin*, January 24, 1955, pp. 127–128.

23. Memo, "U.S. Policy toward Taiwan," the Office of Chinese Affairs, November 21, 1956, CA box 18, NA; Kenneth T. Young Jr., "The Challenge of Asia to United States Policy," address at the forum of the School of International Relations, University of Southern California, August 13, *Department of State Bulletin*, August 27, 1956, p. 347.

24. "National Intelligence Estimate: Chinese Communist Capabilities and Probable Course of Action throughout 1960" (NIE 13–56), January 5,

1956, in *Foreign Relations of the United States, 1955–1957,* vol. 3: *China,* pp. 234–237; Allen Dulles, "The Communists Also Have Their Problems," September 19, 1957, *Department of State Bulletin,* October–December 1957, p. 643.

25. National Intelligence Estimate (NIE 13–56), January 5, 1956; NIE 13–57, March 19, 1957; and NIE 13–2–57, December 3, 1957; *Foreign Relations of the United States, 1955–1957,* vol. 3: *China,* pp. 498, 651.

26. Walter Robertson, "The Power Struggle in the Far East," address at the National War College, August 28, 1956, CA, box 15, NA.

27. Ibid.; "National Intelligence Estimate," p. 251.

28. John Foster Dulles, memo of conversation with Dwight D. Eisenhower re China, June 14, 1955, Dulles Papers, Memo series, box 1, DDE.

29. Dulles's China papers, October 27, 1954, Dulles Papers, White House Series, box 2, DDE.

30. John Foster Dulles, "An Estimate of Chinese Communist Intentions," speech before the Advertising Club of New York in New York City, March 21, 1955, on the occasion of the award to Dulles of the club's Bronze Plaque of Achievement, *Department of State Bulletin,* April 4, 1955, pp. 551–552.

31. Leonard Mosley, *Dulles: A Biography of Eleanor, Allen, and John Foster Dulles and Their Family Network* (New York: Dial Press/James Wade, 1978), p. 437.

32. Ibid. This was part of Dulles's instruction to the American Ambassador to Indonesia. Dulles told him, "As a matter of our general policies, do not tie yourself irrevocably to a policy of preserving the unity of Indonesia. The important thing is that we help Indonesia to the extent that they will allow us to resist any outside influence, especially Communism."

33. Walter Robertson, "The Growing Partnership among Free Nations," speech at the Chamber of Commerce of Greater Philadelphia, January 13, 1955; *Department of State Bulletin,* January 24, 1955, p. 128.

34. Memo re Economic Defense Policy and Program, January 21, 1955, Council on Foreign Economic Policy (CFEP) records, policy papers series, box 12, CFEP 501/1, DDE.

35. Naval Intelligence Agency Report re China trade controls, March 16, 1955, State Department Decimal File 563.21/7107923, RG59, NA.

36. Record of NSC, February 6, 1954; 738.21/5–1954, FE memo re China policy May 19, 1954, State Department Decimal File, RG59, NA.

37. Memo of conversation with John Foster Dulles, August 7, 1956, C. D. Jackson Papers, box 56, DDE.

38. Ibid.

39. Dulles's China Papers, May 24, 1956; Dulles Papers, White House Series, box 5, DDE.

40. Robertson, "The Power Struggle in the Far East."

41. Dispatch re Taiwan situation, from American Embassy in Taiwan to the

State Department, April 2, 1955, State Department Decimal File, 401.62, box 2549, NA.

42. Memo, Walter P. McConaughy of CA to Mr. Robertson and Mr. Tyson of FE, re status report on EDAC Review of U.S. policy on COCOM and CHINCOM Controls, August 24, 1956, CA, box 7, NA.

43. Ibid.

44. Walter Robertson, "The Problem of Peace in the Far East," *Department of State Bulletin,* August 1956, pp. 264–269.

45. Robertson, "The Power Struggle in the Far East."

46. Walter S. Robertson, "Progress in Free Viet-Nam," *Department of State Bulletin,* June 11, 1956, p. 972.

47. David Halberstam, *The Fifties* (New York: Villard Books, 1993), p. 398.

48. John Foster Dulles, confidential testimony at congressional hearing, executive session, House Committee on Foreign Affairs, July 21, 1954, in U.S. House of Representatives, Committee on Foreign Affairs, ed., *U.S. Policy in the Far East,* part 2 (Selected Executive Session Hearings of the Committee, 1951–56) (historical series), pp. 168–169.

49. John Foster Dulles, "The Cost of Peace," *Department of State Bulletin,* June 18, 1956, p. 1000.

50. Walter Robertson, "The Problem of Peace in the Far East," *Department of State Bulletin,* August 13, 1956, p. 268.

51. John Foster Dulles, "Principles in Foreign Policy," *Department of State Bulletin,* April 25, 1955, pp. 671–674; Robertson, "The Problems of Peace in the Far East," p. 268. In this article, Robertson quoted Dulles to make his point.

52. Memorandum, Ralph N. Clough to Walter Robertson, re China trade control differential and related problems, August 28, 1956. CA, box 7, NA.

53. For thoughtful studies of U.S. policy toward Japan in this period, see Roger Buckley, *U.S.-Japan Alliance Diplomacy, 1945–1990* (Cambridge: Cambridge University Press, 1992), and Sayuri Shimizu, *Creating People of Plenty: The United States and Japan's Economic Alternatives, 1950–1960* (Kent, OH: Kent State University Press, 2001).

54. Memo re recent development and future prospects of Japanese trade with Communist China, April 15, 1955, State Department, Office of Intelligence Research, no. 6649, NA.

55. "New Cabinet Must Answer Demand for Trade with Red China," *Jukogyo Shimbun* (Heavy Industries Newspaper), April 29, 1953, State Department, Office of Intelligence Research, no. 4901, NA.

56. Memo re magazine articles on China trade, Foreign Service Dispatch, American Embassy, Tokyo, March 6, 1953, Decimal File 493.94/3–653, NA.

57. Memo re views of leaders of recent Diet-Industry Trade Mission to Peking, January 5, 1954, Decimal File 493.9431/1–554, NA.

58. Li Enmin, *Zhongri minjian jingji waiju, 1945–1972* (Sino-Japanese Non-

Governmental Economic Diplomacy) (Beijing: Remin chubanshe, 1997), pp. 177–189.

59. State Department OIS Report re Foreign Minister Shigemitsui visit, August 23, 1955, OIS No. 5231, NA.

60. JFD Papers, White House Memo Series, Memo re conversation with DDE, November 8, 1953, DDE.

61. Memo re urgency of tariff negotiations to increase Japan's trade, June 18, 1954, State Department Decimal File 511.21/6–1854, NA.

62. Minutes of cabinet meeting, December 5, 1953.

63. Memo, Assistant Secretary Lothair Teebor to Secretary Weeks re domestic industries claiming hardship or threats of hardship because of competition of Japanese imports, July 9, 1954, Commerce Department Decimal File no. 529.63, R640 (366), NA. For instance, according to this memo, in the cotton textile industry, because of the competition from Japanese products, "total employment has declined from 1,252,000 in 1947 to 982,000 in April 1954." In the handmade glass industry, because of the competition, "employment has declined nearly 40% since 1947." The situation became more serious since "in many instances entire communities are dependent upon the Handmade Glassware Industry."

64. Letter, John Foster Dulles to Dodge, July 29, 1954, JFD Papers, Correspondence series, box 6, DDE.

65. Memo of conversation with Eisenhower, March 8, 1954, JFD Papers, White House memo series, box 10, DDE.

66. Letter, John Foster Dulles to Jackson, May 5, 1954, JFD Papers, Correspondence Series, box 7, DDE.

67. Memo re Japanese situation, May 9, 1954 and June 2, 1954, State Department Foreign Service Dispatch, American Embassy, Tokyo, NA.

68. Minutes of cabinet meeting, July 29, 1954, and August 4, 1954.

69. NSC 5429/5, "U.S. Policy toward Far East," November 26, 1954, NA. The NSC claimed, "It would be reasonable to meet the Japanese requests," because "Communist China represents a nearby export market and source of raw materials," because "availability of a Communist Chinese market might ease the pressure of Japanese exports on Free World markets," and because "U.S. expenditures in Japan are of a temporary nature."

70. Record of NSC, August 20, 1954, NA.

71. John Lunaid, *Great Britain and China* (London, 1950), pp. 92–94; Walter Z. Laqueur, *Great Britain and the Rise of Chinese Communists* (London, 1959), p. 162; Michael Lindon, *Three Views of China* (London, 1950), p. 92. For a thoughtful discussion of British response to the rise of the PRC, see Edwin W. Martin, *Divided Counsel: The Anglo-American Response to Communist Victory in China* (Lexington: University Press of Kentucky, 1986), pp. 63–72, 86–93; and Qiang Zhai, *The Dragon, the Lion & the Eagle: Chinese-British-American Relations, 1948–1958* (Kent, OH: Kent State University Press, 1994).

72. House of Commons, vol. 204, column 25, February 6, 1954.

73. *Foreign Relations of the United States, 1952–1954,* vol. 7: *Germany and Austria* (Washington, DC: U.S. Government Printing Office, 1986), p. 1039.

74. Warren Steele, *Great Britain and the People's Republic of China (1949–1955)* (London, 1957), pp. 167–178.

75. *South China Morning Daily* (Hong Kong), November 20, 1954.

76. House of Lords, *Hansard,* vol. 210, column 72, December 4, 1954. The Hong Kong and Shanghai Banking Corporation had been especially critical of the extension to Hong Kong of the Korean War controls. It was argued that China trade controls had disrupted contracts already negotiated, produced a good deal of uncertainty and confusion, upset the industry of the colony by depriving it of raw materials, and jeopardized the livelihood of workers and the functions of the port. (*South China Morning Daily* [Hong Kong], April 6, 1954.)

77. House of Lords, *Hansard,* vol. 201, column 32, September 9, 1954.

78. House of Commons, vol. 200, column 26–29, February 1954.

79. House of Lords, vol. 218, column 19, June 30, 1956.

80. House of Commons, vol. 200, column 24, March 8, 1954.

81. Congressional Record. Debates of the 81st Congress, Second Session 248825–46092, "Results of Questionnaire Mailed to First Congressional District of Iowa." The occupations listed by those replying were as follows: Farmer (1,039); Labor (1,149); Business (735); Professional (487); White Collar (733); Miscellaneous (777).

82. Letter, Walter Judd to Eisenhower, March 15, 1955; DDE Papers, Diary Series, box 2, DDE.

83. Letter, Calvitt Clarke to John Foster Dulles, December 8, 1953, State Department Decimal File 511.67/12–0853, NA.

84. Dulles Papers, White House Memo Series, box 1. Memo of dinner with Sir Winston Churchill, April 12, 1954. Churchill commented on Knowland's threat: "This is certainly not a proper basis for a good relationship."

85. *Manchester Guardian,* May 6, 1953.

86. DDE Diary, February 18, 1956; DDE Papers, Diary series, box 45; Letter, Dwight D. Eisenhower to David Eisenhower, August 15, 1958; DDE Papers, Confidential File, box 62, DDE.

87. Letter, Henry Cabot Lodge Jr., to John Foster Dulles, February 17, 1954, State Department Decimal File 493.009/2–1754, NA.

88. Letter, R. V. Hennes to Smith, February 20, 1954; State Department Decimal File 493.009/2–2054, NA.

89. Letter, Dulles to Lodge, February 27, 1954; State Department Decimal File 493.009/2–2754, NA.

90. Harold Stassen's memo re Mutual Security bill in Congress, April 8, 1954, State Department Decimal File, 493.009/4–0854, NA.

91. Memo re British position with respect to the China Differential, February 4, 1955, CA, box 5, NA.

92. Commerce Department, Central Decimal File 257.11/4–556, NA. Secretary

Weeks's memo re China trade control, April 5, 1956, NA. The Commerce Department pointed out that this had already caused grave troubles for certain U.S. industries. For instance, the American Brush Manufacturers Association protested that while "the prohibition of trade with China keeps hog bristle that is needed for the manufacture of the best brushes out of this country, brushes which are made of China hog bristles are imported into the U.S. from England." With the better and cheaper Chinese hog bristles, British brushes were easily "underselling the American brush market." The association complained bitterly, "We are now living under the specter of economic ruin." (Letter, the American Brush Manufacturers' Association to Secretary Weeks, February 5, 1954, Commerce Department Decimal File 257.11/2–554, NA.)

93. Memo re China Differential, August 23, 1955; OSD, Defense-Executive Office Central Decimal Files, GR 330, box 18. NA.

94. Randall Report re Randall trip to Europe, August 9, 1956, CFEP Records, 1954–1961, Policy Papers Series, box 12. Memo re China Defferential, by Winthrop Brown, June 3, 1956; State Department Foreign Service Dispatch, American Embassy, London, CA, box 6, NA.

95. Letter, John Foster Dulles to Radford, Chairman of JCS, April 8, 1956, JFD Papers, Correspondence series, box 27, DDE. JFD policy paper re U.S. national security, September 5, 1955; JFD Papers, General Correspondence series, box 29, DDE. For Dulles, to ask U.S. allies to apply the China Differential was "a political decision," and he was "not prepared to ask the allies for such a decision."

96. NSC 5429/4, September 15, 1955, White House Office, Office of the Special Assistant for National Security Affairs, NSC Series, Policy Papers Subseries, box 13, DDE. JFD Papers, White House Memo Series, Dulles Memo of conversation with DDE, December 8, 1955, DDE. CFEP Record, 1954–61, Policy Papers series, box 9, memo re U.S. position at Eisenhower-Eden talks, December 28, 1955, DDE.

97. Memo re Eisenhower-Eden talks, January 31–February 1, 1956, DDE Papers, International series, box 27, DDE.

98. The Eisenhower-Eden talks were held January 31–February 1, 1956; see *New York Times*, February 3, 1956.

99. See, for instance, "Trade with Red China: It's a Choice of Two Risks," *Detroit Free Press*, February 3, 1956.

100. *New York Daily News*, February 5, 1956.

101. "National Public Opinion re East-West trade and China trade controls," February 1956, CA, box 6, NA.

102. Congressional Record of February 23, 1956, p. 2771, Senator McClellan speech re East-West trade and China trade controls.

103. DDE Papers, Legislative series, box 6, Eisenhower talks with legislative leaders, April 18, 1956, DDE.

104. Congressional Record of April 5, 1956, p. 8291, Senator McClellan speech re mutural security program.

105. David Lawrence, "Easing of Red Trade Bans Called Peril to Aid Plans," *New York Herald Tribune*, March 5, 1956.

106. DDE Papers, Legislative series, box 31, Eisenhower talks with legislative leaders, April 2, 1956, DDE.

107. DDE Papers, Legislative series, box 32, Eisenhower talks with legislative leaders, March 5, 1957, DDE.

108. Memo, Walter Robertson to Secretary Dulles, re China trade controls, May 6, 1956, CA, box 7, NA.

109. Memo of conversation with Dwight D. Eisenhower, May 27, 1956, and May 28, 1956, JFD Papers, White House Memo series, box 19, DDE.

110. CFEP 501/11, July 23, 1956, Policy Papers series, CFEP Records, 1953–61, box 8, DDE.

111. Memo, Walter Robertson to Secretary Dulles, re China trade controls, May 6, 1956, CA, box 6, NA. EDAC proposal re China Differential, May 23, 1956, CFEP Records, 1954–61, Policy Paper Series, box 19, DDE.

112. Memo Dwight D. Eisenhower re China trade controls, January 2, 1957, DDE Papers, Confidential File, box 63, DDE.

113. Memo re modification of China trade control system, CFEP Records, 1954–61, Policy Paper series, box 8, DDE.

114. Henry Varg, "U.S. New Embargo Policy," *Economist*, May 2, 1957.

115. Letter from Foreign Minister Lloyd to Secretary of State Dulles, May 15, 1957, JFD Papers, Correspondence series, box 29, DDE.

116. Eisenhower re China trade controls, May 16, 1957, DDE Papers, Confidential file, Box 63, DDE.

117. Harold Macmillan, *Riding the Storm*, pp. 317–318.

118. Letter, Eisenhower to Macmillan, May 28, 1957, DDE Papers, Confidential file, box 67, DDE.

119. Memo re British decision, June 2, 1957, OSD, Defense-Executive Office Central Decimal Files GR 335, box 18, NA.

120. Radford memo re "limited sanction," June 3, 1957, JCS Record, Admiral Radford File GR 981, box 25, NA.

121. Eisenhower re British elimination of China diffential at the news conference of June 5, 1957, DDE papers, memo series, box 59, DDE.

122. Harold Macmillan, *Riding the Storm*, p. 320.

123. With regard to Canada's pressure for relaxation of the China embargo in 1957, see Simei Qing, "Changes in Western Embargo Policy toward China, 1954–1958," in Warren I. Cohen and Akira Iriye, eds., *The Great Powers in East Asia* (New York: Columbia University Press, 1990).

124. CFEP Records, 1953–1961, Policy Papers Series, CFEP 557/1, memo re "study of all aspects of policy on U.S. trade with Communist China," August 13, 1957, DDE.

125. Walter Robertson, "Meeting the Threat of Communism in the Far East," *Department of State Bulletin*, February 25, 1957, pp. 295–299.

126. John Foster Dulles, "Our Policy toward Communism in China," speech at

the international convention of Lions International, San Francisco, June 28, 1957, *Department of State Bulletin,* July 15, 1957, pp. 94–95.

127. Eleanor Lansing Dulles, *John Foster Dulles: The Last Year,* foreword by Dwight D. Eisenhower (New York: Harcourt, Brace & World, 1963), pp. 166–184.

128. Halberstam, *The Fifties,* p. 410; Townsend Hoopes, *The Devil and John Foster Dulles* (Boston: Little, Brown, 1973), pp. 403–404; Mosley, *Dulles,* pp. 219–315.

129. When the news appeared in the newspapers that the Eisenhower administration agreed to eliminate the China Differential at the multilateral level, Congress was disturbed again. The China lobby on the Hill was determined to hold out on the U.S. bilateral China Differential. In the Senate, William Knowland claimed that he felt "extremely disappointed" at what the British had done, and he asked what the administration had in mind regarding the bilateral embargo. Secretary Dulles assured him that the United States would hold out, despite its concessions to the allies. In the House, Representative Glenard Lipscomb (R-CA) delivered strong protests to the State Department and asked for a congressional probe. He argued on the House floor in July 1958, "We should never for a moment forget that Communist trade is dedicated to one thing—the strengthening of the Communist strangle-hold over all the people it can manage to trap in its ideological snare. Any economic gains that might accrue to countries of the free world through trade with the Communists are bound to be illusory and short-lived." In November 1958, a House subcommittee left for East Asia to investigate reports that "strategic goods shipped to U.S. allies in the Far East were being consigned to Communist China." DDE Papers, Legislative series, DDE talks with Legislative leaders, March 5, 1958, box 12, DDE.

130. DDE Papers, Legislative Series, June 4, 1958, box 14, DDE.

131. *New York Times,* November 19, 1958.

132. DDE Diary, July 12, 1958, July 14, 1958, and July 16, 1958, DDE Papers, Diary series, box 49, DDE.

133. Stephen E. Ambrose, *Eisenhower: The President* (New York: Simon and Schuster, 1984), pp. 214–245.

134. In 1959 and 1960, when the CCP launched the commune campaign and suffered economic setbacks, Eisenhower became increasingly interested in Chiang Kai-shek's prediction that "there would be disintegration within Communist China" and that "in the ensuing chaos," the KMT could be in a position, with American support, "to move in and take over." The president thought that might indeed be "a possibility." As long as the possibility existed, it was more important to give "full support" to the Nationalist government in Taiwan. See Gordon Gray memo, September 12, 1958, White House, Presidential Staff Secretary File, DDE.

135. Quoted from Chang, *Friends and Enemies,* pp. 170–172.

136. Ibid., p. 172.
137. Memo re the Herter Doctrine, Marshall Green to J. Graham Parsons, Far Eastern Bureau, October 16, 1959, Assistant Secretary of State File 667/1, NA.
138. Ibid.
139. Ibid.
140. Memo, "A New Approach to Our China Policy Objectives," J. Graham Parsons of Far Eastern Bureau to the Secretary of State Designate, December 28, 1960, Assistant Secretary of State File 611.93/12–2860, NA.

8. The Foundation of New China

1. CCP Central Committee's circular, "To Focus on Urban Cities in Our Future Tasks," February 25, 1948, which was drafted by Mao. CCP Files, Economic Policy Section, 1945–1950, CAC, Beijing.
2. Zhou Enlai's speech, September 11, 1953, in *Zhou Enlai jingji wenxuan* (Selected Works of Zhou Enlai on Economics) (Beijing: Zhongyang wenxian chubanshe, 1993), pp. 151–152.
3. Mao, "To Focus on Urban Cities in Our Future Tasks."
4. Most American scholars in Chinese studies agree that beginning in late 1955, particularly after 1957, there emerged two conflicting approaches to China's economic development within the CCP leadership. In their studies, these different blueprints are categorized either as "statist-populist tension" or "market–central planning contention." In the argument of "statist-populist tension," Zhou Enlai, Liu Shaoqi, and Chen Yun were considered state builders, whereas "Mao embodied a populist commitment." In the argument of "market–central planning contention," in contrast, Zhou and Chen were regarded as market reformers, rather than state builders; and Mao became the advocate of "central planning," obsessed with control and order, rather than the populist, preoccupied with continuous revolution. Moreover, most China scholars agree that if after the mid-1950s there were conflicting policy propositions within the CCP, from 1949 to 1955 there was a basic consensus on China's industrialization in Beijing that was to embrace the Stalinist model of command economy. This chapter attempts to transcend both the statist-populist tension and the market-planning contention, and to view it from a different perspective.
5. Mao Zedong, *Selected Works of Mao Zedong*, vol. 2 (Beijing: Foreign Language Press, 1960), p. 669.
6. *Selected Works of Zhou Enlai*, vol. 1 (Beijing: Renmin chubanshe, 1984), pp. 397–404.
7. Report, Bo Yipo to the CCP Central Committee, April 19, 1948; CCP files, economic policy section, 1945–1950, CAC.
8. Bo quoted some entrepreneurs as complaining that "to hire a worker these days is to invite my own elderly father into my house." He also wrote that

the CCP must "abolish party monopoly of merchant exchange in towns and cities." This party monopoly caused merchants to have to go through five different procedures to leave the town or city. They were "forced to pay a service fee to the local party authority." And many public security officers had "taken advantage of such abnormal procedures to acquire their own fortunes." Ibid.

9. Mao Zedong, "Comments on Bo Yipo's Report," April 29, 1948, CAC.

10. CCP North China Finance and Trade Conference, May 1948. Its resolution emphasized, "We must protect private entrepreneurs' property ownership, freedom of operation. . . . We must make serious efforts to promote the development of private industry and commerce in all Communist areas." CCP file, economic policy section, CAC, Beijing.

11. *Selected Works of Mao Zedong,* vol. 4, pp. 103–104.

12. Zhou Enlai, "On PCC Common Program—Its Draft and Characters," October 7, 1949, in *Zhou Enlai xuanji* (Selected Works of Zhou Enlai) (Beijing: Renmin chubanshe, 1984).

13. *Chen Yun wenxuan* (Selected Works of Chen Yun), vol. 2 (Beijing: Renmin chubanshe, 1984), pp. 254–270.

14. Liu Shaoqi, "Zai Tianjing ganbu huiyi shan de jianghua" (Speech at the Cadres' Meeting of Tianjin), April 24, 1949, in *Dangde Wenxian* (Party Documents) (Beijing: Zhongyang dangan guan, Summer 1993), pp. 8–9; also, Huang Xiaotong and Li Wenfang, "Liu Shaoqi 1949 nian Tianjin zhixing" (Liu Shaoqi's Trip to Tianjin in 1949), in *Dangde Wenxian* (Party Documents), pp. 18–19.

15. Liu, "Zai Tianjin ganbu huiyi shan de jianghua" (Speech at the Cadres' Meeting of Tianjin), pp. 4–5.

16. Deng Zihui, "Speech at the Rural Cadres' Working Conference," February 9, 1953, CCP Economic Policy Series, the 1950s, CAC, Beijing.

17. Deng Zihui, "Concluding Report at the Second National Agricultural Working Conference," April 1954, CCP Economic Policy Series, the 1950s, CAC, Beijing. Also see Deng Zihui, "Speech at the Fourth National Agricultural Working Conference," September 15, 1957, CAC, Beijing.

18. Liu Shaoqi, *On Cooperative Economy* (Beijing: Zhongguo caizhengjingji chubanshe, 1987), pp. 7–89.

19. Deng Zihui, "Concluding Report at the First National Agricultural Working Conference," April 1953, CAC, Beijing.

20. Liu, *On Cooperative Economy,* pp. 191–193.

21. Ibid., pp. 269–281.

22. Li Weihan, *Huiyi yu yanjiu* (Recollections and Reflections), vol. 2 (Beijing: Zhonggong dangshi ziliao chubanshe, 1986), pp. 748–755.

23. "The CCP North China Bureau's Report to the CCP Central Committee on Correcting Adventurism in the Campaigns to Organize Mutual Aids and Cooperatives and the CCP Central Committee's Instruction," October 4, 1953, CAC, Beijing; Jiang Boying, *The Biography of Deng Zihui* (Shanghai: Renmin chubanshe, 1988), pp. 305–312.

24. Huang Yuanlan, *Deng Zihui Zhuan* (The Biography of Deng Zhui) (Beijing: Zhongyang wenxian chubanshe, 1996), pp. 105–106.

25. "The Report of CCP Daming County Committee, Hopei Province," March 1953, CCP Economic Policy Series, the 1950s, CAC, Beijing.

26. "The CCP North China Bureau's Report to the CCP Central Committee on Correcting Adventurism in the Campaigns to Organize Mutual Aids and Cooperatives and the CCP Central Committee's Instruction," October 4, 1953, and January 19, 1955, CAC, Beijing.

27. *Zhou Enlai tongyi zhanxian wenxuan* (Selected Works of Zhou Enlai on the United Front) (Beijing: Renmin chubanshe, 1984), pp. 108–109.

28. Cao Yingwang, *Zhongguo de zongguanjia Zhou Enlai* (Zhou Enlai: China's Chief Housekeeper) (Beijing: Zhonggong dangshi chubanshe, 1996), p. 75; *Zhou Enlai jingji wenxuan* (Selected Works of Zhou Enlai on Economics), p. 137.

29. Xue Muqiao, *Xue Muqiao huiyi lu* (Xue Muqiao's Memoir) (Tianjin: Tianjin renmin chubanshe, 1996), pp. 221–222.

30. Su Zhongxian, "Shixi badade lilun yu shijian" (An Analysis of the Theory and Practice of the Eighth CCP's Congress), *Dangshi yanjiu ziliao* (Research Journal on Party Historical Documents), no. 10 (1997): 16.

31. *Chen Yun wenxuan* (Selected Works of Chen Yun), vol. 1, p. 13. He proposed that there be "three principal parts and three supplements" in the economy. "Private enterprise, free production, and free market," he argued, should be encouraged to complement the insufficiency of public enterprise and national planning. For instance, due to Chen's recommendation, the Dongan Market—one of Beijing's biggest shopping centers at the time—restored its "normal business" as it was before the "socialist transformation," when it comprised more than 100 private stores, each with a distinctive character, to meet consumers' different needs.

32. Liu Shaoqi, "Talks with Hunan Provincial Party Leaders," March 1957, in *Liu Shaoqi nianpu, 1898–1969* (The Chronicles of Liu Shaoqi, 1898–1969), vol. 2 (Beijing: Zhongyang wenxian chubanshe, 1996), pp. 352–384. Liu acknowledged that this would be a highly unpopular policy for the CCP's basic constituency—the working class. He thus recommended implementing it with the new workers first, before more drastic reform of the management of public enterprise could take place in the future.

33. "Zhou Enlai's Speech at the State Council Meeting," April 6, 1957, in *Zhou Enlai jingji wenxuan* (Selected Works of Zhou Enlai on Economics), p. 19.

34. *People's Daily* (Editorial), December 20, 1956.

35. "Mao Zedong tanhua, December 7, 1956" (Mao Zedong Conversations), in Su, "Shixi badade lilun yu shijian" (An Analysis of the Theory and Practice of the Eighth CCP's Congress), pp. 18–19.

36. *Selected Works of Liu Shaoqi*, vol. 2, p. 4.

37. Mao Zedong, "Speech at Provincial CCP Leaders' Meeting," July 31,

1955; and "Concluding Remarks at the Seventh CCP Congress of the Sixth Central Committee Meetings," September 1955.

38. *Tangshan Nongmin Bao* (Tangshan Farmers' Daily), April 30, 1955.

39. Mao Zedong, "Remarks on Tangshan Farmers' Daily," in *The High Tide of the Chinese Agricultural Socialist Construction* (Beijing: Renmin Chubanshe, 1956), pp. 8–9.

40. Mao Zedong, "Speech at the Expanded CCP Central Committee Meeting," July 31, 1955; in *Selected Works of Mao Zedong,* vol. 5, p. 101.

41. Zhou Enlai, *Zhou Enlai jingji wenxuan* (Selected Works of Zhou Enlai on Economics), pp. 233–241, 253–254, 278–286, 292–325; Bo Yibo, "Fan Maojin he bada de zhenque juece" (Anti-Rash Advance and the Correct Decision of the Eighth Party Congress), in *Ruogan zhongda juece yu shijian de huigu* (Reflections on Important Decisions and Events), vol. 1 (Beijing: Zhonggong zhongyang dangxiao chubanshe, 1997), pp. 521–561; Xue, *Xue Muqiao huiyi lu* (Xue Muqiao's Memoir), pp. 88, 211–252.

42. One month later, in November 1957, Mao's arguments seemed to be further validated by the Moscow Conference. Khrushchev claimed that the Soviet Union was capable of surpassing the United States in major industrial production in fifteen years. After the Moscow Conference, the Soviets launched a national campaign of "building the first communist society." Eastern European countries quickly followed suit and launched campaigns of industrial production competitions among factory workers.

43. Quan Yanchi, *Mao and Khrushchev* (Huhehaute: Neimonggu renmin chubanshe, 1998), pp. 97–100.

44. It is a system that provides working personnel and their dependents with the primary necessities of life.

45. Chen Jin, ed., *Mao Zedong dushu biji* (Mao Zedong's Reading Notes), vol. 1 (Guangzhou: Guangdong remin chubanshe, 1997), pp. 545–550.

46. Liu Minggang, "Dangde bada erci huiyi pingxi" (An Analysis of the Second Session of the Eighth Party Congress), *Dangshi yanjiu ziliao* (Research Journal on Party Historical Documents), no. 10 (1997). For Mao, many new inventions in science and technology in world history had come from the lower classes, who often had not had formal education and the best equipment. There was a "natural connection between those who were born humble, suffering a great deal and the spirit of daring to think, to act, and to engage in bold creations and inventions."

47. *People's Daily* report, "Chairman Mao Visited the New Commune," June 20, 1958. For Mao, through the "liberalized" enthusiasm and activism of the poor, China could march more rapidly into an "ideal society." In this ideal society, "there will be many communist communes in rural China. . . . Several rural communes will surround a city, to organize an even larger commune." Each of these communes should have its industry, agriculture, and university. In all these communes, "the unity between industry and

agriculture will be achieved; the distinction between cities and villages will be abolished." Many CCP leaders were thrilled by the prospect that "the utopian ideals of great utopian thinkers in human history will eventually be realized and surpassed."

48. *Nongye jitihua zhongyao wenjian huibian* (Important Documents on Agricultural Cooperative Movements), vol. 1 (Beijing: Renmin chubanshe, 1957), p. 249.

49. Chen Xuewei, "Dayuejin yundong shi mo" (The Origin and the End of the Great Leap Forward Campaign), in Qiu Shi, ed., *Gongheguo zhongda shijian he juece neimu* (The Inside Stories of Major Events and Policy-Making Process in the RPC Era), vol. 1 (Beijing: Zhongyang dangshi chubanshe, 1999), pp. 377–378.

50. *Jianguo yilai Mao Zedong wengao* (Mao Zedong Papers since the Establishment of the PRC), vol. 7, *January 1958–December 1958* (Beijing: Zhongyang wenxian chubanshe, 1992), pp. 503–525.

51. Mao Zedong, "Remarks on 'Resolutions of the People's Commune Campaigns," November and December 1958, in ibid., pp. 568–578.

52. Peng Dehuai, *Peng Dehuai zishu* (The Autobiography of Peng Dehuai) (Beijing: Renmin chubanshe, 1981), pp. 265–290; Huang Kecheng, *Huang Kecheng zishu* (The Autobiography of Huang Kecheng) (Beijing: Renmin chubanshe, 1994), pp. 248–270; Li Rui, *Mao Zedong de gongguo shifei* (The Assessments of Mao Zedong's Achievements and Wrongdoings) (Hong Kong: Tiandi dushu youxian gongsi, 1993), pp. 215–225.

53. Cao Yingwang, *Zhongguo de zongguanjia Zhou Enlai* (Zhou Enlai: China's Chief Housekeeper), pp. 16–17, 420–422, 468–469.

54. Xie Chuntao, *Lushan fengyun: 1959 Lushan huiyi jianshi* (Major Events on Lushan: The History of the Lushan Meeting in 1959) (Beijing: Zhongguo qingnian chubanshe, 1996), pp. 140–150.

55. Mao later remarked in private: "We intended to launch an anti-left adventurism campaign when going up Lushan; but we instead launched an antiright opportunism campaign when going down Lushan. This is called 'one may be wise all one's lifetime, but stupid at a crucial moment.'" Quoted from Cao Yingwang, *Zhongguo de zongguanjia Zhou Enlai* (Zhou Enlai: China's Chief Housekeeper), p. 468.

56. Kenneth Lieberthal, "The Great Leap Forward and the Split in the Yan'an Leadership, 1958–65," in Roderick MacFarquhar, ed., *The Politics of China: The Eras of Mao and Deng,* 2nd ed. (New York: Cambridge University Press, 1997), pp. 104, 110.

57. Mao Zedong's speech at the CCP Central Committee meeting, February 1960, in Zhong Zheming, "Mao Zedong tansuo shihe zhongguo guoqing de silu" (Mao Zedong's Search for a Special Type of Chinese Socialism Consistent with the Chinese Situations), in *Mao Zedong Baizhounian jinian* (In Memory of Mao Zedong's 100th Birthday), vol. 2 (Beijing: Zhongyang wenxian chubanshe, 1994), p. 52.

58. Liu Jianhui and Shi Lue, "60 niandaichu de jiuzuo" (The Anti-left Adventurism Campaigns in the Early 1960s), in Qiu, *Gongheguo zhongda shijian he juece neimu* (The Inside Story of Major Events and Policy-Making Process in the PRC History), vol. 1, pp. 451–470.

59. Did the Soviet model have any impact on Mao's radical approach? There have been different interpretations in the U.S. literature. Contrary to his private paper in the State Department file, Schwartz's public writings seem to stress the relevance of the Soviet model to Mao's nationalization and collectivization drive. Benjamin Schwartz, "Modernization and the Maoist Vision: Some Reflecting on Chinese Communist Goals," in Roderick MacFarquhar, ed., *China under Mao: Politics Takes Command* (Cambridge, MA: MIT Press, 1966). In contrast, both Schurmann and Meisner emphasize Mao's search for "a unique Chinese path" in his radical approach after the mid-1950s. Meisner argued that "collectivization in China was accomplished in a manner that stands in striking contrast" to its Soviet precedent. In the Stalinist model, cities rather than countryside, workers rather than peasants, were the first priority. Armed forces had to be sent from the cities to carry out a rural movement that became a virtual "civil war between town and countryside." Mao did claim that in the collectivization campaign "the Soviet Union's experience is our model." To Meisner, however, Mao simply "invoked the ideological authority of Moscow and Stalin to launch a very non-Stalinist mass movement—just as in the pre-1949 years he had hailed Stalin in public pronouncements while defying him in revolutionary practice."

60. *Selected Works of Zhou Enlai on the Untied Front* (Beijing: Renmin chubanshe, 1984), pp. 101–102.

61. Li Weihan, *Huiyi yu yanjiu* (Recollections and Reflections), vol. 2, p. 744. Gao accused Bo of betraying the Chinese working class because Bo had allegedly said that capitalist exploitation had played a "progressive role," which, as everyone at the meeting knew, was what Liu Shaoqi had said in Tianjin in 1949.

62. State Department Working Paper no. 3, CA, box 17, NA.

63. *Pravda*, October 7, 1955.

64. Shu Weikang, "The Gradual Tempo of China's Transitional Period," in *Xinhua Yuebao* (Monthly Gazette) (Beijing), October 1955. The article said, "In the Soviet Union and the people's democracies of southern and eastern Europe, capitalism is being eradicated by violent and forceful means. However, due to the concrete conditions of our country we are able to arrive at the same goal—the eradication of capitalism—by peaceful methods of redemption and socialist transformation."

65. Mao Zedong, "Lun shida guanxi" (On Ten Great Relationships), in *Jianguo yilai Mao Zedong wengao* (Mao Zedong Papers since the Establishment of the PRC), vol. 6 (Beijing: Zhongyang wenxian chubanshe, 1992), p. 82.

66. Ibid., pp. 82–110. Mao stressed, "The democratic management of cooperatives is very important." Indeed, "in our party's history, whenever there was too much centralization or too much decentralization, we suffered tremendous loss." Mao maintained, "We should realize that, to develop heavy industry and light industry, we need markets and raw materials; to reach this goal, we must promote local activism. . . . But now there are too many hands from above which stretch out to local levels, intervene in local affairs, thus the handling of local affairs by the local authorities becomes very difficult. Every day various ministries in Beijing give orders to provincial and municipal authorities; even though the Central Government and the State Council are never aware of these orders, local people regard all these orders as orders of the Central Government. They have to create superficial paper works to deal with bureaucrats, which, just like flood, become so overwhelming, which can almost crush these local authorities' abilities in managing local affairs."

67. In February 1957, Mao further argued that, the ratio of investment in heavy industry, light industry, and agriculture should be "substantially adjusted." The Soviet Union's ratio of investment was nine to one. "Herein lies a problem: the activism and spirit of the Soviet peasants is not high, and neither does the Soviet market flourish." Beginning in late 1958, Mao further proposed a major shift in state investment priorities: agriculture should rank the first, light industry the second, and heavy industry the third. Mao was convinced that, in comparison with the rate of industrial development of the Soviet Union, "the Chinese way may look a little slower in the short run, but will be a little faster in the long run." Mao Zedong, "On the Correct Handling of Contradictions among the People," February 27, 1957; see also Roderick MacFarquhar, Timothy Cheek, and Eugene Wu, eds., *The Secret Speeches of Chairman Mao: From the Hundred Flowers to the Great Leap Forward* (Cambridge, MA: Harvard University Press, 1989), pp. 185–189; and Mao Zedong, "Speech at Chendu Conference," March 10, 1958, in which Mao argued, "The market for our heavy industry is light industry and agriculture. Our domestic market is those hundreds of millions of Chinese people, among whom are 500 million peasants."

68. *Zhou Enlai jingji wenxuan* (Selected Works of Zhou Enlai on Economics), p. 419; also Zhou Enlai's conversation with the Polish ambassador to China, April 28, 1962, quoted from Cao Yingwang, *Zhonggong de zongguanjia—Zhou Enlai* (Zhou Enlai—China's Chief Housekeeper), pp. 107–108.

69. Mao Zedong, "Lun shida guanxi" (On Ten Great Relationships) in *Jianguo yilai Mao Zedong wengao* (Mao Zedong Papers since the Establishment of the PRC), vol. 6, p. 82.

70. Stalin's conversation with Liu Shaoqi and the CCP delegation, July 1949; Stalin's conversation with Zhou Enlai, September 1952; quoted from Shi Zhe, *Zai lishi juren shenbian: Shi Zhe huiyilu* (At the Side of History's

Giants: The Memoirs of Shi Zhe), rev. ed. (Beijing: Zhongyang wenxian chubanshe, 1995), pp. 416–417, 520–521.

71. Mao Zedong, "Wei yinfa Zhang Lu zhuan so fade piyu" (Remarks on the Distribution of the "Biography of Zhang Lu,"), December 7 and 10, 1958, in *Jianguo yilai Mao Zedong wengao* (Mao Zedong Papers since the Establishment of the PRC), vol. 7 (January–December 1958) (Beijing: Zhongyang wenxian chubanshe, 1992), pp. 627–630.

72. Hong Xiuquan, "Tianchao tianmu zhidu" (The Land System in the Heavenly Dynasty), quoted from Mou Anshi, *Taiping Tianguo* (The Taiping Rebellion) (Shanghai: Shanghai renmin chubanshe, 1959), pp. 110–111.

73. MacFarquhar et al., *The Secret Speeches of Chairman Mao,* pp. 15–16.

74. Mao Zedong, "Yao jiehe zhongguo shiji, yongxin du sanbian Stalin de *Sulian shehui zhuyi de jingji wenti*" (To Combine China's Indigenous Situation with Careful Readings of Stalin's Work *On Soviet Socialist Economy*), Mao's letter to the Central Committee, provincial, prefectural, and county party committees, November 9, 1958, in Zhengzhou; quoted from Chen Jin, ed., *Mao Zedong dushu biji* (Mao Zedong's Reading Notes), vol. 1 (Guangzhou: Guangdong renmin chubanshe, 1997), pp. 553–554.

75. Zhang Wentian, "Shehui zhuyi jingji rogan lilun wenti" (Certain Theoretical Issues on the Socialist Economy), August 1961, in *Zhang Wentian xuanji* (Selected Works of Zhang Wentian) (Beijing: Renmin chubanshe, 1985); pp. 519–521, 534–535.

76. *Zhou Enlai jingji wenxuan* (Selected Works of Zhou Enlai on Economics), pp. 151–152, 176.

77. Bo, *Ruogan zhongda juece yu shijian de huigu* (Reflections on Important Decisions and Events), vol. 1, pp. 340–341, 352–362.

78. *Zhou Enlai jingji wenxuan* (Selected Works of Zhou Enlai on Economics), pp. 319–321.

9. Mao's Magic Weapon

1. *Zhou Enlai nianpu, 1949–1976* (The Chronicles of Zhou Enlai, 1949–1976), vol. 1 (Beijing: Zhongyang wenxian chubanshe, 1997), pp. 1–19; John King Fairbank, *The Great Chinese Revolution, 1800–1985* (New York: Harper & Row, 1986), pp. 271–361.

2. *Zhonggong dangshi ziliao* (CCP Historical Documents), vol. 5 (Beijing: Zhongyang dangxiao chubanshe, 1988), p. 149.

3. Zhongyang wenxian yanjiushi, ed., *Liu Da Yi Lai* (After the Sixth Congress), vol. 2 (Beijing: Zhongyang wenxian chubanshe, 1988), p. 55. Wang Ming complained that in the region of Jinggang Mountains of Jiangxi province, which Mao had created after 1927, "most posts of the party leadership are still held by intellectuals." See *Zhong Gong Dang Shi Zi Liao* (CCP Historical Documents), vol. 6, p. 427.

4. *Selected Works of Zhou Enlai,* vol. 1 (Beijing: Foreign Language Press,

1981), pp. 10, 327–328. Also see *Liu Da Yi Lai* (After the Sixth Congress), p. 202.

5. Mao Zedong, "Recruit a Vast Number of Intellectuals," in *Selected Works of Mao Zedong*, vol. 2 (Beijing: Foreign Language Press, 1960), p. 726.

6. *Chen Yun Wenxuan* (The Selected Works of Chen Yun), vol. 1 (Beijing: Renmin chubanshe, 1984), p. 145.

7. Zhou Enlai, "To Build China into a Great, Socialist, Modernized Industrial Nation," September 23, 1954, in *Selected Works of Zhou Enlai*, vol. 2, p. 132.

8. Chen Yi, "Speech at the National Forum on Modern Drama, Opera and Children's Drama," March 6, 1962, Guangzhou, in Zhongyang dangxiao yanjiushi, ed., *Zhou Enlai and Art*, vol. 1 (Beijing: Press of Chinese Academy of Social Science, 1980), pp. 48–99, 288.

9. Mao Zedong, "Speech at the CCP Central Committee Meeting on Issues of Intellectuals," January 20, 1956; and Mao, "Concluding Remarks at the Meeting of Provincial and City CCP Secretaries," January 8, 1957.

10. Zhou Enlai, "Speech at the Forum on Literature and Art and Film Creations," June 19, 1961, in *Zhou Enlai and Art*, vol. 1, pp. 9–10.

11. Zhou Enlai, "Xinjiao de he buxinjiao de yao huxiangzunzhong" (Religious People and Non-believers Should Respect Each Other), May 30, 1956, in *Zhou Enlai tongyi zhanxian wenxuan* (Selected Works of Zhou Enlai on the United Front) (Beijing: Renmin chubanshe, 1984), pp. 309–312.

12. Zhou Enlai, "Construction and Unity," August 24, 1950, in *Selected Works of Zhou Enlai*, vol. 2, p. 21; "Speech at the Forum on Literature and Art and Film Creations," June 19, 1961, in *Zhou Enlai and Art*, vol. 1, pp. 9–10, 29.

13. Zhou, "The New Development of Our People's Democratic United Front," in *Selected Works of Zhou Enlai*, vol. 1, pp. 390, 544.

14. *Zhou Enlai on the United Front* (Beijing: Remin chubanshe, 1987), pp. 137–138, 207, 262, 350–351.

15. Liu Shaoqi, "Talk at the Conference of 7,000 Delegates," January 1962, in *Selected Works of Liu Shaoqi*, vol. 2 (Beijing: People's Press, 1982), pp. 402–403.

16. *Zhou Enlai on the United Front*, pp. 77–98. To make the supervision work, Zhou further suggested that beginning in 1957, the government officials come forward to answer people's deputies' questions and criticism at the People's Congress. If the government officials' reply could not satisfy the people's deputies, in-depth debates should follow. These in-depth debates should be open to the public.

17. Deng Zihui, "Talk at the Expanded Meeting of Central South General Trade Union Preparation Committee," July 1950. Also Liu Shaoqi, "The Internal Contradiction in the State Industry and the Basic Task of the Trade Union," May 1951, in *Selected Works of Liu Shaoqi*, vol. 2.

18. Zhou Enlai, "Changqigongcun, huxiangjiandu" (Long-Term Coexistence

and Mutual Supervision), April 24, 1957, in *Zhou Enlai tongyi zhanxian wenxuan* (Selected Works of Zhou Enlai on the United Front), pp. 347–352.

19. Mao Zedong, "Talks at the Meeting of Provincial and City CCP Secretaries," January 1957.

20. Mao Zedong, "Speech at the Hankou Conference," April 6, 1958.

21. Mao Zedong, "Speech at the Supreme State Council," January 28 and January 30, 1958.

22. Mao Zedong, "Speech at the Hangzhou Conference, CCP Shanghai Bureau," April 1957.

23. Bo Yibo, *Ruogan zhongda juece yu shijian de huigu* (Reflections on Important Decisions and Events), vol. 2 (Beijing: Zhonggong zhongyang dangxiao chubanshe, 1993), pp. 623–632.

24. Roderick MacFarquhar, *The Origins of the Cultural Revolution*, vol. 1: *Contradictions among the People, 1956–1957* (New York: Columbia University Press, 1974).

25. Mao Zedong, "Don't Prohibit Different Opinions Concerning Academic Issues," in *Jianguo yilai Mao Zedong wengao* (Mao Zedong Papers since the Establishment of the PRC), vol. 6 (Beijing: Zhongyang wenxian chubanshe, 1992), pp. 40–41.

26. Zhou Enlai, "Report on the Issues of Intellectuals," January 14, 1956; "The Key to Building Up a Great, Powerful Socialist Nation Lies in the Modernization of Science and Technology," January 29, 1963, in *Selected Works of Zhou Enlai*, vol. 2, pp. 181, 412–416.

27. Zhou Enlai, *Report on the Issues of Intellectuals*, January 14, 1956 (Beijing: Remin chubanshe, 1956).

28. Mao Zedong, "Lun shida guanxi" (On the Ten Great Relationships), in *Jianguo yilai Mao Zedong wengao* (Mao Zedong Papers since the Establishment of the PRC), vol. 6, pp. 82–110.

29. Mao Zedong, *Guanyu zhengque chuli renmin neibu maodun de wenti* (On Correctly Handling the Contradictions among the People) (Beijing: Renmin chubanshe, 1957).

30. Mao Zedong, "Speech at the National Conference on Propaganda Works and Intellectuals," March 12, 1957; *Jianguo yilai Mao Zedong wengao* (Mao Zedong Papers since the Establishment of the PRC), vol. 7 (Beijing: Zhongyang wenxian chubanshe, 1992), pp. 54–68.

31. Qiu Shi, ed., *Gongheguo zhongda shijian he juece neimu* (The Inside Stories of Major Events and Policy-Making Process in the PRC Era), vol. 1 (Beijing: Jingji ribao chubanshe, 1997), pp. 299–300.

32. Ibid., pp. 309–310.

33. Yang Jianye, *Ma Yingchu* (The Biography of Ma Yingchu) (Baoding, Hebei: Huashan wenyi chubanshe, 1997), pp. 146–156.

34. Ye Yongle, *Chenzhong de 1957* (The Heavy Year of 1957) (Nanchang, Jiangxi: Baihuazhou wenyi chubanshe, 1993), p. 68.

35. Ibid., pp. 6–7.

36. Chen Qitong, Chen Yading, Ma Hanbing, and Lu Le, "Our Opinions on Current Works of Art and Literature," *Renmin Ribao* (People's Daily), January 7, 1957.

37. *Liaoning Daily*, February 17, 1957; *Jilin Daily*, February 24, 1957; *Luda Daily*, February 28, 1957.

38. From January 8 to February 28, 1957, while it received more than twenty articles to rebut this article's arguments, the *People's Daily* did not publish any one of them. It was only after Mao's critique that it published a commentary, which "grudgingly" criticized this article. See Ye Yonglie, *Fan yiupai shimo* (The Origins of Antirightist Movement) (Qinghai: Renmin chubanshe, 1997), pp. 124–125.

39. Rod MacFarquhar, Tim Cheek, and Eugene Wu, eds., *The Secret Speeches of Chairman Mao: From the Hundred Flowers to the Great Leap Forward* (Cambridge, MA: Harvard University Press, 1989), pp. 173–174. Mao's ideas on the rectification campaign and the hundred flowers policy encountered strong opposition from the majority of CCP leaders and cadres at all levels. Roderick MacFarquhar, *The Origins of the Cultural Revolution*, vol. 1, pp. 169–260.

40. Bo, *Ruogan zhongda juece yu shijian de huigu* (Reflections on Important Decisions and Events), vol. 2 (Beijing: Zhonggong zhongyang dangxiao chubanshe, 1993), pp. 575–577.

41. Deng Xiaoping, "Jinhou de zhuyaorenwu shi gaojianshe" (The Major Task in the Future Is Economic Reconstruction), April 8, 1957, in Zhongyang wenxian bianji weiyuan hui, ed., *Deng Xiaoping wenxuan* (Selected Works of Deng Xiaoping), vol. 1 (Beijing: Renmin chubanshe, 1994), pp. 261–269.

42. Bo, *Ruogan zhongda juece yu shijian de huigu* (Reflections on Important Decisions and Events), vol. 2, pp. 576–578.

43. Benjamin I. Schwartz, "Thoughts on the Late Mao: Between Total Redemption and Utter Frustration," in MacFarquhar, Cheek, and Wu, *Secret Speeches of Chairman Mao*, pp. 27–28.

44. Deng Xiaoping, "Gongchandang yao jieshou jiandu" (The Communist Party Must Receive Supervision), April 8, 1957, in *Deng Xiaoping wenxuan* (Selected Works of Deng Xiaoping), vol. 1, pp. 270–274.

45. Mao Zedong, "Shiqing zhengzai qibianhua" (Situation Is Now Changing), *Jianguo yilai Mao Zedong wengao* (Mao Zedong Papers since the Establishment of the PRC), vol. 6, pp. 469–475.

46. Mao emphasized that "the great majority of the capitalists" had indeed been "really good" to the CCP. The major headache was "the rightists among the democratic parties and university professors."

47. *Jianguo yilai Mao Zedong wengao* (Mao Zedong Papers since the Establishment of the PRC), vol. 6, p. 538.

48. Ibid., pp. 537–538; Mao Zedong, "CCP Central Committee Circular on the Increase of the Number of the Rightists," July 9, 1957.

49. CCP Central Committee circular on not designating rightists among workers and peasants, September 4, 1957; CCP circular on the criteria for designating rightists, October 15, 1957. Both in Chen Xuewei, "1957 nian xiaji fengyun" (The Summer Storm of 1957), in Qiu, *Gongheguo zhongda shijian he juece neimu* (The Inside Stories of Major Events and Policy-Making Process in the PRC Era), vol. 1, p. 320.

50. While the CCP leadership insisted that the major method in dealing with the "bourgeois rightists" should be "reeducation," not "punishment under the law," local cadres punished them severely according to their own will. Many "rightists" soon lost their jobs in the universities, and this persisted for the following three decades.

51. Mao Zedong, "Suggestions on taking off the rightist caps by stages and in groups and on amnesty of criminals," letter to Liu Shaoqi, August 24, 1959, and September 14, 1959, in *Jiangguo yilai Mao Zedong wengao* (Mao Zedong Papers since the Establishment of the PRC), vol. 8 (Beijing: Zhongyang wenxian chubanshe, 1993), pp. 475–477.

52. *People's Daily,* June 18, 1957.

53. Yang, *Ma Yingchu* (The Biography of Ma Yingchu), pp. 156–172.

54. Zhou Enlai, "Speech at the National Forum on Literature and Art and Creations of Story Films," June 19, 1961; in *Zhou Enlai and Art,* p. 10.

55. Li Zheng, *The Biography of Chen Yi* (Beijing: Dangdai zhongguo chubanshe, 1991), p. 531.

56. Chen Yi, "Talks at Scientists' Meeting in Guangzhou" and "Talks at National Playwrights Convention in Guangzhou," in Liu Shuan, ed., *Chen Yi nianpu* (Chronicle of Chen Yi), vol. 2 (Beijing: Renmin chubanshe, 1995), p. 911; and He Xiaolu, *Yuanshuai waijiaolia* (Marshal Diplomat) (Beijing: Jiefangjunwenyi chubanshe, 1985), pp. 52–68.

57. Ibid., pp. 79–82; Nan Xizhou, *The Life of Zhou Enlai* (Beijing: Zhongguo qingnian chubanshe, 1987), p. 508.

58. Mikhail Zimyanin, "The Political, Economic, and International Standing of the PRC," memo, from the Foreign Ministry Far Eastern Department to Andrei Gromyko, Soviet Foreign Minister, September 15, 1959; report no. 860-dv, TsKhSD; in *CWIHP Bulletin,* no. 6–7, trans. and introduction by Mark Kramer.

59. *Khrushchev Remembers: The Last Testament,* trans. and ed. Strobe Talbott (Boston: Little, Brown and Company, 1974), pp. 270–273, 279, 311; also *Khrushchev Remembers,* trans. and ed. Strobe Talbott (Boston: Little, Brown and Company, 1970), pp. 466–467.

60. Jin Fu, *Wenge qian shinian de zhongguo* (The Ten Years before the Cultural Revolution) (Beijing: Zhonggong dangshi chubanshe, 1998), pp. 58–60.

61. Li Yueran, "Mao Zedong he sulian zhuhua dashi de tanhua" (Mao Zedong's Conversations with the Soviet Ambassador), *Dangshi yanjiu zilao,* no. 3 (1997).

62. Mao Zedong, "Suggested revisions of the CC report at the Eighth Party

Congress," August 21, 1956, in *Jianguo yilai Mao Zedong wengao* (Mao Zedong Papers since the Establishment of the PRC), vol. 6, p. 143.

63. Ibid.

64. Ibid.

65. Bo, *Ruogan zhongda juece yu shijian de huigu* (Reflections on Important Decisions and Events), vol. 1, pp. 517–519.

66. Mao Zedong, summary at the Third Plenum of the Eighth Central Committee, October 9, 1957; quoted from Bo Yibo, *Ruogan zhongda juece yu shijian de huigu* (Reflections on Important Decisions and Events), vol. 2, p. 629.

67. Quan Yanchi, *Mao and Khrushchev* (Huhehaote: Neimonggu renmin chubanshe, 1998), pp. 120–121.

68. Chen Yi, "Speech at the National Forum on Modern Drama, Opera and Children's Drama," March 6, 1962, in *Zhou Enlai and Literature and Art,* pp. 56–57, 86–90.

69. Chen Jin, " 'Tongyixing' yu 'shuangbai fangzhen' " (The Philosophical Issue of "Identity" and "Hundred Flowers Policy") in *Dang de wenxian* (Archival Documents on Party History), no. 4 (Beijing: Zhongyang danganguan, 1993), pp. 49–50.

70. Lewis H. Siegelbaum, *The Stakhanovism* (Cambridge: Cambridge University Press, 1988), pp. 23–26.

71. Fairbank, *The Great Chinese Revolution,* pp. 157–158.

72. Mou Anshi, *Taiping Tianguo* (The Taiping Rebellion) (Shanghai: Shanghai renmin chubanshe, 1959); Wang Qingcheng, "Rujia, mojia, he Hong Xiuquan de shangdi" (Confucian, Mohist, and Hong's God) in *Taiping Tianguo de Lishi he Sixiang* (The History and Ideas of the Taiping Rebellion) (Beijing: Zhonghua shuju, 1985), pp. 275–289.

73. Scott Lowe, *Mo Tzu's Religious Blueprint for a Chinese Utopia* (Lewiston, NY: The Edwin Mellen Press, 1992), pp. 87–89; Yi-Pao Mei, *Motse—The Neglected Rival of Confucius* (London: Arthur Probsthain, 1934), pp. 85–145.

10. Becoming First-Class Citizens of the World

1. For the best study on the origins of the CCP's foreign policy in the American literature, see Michael Hunt, *The Origins of Chinese Communist Foreign Policy* (New York: Columbia University Press, 1996); for an important background on the evolution of the CCP's foreign policy, see Niu Jun, *From Yan'an to the World: The Origin and Development of Chinese Communist Foreign Policy,* ed. and trans. Steven I. Levine (Norwalk, CT: EastBridge, 2005); for a pioneering study on the PRC's diplomacy of "five principles of peaceful coexistence" in the Western literature, see Marsiika, "The Five Principles of Peaceful Coexistence," presented to an international symposium "The PRC at 50," Lund University, Sweden, October 1999; and for

thoughtful and comprehensive studies on Sino-Soviet relations based on Chinese and Russian documents declassified in the 1990s, see Odd Arne Westad, ed., *Brothers in Arms: The Rise and Fall of Sino-Soviet Alliance, 1945–1963* (Stanford, CA: Stanford University Press, 1998) and Yang Kuisong, *Mao Zedong yu Mosske de enen yuanyuan* (The Gratitudes and Grievance between Mao Zedong and Moscow) (Hong Kong: Sanlian shudian, 1999).

2. *Mao Zedong waijiao wenxuan* (A Selection of Mao Zedong's Writings on Diplomacy) (Beijing: Zhongyang wenxian chubanshe, 1995), pp. 160–161; Zhou Enlai, report to Foreign Ministry meeting on China's diplomacy, June 5, 1953; Zhou Enlai, "Speech at the Asian-African Conference," April 19, 1955, in *Zhou Enlai waijiao wenxuan* (A Selection of Zhou Enlai's Writings on Diplomacy) (Beijing: Zhongyang wenxian chubanshe, 1986), p. 116.

3. Zhou Enlai, "The Major Contradiction in Today's World Is That Between War and Peace," June 5, 1953, in *Zhou Enlai waijiao wenxuan* (A Selection of Zhou Enlai's Writings on Diplomacy), pp. 58–62; and Zhou Enlai, "To Learn from All Nations' Strength," speech at the bureau chiefs' meeting at the Supreme State Council, May 3, 1956, in *Zhou Enlai waijiao wenxuan* (A Selection of Zhou Enlai's Writings on Diplomacy), pp. 158–159.

4. Zhou Enlai, "Heping gongchu wuxiang yuanze" (Five Principles of Peaceful Coexistence), December 31, 1953, in *Zhou Enlai waijiao wenxuan* (A Selection of Zhou Enlai's Writings on Diplomacy), p. 63.

5. Ibid.

6. Mao Zedong, "Heping gongchu wuxiang yuanze shi yige changqi de fangzhen" (The Five Principles of Peaceful Coexistence Are a Long-Term Policy), in *Mao Zedong waijiao wenxun* (A Selection of Mao Zedong's Writings on Diplomacy), pp. 177–186.

7. Zhou, "Speech at the Asian-African Conference"; Zhou Enlai, "Talk at the Meeting of the Political Committee of Asian-African Conference," April 23, 1955, in *Zhou Enlai waijiao wenxuan* (A Selection of Zhou Enlai's Writings on Diplomacy), pp. 117, 132; Zhang Wentian, "Guanyu zhixing woguo heping waijiao zhengce zhongde yixie wenti" (Certain Issues in Implementing Our Nation's Peace Diplomacy), March 1956, memo to the meeting of Chinese ambassadors at the Foreign Ministry, which was later approved by the meeting. Zhang Peisen, ed., *Zhang Wentian nianpu* (The Chronicles of Zhang Wentian) (Beijing: Zhonggong dangshi chubanshe, 2000), p. 474.

8. Zhang, *Zhang Wentian nianpu* (The Chronicles of Zhang Wentian), pp. 475–476; Pei Jianzhang, ed., *Mao Zedong waijiao sixiang yanjiu* (Study on Mao Zedong's Diplomacy) (Beijing: Zhonggong dangshi chubanshe, 2002), pp. 32–33.

9. Zhou Enlai, "Xin zhongguo de waijiao" (New China's Diplomacy), speech at the opening ceremony of the establishment of the PRC's Foreign Min-

368 · Notes to Pages 256–259

istry, November 8, 1949, in *Zhou Enlai waijiao wenxun* (A Selection of Zhou Enlai's Writings on Diplomacy), p. 4.

10. Mao Zedong, "Heping gongchu shi yige changqi de fangzheng" (Peaceful Coexistence Is a Long-Term Policy), conversations with U Nu, the premier of Burma, December 1 and 11, 1954, in *Mao Zedong waijiao wenxuan* (A Selection of Mao Zedong's Writings on Diplomacy), pp. 193–194.

11. Conversation, Zhou Enlai with Pakistani prime minister, April 8, 1955, in *Zhou Enlai waijiao wenxun* (A Selection of Zhou Enlai's Writings on Diplomacy), p. 140.

12. *Chen Yi nianpu* (The Chronicles of Chen Yi), vol. 2 (Beijing: zhongyang wenxian chubanshe, 1995), pp. 65–66.

13. *Zhou Enlai nianpu, 1949–1976* (The Chronicles of Zhou Enlai, 1949–1976), vol. 1 (Beijing: Zhongyang wenxian chubanshe, 1997), pp. 625–626.

14. *Zhou Enlai waijiao wenxuan* (A Selection of Zhou Enlai's Writings on Diplomacy), pp. 47–79; *Mao Zedong waijiao wenxuan* (A Selection of Mao Zedong's Writings on Diplomacy), pp. 258, 368, 429, 479–480.

15. Zhou Enlai, "Tong meiguo qingnian daibiaotuan de tanhua" (Conversations with American Youth Delegation), September 7, 1957, in *Zhou Enlai waijiao wenxuan* (A Selection of Zhou Enlai's Writings on Diplomacy), p. 249.

16. Zhou Enlai, "Zhongguoren banwaishi de yixie sixiang," April 24, 1963, in *Zhou Enlai waijiao wenxuan* (A Selection of Zhou Enlai's Writings on Diplomacy), pp. 327–328.

17. Zhang Wentian, "Guanyu zhixing woguo heping waijiao zhengce zhongde yixie wenti" (Certain Issues in Implementing Our Nation's Peace Diplomacy), March 1956, memo to the meeting of Chinese ambassadors at the Foreign Ministry, in *Zhang Wentian nianpu* (The Chronicles of Zhang Wentian), p. 474.

18. Several joint Sino-Soviet companies in Xinjiang were also placed under exclusive Chinese control. Wang Taiping, ed., *Xin Zhongguo waijiao wushinian* (Fifty Years of New China's Diplomacy), vol. 2 (Beijing: Beijing chubanshe, 1999), pp. 802–810.

19. In Zhou's view, Khrushchev's economic aid policy gradually shifted to a different direction. The new emphasis was an international division of labor within the socialist bloc. Because of this, unlike Stalin, Khrushchev asked China not to build many machinery factories, since the Soviet Union already had an adequate number.

20. Zhou Enlai, "Zhengqu waiyuan, dan bu yilai" (Try to Get Foreign Aid, but Do Not Rely on Foreign Aid), speech at the State Council's standing committee meeting, October 11, 1956, in *Zhou Enlai waijiao wenxuan* (A Selection of Zhou Enlai's Writings on Diplomacy), pp. 172–174.

21. Mao Zedong, " 'Yibiandao,' dui bu dui?" (Is It Correct to Have a Policy of "Leaning to One Side?"), speech at the second national convention of the Chinese National Industrial and Commercial Association, December 8,

1956, in *Mao Zedong waijiao wenxuan* (A Selection of Mao Zedong's Writings on Diplomacy), pp. 278–279.

22. Ibid.

23. Mao said that in an appraisal of Stalin's work it was wrong either to affirm everything or to negate everything. According to Liu, "The Soviets told us in the past that everything Stalin did was great, correct; now they are telling us that everything Stalin did was mean, wrong, and that he committed countless crimes." In the past, "we did not follow Stalin's orders and instructions; why should we now follow the Soviets' new orders?" Yang Xiuhui, ed., *Waijjiao fengyun renwu* (Chinese Diplomacy in a Turbulent World) (Beijing: Zhongguo wenshi chubanshe, 1997), pp. 6–10, 17–18.

24. Mao Zedong, "Xiqu lishi jiaoxun, fandui daguo shawenzhuyi" (Learn from Historical Lessons and Oppose Great Power Chauvinism), conversation with Yugoslav party delegation, September 1956, in *Mao Zedong waijiao wenxuan* (A Selection of Mao Zedong's Writings on Diplomacy), pp. 260–261.

25. Zhou Enlai, "On the Present International Situation, China's Foreign Policy, and the Liberation of Taiwan," delivered at the Third Session of the First National People's Congress on June 28, 1956 (Beijing: Foreign Language Press, 1956), p. 19.

26. Shi Zhe, *Lingxiu Mao Zedong* (Leader Mao Zedong) (Beijing: Hongqi chubanshe, 1997), pp. 140–142; Mao Zedong, "Xiqu lishi jiaoxun, fandui daguo shawenzhuyi" (Learn from Historical Lessons and Oppose Great Power Chauvinism), September 1956, in *Mao Zedong waijiao wenxuan* (A Selection of Mao Zedong's Writings on Diplomacy), pp. 260–261.

27. Wu Lengxi, *Shinian Lunzhan: Zhongsu guanxi huiyilu, 1956–1966* (Memoir on Sino-Soviet Relations, 1956–1966) (Beijing: Zhongyang wenxian chubashe, 1999), pp. 10–13. The author was the head of Xinhua news agency from 1948 to 1956, editor-in-chief of the *People's Daily* from 1957 to 1966, a Politburo member at the Eighth Party Congress in 1956, and a participant in this emergency Politburo meeting on October 20, 1956.

28. *Zhou Enlai nianpu, 1949–1976* (The Chronicles of Zhou Enlai, 1949–1976), vol. 1, pp. 629–630.

29. Wu, *Shinian Lunzhan: Zhongsu guanxi huiyilv, 1956–1966* (Memoir on Sino-Soviet Relations, 1956–1966), p. 13; and Shi, *Lingxiu Mao Zedong* (Leader Mao Zedong), pp. 146–148.

30. Pei Jianzhang, *Zhonghua remen gongheguo waijiaoshi, 1949–1956* (The Diplomatic History of the PRC, 1949–1956) (Beijing: Shijie zhishi chubanshe, 1994), p. 62; Shi, *Lingxiu Mao Zedong* (Leader Mao Zedong), pp. 148–149.

31. Mark Kramer, "New Evidence on Soviet Decision-Making and the 1956 Polish and Hungarian Crises," *Cold War International History Project Bulletin*, no. 8–9, pp. 18–19.

32. Ibid., pp. 18–21.

33. Khrushchev recorded his discussion with Liu Shaoqi on the night of October 30 in his memoir: "We sat up the whole night, weighing the pros and cons of whether or not we should apply armed force to Hungary." "Every time we thought we'd made up our minds about what to do, Liu Shao-chi would consult with Mao Tse-tung." And "we finally finished this all-night session with a decision not to apply military force in Hungary." On the evening of October 31, when he saw Liu off at the airport, he informed him of the more recent decision to send Soviet armed force to Hungary. Liu responded, "I can't get Comrade Mao Tse-tung's consent at this moment. . . . But you may assume that you have our backing." Nikita Khrushchev, *Khrushchev Remembers: The Last Testament*, trans. and ed. Strobe Talbott (Boston: Little, Brown and Company, 1974), pp. 418–419.

34. *Zhou Enlai nianpu, 1949–1976* (The Chronicles of Zhou Enlai, 1949–1976), vol. 2, pp. 4–5.

35. Li Yueran, "Wo zai Zhou zongli shenbian gongzuo de pianduan huiyi" (Memoir of My Years Working with Premier Zhou), in Foreign Ministry, ed., *Xin zhongguo waijiao fengyun* (Stormy Events in New China's Diplomacy) (Beijing: Shijie zhishi chubanshe, 1990), pp. 93–94; also, *Zhou Enlai nianpu, 1949–1976* (The Chronicle of Zhou Enlai, 1949–1976), vol. 2, pp. 7–15. Khrushchev complained that some East European leaders "only wanted to get gold from us, and then used this gold to cultivate relations with the West." For Zhou, "If we have different opinions about them, we should tell them in front of their face, to consult with them."

36. *Zhou Enlai nianpu, 1949–1976* (The Chronicles of Zhou Enlai, 1949–1976), vol, 2, pp. 5–6. Khrushchev agreed that the Chinese troops should withdraw from North Korea. But he told Zhou that the Soviet troops' withdrawal from East Germany could not be carried out immediately. It would depend on the specific situation in Europe.

37. Robert H. Donaldson and Joseph L. Nogee, *The Foreign Policy of Russia: Changing Systems, Enduring Interests,* 2nd ed. (Armonk, NY: M. E. Sharpe, 2002), p. 32.

38. Mao Zedong, "Guanyu sulian qingqiu zai zhongguo jianli tezhong changbowuxiandiantai wenti" (On the Soviet Request for Building a Long-Wave Radio Station in China), June 7, 1958, in *Mao Zedong waijiao wenxuan* (A Selection of Mao Zedong's Writings on Diplomacy), pp. 316–317, 634 (fn. 172 and 177).

39. Mao Zedong, conversation with Soviet ambassador P. Yudin, July 22, 1958, in *Mao Zedong waijiao wenxuan* (A Selection of Mao Zedong's Writings on Diplomacy), pp. 322–323.

40. Mao was particularly angry at Khrushchev's proposal that China and the Soviet Union should have a "50/50 share" in the joint fleet. "Even when the Japanese signed that notorious unequal treaty with Yuan Shikai in 1915," Mao confided in private, "they let China have 51 percent of the share, to pretend that they recognized China's sovereignty." He asked Yudin, if the CCP ever agreed to the Soviet request, "how can we ever

explain to the Chinese people about this joint fleet?" See Wang Hebin, *Ziyunxuan zhuren wo suo jiechu de Mao Zedong* (My Conversations with Mao Zedong in the Room of Ziyun) (Beijing: Zhonggong zhongyang dangxiao chubanshe, 1991), p. 142.

41. Mao Zedong, conversation with Soviet ambassador Yudin, July 22, 1958. Mao assured Yudin that in wartime, all Chinese naval ports and airfields "the Soviets could use as their own," while the Chinese could enjoy "the same privileges" in the Soviet Union. As soon as the war was over, however, both sides' troops should "immediately return to their own country."

42. Khrushchev, *Khrushchev Remembers*, pp. 258–260. According to Li Yueran, Mao's and Zhou's Russian interpreter, on August 2, at a meeting in the swimming pool, Mao said, "So many foreigners have come to China, trying to dominate the Chinese, but none of them could succeed in the end. The Chinese nation has been the most difficult to be assimilated in the world." Later, Khrushchev interpreted this as the major evidence that Mao had "the chauvinist ambition of conquering the world." Li Yuerang, "Wo wei Maozhuxi dangfanyi de rizi" (I Was Chairman Mao's Interpreter), *Journal of Yanhuang chunqiu* (August 1997): 68.

43. Wei Wei, *Ne Rongzhen zhuan* (The Biography of Ne Rongzhen) (Beijing: Dangdai zhongguo chubanshe, 1994), pp. 574–579. By the end of 1956, Soviet attitudes toward the CCP were warming up, as Liu Xiao, the Chinese ambassador to Moscow, observed. It was during Zhou's visit to Moscow in early 1957 that the Soviet leaders first offered to train Chinese students in missile technology.

44. This agreement was followed by a comprehensive agreement on Soviet aid in 122 scientific and technological projects in January 1958. Chen Mingxian, ed., *Xin Zhongguo 45 nian yanjiu* (Study on 45 Years of New China) (Beijing: Ligong daxue chubanshe, 1994), pp. 242–243.

45. *Dangdai zhongguo waijiao* (Contemporary Chinese Diplomacy) (Beijing: Zhongguo shehui kexue chubanshe, 1987), pp. 114–115.

46. "The Negotiations between CPSU and CCP Delegations, September 1960, Moscow," *CWIHP Bulletin*, no. 10.

47. "A New 'Cult of Personality': Suslov's Secret Report on Mao, Khrushchev, and Sino-Soviet Tensions, December 1959," translated and with an introduced by Vladislav M. Zubok, *CWIHP Bulletin*, no. 8–9.

48. It was against this backdrop that the article by the CCP Central Committee's magazine *Red Flag* in April 1960, entitled "Long Live Leninism," was interpreted in an entirely different light in Moscow. While it targeted Tito's "revisionism," it still talked about the "leading role" of the Soviet Union in the socialist bloc. And it reminded Moscow of Dulles's "plot" to split the Sino-Soviet alliance that had aimed to isolate China first and to defeat a weakened Soviet Union eventually. However, from the Soviet perspective, as a Soviet diplomat recalled, this article "removed any doubts" that Soviet officials and diplomats still had about "the magnitude of the rift between the two countries." See Song Qingling, "The Basis of Eternal

Friendship," *Renmin Ribao* (People's Daily), February 24, 1960; and Mark Kramer, "The USSR Foreign Ministry's Appraisal of Sino-Soviet Relations on the Eve of the Split, September 1959," *CWIHP Bulletin*, no. 6–7.

49. In the aftermath of the Romanian Party Congress in June 1960, in which Khrushchev had a public exchange with Peng Zhen, the head of the CCP delegation, concerning the issue of "peaceful transition to socialism," the Soviet government sent a letter to the Chinese government on July 16, 1960, declaring that Moscow was to withdraw all Soviet experts from China.

50. Hu Shiyan, *Chen Yi zhuan* (The Biography of Chen Yi) (Beijing: Dangdai Zhongguo chubanshe, 1998), p. 548; "The Short Version of the Negotiations between CPSU and CCP Delegations, September 1960," *CWIHP Bulletin*, no. 10.

51. Vladislav Zubok and Constantine Pleshakov, *Inside the Kremlin's Cold War: From Stalin to Khrushchev* (Cambridge, MA: Harvard University Press, 1996), p. 210.

52. Ishwer C. Ojha, *Chinese Foreign Policy in an Age of Transition: The Diplomacy of Cultural Despair* (Boston: Beacon Press, 1969), pp. 124–125.

53. For China's role in the first Indo-China war and the Geneva Conference, see Zhai Qiang, "China and the Geneva Conference of 1954," *China Quarterly* (March 1992).

54. Luo Guibo, "Chushi yuenan zhichu" (The Beginning of My Mission to Vietnam), in *Hongzhua yizong* (Hangzhou: Jiangsu renmin chubanshe, 1995), pp. 1–27; *Zhongguo junshi guwentuan yuanyue kangfa douzheng shishi* (Historical Facts about the Role of the Chinese Military Advisory Group in the Struggle to Aid Vietnam and Resist France) (Beijing: Jiefangjun chubanshe, 1990), pp. 1–7. Ho Chi-minh wanted the military advisory group to help prepare for the worst scenario: if the Diem government in the South, backed by the United States, was to launch a military attack against the North. In March 1955, the military advisory group participated in the strategic design for such a scenario and supported the modernization of the North Vietnamese army as the long-term guarantee for national defense.

55. Guo Ming, Luo Fangming, and Li Baiyin, eds., *Xiandai zhongyue guanxi ziliao xuanbian, 1949–1978* (Selected Documents of Contemporary Sino-Vietnamese Relations, 1949–1978), 3 vols. (Beijing: Shishi chubanshe, 1986), pp. 174–178, 300–302.

56. "Zhongguo zhengfu zhichi yuenan minzhu gongheguo heping changyi de shengming" (The Statement of the PRC Government on Its support for the Vietnamese Democratic Republic's Proposal of Peaceful Unification), March 9, 1958, in Guo, Luo, and Li, *Xiandai zhongyue guanxi ziliao xuanbian, 1949–1978* (Selected Documents of Contemporary Sino-Vietnamese Relations, 1949–1978), p. 123.

57. *Mao Zedong baizhounian jinian* (Commemorate Mao Zedong's Centennial

Birthday), vol. 3 (Beijing: Zhongyang wenxian chubanshe, 1994), pp. 224–228.

58. Guo Ming, ed., *Zhong yue guanxi yanbian 40 nian* (Forty Years of Sino-Vietnamese Relations) (Nanning: Guangxi renmin chubanshe, 1983), pp. 66–68.

59. Hoang Van Hoan, "Distortion of Facts about the Great Friendship between Vietnam and China Is Impermissible," quoted from Zhai Qiang, *China and the Vietnam Wars, 1950–1975* (Chapel Hill: University of North Carolina Press, 2000), p. 83.

60. Mao, "Heping gongchu shi yige changqi de fangzheng" (Peaceful Coexistence Is a Long-Term Policy), pp. 177–196.

61. Ibid.

62. Ibid.

63. Ibid., p. 196.

64. Mao Zedong, "Zhiyao shuangfang yiuhao, bianjie wenti jiuhao jiejue" (It Will Be Easy to Solve Border Issues, So Long as We Have Friendly Relations) excerpt of conversation with Burmese Premier U Nu, September 29, 1960, in *Mao Zedong waijiao wenxuan* (A Selection of Mao Zedong's Writings on Diplomacy), pp. 444–445.

65. Department of State Staff Summary, Far East, September 3, 1958, NA.

66. What Nehru referred to were the U.S. State Department's public statements on Tibet's legal status at the time. As a State Department paper, "Policy Review Paper on Tibet," (January 31, 1951), indicated, the international treaties in place before the establishment of the PRC recognized that "Tibet forms part of Chinese territory." See CA, "Policy Review Paper on Tibet," January 31, 1951; Records of the Office of Chinese Affairs, NA.

67. Sardar Vallabbhai Patel, India's home minister and Nehru's most senior colleague in the cabinet, wrote to Nehru in December 1950 that Indian defense had so far been "based on the calculations of a superiority over Pakistan." But now "for the first time, after centuries, India's defense has to concentrate itself on two fronts simultaneously."

68. Zhou Enlai, "Xizang wenti yu zhongyin guanxi" (The Tibetan Issue and Sino-Indian Relationship), May 6, 1959, in *Zhou Enlai waijiao wenxuan* (A Selection of Zhou Enlai's Writings on Diplomacy), pp. 271–272.

69. Zhou, "Heping gongchu wuxiang yuanze" (Five Principles of Peaceful Coexistence), in *Zhou Enlai waijiao wenxuan* (A Selection of Zhou Enlai's Writings on Diplomacy), p. 63; Lu Jianhong, *Zhou Enlai de tanpan yishu* (The Art of Negotiation in Zhou Enlai's Diplomacy) (Beijing: Zhongyang wenxian chubanshe, 1996), pp. 274–277.

70. *Zhou Enlai nianpu, 1949–1976* (The Chronicles of Zhou Enlai, 1949–1976), vol. 2, pp. 1–2. Zhou further suggested that the Tibetan Autonomous Region (TAR) should be established as soon as possible. The Dalai Lama said that the TAR would be established by the end of 1957.

71. Ibid.; Jawaharlal Nehru: "Happenings in Tibet," April 27, 1959, in Nehru,

India's Foreign Policy: Selected Speeches, September 1946–April 1961 (Delhi: Publications Division, Ministry of Information and Broadcasting, Government of India, 1961), pp. 322–324.

72. Qiu Shi, ed., *Gongheguo zhongda shijian he juece neimu* (The Inside Story of Policy Making in the PRC's Important Events), vol. 1 (Beijing: Jingji ribao chubanshe, 1997), pp. 78–82.

73. A. Tom Grunfeld, *The Making of a Modern Tibet* (Armonk, NY: M. E. Sharpe, 1996), pp. 154–158; Chris Mullin, "The CIA: Tibetan Conspiracy," *Far Eastern Economic Review* (September 5, 1989): 30–34. Mullin's study was based on his intensive interviews with the participants in these events.

74. Jamyang Norbu, "The Tibetan Resistance Movement and the Role of the CIA," in Robert Barnett, ed., *Resistance and Reform in Tibet* (London: Hurst, 1994), pp. 194–195; Qiu, *Gongheguo zhongda shijian he juece neimu* (The Inside Story of Policy Making in the PRC's Important Events), vol. 1, pp. 112–114.

75. Nehru, "Happenings in Tibet," in Nehru, *India's Foreign Policy*, pp. 325–326.

76. Ibid., pp. 323–325.

77. S. V. Chervonenko, "Memorandum of Conversation with the General Secretary of the CC CCP, Member of the Politburo of the CC CCP, Deng Xiaoping," June 1960, *CWIHP Bulletin*, no. 10.

78. Mao Zedong, "India Is Not Our Enemy, but Our Friend," in *Mao Zedong waijiao wenxuan* (A Selection of Mao Zedong's Writings on Diplomacy), pp. 376–377.

79. Nehru, *India's Foreign Policy*, pp. 326–327.

80. Lei Yingfu, *Tongshuaibu canmou de zhuihuai* (Remember My Works as the General Chief of Staff of PLA) (Hangzhou: Jiansu renmin chubanshe, 1993), pp. 98–114. Mao also emphasized that within the twenty kilometers, "the Chinese frontier forces must not open fire, must not go on patrol, must not go hunting, must not have military exercises, and must not engage in shooting practice."

81. Premen Addy, "British and Indian Strategic Perceptions of Tibet," in *Resistance and Reform in Tibet*, pp. 39–46.

82. Grunfeld, *Making of a Modern Tibet*, p. 164.

83. Li Enmin, *Zhongri minjian jingji waijiao, 1945–1972* (Sino-Japanese Nongovernmental Economic Diplomacy, 1945–1972) (Beijing: Renmin chubanshe, 1997), p. 57.

84. Zhou Enlai, "Zhongri guanxi de guanjian shi heping gongchu" (The Key to Sino-Japanese Relations Is Peaceful Coexistence), conversation with the Japanese Diet delegation, October 11, 1954, in *Zhou Enlai waijiao wenxuan* (A Selection of Mao Zedong's Writings on Diplomacy), pp. 87–91.

85. Li, *Zhongri minjian jingji waijiao, 1945–1972* (Sino-Japanese Nongovernmental Economic Diplomacy, 1945–1972), pp. 180–181.

86. Zhou Enlai, "Talk at the Meeting of the Political Committee of Asian-African Conference," in *Zhou Enlai waijiao wenxuan* (A Selection of Zhou Enlai's Writings on Diplomacy), p. 132.

87. Feng Zhaokui, Liu Shilung, Liu Yingchun, Jiang Peizhu, Jin Xude, and Zhou Yongsheng, *Zhanhou riben waijiao, 1945–1995* (Japan's Postwar Diplomacy, 1945–1995) (Beijing: Zhongguo shehuikexueyuan chubanshe, 1996), pp. 280–281, 567–575; Li, *Zhongri minjian jingji waijiu, 1945–1972* (Sino-Japanese Nongovernmental Economic Diplomacy), pp. 223–226.

88. Sheng Jinding, "Duiri wangshi zhuiji" (Memoir of My Time in Japan), *Zhuanji wenxuan* (Biography Literature), 31, no. 4 (1977).

89. Li Enmin's extensive interviews with Japanese businessmen, former Diet members, and members of Sino-Japanese Friendship Association, in *Zhongri minjian jingji waijiaou (1945–1972)* (Sino-Japanese Nongovernmental Economic Diplomacy), pp. 235–239.

90. If Sino-Japanese trade had not been suspended for two and half years from 1958 to 1960, as a president of a Japanese steel company recalled, the momentum of Sino-Japanese commercial and technological exchanges would have developed so fast in the 1960s that "the normalization of Sino-Japanese diplomatic relations might have well been in the 1960s, rather than in the 1970s." Ibid., pp. 244–246.

91. *Mao Zedong waijiao wenxuan* (A Selection of Mao Zedong's Writings on Diplomacy), pp. 213, 223, 229.

92. Zhou, "On the Present International Situation, China's Foreign Policy, and the Liberation of Taiwan," pp. 17–18.

93. Zhou Enlai, "Yaoqing meigong jizhe fangwen zhongguo" (Invite American Journalists to Visit China), *Renmin ribao* (People's Daily), August 6, 1956.

94. *Mao Zedong waijiao wenxuan* (A Selection of Mao Zedong's Writings on Diplomacy), pp. 227–237.

95. Ibid., p. 246.

96. *Zhou Enlai nianpu, 1949–1976* (The Chronicles of Zhou Enlai, 1949–1976), vol. 1, pp. 23–24.

97. State Department Staff Summary, September 3, 1958, NA.

98. Shi Zhifu, ed., *Zhonghua renmen gongheguo duiwai guanxishi (1949–1989)* (Diplomatic History of the PRC, 1949–1989) (Beijing: Beijing University Press, 1996), pp. 104–105.

99. Zhou Enlai, "Jianjue fandui zhizao 'liang ge zhongguo' de yinmou" (Resolutely Oppose the "Two Chinas" Plot), conversation with British charge d'affaires, January 5, 1955, in *Zhou Enlai waijiao wenxuan* (A Selection of Zhou Enlai's Writings on Diplomacy), pp. 95–96.

100. For an excellent analysis of the first Taiwan Strait Crisis, see Gordon H. Chang and He Di, "The Absence of War in the U.S.-China Confrontation over Quemoy and Matsu in 1954–1955: Contingency, Luck, Deterrence?" *American Historical Review* (October 1993).

101. Ibid.

102. Zhou Enlai, "Jianjue fandui zhizao 'liang ge zhongguo' de yinmou" (Resolutely Oppose the "Two Chinas" Plot), in *Zhou Enlai waijiao wenxuan* (A Selection of Zhou Enlai's Writings on Diplomacy), pp. 101–105; Zhou Enlai, conversation with Edgar Snow, August 30, 1960, in *Zhou Enlai waijiao wenxuan* (A Selection of Zhou Enlai's Writings on Diplomacy), pp. 296–297.

103. *Zhou Enlai waijiao wenxuan* (A Selection of Zhou Enlai's Writings on Diplomacy), pp. 296–297; and He Di, "The Evolution of PRC Policy toward the Offshore Islands," in Cohen and Iriye, *Great Powers in East Asia, 1953–1960*, pp. 231–232.

104. Lin Xiaoguang, "Zhongguo gongchandang duitai zhengce de lishi yanjin" (The Historical Evolution of the CCP's Policy toward Taiwan), *Dangshi yanjiu zilao* (Archival Documents on Party History), no. 3 (1997): 5–6.

105. They were Wu Guozhen, the governor of Taiwan, who had been driven out into exile in 1954, and Sun Liren, the Commander-in-Chief of the Nationalist Army, who had been sentenced to prison in 1955; Xue Jianhua, *Cheng Siyuan zhuan* (The Biography of Cheng Siyuan) (Beijing: Guojiwenhua chuban gongsi, 1994), p. 114; Cheng Siyuan, *Wode huiyi* (Memoir) (Beijing: Huayi chubanshe, 1994), pp. 248–250.

106. Cao Juren, "Yiheyuan yixitan: Zhou Enlai zongli huijianji" (The Conversation in the Summer Palace: The Meeting with Premier Zhou Enlai), *Nanyang Shangbao*, August 14, 1956.

107. Lin Xiaoguang, "Zhongguo guochandang duitai zhengce de yanbian" (The Historical Evolution of the CCP's Policy toward Taiwan), *Dangshi yanjiu zilao* (Archival Documents on Party History), 3 (1997): 6–7. Song's brother, a former KMT general, was a prisoner of war in Liaoning. Chiang thought that if his trip to the mainland were discovered by American journalists, Song could always cover up by saying that he was visiting his brother there.

108. Yang Qinhua, "1978 nianqian haixia liangan mouhe zuji shilu" (The Record of Peace Negotiations between the Two Sides of the Taiwan Strait before 1978), *Journal of Yanhuang chunqiu*, no. 8 (1997): 21.

109. Cheng, *Wode huiyi* (Memoir), pp. 250–251; Mao Lei and Fan Xiaofang, eds., *Guogong liang dang tanpan tongshi* (Negotiation History between the CCP and the KMT), vol. 2 (Lanzhou: Lanzhou University Press, 1996), chap. 1.

110. *New York Times*, August 22, 1957.

111. Zhou, "Conversation with American Youth Delegation," in *Zhou Enlai waijiao wenxuan* (A Selection of Zhou Enlai's Writings on Diplomacy), pp. 239–252.

112. Pei Monong, *Zhou Enlai waijiao xue* (Zhou Enlai's Diplomatic Theory and Practice) (Beijing: Zhongyang dangxiao chubanshe, 1998), pp. 320–326.

113. Kenneth T. Young, *Negotiating with the Chinese Communists* (New York: McGraw-Hill, 1968), pp. 133–134.

114. Hu Shiyan, *Chen Yi zhuan* (Biography of Chen Yi), pp. 533–535.

115. Liao Xinwen, "Xiao paoji yunyu dazhanlun: Dui 1958 nian Mao Zedong juece paoji jinmen de lishi kaocha" (Small Shelling, Big Strategy: The Historical Examination of Mao Zedong's Strategic Thinking in the Jinmen Shelling of 1958), in *Mao Zedong baizhounian jinian* (Commemorate Mao Zedong's Centennial Birthday), pp. 691–692; Wu Lengxi, "Inside Story of the Decision Making during the Shelling of Jinmen," *Zhuanji wenxue* (Biographical Literature), no. 1 (1994): 5–11.

116. Yang Zhaolin, *Jianli qiangda de haijun* (To Build a Strong Navy) (Beijing: Zhongyang wenxian chubanshe, 1994), pp. 218–219.

117. Ibid., pp. 220–221.

118. Mao Zedong, "Speech at the 15th Supreme State Council meeting," September 5, 1958, in *Jianguo yilai Mao Zedong wengao* (Mao Zedong Papers since the Establishment of the PRC), vol. 7 (Beijing: Zhongyang wenxian chubanshe, 1998), pp. 384–385.

119. Ye Fei, *Ye Fei huiyilu* (Memoirs of Ye Fei) (Beijing: Jiefangjun chubanshe, 1988), pp. 661–662. (Ye Fei was the PLA's commander-in-chief in the Jinmen shelling of 1958.)

120. Mao Zedong, speech at the Supreme State Council meeting, September 8, 1958; quoted from Liao, "Xiao paoji yunyu dazhanlun (Small Shelling, Big Strategy), in *Mao Zedong baizhounian jinian,* p. 700.

121. Jinmen and Mazu were very close to the mainland. Chiang Kai-shek thought that to give them up could mean that the KMT's stay on Taiwan would be permanent, or two Chinas would be a reality. Chiang Kai-shek thus loudly protested Dulles's suggestion of withdrawing from Jinmen and Mazu. He insisted that the KMT would never give up its one China policy.

122. Mao's speech at the Supreme State Council meeting, September 8, 1958.

123. Zhang delivered his message to the KMT government on Taiwan via his personal friends in Hong Kong. Mao and Fan, *Guogong liang dang tanpan tongshi* (Negotiation History between the CCP and the KMT), vol. 2, p. 304.

124. Mao Zedong, "Remarks at the Meeting of Provincial and Municipal Party Secretaries," February 1959; Mao Zedong, conversations with Moroccan Communist Party delegation, February 27, 1959. Both quoted from Yang Qinhua, "1978 nianqian haixia liangan mouhe zuji shilu" (The Record of Peace Negotiations between the Two Sides of the Taiwan Strait before 1978), *Journal of Yanhuang chunqiu,* no. 8 (1997): 22.

125. Bo Yibo, "Fangzhi 'heping yanbian' wenti de tichu" (Warning on "Peaceful Evolution": Its Origins in CCP's Discussions), in *Ruogan zhongda juece yu shijian de huigu* (Reflections on Important Decisions and Events), vol. 2 (Beijing: Zhonggong zhongyang dangxiao chubanshe, 1993), pp. 1140–1147.

126. Ibid.

127. Mao Zedong, "Huanhe dui shehuizhuyi guojia he zibenzhuyi guojia de renmin douyiuli" (Détente Is Beneficial to Both Socialist Countries' and Cap-

italist Countries' Peoples), conversation with the General Secretary of the Australian Communist Party, October 26, 1959, in *Mao Zedong waijiao wenxuan* (A Selection of Mao Zedong's Writings on Diplomacy), pp. 387–388.

128. Ibid.

129. Mao Zedong, "Diguo zhuyi shi bukepade," conversation with delegates of twelve African countries, May 7, 1960, in *Mao Zedong waijiao wenxuan* (A Selection of Mao Zedong's Writings on Diplomacy), pp. 408–409.

130. Tong Xiaopeng, *Fengyu sishinian* (Forty Years of Braving Wind and Rain), vol. 2 (Beijing: Zhongyang wenxian chubanshe, 1996), p. 292. The author was Zhou Enlai's chief of staff, deputy minister of the united front, and top aide on Mainland-Taiwan relations in the 1950s and up to Zhou's death in 1976.

131. *Zhou Enlai nianpu, 1949–1976* (The Chronicles of Zhou Enlai, 1949–1976), vol. 2, p. 15.

132. Ojha, *Chinese Foreign Policy in an Age of Transition,* pp. 52–53.

133. Michael H. Hunt, *The Genesis of Chinese Communist Foreign Policy* (New York: Columbia University Press, 1996), pp. 3–5.

134. Robert McNamara with Brian VanDemark, *In Retrospect: The Tragedy and Lessons of the Vietnam War* (New York: Random House, 1995), pp. 32–33.

135. Warren I. Cohen, *Dean Rusk* (Totowa, NJ: Cooper Square Publishers, 1980), p. 329.

136. Hans J. Morgenthau, "Ideology and the National Interest," in Hans J. Morgenthau and Jerald C. Brauer, *U.S. Policy in the Far East: Ideology, Religion, and Superstition* (New York: Council on Religion and International Affairs, 1968), pp. 24–35.

137. Douglas Jehl, "Secret Papers about China Are Released by the C.I.A.," *New York Times,* October 19, 2004; see also Robert L. Suettinger, "Introduction to Selected China NIEs, 1948–1976," National Intelligence Council, *http://www.dni.gov/nic/NIC_foia_china.html.*

Conclusion

1. Thucydides, *The Peloponnesian War,* rev. ed., trans. Richard Crawley with introduction by T. E. Wick (New York: Random House, 1982), pp. 1–3.

2. Barry Rubin, *Paved with Good Intentions: The American Experience and Iran* (New York: Oxford University Press, 1980), p. x.

3. Richard Immerman, "Psychology," in Michael Hogan and Thomas Paterson, eds., *Explaining the History of American Foreign Relations,* 2nd ed. (Cambridge: Cambridge University Press, 2004), p. 116.

4. Emily S. Rosenberg, "Considering Borders," in Hogan and Paterson, *Explaining the History of American Foreign Relations,* p. 176.

5. Quoted from Alastair Iain Johnston, "Is China a Status Quo Power?" *In-*

ternational Security 27, no. 4 (Spring 2003): 55. For an excellent study of perceptions between the United States and China in the 1990s, see David Lampton, *Same Bed, Different Dreams* (Berkeley: University of California Press, 2003).

6. Pan Yue, "Environmental Culture and China's National Renaissance," speech, Green China Forum symposium, October 25, 2003, quoted from Zhang Xiaoming, *Zhongguo gaoceng xinzhinang* (New Brainpower of China), vol. 1 (Beijing: Ligongdaxue chubanshe, 2004), pp. 7–9.

7. Zhang Xiaoming, *Zhongguo gaoceng xinzhinang* (New Brainpower of China), vols. 1 and 2; Zhang Zhanbin, ed., *Zhongguo jianjin gaige qianyan redian wenti baogao (neibu ziliao)* (Report on Controversial Issues in China's Gradualist Economic and Political Reforms) (For Internal Reference), vols. 1 and 2 (Beijing: Zhongguo guanli kexue yanjiuyuan chubanshe, 2002); Dong Fangzhi, *Yu Zongli tanxin* (A Heart-to-Heart Conversation with Premier Zhu Rongji) (Guangzhou: Guangdong luyou chubanshe, 1999); He Yiqun, *Qianlong zaiyun: Jiaofenghou de zhongguo* (Dragon in the Ocean: Major Controversies in China's Economic and Political Reforms), vols. 1, 2, and 3 (Beijing: Hongqi chubanshe, 1998); Luo Yuzhong, Wan Qigang, and Liu Songshan, *Renquan yu fangzhi* (Human Rights and Rule of Law) (Beijing: Beijing University Press, 2001); Zhang Lihua, *Shi chang Jingji yu Min Zhu Zhengzhi* (Market Economy and Democratic Polity) (Beijing: Minzhu yu jianshe chubanshe, 2002).

8. Ma Lichang and Ling Zhijun, *Jiaofeng: Dangdai zhongguo sanci sixiang jiefang shilu* (Clash: A Record of Three Liberations of Ideas in Contemporary China, 1978–1998) (Beijing: Zhongguo gaige chubanshe, 1998); Lin Zha, ed., *Jiaofen hou de jiaofeng: Hou gaige zhongguo* (Clash after Clash: China in the Age of Reform) (Beijing: Hongqi chubanshe, 2003).

9. Peter Hays Gries, *China's New Nationalism: Pride, Politics, and Diplomacy* (Berkeley: University of California Press, 2004); Fang Ning, Wang Bingquan, and Ma Lijun, *Chengzhang de zhongguo: Dangdai zhongguo qingnian de guojia minzu yishi yanjiu* (Growing China: A Study on Current Chinese Youths' Concepts of Nations and Nationalism) (Beijing: Renmin chubanshe, 2002).

10. Johnston, "Is China a Status Quo Power?" pp. 5–56. For a similar argument about the danger of security dilemma dynamics in U.S.-China diplomacy in the post–Cold War world, see Thomas Christensen, "China, the U.S.-Japan Alliance, and the Security Dilemma in East Asia"; Robert S. Ross, "Engagement in U.S. China Policy," in Alastair Iain Johnston and Robert Ross, eds., *Engaging China* (New York: Routledge, 2002); Lampton, *Same Bed, Different Dreams;* Kenneth Lieberthal, "Why the U.S. Malaise over China?" *YaleGlobal Online,* January 19, 2006, *http:// yaleglobal.yale.edu.*

11. Alexander George, "Ideology and International Relations: A Conceptual Analysis," *Jerusalem Journal of International Relations,* 9, no. 1 (1987).

12. Edward H. Carr, *The Twenty Years' Crisis, 1919–1939,* 2nd ed. (1946; repr. New York: Harper & Row, 1964), pp. 212–213.
13. Carr, *Twenty Years' Crisis,* p. 200.
14. Quoted from Paul R. Viotti and Mark V. Kauppi, *International Relations Theory,* 3rd ed. (Boston: Allyn and Bacon, 1999), pp. 19–20.

Primary Sources

The National Archives of the United States, College Park, Maryland (NA)

United States State Department, Record Group 59 (RG59)

RECORDS OF THE POLICY PLANNING STAFF
59.3.6 Records of Offices Responsible for Far Eastern and Pacific affairs
   Central File of the Office of East Asian Affairs, 1947–1964
   Records of the Bureau of Far Eastern Affairs, 1942–1958 (FE)
   Records of the Division of Chinese Affairs, 1944–1950, 1951–52, 1953–1960 (CA)
59.3.7 Records of Offices Responsible for Economic Affairs
   Records of the Assistant Secretary of State for Economic Affairs, 1944–1950
   Records of the Office of Economic Security Policy, 1945–1947
   Records of the Office of International Trade Policy, 1940–1949
59.5.1 Records Relating to Commissions, Missions, and Committees
   Records of the Missions of General George C. Marshall to China, 1945–1947

United States Defense Department: Record Group 218 and 330 (RG218 and RG330)

218.3 Records of the Chairman, Joint Chiefs of Staff (JCS)
   Correspondence, memorandums, and messages of JCS Chairmen Adm. Arthur W. Radford, 1953–1957; Gen. Nathan F. Twining, 1957–1960.
330.6.1 Records of the Executive Office
   Export control security lists, 1951–1954

The Harry S Truman Library, Independence, Missouri (HST)

Presidential Papers, 1945–1953

Confidential Files, 1945–1953
Korean War Files, 1947–1952
National Security Council Files, 1947–1953
Naval Aide to the President Files, 1945–1953

Papers of Dean Acheson, Secretary of State, 1949–1953

Memorandums of Conversations, 1949–1953

Oral Histories

W. Walton Butterworth
O. Edmund Clubb
John F. Melby
Paul H. Nitze

The Eisenhower Library, Abilene, Kansas (DDE)

Presidential Papers (Ann Whitman File), 1953–1960

Committee of Foreign Economic Policy Series (CFEP)
DDE Diary Series
Dulles-Herter Series
International Series
NSC Series
Ann Whitman Diary Series

Papers of John Foster Dulles, Secretary of State, 1953–1959 (JFD)

Subject Files
Telephone Conversations
White House Memoranda

C. D. Jackson Papers

Donovan, Robert J. Manuscript of *Eisenhower: The Inside Story*, 1956. Journalist, President, White House Correspondents' Association, 1954.

The Seeley Mudd Library at Princeton University, New Jersey (SML)

Papers of Allen Dulles

Council on Foreign Relations Files

Oral Histories

Bowie, Robert R. (1909–)—Assistant Secretary of State for Policy Planning
Judd, Walter H. (1898–1994)—U.S. Congressman

Russian Archival Documents

Shen Zhihua, ed. *The Korean War: Newly Declassified Documents from Russian Archives*. Vols. 1–3. Taipei, Taiwan: Institute of Modern History, Academia Sinica, 2004.

The Second National Archives of China, Nanjing, China (SNAC)

KMT Defense Ministry's Reports on Local Situations in the aftermath of KMT's Takeover of CCP Areas, 1947–48
KMT Intelligence Reports on the CCP's Intentions during the Marshall Mediation
KMT Papers on Nationalist China's Economic Reconstruction, 1945–1948
KMT Papers on Sino-American Commercial Treaty Negotiations, 1945–46
KMT Papers on the Marshall Mediation in China, 1945–1947

The Central Archives of China, Beijing, China (CAC)

CCP Intelligence Reports on the KMT Intentions during the Marshall Mediation
CCP Papers, Economic Policy Series, 1950s
CCP Papers on Economic Reconstruction in CCP Areas, 1945–1950
CCP Papers on Implementing "Three-Three Political System" in CCP Areas, 1946–1949
CCP Papers on Land Reform Campaigns, 1946–1949
CCP Papers on the Marshall Mediation in China

The PRC Foreign Ministry Archives, Beijing, China (PRCFM)

Papers on the Bandung Conference, 1954–55
Selected Papers on Sino–Eastern European Relations, 1949–1955
Selected Papers on Sino-Soviet Relations, 1949–1955

Chinese Documents

Chen yi nianpu (The Chronicles of Chen Yi). Vols. 1–2. Beijing: Zhongyang wenxian chubanshe, 1995.
Chen Yun wenxuan (Selected Works of Chen Yun). Vols. 1–2. Beijing: Renmin chubanshe, 1984.
Dangdai zhongguo waijiao (Contemporary Chinese Diplomacy). Beijing: Zhongguo shehui kexue chubanshe, 1987.

Gongheguo wushinian zhengui dangan (Fifty Years of the PRC: Primary Archival Documents). Vols. 1–2. Beijing: Zhongguo dangan chubanshe, 1999.

Jianguo yilai Liu Shaoqi wengao (Liu Shaoqi Papers since the Founding of the PRC). Vol. 1, 1949–1950. Beijing: Zhongyang wenxian chubanshe, 1998.

Jianguo yilai Mao Zedong wengao (Mao Zedong Papers since the Establishment of the PRC). Vols. 1–12. Beijing: Zhongyang wenxian chubanshe, 1987–1997.

Jianguo yilai Zhongyao wenxian xuanbian (Selections of Major Documents since the Founding of the PRC). Vols. 1–15. Beijing: Zhongyang wenxian chubanshe, 1987–1997.

Liu Shaoqi nianpu, 1898–1969 (The Chronicles of Liu Shaoqi, 1898–1969). Vols. 1–2. Beijing: Zhongyang wenxian chubanshe, 1996.

MacFarquhar, Roderick, Timothy Cheek, and Eugene Wu, eds. *The Secret Speeches of Chairman Mao: From the Hundred Flowers to the Great Leap Forward.* Cambridge, MA: Harvard University Press, 1989.

Mao Zedong Junshi Wenji (Collected Military Manuscripts of Mao Zedong). Vols. 1–6. Beijing: Zhongyang wenxian chubanshe, 1993.

Mao Zedong waijiao wenxuan (A Selection of Mao Zedong's Writings on Diplomacy). Beijing: Zhongyang wenxian chubanshe, 1995.

Mao Zedong Xizang gongzuo wenxuan (A Selection of Mao Zedong's Writings on Tibet). Beijing: Zhongyang wenxian chubanshe and Zangxue chubanshe, 2001.

Mao Zedong zai qida de baogao he jianghuaji (Mao Zedong's Reports and Speeches at the Seventh Party Congress, April–June 1945). Beijing: Zhongyang wenxian chubanshe, 2000.

Peng Ming, ed. *Zhongguo xiandaishi ziliao xuanji, 1945–1949* (A Selection of Contemporary Chinese Historical Documents, 1945–1949). Vol. 6. Beijing: Zhongguo renmindaxue chubanshe, 1989.

Re Di, ed. *Zhou Enlai yu Xizang* (Zhou Enlai and Tibet: Zhou Enlai's Writings and Speeches on Tibet). Beijing: Zhongguo zangxue chubanshe, 1998.

Zhonggong bada shi (The Chronicles and Primary Documents of the Eighth Party Congress). Beijing: Zhongyang wenxian chubanshe, 1997.

Zhonggong zhongyang wenjian xuanji (Selected Documents of the CCP Central Committee). Vols. 12–15. Beijing: Zhongyang dangxiao chubanshe, 1985–1988.

Zhongguo jianjin gaige qianyan redian wenti baogao (Report on the Most Controversial Issues in Current Chinese Gradualist Reform). Vols. 1–2. Beijing: Zhongguo guanlikexue chubanshe, 2002 (internally circulated).

Zhongguo junshi guwentuan yuanyue kangfa douzheng shishi (Historical Facts about the Role of the Chinese Military Advisory Group in the Struggle to Aid Vietnam and Resist France). Beijing: Jiefangjun chubanshe, 1990.

Zhou Enlai jingji wenxuan (Selected Works of Zhou Enlai on Economics). Beijing: Zhongyang wenxian chubanshe, 1993.

Zhou Enlai nianpu, 1898–1949 (The Chronicles of Zhou Enlai, 1898–1949). Beijing: Zhongyang wenxian chubanshe, 1989.

Zhou Enlai nianpu, 1949–1976 (The Chronicles of Zhou Enlai, 1949–1976). Vols. 1–3. Beijing: Zhongyang wenxian chubanshe, 1997.

Zhou Enlai 1946 nian tanpan wenxuan (A Selection of Zhou Enlai's Writings during His Negotiations with the KMT in 1946). Beijing: Zhongyang wenxian chubanshe, 1996.

Zhou Enlai waijiao wenxuan (A Selection of Zhou Enlai's Writings on Diplomacy). Beijing: Zhongyang wenxian chubanshe, 1986.

CCP Memoirs

Bo Yibo. *Qishinian fendou yu sikao* (Reflections on Seventy Years of Struggles and Soul-searching). Beijing: Zhonggong zhongyang dangxiao chubanshe, 1999.

———. *Ruogan zhongda juece yu shijian de huigu* (Reflections on Important Decisions and Events). Vols. 1–2. Beijing: Zhonggong zhongyang dangxiao chubanshe, 1991, 1993.

Chen Geng. *Chen Geng Riji* (The Diary of General Chen Geng). Beijing: Jiefangjun chubanshe, 1984.

Du Ping. *Zai Zhi yuan jun Zongbu* (In the Headquarters of the People's Volunteer Army). Beijing: Jiefangjun chubanshe, 1991.

Hong Xuezhi. *Kangmei yuanchao zhanzheng huiyi* (Recollections of the War to Resist U.S. Aggression and Aid Korea). Beijing: Jiefangjun wenyi chubanshe, 1990.

Hu Qiaomu. *Hu Qiaomu huiyi Mao Zedong* (Hu Qiaomu Remembers Mao Zedong). Beijing: Renmin chubanshe, 1995.

Huang Hua. "My Contact with John Leighton Stuart after Nanjing's Liberation." Trans. Li Xiaobing. *Chinese Historians* 5, no. 1 (Spring 1992): 47–56.

Huang Kecheng. *Huang Kecheng zishu* (The Autobiography of Huang Kecheng). Beijing: Renmin chubanshe, 1994.

Kang Maozhao. *Waijiaoguan huiyilu* (A Diplomat's Memoir). Introduction by Huang Hua. Beijing: Zhongyang wenxian chubanshe, 2000.

Li Rui. *Lushan huiyi shilu* (A Truthful Account of the Lushan Conference). Hong Kong: Tiandi Tushu, 1993).

Li Weihan. *Huiyi yu yanjiu* (Recollections and Reflections). Vols. 1–2. Beijing: Zhonggong dangshi ziliao chubanshe, 1986.

Li Yueran. *Memoir: Zhongsu waijiao qinliji* (Witness Sino-Soviet Diplomacy: Mao's Russian Interpreter's Testimony). Beijing: Shijie zhishi chubanshe, 2001.

Liu Xiao. *Chushi sulian ba nian* (Eight-Year Diplomatic Mission to the Soviet Union). Beijing: Zhonggong dangshi chubanshe, 1986.

Luo Guipo. *Hongzhua yizong* (Recollections of My Mission to Vietnam). Nanjing: Jiangsu renmin chubanshe, 1995.

Nie Rongzhen. *Nie Rongzhen yuanshuai huiyilu* (The Memoir of Marshall Nie Rongzhen). Beijing: Jiefangjun chubanshe, 2005.

Peng Dehuai. *Peng Dehuai zishu* (The Autobiography of Peng Dehuai). Beijing: Renmin chubanshe, 1981.

Shi Zhe. *Lingxiu Mao Zedong* (Leader Mao Zedong). Beijing: Hongqi chubanshe, 1997.

——. *Zai lishi juren shenbian: Shi Zhe huiyilu* (At the Side of History's Giants: The Memoirs of Shi Zhe). Rev. ed. Beijing: Zhongyang wenxian chubanshe, 1995.

Tong Xiaopeng. *Fengyu sishinian* (Forty Years of Braving Wind and Rain). Vols. 1–2. Beijing: Zhongyang wenxian chubanshe, 1996.

Wang Bingnan. *Zhongmei huitan jiu nian huigu* (Review of the Nine-Year Sino-American Ambassadorial Talks). Beijing: Shijie zhishi chubanshe, 1985.

Wang Dongxing. *Wang Dongxing Riji* (The Diary of Wang Dongxing). Beijing: Zhongguo shehuikexue chubanshe, 1993.

Wu Lengxi. *Shinian lunzhan* (Ten Years of Debates: Recollections of Sino-Soviet Relations, 1956–1966). Beijing: Zhongyang wenxian chubanshe, 2000.

Wu Xiuquan. *Huiyi yu huainian* (Recollections and Cherishing the Memories). Beijing: Zhonggong zhongyang dangxiao chubanshe, 1995.

——. *Zai waijiaobu ba nian de Jingli, 1950.1–1958.10* (Eight Years' Experience in the Foreign Ministry, January 1950–October 1958). Beijing: Shijie zhishi chubanshe, 1988.

Xiao Xiangqian. *Wei Zhongri shidai yiuhao nulifendou* (Recollections of Sino-Japanese Negotiations: Fighting for Sino-Japanese Enduring Friendship). Nanjing: Jiangsu renmen chubanshe, 1994.

Xu Xiangqian. *Lishi de huigu* (In Retrospect). Beijing: Jiefangjun chubanshe, 1998.

Xue Muqiao. *Xue Muqiao huiyi lu* (Xue Muqiao's Memoir). Tianjin: Tianjin renmin chubanshe, 1996.

Yang Dezhi. *Huiyilu* (The Memoir of Yang Dezhi). Beijing: Jiefangjun chubanshe, 1992.

Yang Di. *Zai Zhi yuan jun zongbu de suiyueli* (My Years in the Headquarters of the People's Voluntary Army: A Truthful Account of the Events Unknown to the Outside World). Beijing: Jiefangjun chubanshe, 1998.

Yang Gongsu. *Yige waijiao teshi de huiyi* (An Ambassador's Memoir). Hainan, Guandong: Hainan chubanshe, 1999.

Yang Shangkun. *Huiyi lu* (Yang Shangkun's Memoir). Beijing: Zhongyang wenxian chubanshe, 2001.

——. *Yang Shangkun riji* (The Diary of Yang Shangkun). 2 vols. Beijing: Zhongyang wenxian, chubanshe, 2001.

Ye Fei. *Ye Fei huiyilu* (Memoirs of Ye Fei). Beijing: Jiefangjun chubanshe, 1988.

Yu Guangyuan, Wang Enmao, Ren Zhongyi, and Li Desheng. *Gaibian zhongguo mingyun de sishiyi tian* (The Forty-One Days That Changed China). Shenzhen, Guandong: Haitian chubanshe, 1998.

Index

Acheson, Dean: views on modernity and identity, 7; on promotion of Titoism, 98–99, 108; on military withdrawal from Taiwan, 102–103, 136; on "defensive perimeter" in the Western Pacific or "enclave strategy," 103–104; on Asian consciousness, 104–105; defending NSC 41, 105–106; disagreement with Congress, 106–107; on U.S. military buildup, 109; and secret communications channel with the CCP, 132; response to Ward spy case, 149; Korean War decisions, 162–164. *See also* State Department, U.S.

"Agreement on Commerce and Transportation between India and Tibet of China," 254, 273

America. *See* United States

America's Response to China, 8

Anarchism, after Revolution of 1911, 25

Antirightist campaign, 236, 243, 247–250, 283–284

Anti-Right Opportunist Campaigns, 219

Asian consciousness, 104–105

Atom bomb, 87

Atomism, 14

Attlee, Clement, 187, 256

Bangdung Conference, 271

Barr, David, 96

Barracks, CCP's seizure of, 134–136

Bevin, Ernest, 187

Blueprints, economic, 205–227

Blueprints, political, 228–241

Bolton, Rep. Frances, 170–171

Bowie, Robert, 173, 180

Bo Yibo, 206, 248

Bretton Woods Monetary Agreement, 33–34

Burma, 270–272

Byrnes, James, 59–60

Cadres, CCP, vs. intellectuals, 231–233, 235, 239–240, 244–245, 293

Cao Juren, 283

Carr, Edward, 305

Catholic spy case, 133–134

CCP. *See* Chinese Communist Party (CCP)

Central Daily, 90

Central Intelligence Agency (CIA), 109, 163, 295

CFEP. *See* Committee of Foreign Economic Policy (CFEP)

Chang, Gordon H., 3, 202

Cheng Siyuan, 283

Chen Mingshu, Gen., 132–133

Chen Yi, 230, 233, 244, 249, 256, 258, 285

Chen Yun, 207, 210

Chiang Kai-shek: on industrialization, 38–42; and united front, 65, 66; Mao's views on, 69; in coalition negotiations,

Chiang Kai-shek (*continued*)
76–82; support for PCC Resolution, 77–78; on army ratios, 79–80; elected president, 89; and Taiwan Strait crises, 283

China, 30–56, 119–121, 169–170, 301–302

China-American Council of Commerce and Industry, Inc., 35

China Committee (CHINCOM), 183, 196

China Desk. *See* State Department, U.S.

China Differential, 183, 187, 191–192, 195–197

China's Destiny, 65

China's Financial and Economic Daily, 303

China threat, 301

China-U.S. relations: deterioration of, 2, 298; importance of history to, 8–9; misjudgments in, 8; study of antagonism in, 8; diplomatic relations discussions, 128–129, 131–132; actions against consulates, 130–131; secret communications channel, 132–133, 148; pre–Korean War objectives, 137; deterrence and moderation in, 140–141; policy similarities of, 143; demand for equality, 148–150; Korean War misjudgments, 167–168; in the 1950s, 279–289; two-leg theory, 289; Vietnam conflict, 292–296; future of, 301–306; danger of security dilemma dynamics to, 304; importance of examining policy assumptions, 305. *See also* Self-fulfilling prophecy

China-USSR relations: Chiang government recognition, 71; and Port Arthur base, 71; U.S. plan for split between, 99, 102, 105, 112, 143, 150, 173–174, 179, 202–203; China's need for Soviet support, 119, 121–122, 123–124; "leaning to one side" policy, 121–127; in the 1950s, 258–268; deterioration of, 263–268. *See also* Titoism, promotion of

CHINCOM. *See* China Committee (CHINCOM)

Chinese, overseas, 173

Chinese Communist Party (CCP): Zhou Enlai on relationship between CCP land revolution and national revolution, 26; united front, 26, 65–67, 73–74; anti-legalism of, 27; Truman's view of, 61–

62; in coalition negotiations, 76–82; Manchurian civil war, 77, 82–88; support for PCC Resolution, 78–79; considers American model, 78; military of, 85–87; position on Tito, 113–114; relations with Third Force, 114–118; need for Soviet support, 119, 121–122; seizure of American barracks, 134–136; insistence on New Democracy, 138–139; and John Leighton Stuart, 145–147; distrust of U.S. China policy, 147; defense of 38th parallel, 151, 153–161, 164–168; Taiwan campaign buildup, 153; conflicting visions of domestic reconstruction in, 205–241; response to Soviet criticism, 246; anti-intellectualism in, 248; mediates in Soviet bloc, 261, 262; relationship between domestic and foreign policies, 289–292; post–Cold War reform in, 302–303. *See also* Blueprints, economic; Blueprints, political; Deng Xiaoping; Mao Zedong; Zhou Enlai

Chinese Exclusion Laws, 49–50

Chinese Industrial Association, 40, 43

Chinese Northeast Border Defense Army (NEBDA), 154

Chinese People's Volunteer Army, 157

Christianity, in China, 18, 27, 251, 299

Class warfare, 212, 217, 302

Clubb, Oliver Edmund, 135, 144, 164

Coalition government, Chinese, 69, 73–74, 76–80, 117

COCOM. *See* Consultative Group Coordinating Committee (COCOM)

Cohen, Paul A., 2–3

Cohen, Warren I., 8, 294

Cominform, 113, 118

Command economy, Stalinist, 220–221

Commerce Department, U.S., 186, 191

Commerce, Navigation and Friendship Treaty, 33–34

Committee of Foreign Economic Policy (CFEP), 180, 194, 196–197

Common Program, 117, 206, 207

Communes, public institutions in, 218

Communist Party of Yugoslavia (CPY), 96, 113–114

Confrontation thesis, 138, 141

Congress, U.S., 54, 106–107

Connally, Sen. Tom, 50

Constitution, U.S., 28–29

Constitutional rule, and democratic transition, 24–25
Consultative Group Coordinating Committee (COCOM), 183–184, 196
Containment strategy, or peripheral military containment strategy, 178–179, 180, 183, 269, 293, 296
Core policy assumptions, discovering, 4–5
Council on Foreign Relations Study Group on Sino-Soviet Relations, 172
Cultural filters, 3
Cultural predisposition, concept of, 5–6
Cultural values, in policymaking, 6–9
Culture, Chinese, 29–32, 254–255, 291–292, 294–295, 299, 315n56
Culture, defined, 5–6

Da Gong Bao, 51–52, 72, 77, 115
Dalai Lama, 272–275
Defense Department, U.S., 191–192, 195
Defensive perimeter, 103–104, 151, 169, 180, 183
Democracy, 24, 27–28, 28–29, 62–67
Democratic League, 88–90, 92, 115
Democratic Republic of Vietnam (DRV), 268–270
Democratic transition, theory of, 24–25
Deng Xiaoping, 29–30, 122, 127, 249, 266, 267
Deng Zihui, 208–209, 210
Dewey, John, 4
Dietman's League for the Promotion of Sino-Japanese Trade, 185
Diplomacy, Chinese: and diplomatic tradition, 13, 291–292, 294–295, 315n56; and economic and political blueprints, 253–254; foreign policy setbacks, 253; peaceful coexistence policy, 253, 254–258; equality of nations, 256–257; conflict management, 257–258; and the Soviet Union, 258–268; in North Vietnam and North Korea, 262–263; in Vietnam, 268–270; in Burma, 270–272; in India, 272–276; in Japan, 276–279; in the United States, 279–289; two-leg theory, 289, 292; nationalism in, 291–292; critique of exporting revolution, 293
Double Ten Agreement, 76–77
Dulles, Allen, 176
Dulles, John Foster: on modernity and identity, 7; belief in Chinese expansion

plans, 177–178, 181–183; reversal of enclave strategy, and installation of peripheral military containment strategy, 179–180, 183, 269, 293, 296; on American responsibility, 182–183; on Japanese trade, 185–186; disagreement with Lodge, 191; talks with Eden, 191, 192; on British trade, 195; on PRC recognition, 198–199; death of, 199; quoting Pericles, 199; and Taiwan Strait crises, 282, 284–285; discussed by CCP, 288; misperception of Chinese intentions, 293–294

Economic Defense Advisory Committee (EDAC), 180–181, 183, 194
Economic reconstruction, in world politics, 305
Economy, Chinese: Taiping rebels' radical populist vision of, 18, 22, 223–224; Constitutionalists' social market vision of, 18–19, 22; Republican revolutionaries' vision of mixed economy, 19–20, 22–23; Principle of People's Livelihood, 19–20, 29; government's role in, 19–20; similarities and differences with United States, 22–23; Deng's and Sun's visions of, 30; U.S. restrictions on, 101–102, 109, 110–111; Eisenhower's views on, 174–175; State Department views on, 176; CCP's gradualist blueprint of, 205–213, 225–226; CCP's radical populist blueprint of, 213–220, 225–226; Great Leap Forward, 217–219; relations with Soviet model of industrialization, 220–224; comparison of gradualist and radical populist blueprints, 225–226. See also Command economy, Stalinist; Gradualist economic blueprint; Mixed economy; Populist economic blueprint
Economy, U.S., 20–23
EDAC. See Economic Defense Advisory Committee (EDAC)
Eden, Anthony, 189, 191, 192
Egalitarianism, absolute, 23
"Eight Principles for Chinese Foreign Economic Aid," 255
Einstein, Albert, 8
Eisenhower, Dwight D.: inducement policy of, 170–175, 295; on Chinese nationalism and communism, 171–175;

Eisenhower, Dwight D. (*continued*)
on NSC 68 and Soviet intention, 174;
on new concept of national security,
174–175, 345–346n12; on China
embargo, 184, 190–191, 192–194, 196;
on Japanese trade, 186; on British
trade, 190–196; and Reciprocal Trade
Act, 200; racist comments of, 201–202;
support for Taiwan, 201; changed view
of CCP, 287
Eisenhower administration, 170, 180, 203,
204, 226–227, 292–296
Eisenhower-Eden communique, 192
Embargo, China, 178–179, 180–183, 183–
196. *See also* China Differential
Enclave military strategy, 103–104, 183;
vs. strategy of peripheral military
containment, 175–182
Equality, Chinese search for, 148–150, 299

Fairbank, John King, 141, 251
Fei Xiaotong, 239–240
Filters, cultural, 3
Formosa. *See* Taiwan
Four Freedoms policy, 209
Freedom, Chinese, American conceptions
of, 11–17
Fugh, Philip, 145

Gao Gang, 130, 154, 220–221
Geertz, Clifford, 6
"The General Principles Regarding China's
Postwar Industrialization," 39–42, 45–
46
Geneva Agreement, 181
George, Alexander, 304–305
Global civil society, constructing, 306
Golden Mean doctrine, 32
Goldstein, Judith, 7
Go West Campaign, 302
Gradualist economic blueprint: mixed
economy, 205–208; peaceful
redemption, 209–210; voluntarism, 210–
211; and rural cooperative movement,
210; problems with implementing, 211–
213; impact of, on economy, 213;
overturned by Party Congress, 216;
comparison with populist blueprint, 225–
226; prosperity under, 290
Gradualist political blueprint: key
components, 229; history of CCP policy
toward intellectuals, 229–231, 248–249;

Hundred Flowers policy, 238–241;
problems with implementing, 241–242;
response to Soviet critiques of, 246;
philosophical underpinnings, 248–252
Grantham, Alexander, 171
Great Britain, and China embargo, 187–
196
Great Leap Forward, 217–219
Green GDP growth rate, 302
Greenstone, J. David, 15
Gromyko, Andrei, 126
Guanchajia magazine, 89
Guangming Daily, 241

Hamilton, Alexander, 14, 21
Harding, Harry, 8
Hartz, Louis, 15
Hatoyama, Ichiro, 185, 278
Herter, Christian, 202, 266
Herter Doctrine, 202–204
Hoang Van Hoan, 270
Ho Chi-minh, 181, 268–270, 294
Hoffman, Paul, 97, 98
Hong Kong, 188
Hong Rengan (Hung Jen-gan), 18
Hong Xiuquan, 12–13, 18, 23–24, 27, 70,
223–224
Huang Hua, 128–129, 145, 149–150
Huan Xiang, 135
Hu Hanmin, 63, 64
Hume, David, 20, 21
Hundred Flowers policy: American
attitude toward, 176, 237–238, 252;
purpose and function of, 238–239;
intellectuals' ideas for, 240–241, 248–
249; Soviet response to, 245–248; and
nuclear program, 247–248. *See also*
Gradualist political blueprint
Hungarian uprising, effects on China, 242,
262, 281
Hunt, Michael, 2, 291–292
Hu Qiaomu, 84–85, 86, 126, 136, 159
Hurley, Gen. Patrick, 57, 70, 97–98
Hu Shi, 12–13

Ideology, 4; defined, 5
Immerman, Richard, 300
Immigration law, U.S., 48, 49–50
India, 272–276
Industrialization, Chinese: U.S. business
community on, 34–38; financing for, 35–
36, 37, 43–45; tariff reductions for, 35,

36, 43; privatization for, 36–38, 45–46; Chinese Nationalist views on, 38–42; Chinese-U.S. visions for, 43–46; and national treatment, 47–49; U.S. loan for, 50–51; Mao's views on, 68–69; and U.S. trade policy, 100–102; necessity for modern China, 205; and gradualist economic blueprint, 212–213; differences from Soviet industrialization, 221–222; need for peaceful environment, 280

"Industrial Reconstruction Program in Postwar China," 40–42

Intellectuals: history of CCP policy toward, 229–231, 248–249; Chen Yi's experience as, 230–231; recruitment of, by CCP, 230–231; vs. CCP cadres, 231–233, 235, 293; coercion of, 231; China's need for, 236; encouraged to surrender, 236; response to Hundred Flowers policy, 239; criticism of, 241–242; reinstated by Deng, 248–249. See also Third Force, Chinese; Urban Chinese

Intermediate zone theory, 85

Iriye, Akira, 3

Isaacs, Harold, 6, 7

Japan, 276–279

Jefferson, Thomas, 14, 21, 28

Jehl, Douglas, 295

Jervis, Robert, 8, 95–96

Jilin Daily, 241

Jinmen, shelling of, 281–282

Johnson, Alexis, 284

Johnson, Louis, 105, 109

Johnston, Alastair Iain, 5

Joint Chiefs of Staff, 191–192, 195

Journalists, U.S., invited to China, 180, 197–198, 279–280

Judd, Rep. Walter, 170–171, 190

Kang Yuwei, 12, 18–19

Kano, Hisaakira, 184

Kant, Immanuel, 15–16

Kennan, George, 109, 161

Keohane, Robert, 7

Khamba uprising, 273–274, 276

Khrushchev, Nikita, 199, 202–203, 245–247, 263–268

Kim Il-Sung, 86, 151, 157

Kishi, Nobusuke, 278

Kissinger, Henry, 109–110

KMT. See Kuomintang (KMT)

Knowland, Sen. William, 106, 174, 190, 193

Korea, bill for aid to, 106

Korean War, 95–96, 151–168, 184. See also 38th parallel

Kovalev, Ivan, 122, 125, 127, 129–130

Kuomintang (KMT): united front with CCP, 26, 65–67; and elections, 27; and postwar industrialization, 40–46; U.S. support of, 59–60, 111–112; U.S. relations with, 60–62; vision of democracy, 62–67; and judicial reform, 63; early CCP negotiations, 76–82; military clashes with CCP, 77; takeover of Manchurian cities, 82; reactions to Manchurian civil war, 84–85; military strength of, 87; land reform efforts of, 91; collapse of government, 96

Landed elite, 25–26, 27

Land reform, 26, 67–68, 69–70, 75–76, 90, 91, 230, 326–327n102

Lao Zi, 255, 257

"Leaning to one side" policy, 121–127, 259

"Left-adventurism," 211

"Left extremism," 219

Leninist doctrine, 175–176

Levine, Steven, 2, 5

Liang Qichao, 12, 18–19, 27

Liang Shumin, 115–116

Liaoning Daily, 241

Liberal peace, 15–16

Li Jishen, 283

Li Lisan, 167

Lin Biao, 155

Lippman, Walter, 1

Lipset, Seymour Martin, 15, 17

Liu Shaoqi: On Internationalism and Nationalism, 114, 119–121; negotiates with Stalin, 123; Stuart's view of, 145; Tianjin talks, 208, 221; on Soviet bloc uprisings, 212; on the NPC, 234; mediates in Soviet bloc, 261–262

Liu Yalou, 86

Li Zehou, 17

Li Zicheng, 114–115

Li Zongren, 89, 282–283, 284

Lloyd, Selwyn, 195

Locke, John, 15

Lodge, Henry Cabot, Jr., 190
Lo Haisha, 132–133
Luo Longji, 88–89, 92, 241
Lushun, Soviet base at, 124, 126, 151, 160

MacArthur, Gen. Douglas, 153, 154, 162, 164
MacFarquhar, Roderick, 237–238
Macmillan, Harold, 195
Magill, R. N., 99–100, 107–108
Malinovski, Marshal R., 263
Mamoru, Shigemitsui, 185
Manchuria, 71, 81–85, 88, 159–160
"The mandate of heaven," 24
Mao Zedong: on industrialization, 68–69; theory of New Democracy, 68–70; on Chiang's role, 69; city takeover plan of, 71–72; in coalition negotiations, 76–82; intermediate zone theory of, 85; people's war theory of, 86–88; on internationalism, 120–121; and Sino-Soviet treaty, 124–127; questions U.S. trade intentions, 127; agreement with barracks seizure, 135; communication with Stalin, 136–137, 154–156, 165–166; confrontation thesis with regard to Mao's policy toward the United States, 138–139; meeting with Kim Il-Sung, 152; decision to enter Korean War, 156–161; on mixed economy, 205–206; concern for peasants' welfare, 213–216; on the gradualist economic blueprint, 213; and the Great Leap Forward, 217–219; on Stalinist command economy, 222–223; influenced by Mohist philosophy, 226; calls for strikes and demonstrations, 235–236; and Hundred Flowers policy, 237–245; disagrees with Soviets, 246–248; criticizes Soviet metaphysics, 249–250; misjudgment of intellectuals, 250; disillusionment with United States, 259; and Sino-Soviet submarine fleet, 263–265; cult of personality, 267; peace initiative of, 279–281; reaction to two Chinas concept, 285; CCP discussion on Dulles, 288; two-leg theory, 289; comparisons to Hitler, 295
Marriage Law, 117
Marshall, Gen. George, 57, 59, 77, 79–80, 82–84, 162

Marshall mission, 57–58, 60, 91–94
Martin, Rep. Thomas, 189
Mass movement, in China, 63–64
Ma Xulun, 92
May, Ernest, 8
Ma Yingchu, 240, 243
Mazu, shelling of, 281–282
McCarthy, Sen. Joseph, 107, 189, 294
McClellan, Sen. John, 193
McClintock, Robert, 173
McConaughy, Walter, 162–163, 181
McNamara, Robert, 169, 294
Mencius, 255
Metaphysics, Soviet, 249–250, 255
Mikoyan, Anastas, 126, 258
Military rule, and democratic transition, 24
Mixed economy, 19–20, 22, 39–40, 45–47, 206–209
Modernity, and freedom, 13
Modernity, and identity, 6–7, 30–32, 298–299, 303–304. See also Visions, cultural
Mohist philosophy, 226, 251
Molotov, V. M., 136
Monarchy, constitutionalist, 23–24
Moral citizenry, 27, 29
Morality, as policy justification, 6, 297; and as policy rationality, 6–7, 297–298
Morgenthau, Hans, 165, 294–295
Most-favored-nation treatment, 47–49, 51

Nagasaki national flag incident, 278
National Foreign Trade Convention, U.S., 34–35
National Foreign Trade Council, 35
Nationalism, Chinese, 141–142, 160, 171–172, 291–292, 299–300
Nationalists. See Kuomintang (KMT)
Nationality Act (1940), 49
National People's Conference (NPC), 234
National Security Council (NSC), 97
National treatment, 47–49, 51
Naval Intelligence Agency, 179
Nehru, Jawaharlal, 155, 254, 272–276
New center, in Chinese politics, 302–303
New Deal, 21–22
New Democracy, 67–69, 114–115, 117, 120, 138–139, 205–206
"A New Look at U.S. Economic Security Policies and Actions," 180
Newspapers, Chinese: Da Gong Bao, 51–52, 72, 77, 115; Chen Yen Pao, 52;

Hsin Wen Pao, 52; *Shang Wu Ji Pao*, 53; *Central Daily*, 90; *Jiefang ribao*, 90; *People's Daily*, 239, 241; *Guangming Daily*, 241; *Jilin Daily*, 241; *Liaoning Daily*, 241; *China's Financial and Economic Daily*, 303

Ngo Dinh Diem, 181–182, 269

Nie Rongzhen, 155, 156–157

Nitze, Paul, 109

Nixon, Richard, 6

North China Finance and Trade Conference, 206

NSC 41, 105–106

"NSC 48/2—U.S. Policy toward Asia," 105–106

NSC 68, 109–110, 161, 174

NSC 81/1, 162

Nye, Joseph, 301

Office of Naval Intelligence (ONI), 109

Ojha, Ishwer, 291

On Coalition Government, 67–68, 118

"On Ibsenism," 12–13

"On Internationalism and Nationalism," 119–120

On New Democracy, 205–206

On Socialist Economy, 224

On the People's Democratic Dictatorship, 118

"On the Question of Agricultural Cooperatives," 215

On the Relationship between Group Rights and Individual Rights, 12

Organicism, 14–15

"Our Policies toward Communism in China," 198–199

Pakistan, 256

Panikkar, K. M., 155, 162–163

Pan Yue, 302

Particularism, cultural, 10

Peaceful coexistence: philosophical foundation of, 254–255, 290; five principles of, 254, 258, 260; importance to China's future, 254; preconditions for, 255–256; "Eight Principles for Chinese Foreign Economic Aid," 255; and great power chauvinism, 256–257; American views on, 257; applied to Soviet bloc, 260–261, 262; applied to Asian neighbors, 268–279; applied to

United States, 279–281; shifted to policy of "two legs," 288–289

Peasants, Chinese: and urban Chinese, 26, 31, 293, 299, 302; quasi-judicial powers of, 27; and industrialization, 44–45; failure of KMT plan for, 63–65; Mao's plans for, 68–70; become landowners, 90–91; and the gradualist economic blueprint, 208–211; concerns for welfare of, 213–216; and the Great Leap Forward, 217–219; use radical economic blueprint, 224; need for partnerships with urban China, 228, 248

The Peloponnesian War, 297

Peng Dehui, 155, 156, 158, 160, 218, 263, 287

People's Daily, 239, 241

People's Liberation Army (PLA), 96, 128, 130–131

People's Republic of China (PRC), 5, 117, 295. *See also* Blueprints, economic; Blueprints, political; Diplomacy, Chinese

People's war theory, 86–88

Pham Van Dong, 262

Polish uprising, 260–262

Political Consultative Conference (PCC), 76, 77–78, 117, 233–234

"Political Designers Academy," 240

"The Political, Economic, and International Standing of the PRC," 266

Polity, modern, 23–28

Population control, 240, 256

Populist economic blueprint, 225–226

Port Arthur. *See* Lushun, Soviet base at

Powell, Colin, 304

Principle of People's Livelihood, 20, 22–23, 29, 38–39, 45–46, 55–56. *See also* Mixed economy

Prochnow, Herbert, 192

Psychology, of containment strategy, 179

Public Opinion, 1

Qin Xiaoying, 303

Quotas, for immigration, 48, 50, 54

Racism, in Chinese-U.S. relations, 49–50, 51, 54, 201–202

Radical populist political blueprint, 236–237, 248, 249, 267–268, 289–290

Rankin, Karl, 55

Reciprocal Trade Act and Mutual Security Bill, 200
Reconstruction, of China, 58–76
Religion, in a republic, 28
Religious freedom, 134
Remer, Charles, 43, 45–46
Republic of China, second, 62
"Respectful Address to the Chinese Communist Party," 115–116
Revolution of 1911, 24–25
Rights, individual and group, 11–13
Robertson, Walter, 175–177, 178, 181, 194, 198
Rodgers, Daniel, 15
Romance of Three Kingdoms, 116
Roosevelt, Franklin D., 21–22
Roosevelt, Theodore, 21
Rosenberg, Emily S., 301
Roshchin, Nikolai, 152, 156
Ross, Robert S., 8
Rostow, W. W., 55–56
Rousseau, Jean-Jacques, 20
Rozman, Gilbert, 7
Rubin, Barry, 298
Ruji Qing, 75
Rural Chinese. *See* Peasants, Chinese
Rusk, Dean, 111
Russian Revolution of 1917, 25

Schaller, Michael, 3
Schuman, Robert, 110
Schwartz, Benjamin, 172
Self-fulfilling prophecy, in U.S.-China interactions, 296, 301
September 11, effects on Chinese diplomacy, 301, 304
Shen Zhihua, 151
Shepilov, Dmitrii, 261–262
Shi Cuntong, 25
Shi Zhe, 136
Sihanouk, Prince, 272
Sino-American Industrial and Commercial Association, 35
Sino-American Treaty of 1880, 49
Sino-Soviet Agreement on Soviet Aid in Hi-Tech Defense Industry, 264
Sino-Soviet Friendship and Alliance Treaty (1945), 71, 119
Sino-Soviet Treaty of Friendship, Alliance, and Mutual Assistance (1950), 124–127
Socialism, 4, 30, 90; concept of, without class struggle vs. with class struggle, 225–226, 248–252
"Some Ideological Aspects of Sino-Soviet Relations," 172
Song Qingling, 91
Song Yishan, 283
Southeast Asia Treaty Organization (SEATO), 275
South Korea, 103–104
South Vietnam, 169. *See also* Peripheral military containment strategy; Vietnam; Vietnam War
Soviet Union: and Port Arthur base, 71; recognition of Chiang government, 71; influence on coalition negotiations, 81–82; and Manchurian civil war, 84–85; lack of military aid to CCP, 85–86; split with Yugoslavia, 96–97; report of atomic attack by, 109; reactions to New Democracy, 118; differences from Chinese industrialization, 221–222; emphasizes socialist industrialization, 221; response to Hundred Flowers policy, 245–248; Sino-Soviet submarine fleet, 263–265. *See also* Stalin, Joseph
Stalin, Joseph: involvement in CCP-KMT negotiations, 72; and Manchurian civil war, 84–85; distrust of CCP, 113, 122; reactions to New Democracy, 118–119; negotiations with Liu, 123–124; and Sino-Soviet treaty, 125–127; communication with Mao, 136–137, 154–156, 165–166; on Acheson's speech, 136–137; Korean War involvement, 151–152, 154–156, 157–158, 166–167; on Chinese industrialization, 223, 224
Stassen, Harold, 191
State Department, U.S.: and Chinese industrialization, 37–38, 43–46, 49–50; China reconstruction vision in post–World War II years, 58–62; and promotion of Titoism, 98–99; and pre–Korean War China trade policy, 99–102, 107, 111–112; conflicting policy assumptions of, 141–142; reaction to Zhou Enlai Demarche, 144–145; China policies discredited, 168; perception of PRC foreign policy intentions in the 1950s, 175–178, 203–204, 293; disagreement with Lodge, 190–191;

concept of two Chinas, 285. *See also* Acheson, Dean; Dulles, John Foster

Strikes and demonstrations, Mao calls for, 235–236

Strong, Anna Louise, 87

Stuart, John Leighton, 89, 96, 128, 132–133, 145–147

Stuart, W. W., 100

Submarine fleet, Sino-Soviet, 263–265

Suettinger, Robert L., 295–296

Suhrawardy, H. S., 256

Sun Fo, 40, 43, 66, 79, 80

Sun Yat-sen: on nonaggression, 4; on freedom, 13; on freedom of wealth, 16; on mixed economy, 19–20, 22–23; on democracy, 23–24; and democratic transition theory, 24–25, 62–63; proposes united front, 26; on morality, 27; Three Principles of the People, 31, 299, 304; Theory of Democratic Transition, 62–63; KMT support of theories, 62; Mao's emphasis on, 73; defended by Liu, 120. *See also* Principle of People's Livelihood

Sun Yat-sen, Madam, 117

Supreme National Defense Council, 39, 41–42

Suslov, Mikhail, 267

Taiping rebellion, 18, 23–24, 251, 299

Taiwan: industrialization of, 55–56; bill for aid to, 106; blockade of east China, 121–122; Chinese desire to split U.S. alliance, 143; views on Titoism, 180; Cairo Declaration (1943), 281; shelling of Jinmen and Mazu, 281–282, 285–287; Beijing's peace initiative toward, 282–283. *See also* Chiang Kai-shek

Taiwan Strait crisis, first, 281–282

Taiwan Strait crisis, second, 285–287

Teetor, Loshair, 186

The Theory of China's Economy, 38–39, 45

Theory of Democratic Transition, 24–25, 62–63

"Theory on Population Control," 240

Third Force, Chinese: composition of, 58, 74; feelings toward CCP, 74–75; political program of, 74; on land reform, 75–76; belief in coalition government, 76; support for PCC Resolution, 78; and Manchurian civil

war, 85; opposition to U.S. aid bill, 91–93; relations with CCP, 114–118; continued CCP alliance, 138–139. *See also* Intellectuals; Urban Chinese

38th parallel: importance of, 151–164; CCP's defense of, 151; troops cross, 154–155, 157; U.S. decision on, 161–164; thesis on, 164–168. *See also* Korean War

Three Principles of the People, 31, 299, 304

Thucydides, 297

Tibet, 272–276

Titoism, promotion of, 98–99, 106, 145, 173, 180, 187–188

Tocqueville, Alexis de, 15, 28

Treaty negotiations, commercial, 47–53

Truman, Harry S., 61–62, 103, 147, 153, 164

Truman administration, 33–56, 83, 84, 96–99, 161–164. *See also* United States

Truman Doctrine, 62

Tutelage rule, 24, 62–63, 65. *See also* Theory of Democratic Transition

The Twenty Years' Crisis, 1919–1939, 305

Two-leg theory, 289, 292

United front, CCP and KMT, 65–67, 68–69, 70

United States: attitude toward communism, 4; worldview of, 31–32; lack of feudal heritage, 31; post–World War II agenda of, 33; and Chinese industrialization, 34–38; and China's democratization, 58–62, 88–94; pre–Korean War new economic strategy toward CCP, 97–98, 99–102; pre–Korean War new military strategy toward Taiwan, 102–105; enclave military strategy vs. peripheral military containment strategy, 103–104, 177–183; implementation of new China policy, 105–111; conflicting assessments of PRC's nature and intentions in the 1950s, 170–178, 196–204; strategy of containment by, 178–179, 180, 183, 269, 293, 296; non-recognition of PRC, 198–199; post–Cold War relations with China, 279–289; and Taiwan Strait crises, 282, 284; misjudgment of Chinese intentions, 292–296, 300, 304–305

Universalism, cultural, 10
U Nu, 270–272
Urban Chinese: conflict with rural Chinese, 26, 31, 293; treaty protests by, 51–53; support of KMT, 63; split with KMT, 89–90, 92; anti-Americanism of, 122; need for rural coalition, 248; benefits of coalition with peasants, 299; widening gap with peasants in the 1990s, 302. See also Intellectuals; Third Force, Chinese
"U.S. Policy Regarding Trade with Chinese Communists," 105
USSR. See Soviet Union

Vietnam: U.S. interest in, 110; elections scheduled for, 181; peripheral military containment against PRC in, 183, 269, 293; China diplomacy in, 268–270; French activity in, 268; origins of Vietnam War revisited, 292–296
Vietnamese National Liberation Front, 269
Vietnam War: origins revisited, 169, 292–296; installation of peripheral military containment strategy in, 169–183; and Sino-Soviet relations, 266–268, 270; China's new Vietnam policy, 268–270; and Sino-American relations, 288–289. See also Vietnam
Vincent, John Carter, 60, 88, 93
Visions, cultural: of modernity and identity, defined, 6–7; Chinese and American, on freedom, 11–17; on modern economy, 17–23; on democracy, 23–29; Chinese and American, similarities and differences, 29–32; impact of, on policy choices, 300–301
Voltaire, 20
Voroshilov, K. Y., 246–247, 261

Walstrom, Joe, 192
Wang Guofan cooperative, 214
Ward, Angus I., 129, 130, 139–140
Ward spy case, 131–132, 133, 138, 139–140, 149
War of Resistance, KMT-CCP alliance in, 65
Wedmeyer, Albert C., 57
Wen Yiduo, 88
White Terror, 70
Whiting, Allen S., 164–165

Wilson, Woodrow, 15–16, 21, 23
Women's liberation, 117
Wong Wenhao, 43–44
Worldview, differences in, 29–32. See also Visions, cultural
Wu Xiuquan, 122–123

Xinhua Yuebao, 221

Yalta Agreement, 84, 85, 151
Yan Fu, 12
Yang Kuisong, 140
Yang Shangqui, 244
Yin Chung-jun, 55–56
Yin-Yang balance, 29, 30, 32, 249
Young, Kenneth, 285
Yudin, Pavel, 126, 263, 264
Yu-pin, Bishop Paul, 49–50

Zhang Baijia, 79
Zhang Bojun, 240, 243–244, 258
Zhang Dongsun, 74, 92
Zhang Lu, 223
Zhang Taiyan, 11–12
Zhang Wenjin, 149
Zhang Wentian, 225, 255
Zhou Enlai: on the landed elite, 26; in coalition negotiations, 77, 80–81; support for PCC Resolution, 78; and secret communications channel, 132–133; communication with Stalin, 136–137, 158; comments on China-U.S. relations, 137; talks with Roshchin on Korea, 153–154; ultimatum on 38th parallel, 155; invites U.S. journalists to China, 180, 197, 279–280; on mixed economy, 206; on gradualist economic blueprint, 211, 212; defends intellectuals, 229–234, 244; call for legal system, 233–234; five principles of peaceful coexistence, 254, 258; on conflict management, 257–258; reducing Soviet dependence, 258–259; mediates in Soviet bloc, 262; and relations with Japan, 277–279; and Taiwan Strait crises, 282–283; reaction to two Chinas concept, 285; on Soviet foreign policy philosophy, 290–291
Zhou Enlai Demarche, 144, 150
Zhu De, Marshal, 218
Zhukov, G. K., 247
Zimyanin, Mikhail, 245, 266